The Essence of Chaplin

ALSO BY JOHN FAWELL

*The Art of Sergio Leone's **Once Upon a Time in the West**: A Critical Appreciation*
(McFarland, 2005)

The Essence of Chaplin

The Style, the Rhythm and the Grace of a Master

JOHN FAWELL

McFarland & Company, Inc., Publishers
Jefferson, North Carolina

LIBRARY OF CONGRESS CATALOGUING-IN-PUBLICATION DATA

Fawell, John Wesley, 1959–
The essence of Chaplin : the style, the rhythm
and the grace of a master / John Fawell.
  p.   cm.
Includes bibliographical references and index.

ISBN 978-0-7864-7634-3 (softcover : acid free paper) ∞
ISBN 978-1-4766-1743-5 (ebook)

1. Chaplin, Charlie, 1889–1977—Criticism and interpretation.   I. Title.
PN2287.C5F39 2014   791.4302'33092—dc23   2014031514

BRITISH LIBRARY CATALOGUING DATA ARE AVAILABLE

© 2014 John Fawell. All rights reserved

*No part of this book may be reproduced or transmitted in any form
or by any means, electronic or mechanical, including photocopying
or recording, or by any information storage and retrieval system,
without permission in writing from the publisher.*

On the cover: Director Charles Chaplin (at camera)
directing an unidentified film, 1920s (Photofest)

Printed in the United States of America

*McFarland & Company, Inc., Publishers
Box 611, Jefferson, North Carolina 28640
www.mcfarlandpub.com*

Table of Contents

Introduction   **1**

One: The Biography   **11**
Two: Charlie's Role-Playing   **25**
Three: Chaplin's Satire   **37**
Four: Beyond Satire: What Charlie Believes In   **53**
Five: Chaplin and the Intimacy of the Camera   **65**
Six: The Concrete and the Suggestive   **81**
Seven: Chaplin's Filmmaking Skills   **94**
Eight: Chaplin's Sense of Balance   **116**
Nine: Balance in the Character of Charlie   **129**
Ten: Charlie and Women   **145**
Eleven: Charlie, Dogs and Children   **168**
Twelve: Charlie and Men   **185**
Thirteen: Chaplin and Rhythm   **200**
Fourteen: Dance   **208**
Fifteen: Chaplin's Music   **217**
Sixteen: Two Musical Sequences   **227**

Chapter Notes   **243**
Bibliography   **247**
Index   **249**

Introduction

The Dominance of the Chaplin Biography

Anyone who aims to write a book on Charlie Chaplin had better do some soul-searching as to the book's necessity, given the vast bibliography on Chaplin, perhaps the largest on any single filmmaker. Unlike other directors in the Hollywood canon, who had to wait for French intellectuals in the 1950s to take them seriously, Chaplin was popular with critics, intellectuals and artists from the start of his career. The mass of critical works on him accumulated rapidly and the pile-up hasn't abated since.

That said, if Chaplin criticism is noteworthy for its immensity, it is characterized, as well, by a certain uniformity and redundancy. Despite the vast number of books on Chaplin, careful analysis of his artistry is not always easy to find. There are a variety of reasons why the attention of Chaplin critics is often diverted from Chaplin's films themselves.

First, Chaplin's biography is so fascinating that it tends to overwhelm his work. Chaplin studies often reflect a greater interest in Chaplin's fame than the artistry that earned him that fame. Even critical works on Chaplin tend towards the biographical, lining up their analysis of his films along the axis of his life's story and filling in commentary on the films with biographical back-story about the making of the film or its reception.

As early as 1973, one critic called for a moratorium on Chaplin biographies that were appearing with a frequency in inverse proportion to what they added to our understanding of Chaplin.[1] That call has gone unheeded and the last forty years have seen a steady stream of Chaplin biographies that, excepting David Robinson's *Chaplin, His Life and Art*, a standard-setting fusion of biography and criticism,[2] have not added a great deal to our understanding of Chaplin's films.

One thing that has changed in Chaplin biographies is that they have gotten nastier. A time-tested way for biographers to stake out new ground in their subject is to delve into that subject's darker side, and so the last few decades have seen an uptick in biographies that revel in the less attractive sides of Chaplin's character, particularly the vanity and imperiousness of his later years.[3]

A more fortuitous turn of events has been an increasing tendency in biographies that try to delve more deeply into the historical detail surrounding Chaplin's life.[4] Influenced by the trend of New Historicism over the last four decades or so, more books have appeared that are exhaustive in their research into the cultural locations and events of Chaplin's life, turning up, for example, more and more information on the South London locale of Chaplin's childhood and the music hall scene into which he was born, or accessing troves of papers having to do with the U.S. government's suspicions about Chaplin during the 1940s and '50s.

These are often meticulously researched books that are fascinating to the Chaplin aficionado, and interesting works of cultural analysis in their own right, but they have in common with the more spurious, scandal-mongering biography a certain indifference to the actual artistic creations of Chaplin. Both types of studies operate under the assumption that if you are going to say something new or interesting about Chaplin, it won't be in regard to the films themselves.

Another unwelcome consequence of the fascination with Chaplin's biography is that the biography has dictated, perhaps too much, the way we look at his films. For example, Chaplin's socialist and communist leanings, and his contentions with the U.S. government during a period that fascinates Americans (the era of McCarthyism and the House Un-American Activities Committee), have led to a preoccupation with Chaplin's politics and a tendency to study his films, retroactively, as those of a political filmmaker. Chaplin's film alter ego Charlie, an economically crushed, forgotten man of the streets, seems to confirm that tendency, as does Chaplin's film *Modern Times*, perceived by many as Chaplin's crowning accomplishment, with its scenes that focus on the dehumanization of the worker.

But though Chaplin did become politically active in his middle years, he always admitted that his politics were not well thought out, that he belonged to no political party, that he had never voted and that, in his silent films at least, he had no interest in speaking politically. His later, sound films are more overtly topical. But his silent film comedies with Charlie, the cream of his great output, are consistently apolitical. There are sporadic moments of social commentary, for example when officials herd Charlie and the other immigrants like cattle in *The Immigrant*, and the famous human-cog-in-the-machine scenes from *Modern Times*; but these moments are infrequent in Chaplin's silent films and don't necessarily add up to a political vision. They are on a par with the social commentary of other Hollywood practitioners with liberal tendencies, say John Ford in *Stagecoach*, a film in which Ford and his scenarist Dudley Nichols side with a prostitute, a drunk and an outlaw against the likes of bankers, genteel ladies and a women's league of decency. In Ford's films, as in Chaplin's, there is less a specific politics than there is a kind of general indignation towards piety and self-righteousness—one of the characteristics, I might add, of many of the studio era's best films.

An Indifference to Aesthetics

The preoccupation with Chaplin's biography, then, is one reason for the tendency, among Chaplin critics, to approach Chaplin's films from a historical and sociological direction. Another reason for the default tendency to look at Chaplin's films from a sociological perspective may be that it is not easy to explain their significance according to other criteria. His films are not characterized by overt content. Their ideas are not explicitly articulated, but built into gags, the meaning of which demands careful inference and extrapolation. There are ideas in these films but they are rarely stated outright. They have to be found out. Indeed, the finding out, as Chaplin well knew, is a great part of the fun. When ideas are more explicitly stated, as in Chaplin's later films, this explicitness tends to be to the film's detriment. Chaplin, the world has long since agreed, was a unique mime, satirist and filmmaker, but a more conventional philosopher.

Also, film scholarship, in general, has always been confused by the content-less film. It has tended to bring literary criteria to a non-literary art form and to value film for its depth of ideas or its social context or commentary. Many of film criticism's most egregious lapses have been in underrating comedy, which does not parade obvious or explicit ideas and which is often better valued for its formal qualities, its sense of rhythm and structure. We are often on firmer ground when we consider Chaplin's films in terms of their musicality, their rhythm, timing, structure and symmetry, than we are when we discuss them in terms of their content.

Few Chaplin aficionados, for example, actually consider *Modern Times* Chaplin's greatest film but it still remains the Chaplin film a student will most likely first see in high school. Why? Because it explicitly expresses what many viewers see in it as "themes": the dangers of industrialization, for example, or the objectification of the worker. These themes dovetail nicely with Chaplin's famed quasi–Communist politics that got him into trouble with the House Un-American Activities Committee and the United States in general and which contributed to his exile from America late in his career. By the time you tie all this together, you have a nice social science unit. But you've distanced yourself from a nuanced study of Chaplin's films, so gorgeous in their aesthetic detail and so ambitious in their commentary, not just on industrialization, but on the foibles of human nature in general.

Chaplin's conservative aesthetic has also provided an obstacle to a full appreciation of his style. Chaplin's aesthetic is classical. He favored a camera that didn't move a great deal and long takes, often in far or medium range shots. One of the best sequences in his films, for example, the restaurant sequence from *The Immigrant*, is so fixed in its point of view, and distant from its subject, that it is easy to see how it might be considered stagey. The genius of that sequence lies in Chaplin's meticulous choreography and his willingness to strain for such quiet gestures that the audience has to be on the top of their game, highly observant themselves, to realize the sequence's full potential.

Chaplin was a hero of sorts to practitioners of the classical Hollywood studio style of directing. Directors like Ernst Lubitsch and Alfred Hitchcock never tired of turning to his films for examples of how a good studio film should be made. They praised, in particular, his gift for economy of expression and elegant inference, two sacred principles to the great studio-era Hollywood directors. The ingenuity of this kind of quiet aesthetic fell out of vogue around the same time the Hollywood studio era met its demise and the French New Wave set off an orgy of expressive camerawork and editing that is still with us today. We still have a tendency to equate serious filmmaking, "the art film," with showy technique, with expressive camera angles and conspicuous editing.

And Chaplin didn't help matters by being, in the latter stages of his career, resistant to change and the evolution of new film equipment, so that his films, from *Modern Times* on, often look stale, stagey and antique. Hence, the period in the sixties and seventies where it was *de rigueur* to prefer Buster Keaton's comedies, characterized by a more manic energy, huge cinematic conceits and a more free-wheeling exercise of the film camera than Chaplin's.

But Chaplin's Zen-like understanding of the potential in stillness that the camera unlocks is every bit as cinematic as Keaton's films, probably more so if we rank films according to the subtlety of their gesture or for their ability to record marvels that are unseen by the naked eye. Though Chaplin criticism has intermittently awakened to the sophisticated cinematic technique inherent in Chaplin's conservative aesthetic,[5] there is still much work to do in getting at the beauty and profundity of Chaplin's comic scrimshaw, much more the *raison d'être* of his work than his views on poverty or the plight of the working man.

The Linear Study

One other weakness that is endemic to Chaplin criticism is a tendency to look at his work and career sequentially. This tendency towards linear studies of Chaplin in criticism of his work is due in part to the fascinating biography. It's hard not to examine the films within the context of the extraordinary arc of his life. And then Chaplin conveniently arranged his career into such nicely delineated chapters, with each studio at which he toiled (Keystone, Essanay, Mutual, First National, United Artists) representing a discrete advancement in the sophistication of his comedy and his delineation of Charlie's character. The films during each of these periods have their own particular flavor and critics have always loved to chart the development of Chaplin's comedic talents, and of his complex characterization of Charlie, from studio to studio. And so a massive portion of critical works on Chaplin follows the same organizational process, a forced linear march through his films, sequentially, starting from his first at Keystone, to his last film, *A Countess from Hong Kong*, with a good deal of biographical back-fill along the way.

The detriments to this organizational method are obvious. First, since studies like this organize themselves according to the development of Chaplin's career, they are, by nature, quasi-biographies and constantly abandon their analysis of the film to consider Chaplin's life at the time of the films, often finding their relevance only in the facts surrounding the production of the films. The method also leads to a good deal of numbing plot summary as these critics are forced to summarize the plot of each film in order to provide the context for their analysis. Often plot summary substitutes *for* analysis.

And this method results in a good deal of repetition, as ideas raised in analysis of one film reappear haphazardly in analyses of others as well. The problems that occur in these studies are familiar to any professor who has graded papers in which students adopt a chronological approach to a book or story they analyze: The ideas are interjected willy-nilly, tagging along the narrative, whereas the ideas should be leading the way, drawing from the narrative to support themselves when necessary and avoiding plot summary altogether.

But perhaps the most frustrating consequence of this linear, sequential approach to Chaplin's films is its tendency to spend a disproportionate amount of time on Chaplin's lesser work. The film-by-film approach characteristic of these linear studies of Chaplin is frustratingly democratic. Each film gets its equitable due, when, in reality, certain films deserve more attention than others.

The fault is usually not so much in the analysis of earlier films. Most critics identify the Keystone films as merely the place to see the stirring of Chaplin's comic genius, the first source of some of his best bits. They rarely overstate the merits of those films. But the time accorded to Chaplin's later sound films in these books, films that most critics agree represent Chaplin's talent in decline, seems disproportionate. This outsized attention to later works reflects, at least partially, a bias in favor of the feature-length film. But the attention given these works is also due to the fact that these later films were made at times when Chaplin's biographical story is of great interest to students of Chaplin. So the films represent telling appendages to his biography, for example, the way the negative critical reception to *Monsieur Verdoux* contributed to the U.S. government's suspicions of Chaplin's character and politics in the late 1940s. When you add the fascination with Chaplin's biography to the new historical tendency of the last few decades to exhaustively study documents and history surrounding Chaplin's films, you arrive at books that spend an exorbitant amount of time analyzing that period of Chaplin's career when he is making his weakest films.

Charles J. Maland's study *Chaplin and American Culture: The Evolution of a Star Image*,[6] for example, is a meticulously researched study of the evolution of America's relationship with, and perception of, Chaplin and so, by stated intention, more a work of sociology than film criticism. It's filled with interesting context for Chaplin's life work. Still, we can't help but be struck by the fact that Maland has finished dealing with those films that represent the cream of Chaplin's output by about one-third of the way through the book. So a majority of the book, as is the case of so many studies of Chaplin, concerns itself with years that, for the student of Chaplin's art, are less important.

Even books specifically devoted to analysis of Chaplin's films tend, typically, to devote a third or more to Chaplin's sound films, all of which are intriguing creations but also pale reflections, in terms of their artistic merit, of Chaplin's talent at its height, a talent that had to do with communication via silent film.

My point is not to criticize wholesale the tendency to study Chaplin's later films, all of which are fascinating exercises and worth reflecting on in getting at Chaplin's art, but to explain why, in this study, I will focus to a much greater extent on those films that critics generally agree represent the cream of Chaplin's crop: the silent film comedies with Charlie, and even more specifically, those at Essanay, Mutual, First National and United Artists. I don't completely ignore the Keystone films or the late sound films but the book aims for the analysis of Chaplin's films to be in proportion to their artistic merit.

The one exception to my tendency to stick to the silent films with Charlie is the good-sized amount of space I devote to Chaplin's one silent feature film that doesn't involve Charlie, *A Woman of Paris.* This film warrants study in any book aiming to get at Chaplin's artfulness in film for two reasons: First, it is a silent film and Chaplin's genius was for silent film. We can see much in his approach to silent film in *A Woman of Paris* that illuminates his skill at capitalizing on the silent film medium in his films with Charlie. Secondly, Chaplin made this film when he was in his prime.

In this one silent film in which he was not the star, he seemed to want to show the world how much he had learned about the nature of silent cinema, its potential for a new kind of subtle, visual communication. Freeing himself from Charlie allowed him to indulge in pure style. The film was met with critical, but only limited financial, success and Chaplin took the public's semi-indifference to heart and didn't repeat the experiment. But it's a highly effective film, a stylish, understated, classically told melodrama that proves Chaplin could have been among the best silent film dramatists of the time, in the company, if not the better, of subtle masters of melodrama like Fred Niblo and Victor Sjostrom. The film exhibits exactly the cinematic sophistication that critics skeptical about Chaplin often say is absent from his films. It's particularly useful in highlighting the inferential nature of Chaplin's films, and their tendency, in the manner of Naturalism, to express large ideas via small, well-chosen physical detail. Both of these aesthetic tendencies are a large part of what makes Chaplin's films with Charlie great as well.

Summary of Approach

In short, then, this book will concentrate on Chaplin's films a great deal more than it will on Chaplin's biography, turning to the biography (after a brief summary of it in the first chapter) only when it provides necessary context for understanding Chaplin's art. And it will organize itself according to what I think are the key ideas and ingredients of Chaplin's art rather than follow a linear trail from Chaplin's first to his last films. Its goal is not to summarize the arc of his career but to offer a lexicon of his filmic nature.

This approach can be problematic as the Charlie of the early films is not exactly the same as the Charlie of the later films. Charlie evolves over the years. He's much more punkish and belligerent in the early films, much more the sentimental harlequin in the later ones. But I take the approach that Charlie is, for the most part, a whole character throughout Chaplin's films, just one who develops over time. The young Charlie is no more cleanly detached from the old Charlie than we are from younger versions of ourselves. The essential dichotomy of, and balance in, Charlie's character is there from early on. Chaplin's gift for pathos is evident as early as the Essanay films. From a very early point we feel empathy for Charlie. And gentle as he is in his later films, he still has bouts of roguish sadism, for example in the drunk-on-riveting scene from *Modern Times* in which he returns to the lascivious faun persona of his youth.

This work will also concentrate on those films that critics have tended to agree are most worthy of study. Overall, the book defines the heart of Chaplin's cinema as his silent works that involve Charlie, paying particular attention to Chaplin's work at Mutual, First National and the earlier days of United Artists. It takes certain films in particular as gospel, certainly the great silent film features (*The Kid, The Gold Rush, The Circus, City Lights, Modern Times*) but also certain, nearly perfect, shorter, earlier films like *The Immigrant, The Pawn Shop, The Pilgrim,* and *A Dog's Life*. I reserve the right to touch on some films over and over, from the vantage point of different ideas, and to comment on others just briefly, and still others not at all. Certain gags in Chaplin's films also prove to be so pivotal that they come up several times in this book, each time within the context of a different idea on Chaplin's cinema. The book aims to stay closest to those moments in Chaplin's films where he was operating at his very best, firing on all cylinders.

Another unavoidable problem with this kind of study, which aims to look at Chaplin's greatest films as a whole, is that it precludes stem-to-stern analysis of any one Chaplin film. But, again, library shelves are fairly groaning under the weight of books that offer film-by-film analysis. There are now even entire books devoted to single films, like Maland's excellent study of *City Lights* for the BFI film classics series. My goal here is to analyze the films Chaplin made when his talent was white hot, and to draw from that analysis a small lexicon of Chaplin's greatest skills as a filmmaker, an introduction to the essentials of his craft. I mean the book for the scholar who I hope will be interested in my particular take on Chaplin. But I intend it, just as much, for the general reader who is looking for a cogent introduction to Chaplin, who is seeking to understand why it is that critics take Chaplin as seriously as they do. I mean the book as a series of answers to the question, "What are the ingredients that make Charlie Chaplin such a revered filmmaker?"

Arguments

In answering that question, I will argue that Chaplin's goals as a comedian and filmmaker were a great deal more ambitious than can be appreciated within the confines of a sociological framework. Chaplin, via his gift for mimicry and satire, was able to comment widely on human nature. He approaches the great artists of any medium, in any time, in his ability to touch on subtle aspects of the human condition, to show us ourselves in ways that both chasten and humble us (via his acute sense of human pretension) and soothe and comfort us (via his gift for pathos and insistence on the significance of pity and empathy). Charlie is much more than the victim of an economic situation, more than the representative of a particular time. He's the soul in action, one of the most complex and engaging representations of the human condition any art has seen.

And I will argue that in straining to underscore content in Chaplin's films, and to tie that content to the momentous events of Chaplin's life and times, critics have often under-appreciated Chaplin's aesthetic accomplishments, which Chaplin always felt were his greatest. A good deal of the book will be spent on the structure of Chaplin's comedy, its musical grace and sophisticated rhythm, the way it elevates via feeling rather than ideas. Like so many great filmmakers, Chaplin often said that film was closer to music than the other arts. The merit of his cinema, the depth of its emotion, the extent of its meaning are, perhaps, all the more apparent in an analysis of his films that stresses its formal properties more than its sociological content.

I want also, in this book, to underline Chaplin's significance, not just as a comedian, but as a filmmaker. Because Chaplin's aesthetic was a conservative one, critics have tended to underrate his cinematic skills, citing his genius as that of a stage comedian caught on film. But if Chaplin's aesthetic was quiet, it was also influential. With his eye for small details that pack huge emotional wallops and his gift for fey, elliptical gags that leave room for the viewer's skills of observation, Chaplin is one of the founding fathers of the studio era's elegant classical aesthetic. When Peter Bogdanovich asked Hollywood pro Leo McCarey if he ever learned anything from Chaplin, McCarey responded, simply, "Yes, good taste."[7]

Of course, commercial filmmakers are not the only ones to venerate Chaplin's style. One of the most fascinating aspects of his career is that Chaplin always appealed to both a popular audience and intellectual critics and to both the commercial and the more experimental directors who came in his wake. When Robert Bresson, the godfather of the European art film, was asked by a film journal to cite the ten best films in history, Bresson listed only Chaplin films. Avant-garde filmmaker Jean Marie Straub felt Chaplin was the greatest editor in film history, interesting praise given how often Chaplin is faulted by critics for errors in continuity.

Moreover, there is ample evidence, in Chaplin's oeuvre, of overtly artful and expressive shots that suggest he could have been, had he chosen that direction, a more expressively visual director, in the manner of Buster Keaton. Restraint, however, is the hallmark of Chaplin's style. Perhaps his greatest claim to fame as a filmmaker is his pioneering understanding of the sensitivity of the film camera to the nearly invisible, his skill in coaxing from the camera, moments of fleeting, ineffable grace and beauty.

In the end, the goal of this book is to carve out the heart of Chaplin's filmic skill. It operates under the assumption that the best way to do that is to focus the reader's attention on that maddeningly swift and miniature comic play at the heart of his best gags, in his best films. It aims to bring the hidden mechanics of Chaplin's technique to the foreground, to articulate as clearly as possible just how carefully wrought Chaplin's films are.

Easier said than done. Trying to still Chaplin's comedy long enough to understand it is like trying to capture lightning in a bottle, or study a dead animal drained of its life colors. No doubt one reason scholars turn so often to Chaplin's life rather than his films is that they have thrown up their hands at the futility of putting into words what Chaplin so aptly recorded in mime. I can't promise that I won't tax the reader myself in some of my close readings of Chaplin's filmic texts. Trying to distill Chaplin's particular comic genius will always be something of a holy grail, eternally frustrating to Chaplin scholars and their readers alike. Thomas Burke wrote, "[T]o attempt to isolate the essence that has placed Charlie above all others of the world is hopeless."[8] Waldo Frank wisecracked about "the intellectuals of New York and Paris turning his stunts into logarithmic mazes as if he were Einstein."[9] And Gerald D. McDonald wrote that "to see a Chaplin comedy, then to try to tell what you have seen, is a difficult thing to do."[10]

McDonald is right. Chaplin was so rapid and mercurial in his comedy that it is evident in certain scenes that he himself didn't even plan on some of his best gestures and comic effects. He often reaches such a state of physical agitation and inspiration that a kind of instinctual genius takes over; his body outpaces his consciousness and expresses itself in rapid little gestures that pass too quickly for the naked eye. But the camera picks them up. And the viewer can too, *if* they attend very closely to the recorded image.

And, then, if viewers reflect on that gesture, they may find that it implies a lovely little idea that even Chaplin, a mime not a philosopher, couldn't have put into words.

He said in one interview, "It always starts—for me at least, not from an idea, but from an emotion, and of that emotion the idea is born."[11] Chaplin's cinema is not one that seeks to express ideas, but rather a cinema of gestures, from which ideas are thrown, like sparks, with great ferocity and abundance. We get at Chaplin's cinema when we study the gags, when we follow the comedy to the ideas.

It's in the intricacies of Chaplin's gags that the real story of his genius is told. Chaplin's gift was not just for mimicry but for filmmaking, for knowing how to capture those intricacies with the movie camera. Chaplin's films contain some of the quietest, most elusive and elegantly expressed moments in film history. The *bon mots* and speeches of his latter films attest to a searching mind, a quippy literacy and a noble spirit. But it's not in the obvious content of these didactic exercises that we best confront Chaplin's genius. Ironically, it's much more humble fare that proves Chaplin's greatness, those little moments of nearly invisible grace and charm in his gags with Charlie. Those moments testify not only to glorious mimetic skills, but also a wide study and appreciation of human nature, and perhaps most surprisingly, a pioneering understanding of the movie camera's ability to capture that understanding in finely inscribed detail.

Chapter Breakdown

After a first chapter in which I make some summary points on Chaplin's biography and the arc of his career, the book will break down into five sections.

In the first section, Chapters Two through Four, I consider the satirical aspects of Chaplin's comedy, paying particular attention to his gift for role-playing and the way he satirizes the roles we play (and take seriously) in our lives. I stress the wide-ranging nature of Chaplin's satire, the vast array of human pretension he has at his mimetic disposal and how important the satirical impulse is to Chaplin's cinema, a principal goal of which is to mortify our sense of vanity.

At the same time, I argue, in Chapter Four, against the commonly held notion that Charlie is only a satirical creature who picks up and abandons identities at the drop of a hat, who, in the end, neither represents or believes in any viable approach to life himself. Charlie does, at times, behave sincerely and it is incumbent on the viewer of Chaplin's films to attend to what it is that Charlie does believe in, what virtues he feels are left us if we manage to leave off our posturing and role-playing. That discussion leads inevitably to consideration of that constellation of things that Chaplin held sacred: material comforts, physical pleasure, art, beauty, love, empathy and humility.

The second section of the book (Chapters Five through Seven) turns its attention to Chaplin's cinematic talents. In these chapters I argue that critics have tended to underestimate Chaplin's technical skills as a filmmaker. His approach to cinema could rightly be termed classical and is of a piece with the quiet, deliberate technique that came to define the studio era that succeeded him, an era upon which he had no small influence.

Chapter Five argues that Chaplin's greatest distinction as a filmmaker is his sensitivity to the intimacy of the movie camera, his gift for the kind of fine comic minutiae only the movie camera is capable of capturing. Chapter Six studies his talent, born from his subtle sense of humor, but translated into the mechanics of film, for ellipticism, the art of suggestion. It's this aspect of his filmmaking—his economy, his gift for omission—that has always been most venerated by the legions of filmmakers, commercial and avant-garde alike, who take Chaplin as their directorial hero. In Chapter Eight, I note the many examples of expressive and artful technique in Chaplin's films that testify, not only to a capacity for a more artful technique than critics have often granted Chaplin, but to a determination to keep that capacity in check, the way Chaplin's filmic skills were matched by a sense of filmic humility.

The third section (Chapters Eight and Nine) discusses Chaplin's great sense of balance. Balance, the hallmark of classical cinema, is evident in Chaplin's tempered blend of comedy and pathos in his films, his great sense of taste, and in the extraordinarily complex character of Charlie, who is defined by his paradoxical nature, his ability to hold a score of opposing tendencies in delicate counterpoise. In this section of the book I emphasize how Chaplin makes Charlie's empathy and pathos palatable to us by more than balancing it with his sense of Charlie's appetitive nature.

In the fourth section, Chapters Ten through Twelve, I reflect on the fictional world of Chaplin's alter ego, or film surrogate, Charlie. I interpret this world as a kind of battleground divided into two camps, Charlie's enemies and his allies. Charlie's enemies are almost entirely male figures of authority: employers, co-workers, fathers and policemen. Charlie's allies tend to be powerless figures. I explore three of these allies in particular: children, dogs and women. In Chapter Eleven, I discuss Charlie's intense relationships with women, touching on Charlie's own femininity, and the way he uses that femininity to comic effect. I stress even more the way in which Chaplin's cinema can be seen as something of an ode to femininity. In Chapter Twelve, I discuss Charlie's close affinity with children and dogs, emphasizing the way Chaplin channels children's and dogs' behavior in his comedy. Chapter Fourteen examines Chaplin's complex reaction to masculinity, including his pitch-perfect imitations of male posturing and the comic war he wages with male figures of authority, particularly employers and policemen.

In the fifth and final section (Chapters Thirteen through Fifteen) I look at the musicality of Chaplin's cinema: his gift for rhythm, the way he involves dance in his cinema, the musical scores he wrote for his films. I consider not only the soundtracks he wrote for *City Lights* and *Modern Times* at the time of those films' releases, but the music he scored, retroactively, for his other feature films and his First National films; these scores have deepened the experience of those films (usually not the case when directors tamper with their earlier works). The book concludes, in Chapter Sixteen, with extensive analysis of two famous scenes from Chaplin's *City Lights*, the boxing sequence and the closing sequence, both representative of the care Chaplin put into the musical rhythm of his films.

One

The Biography

Though the principal purpose of this book is to analyze Chaplin's films, not his life, I will at times refer to it in my analysis of his films and so it may be useful to offer some thoughts on the more significant episodes from his biography. Also, I would like this study to be of use, not just to Chaplin scholars, but to readers coming to Chaplin for the first time. And for those readers I offer a brief summary of his life and filmic career, annotated with some observations about how that biography has been interpreted.

It is easy to understand why Chaplin studies have been so overwhelmed by his biography. It really is one of the great stories of the 20th century, fascinating in a variety of ways. There is, for example, his vast international celebrity. It's not easy to encapsulate Chaplin's fame at its peak. His films were lowbrow and accessible enough to appeal to the masses, subtle and charming enough to excite the most sensitive aesthete. He appealed to everyone.

Also, silent film provided no language obstacles to the craze for Chaplin's charming humor that swept through the world in 1915 and 1916 and so he enjoyed an international celebrity that would be hard to attain in the sound era. As his friend Thomas Burke wrote of him in 1932, Chaplin "is the first man in the history of the world of whom it can be truly and literally be said that he is world-famous. Charlie is known in regions where Napoleon and Beethoven and Mussolini have never been heard of. He is known in the Solomon islands, in the interior of New Guinea and the inner cities of Tibet, and in the recesses of Africa."[1] More recently, Simon Louvish, in reflecting on how Chaplin penetrated "into the nooks and crannies" of colonialist cultures, cites as examples of Chaplin's universal fame, his influence on the Lakhaon Bassac folkloric theater of Cambodia and Turkish shadow puppet theater.[2]

The images of Chaplin speaking at a bond rally in 1918 in New York or navigating the London throngs that surrounded him in his first return to England after his success are powerful because of the vastness of the crowds, and also the crowd's kinetic nature caught in the photo. The photos are striking for how they catch a dynamic fluidity to the crowd, all tending towards Chaplin. The only pictures of celebrity worship that

I can think of that are comparable in their combination of vast scale and dynamism are those during the Beatles phenomenon, though Chaplin's crowds express none of the hysteria of the Beatles crowds. In fact the uniform expression of Chaplin's crowds is an open-faced, astonished delight. He looks, in these pictures, exactly like what he was, the most popular man in the world.

Chaplin's enormous success and wealth make him fascinating. He represents the ultimate rags-to-riches story. Chaplin's father, a music hall performer of some renown, was for the most part an absentee parent, a deadbeat dad when it came to child support, an alcoholic who died when Charlie was twelve, bequeathing Charlie, at least, with an acute understanding of the nature of the drunk that would serve Charlie well as he developed his comedy routines. Of course, the South London of his time provided a good number of models for that particular vein in his comedy.

His mother was also a performer, though less famous than his father. She was a more inspirational figure in his life and he lovingly protected many fine memories of her, some more mythical than fact-based. But she was no bastion of consistency either, bearing three children with three different men, sometimes supporting Charlie and his half-brother Sydney through the generosity of male friends, and succumbing to a madness, perhaps derived from syphilis, that would render her a burden rather than a support to Chaplin after the age of fourteen.

In short, Chaplin experienced a Dickensian childhood that included stints at charity centers and orphanages, a wicked stepmother and a mother gone insane. He had to work from the age of nine or so, sometimes as a performer, sometimes through a variety of small jobs, including one that serves as a premonition of his films: selling flowers at pubs. By sixteen he was an actor of some repute, and by nineteen an important member of Fred Karno's troupe of polished music hall performers; he would apprentice there in a thorough, meticulous brand of comedy that provided the foundation of his comic identity. The penury that led to this professional precociousness was obviously one part tragedy and one part great fortune, as his vast and early success as an entertainer no doubt explains how he could, by the age of twenty-six, be the most successful comic performer in the world. Like the other genius of Hollywood, Orson Welles, Chaplin was out plying his living like an adult from early adolescence on.

The numbers of Chaplin's financial remuneration in Hollywood are stunning. In 1916, Mutual Film Corporation signed him to his third major contract in Hollywood after stints with Keystone and Essanay, agreed to pay him $670,000 for his first year's work and to lay out $1,530,000 for the total cost of forming the Chaplin producing company. As David Robinson has noted, "no person in the world other than a king or emperor—unless perhaps Charlie Schwabb of the U.S. Steel Corporation—had ever received even half that salary."[3] Rarely has the rags-to-riches story been so literally true. From this point on, Chaplin was something Hollywood has rarely seen, a truly independent artist, able to do what he wanted and how he wanted. As he said at the time, "What this contract means is simply that I am in business with the worry left out and with the dividends guaranteed. It means that I am left free to be just as funny as I dare."[4]

This financial freedom is no small part of Chaplin's success as a filmmaker. He was able to bankroll his perfectionism and to shoot the large amounts of footage he felt were necessary to perfect his gags on screen. During the making of *The Immigrant* in 1917 he scrapped an entire week of filming when he decided Henry Bergman was not a frightening enough figure in his role as the waiter who oppresses Charlie. Chaplin's ratio of film shot per film used is epic by the standards of any day, all but financially impossible today. He edited *The Gold Rush* down to 8,555 feet from 231,505 feet, *A Woman of Paris* to 7,557 from 130,000. These numbers were unparalleled at the time and still are. No studio would have allowed a director this kind of liberality. None would today either. And these numbers explain to a great extent how Chaplin was able to arrive at such pinpoint precision in his elaborate choreography or such fine scrimshaw in the recording of his mime.

Theodore Huff notes that the scene in *The Kid*, in which Jackie Coogan makes pancakes and Charlie rises from bed for breakfast, was "said to have taken two weeks and fifty thousand feet of film to shoot." All for a scene "scarcely a minute in length." Huff also describes how Chaplin, in filming *The Count*, spent three weeks on a scene where Charlie kicks a man while dancing and then whirls the girl about in one clean, fluid gesture, "a simple effect in appearance," as Huff describes it, but one that "involved hiring a band, learning certain dance steps, perfecting certain facial expressions, timing the action with the moving camera, etc."[5] Anecdotes like this provide very clear examples of what made Chaplin's films great: an obsession with clean, articulate gags, characterized by stunning rapidity and microscopic attention to detail.

Despite the importance of understanding film as a collaborative medium, it's striking how often great Hollywood films (Hitchcock and Capra in their prime, for example) came about when directors were granted more freedom in production. Chaplin provides more proof that, for all the genius of the system, some of Hollywood's greatest work occurred when its best filmmakers were allowed to find their own head of steam.

That said, Chaplin might also be seen as finally choking on his freedom. His career is marked by many dramatic moments on set where he put his cast through an astonishing number of retakes of dubious necessity. In many ways, the freedom in time his wealth afforded him got the best of him. Chaplin's career is one of decreasing productivity and the decrease correlates to the increase in wealth: 14 films for Essanay in 14 months; 12 for Mutual in a year and a half; eight for First National in five years, from 1918 to 1923. His five great silent films for United Artists were made over the course of 13 years from 1923 to 1936. His four sound films over the course of 27 years, from 1940 to 1967.

Of course there's nothing scandalous in these numbers. He evolved into making more complex feature films. The time spent on them is reflected in much of the product, particularly his late silent features. And he's certainly not the only director whose output decreased with age. But his productions were also increasingly troubled by problems only someone with his financial freedom could create: lengthy shutdowns as he worked out problems, unproductive bouts of obsessive procrastination. By the end of his career, most critics agree he became somewhat lost in himself, so used to having his way in filming that he fell out of touch with the evolution of film techniques. Ironically, the films he spent the longest time on, those of the sound era, often look cheap and antiquated in their production values, despite the time spent on them.

Perhaps the most fascinating aspect of Chaplin's biography is its Zelig-like nature. Chaplin's popularity was enormous, crossing all educational, economic, artistic and national lines. He seems to have been sighted with, or celebrated by, every significant figure of the first two-thirds of the 20th century. The photo album of Chaplin's life is almost comical in its documentation of his ubiquity. There's Chaplin with Gandhi in East London, with Chou En Lai in Geneva, with Albert Einstein at the premiere of *City Lights*, on set in Hollywood with the visiting Helen Keller or Anna Pavlova. Accounts of his life and travels only add to the roll call. There he is performing his famous dance of the rolls in Picasso's apartment in Paris, dining with Picasso and Sartre in Chaplin's hotel in Paris, lounging with Jean Cocteau on a boat headed to Hong Kong, playing parlor games with Prince Edward of Wales at the prince's country estate in Belvedere, sharing dry martinis with Roosevelt in the White House or lunch with Herbert Hoover on the top floor of the Times building in New York. He never met Stalin but Stalin is reported to have said that Chaplin was the only person in the world he longed to meet.[6]

And has any popular filmmaker, much less a film comedian, enjoyed the adulation from his day's intellectual elite and literati that Chaplin did? Winston Churchill took pride in his friendship with Chaplin and penned a lengthy essay on him, finding in his films "moments of an almost unbearable poignancy."[7] Freud wrote on him too, describing him as "undoubtedly a great artist." George Bernard Shaw saw him as "the only genius developed in motion pictures."[8] T.S. Eliot praised him for having "invented a rhythm" in filmmaking.[9] Mayakovsky praised the great emotional effects Chaplin achieved from small, insignificant visual detail.[10] Chaplin spent time with H.G. Wells in London, with Robinson Jeffers and John Steinbeck at their homes in California, with German exiles Bertolt Brecht and Thomas Mann and British writers Stephen Spender and Aldous Huxley in Hollywood.

The Cubist, Surrealist and Dadaist painters venerated him. Diego Rivera was a friend. Fernand Leger involved his image in many of his paintings and felt that Chaplin reached "the depths of life, the drama of human destiny, by means of the plastic rhythm of gesture and the most total silence."[11] Chaplin hobnobbed with and took musical advice from Rachmaninoff, Stravinsky and Schoenberg. James Barrie wanted him to play Peter Pan. Nijinsky praised his dance. Leading literary lights Graham Greene and Edmund Wilson wrote careful analyses of him. Intellectuals in the vanguard of the American press, including James Agee, Robert Sherwood and Alexander Woollcott, were adulatory to the point of being cultish. Hart Crane wrote a poem on him, "Chaplinesque."

Chaplin's biography also fascinates because of the general constitution of his nature that so often has been summed up as "genius." He was the most charming comedian that the film world has ever seen and also one of the most perceptive and pioneering directors. He arrived at a point where, with the aid of trained composers, he scored his own films, creating rich, complex symphonic works that are still performed in concert. He penned several hit songs, including "Smile" and "This Is My Song," that have survived as part of the classic American songbook. He played several instruments, including the piano, the violin and the cello, with some expertise. "As soon as I touched the piano, I could play," he told Lillian Ross. "The same with the violin."[12] His physical prowess is awe-inspiring. The greatest mime of the century, he seemed to handle any physical challenge with ease and his films offer testimony to his skill in acrobatics, swimming, wrestling, and skating, just to name a few talents. These

Fascination with Chaplin's romantic life, for example his relationship with Marion Davies, has been a large part of why his biography fascinates, to the point of overwhelming critical analysis of his films. Here Chaplin and Davies are in the projection room at the Hearst castle.

kinds of natural gifts, fusing the realms of aesthetics and athletics, combined with the god-like power of his international celebrity (probably the greatest the world has even known, coming as it did, just at the dawn of the cinematic image and before language would separate national cinemas from one another), explain the tendency to call him a "genius."

And of course his many sexual and political imbroglios fascinate as well. Just listing the ages of his four wives (16, 16, 26, and 18) raises eyebrows, even if the last, to Eugene O'Neill's daughter Oona, did turn out to be a lasting and stable marriage. The first two marriages, particularly the second, resulted in highly publicized, messy divorces. Combined with an even more embarrassing paternity suit brought by a troubled stalker, Joan Barry, Chaplin's sex life was sensational fodder to the press and one of the biggest contributions to his inevitable decline in public favor. In fact, what the government perceived as Chaplin's moral lapses had as much to do with its unwillingness to grant a reentry visa to Chaplin when he left the country in 1952 as his politics.

In between his four wives, Chaplin provided his biographers with their favorite thing, countless affairs, notable for their quantity and for their wide range. He engaged in liaisons with anonymous starlets (such as his first two wives) and great actresses of his time (Pola Negri, Louise Brooks, Marion Davies), with artists (Rebecca West), bohemians (Claire Sheridan) and famous gold-diggers (Peggy Hopkins Joyce, the inspiration for *A Woman of Paris*).

And just as he seemed to know every significant public figure of the 20th century, so his biography seems entwined around the key historic events of the 20th century. One of the first of the many public controversies he would experience occurred during World War I when the British press sent him a white feather of sorts, faulting him for not having volunteered to serve in the war. He compensated by throwing himself into bond drives and other fundraising activities. And he made *Shoulder Arms*, a film that still represents one of the most clever and original (and visually striking) takes on World War I.

He was the object of an assassination plot in Japan while visiting there in 1932, the purpose of which was to draw America into war. He took advantage of his many similarities to Adolf Hitler (the mustache, martinet build and confident carriage) to great effect in *The Great Dictator*, a film that stands alone in its attack on Germany during a time where Hollywood was close to collaborationist in its desire to protect its German interests. *The Great Dictator* is a flawed film but images from it have nevertheless been burned into the national consciousness. Like *Shoulder Arms*, and perhaps *A King in New York*, the film testifies to Chaplin's ability to stamp his identity into the most momentous world events of his time.

Chaplin's left-leaning politics led to lifetime sympathy with Russia and he outpaced even the most credulous of American radicals in his faith in the Soviet government, publicly lauding Khrushchev in flowery terms as late as 1954. His Communist and Russian sympathies, coupled with his unwillingness to seek citizenship in America (he saw himself, like the Tramp, an artist and anarchist who stood outside national sympathies) and his increasingly bad moral reputations, led to tangles with the House Un-American Activities Committee and ultimately to his exile from the U.S. How much of this exile was self-imposed is one of these subjects of endless debate in Chaplin studies. Chaplin might easily have been able to force the government's hand by reapplying for entry but many critics feel the "king in exile" role appealed to him and that living in Switzerland provided financial advantages as well.

The fall of Chaplin is yet another aspect of his biography that makes it so absorbing. One of art's greatest rags-to-riches story is succeeded by one of the century's most epic falls from grace. Who can match Chaplin's ascension to heights of popularity in this country? And yet what other artist of his stature has been so thoroughly renounced and rejected by the U.S.? Chaplin was known to hatch some pretty wild ideas for films that never came off, most famously his notion to take on the role of Napoleon. Late in his career he horrified friends by suggesting he might like to play the role of Christ. But we have to at least sympathize with the impulse. "Isn't it awful," Chaplin's friend Thomas Burke recalls Chaplin saying to him in 1931 during Chaplin's return to England, "that these people should hang around me and shout 'God bless you Charlie!' and want to touch my overcoat and laugh and even shed tears. And why? Simply because I cheered 'em up. God, Tommy, what kind of filthy world is this—that makes people lead such wretched lives that if anybody makes 'em laugh they

Chaplin's return to America in 1971, capped by a Lifetime Achievement Award presented at the Oscars, was a triumph. The U.S., in the sixties and seventies, had rediscovered its affection for Chaplin. Here Chaplin is photographed with his wife Oona and other award winners of that year: Cloris Leachman, Ben Johnson and Gene Hackman.

want to kneel down and touch his overcoat, as though he was Jesus Christ raising 'em from the dead."[13] Chaplin was honest enough to see the implicit dark side of his popularity on the way up before experiencing its more explicit nastiness on the way down. The same man whose garments were grabbed for their talismanic powers finished by leaving the country branded a pervert and seditionist.

In the sixties Chaplin got to ride one more cultural current as the tide of public opinion swung back in his favor. America had arrived at a new era, one which was in perfect sync with Chaplin's history of pacifism and political rebellion. America was now willing to see Chaplin as he had always seen himself, the victim of a witch hunt, a fairly accurate summary of the situation, regardless of how naive Chaplin's politics were or how well he had protected his money in Switzerland. He had shown a good deal of political backbone during the era in which he was hounded by the government and stood up to McCarthyism in no uncertain terms. The film world invited him back to America for a whirlwind tour of honors culminating in a Lifetime Achievement Award at the Academy Awards which moved him to tears. The honor was, to say the least, a legitimate one.

Controversy dogged him after his death when his grave was dug up and his body stolen for ransom by a couple of hapless extortionists. Chaplin was still subject to an obsessive attention that was as destructive as it was adulatory.

With a life like this, it is easy to see how Chaplin's biography has dominated the writing about him. But the problem is that it tempts critics to keep raking over the various fascinating elements of Chaplin's life and to disregard the work that led to all this celebrity in the first place. Chaplin has suffered the same fate that Hemingway has: A kind of cottage industry of critical debate has sprung up beside his work, overshadowing it, concerning itself endlessly with the ambiguities and inconsistencies of Chaplin's eventful life story.

Chaplin gilded the lily quite a bit in recapping his life in his interviews and biography and so there is a lot of straightening out to be done in getting to the actual truth of the events of his life. And the inevitable result of all this effort to catch Chaplin out in his inconsistencies is a newer breed of biography that is somewhat hostile to its subject. So much of the ink spilled on Chaplin has to do with whether he was what he said he was and whether his work was consistent with his character. Was he as poor as he made out? Was he negligent towards his madhouse mother? Was he disloyal to his longtime co-workers, a tyrant on the set? Was the great progenitor of love a tyrant to his kids? Was he cheap? How seriously do we take quasi-communist politics when they are those of one of the richest men in America? The questions like this are endless and comprise a great deal of the critical attention to Chaplin.

Critics have long cackled over the flaws in Chaplin's "genius": the awful spelling and grammar in the few letters he wrote; that he didn't read nearly as much as he let on; that he was addicted to thesauruses and had a middle-class habit of cultivating and showing off his vocabulary; that he posed with his cello more often than he played it; that he couldn't read music. His political philosophy was lambasted for its idealism and naiveté. The more he unleashed didactic speeches such as the ones that conclude *The Great Dictator* or *Monsieur Verdoux*, the harder it was to take him seriously as a "genius."

I won't weigh in on these biographical debates in great detail in this work. I will say that, after wading through some of these studies, one begins to wonder why the biographer turned to a subject he or she disdains so much in the first place. It's hard not to smile, for example, at this reader's ingenuous assessment of Kenneth Lynn's biography in the reader's commentary section of an online bookstore: "I gradually wondered what it was that bothered me about the writing. Suddenly it dawned on me. Kenneth Lynn hates Charlie Chaplin."[14]

Taking these biographies in bulk, giving priority to firsthand accounts rather than skewed biographical interpretation of those accounts, Chaplin does not come off a great deal worse than the rest of us poor sinners. That is to say he vies with his great creation, Charlie, as a mixture of good and bad held in complex equilibrium. The most trustworthy voices from Chaplin's life are neither those who lionize him nor those who debase him but objective analysts like Thomas Burke, his friend from early in his career, or most of Chaplin's children, who were capable of offering devastatingly honest assessments of his weaknesses side by side with great appreciation for his charm, warmth, sentimentality and wisdom.

Chaplin himself is often the best defense against biographers bent on demystifying him because, despite his self-centeredness, he was, paradoxically, often capable of, and noted for, a great humility as well, always the first to pooh-pooh the idea that he was a genius ("Many a jack of all trades have been mistaken for a genius"[15]), the first to admit that his politics were not particularly profound ("I have no political persuasions whatsoever"[16]), the first to downplay his supposed virtuosic musical skills ("I la-laed and Arthur Johnson wrote it down"[17]).

Chaplin had the confidence of the self-made man and, though he exhibited the self-made man's weakness for inflated vocabulary and dodged troubling aspects of his life in his autobiography, in person he rarely paraded as more than he was. Early accounts of Chaplin, in particular, stress his lack of pretense. "He hadn't a scrap of affectation," wrote one interviewer in 1917.[18] "Most of us have some touch of humbug about us," wrote Thomas Burke in 1931, "Chaplin had none."[19] These comments don't accord perfectly with his later years in Switzerland where he could exhibit tyrannical tendencies with his family and was bitten by an insecurity, derived from diminishing talent, that often made him more pompous in his comments about life and filmmaking than he had been earlier in life. But to the bitter end he was capable of a refreshing absence of pretense, for example in the last pages of his biography, a book that annoys many by its endless recounting of celebrity encounters, but which includes, towards its end, this bracing bit of honesty: "I have no design for living, no philosophy— whether sage or fool, we must all struggle with life. I vacillate with inconsistencies."[20]

I note that there is, in his biographers, a correspondence between knowledge of his films and the depth and well-roundedness of the biography. In other words, the more deeply the critic understands and appreciates Chaplin's films, the more sympathetic the biography tends to be. The less the critics seem to exhibit an appreciation of Chaplin's films, the less predisposed they are to a sympathetic reading of his life. You might argue that fans of Chaplin are unduly influenced by his work. I would argue that, as is the case with most great artists, you get the best of Chaplin in his works of art. That's why they are the more worthy object of study.

It is remarkable how many traits Chaplin and his alter ego, Charlie, share and, at the same time, how much better the Tramp wears those traits. The Tramp is, for example, as Chaplin was, a fairly erotic creature, viscerally responsive to the flash of a young woman's ankle. But he's also a child who seems happiest just to tease and frolic with the young woman who comes his way. And his affection comes hand in hand with a Galahad-like tendency towards protectiveness that wasn't always apparent in Chaplin's real-life dealings with women. Charlie is an anarchist of sorts, master of all roles, faithful to none, a satirist bent on sending up all we take seriously. His attempts to fashion a role for himself as anarchist, decrying patriotism and refusing American citizenship, earned him the enmity of Americans and got him kicked out of the country. Charlie's cynicism is a welcome antidote to his sentimental tendencies. But Chaplin's own mordant cynicism often got him in hot water, the public reaction to the sophisticated pessimism of *Monsieur Verdoux* being a case in point.

Chaplin's films have often put me in mind of Baudelaire's poem "The Albatross" which compares the artist to the great sea bird which flies gracefully over vast expanses of ocean but is laughably awkward on small patches of ground. Charlie too is light and dexterous, an idealized dancer in his dreams or in his most spirited moments of fancy, but as in so many of his dream sequences, he always finishes by being roughly dropped on the ground where, like the albatross, he is at the mercy of his oversized feet. The metaphor also seems to apply to Chaplin *vis à vis* his fictional creation, Charlie. Charlie distills and idealizes qualities in Chaplin that were not enacted so gracefully in real life. "If only he could be as tolerant as 'Charlie,'" Burke said of Chaplin, "he would be happier,"[21] citing one more area in which Chaplin was outstripped by his own creation. Charlie, in many ways, represents the best of Chaplin's nature, a nature that often clashed as awkwardly with the world around it as Charlie's did with his. Like Charlie, and like all great artists, Chaplin was at his best, and only found real ease, in his dreams.

The Chronology of Chaplin's Films

Chaplin's filmic biography is engaging also, hence the tendency of critical works on Chaplin to proceed chronologically through his career on a film-by-film basis. My analysis of Chaplin will be organized according to ideas that I want to emphasize about his films rather than the chronology of his career and will focus on the silent films with Charlie, rather than the entirety of Chaplin's film output. But a thumbnail sketch of the chronological arc of his entire career might provide some useful context before my more specific analysis.

Spotted on tour with Fred Karno's traveling band of highly polished music hall comedians (a group that included Stan Laurel), Chaplin was recruited by Mack Sennett for Keystone. Chaplin's Keystone films represent the first solidification of Chaplin's talent as he carves out a spot as the leading light of Sennett's comedians and starts to learn the rudiments of filmmaking. Chaplin's film skills and his portraiture of Charlie both evolve significantly at Essanay where he first gets to make films according to the dictates of his own particular vision. The Mutual comedies represent a kind of arrival of the fully developed Chaplin. The films of this era are often the favorite of Chaplin aficionados. In these films Chaplin has arrived at a maturity of ideas and a polished presentation that would define the golden age of his career. Charlie, in the Mutual comedies, still has some of the freewheeling chaos and pugnacious aggressiveness about him that he would lose as both Chaplin and his alter ego aged and mellowed over the years. The Mutual films seem to be characterized by a creative glee. Perhaps their most telling characteristic is how often Charlie erupts into gleeful non sequiturs of inspired dance that seem to be as expressive of Chaplin being at the height of his fame, wealth and creative powers as they are of the Tramp's carefree nature.

The First National films are even more polished and the better ones are characterized by cleaner narrative lines and more ambitious mixtures of emotion. The central gags are often slower but at the same time more carefully choreographed. The comic abandon of the Mutual comedies gives way to ice-cold comic dances of almost mathematical precision. In fact, the entire arc of Chaplin's silent film career could be described as one in which he continuously slows himself down, gradually learning to draw more from the camera, moving closer to it, trusting it to spy the quietest gesture, increasingly learning to soak laughs out of patient timing.

By the time Chaplin was his own boss at United Artists, the company he founded with Mary Pickford, Douglas Fairbanks and D.W. Griffith, he was in the business of full-length feature films. For other Chaplin fans, the late First National and early United Artists films represent Chaplin's zenith, in particular *The Kid*, *The Gold Rush* and *City Lights*. These seem the films Chaplin was destined to create, the ones all others were leading up to. Here the emotions are deepest, the narratives most interesting, the complexities of the Tramp's character richer than ever. The Mutual, First National, and United Artists silent films represent the great core of Chaplin's work, and the primary object of study for this book.

Sound Films

Chaplin's last two silent films, *City Lights* and *Modern Times*, were made during the sound era. Both have complete soundtracks and explore the comic potential of sound. Snatches of dialogue exist in the periphery of *Modern Times*. Still, in the end, starring Charlie as they do, and limiting themselves almost entirely to the parameters of silent film, they seem more the final expressions of Chaplin's silent cinema. The three entirely sound pictures that Chaplin made for United Artists (*The Great Dictator*, *Monsieur Verdoux*, and *Limelight*) and the two he made with British financing at the end of his career (*A King in New York* and *A Countess from Hong Kong*) represent the last era in Chaplin's work, the era of his talkies. These are not Chaplin's greatest films and the decline here is not just due to the mismatch of Chaplin and sound. Chaplin was 40 years old by the time sound came around, 42 in *City Lights*, and 47 in *Modern Times*. Picasso, with characteristic ungenerous honesty, noted in 1952 when *Limelight* came out that "the real tragedy lies in the fact that Chaplin can no longer assume the physical appearance of the clown because he's no longer slender, no longer young, and no longer has the face and expression of his 'little man,' but that of a man who's grown old. His body isn't really him anymore."[22]

Some of this diminution in Chaplin's screen presence is apparent even by the time of *City Lights*. Chaplin looks a little stouter in that film than he had before, a little more subject to the laws of gravity, a little longer in the tooth. His moustache is at times a little too shellacked. And there are signs of age in his temperament as well, little bits of cloying mime and unctuous charm that the camera ruthlessly catches and which show that Chaplin is a bit more self-conscious and calculating in his effects. They suggest that the Tramp's absolute freedom, his clean anarchistic abandon, is just about spent.

Modern Times, though justly venerated, and the subject of much analysis in this book, probably represents the beginning of Chaplin's decline. Five years had passed since his last film. Chaplin physically embodies the Tramp even less so than he did in *City Lights*. And while *City Lights* seemed, in its day, a charming homage to a disappearing art form, *Modern Times* appeared to represent a stubborn fixation to the past. "By the time *City Lights* came out in 1931," writes Andrew Sarris, "audiences had become nostalgia for the lost glories of the silent screen. By 1936, everyone had adapted so completely to the sound film that Chaplin's intransigently silent mimetics in *Modern Times* seemed willful, reactionary, and technologically cowardly."[23] *Modern Times* has some of Chaplin's most sophisticated and perfectly carried-out gags, but it also provides glimpses of the didacticism, poor production values, and awkward response to sound that would mar the films that succeeded it.

Chaplin, out of a combination of fatigue and perfectionism, was making fewer films by the time of the talkie era and, most of his contemporaries and his critics agree, was falling out of step with technological developments in films. Certain that his films would sink or swim according to the merits of his own comedy, he was famously indifferent to continuity and set design. His attention to the soundtracks of these films, which is often their most refined feature, may also have made him more indifferent to certain visual aspects of the film. The sets in all of his talkies often have a shoddy, B-film quality. The use of rear projection, which is often quite accomplished in his earlier silent films, becomes glaringly artificial.

There are, nevertheless, innovative uses of sound in these films. Chaplin applied his aesthetics of omission and inference to sound just as he had to silent film and with some clever effect, for example the way he infers what orators are saying via kazoo sounds in *City Lights* or what Hinkel is saying, via a nonsensical version of German, in *The Great Dictator*. He liked aural puns, just as he had visual ones, for example the moment in *City Lights* when he swallows a whistle and summons dogs and taxis against his will. Chaplin's sound gags were innovative enough to influence French comic filmmaker Jacques Tati, one of film's greatest innovators in sound. We strongly detect the spirit of Chaplin in many of the sound gags in Tati's films just as we do in his affection for Chaplin-like visual puns. But many of Chaplin's sound gags are also leaden and tedious (the swallowed whistle gag, again, alas) and, in general, he never exhibited the facility in sound comedy that he had in silent comedy.

Modern Times nevertheless remains our last view of Chaplin in his prime, our last whole view of the character of Charlie, and our last chance to see Chaplin toil in the domain of silent cinema. The rest of Chaplin's sound films are much more qualified in their success. It can be amusing at times to watch the contortions that devotees of Chaplin go through to convince themselves that Chaplin's talkies are tantamount to the quality of his silent work. That said, each of the films is utterly original, a *sui generis* testimony to the brazenly original nature of Chaplin's artistic temperament, as well as his artistic and financial independence. This seems like the right place to say a few words about these films as they will be, for the rest of this study, relegated to the background.

The Great Dictator, like *Modern Times*, has enjoyed a boost in value, it seems to me, because it traffics in overt political and thematic ideas, always the quickest way to get critics to take a film seriously. There are not many great sequences in the film and the fact that Chaplin puts so many fine character actors to so little use reminds us that the key to Chaplin's best films had always been Chaplin himself. He would never be a Preston Sturges who knew how to get the most out of an ensemble cast.

But the film testifies to one of Chaplin's greatest virtues: his tendency to take on the seemingly unassailable, to act on his belief that nothing is beyond satire. The rise of Hitler was an unbelievably touchy subject from which to fashion a comedy and even Chaplin later admitted that, had he known about the death camps, he would not have made the film. It deserves praise if for no other reason than that no other Hollywood filmmaker had the freedom or courage to shove a pie in Hitler's face as Chaplin did. Still, its really great sequences (the dance with the globe, the shave set to Brahms' "Hungarian Rhapsody") are the silent ones set to music, scenes that exhibit Chaplin's gift for two forms of non-verbal communication, mime and music.

Moreover, the climactic speech, though filled with admirable and well-expressed ideas (at this point in time it is perhaps the most popular Chaplin clip on YouTube), is also delivered with an unctuous sanctimony that seems a betrayal of the principles of Chaplin's silents. In his greatest films, Chaplin put a premium on encasing ideas and emotions in fine physical detail and not spitting ideas out in words, which were, of course, available in silent films as well, in title cards. Chaplin's barber in the film had been, throughout the film, a man of few words and so Chaplin meant this great burst of articulation at the end to catch us by surprise, and perhaps provoke the thought that, after all these years of silence, Chaplin was more articulate than we had ever realized. But how much more effective is the singing waiter scene in *Modern Times* when Chaplin introduced his voice to the world for the first time in a song that was a mishmash of languages and, by its very nonsense, mocked the significance of language itself.

Monsieur Verdoux is, to my mind, one of Chaplin's more successful sound films, an often very sophisticated exercise in the vicious mordancy that is at the heart of Charlie's lasting appeal. In fact, Monsieur Verdoux seems, of all Chaplin's characters from his talkies, the closest to the spirit of Charlie—in his amorality, his jumpiness, his mocking nature, his love of flowers, his energetic, fastidious nature. Monsieur Verdoux plays the role of the dandy with the same aplomb that Charlie had. He is perhaps Chaplin's most successful middle-aged reincarnation of Charlie. Chaplin seems more at ease with himself in this film than he does in any of his talkies, as he loses himself in the busy, effete efficiency of the elegant gentleman role that was second nature to him, indeed even part of his public persona. Still, the majority of the film's scenes are quite static and Martha Raye torpedoes it with a loud humor that seems more of a piece with a Three Stooges short than this elegant little conceit. And this film, like *The Great Dictator,* finishes with an extremely literate speech, rendered with an air of unctuous self-satisfaction, that somehow makes the speech as grating as it is impressive.

Limelight is an even creakier, more stale exercise than Chaplin's first two talkies but, at the same time, an often touching reflection on Chaplin's career that capitalizes on the pathos inherent in his role in it, as a faded clown. Some of its best lines are self-reflexive ones, like Calvero saying "must be the Tramp in me" or when he's referred to as "that old reprobate." At the same time, it's a very wordy film and Chaplin postures like a sage in it, handing down one adage after another to his young charge, played by Claire Bloom. These adages are, like the speeches from *The Great Dictator* and *Monsieur Verdoux*, often lovely and thought-provoking, but at the same time expressed with a sanctimony that would have provoked the early Chaplin to mimicry.

I'd have to agree with Gerald Mast's assessment (much of which applies to Chaplin's other sound films as well) that it "is probably a better film in the light of the 40-year career that went before it," a reminder "that the totality of Chaplin's work is more impressive than any individual film."[24]

A King in New York has all the faults that came to define Chaplin's sound films: an awkward, ponderous pace, bland sets, and poor technical skills. The satire on the shallowness and pervasiveness of American popular culture is often tired and too broad (not to mention reflective of an aging sensibility obviously out of touch with that culture). On the other hand, despite its political subject matter, it's a less preachy film than the talkies that precede it and signals, with *A Countess from Hong Kong*, a refreshing return, in Chaplin's last phase, to light comedy. Critics often fault Chaplin for the "sour grapes" nature of the film but he actually avoids the sanctimony and speechiness of his previous sound films by putting his ideas into the mouth of a precocious ten-year-old boy, a pint-sized Marxist given to political rants. It's a great idea, a sly, round-about way, on Chaplin's part, of taking the mickey out of his political self-righteousness. In fact, the satire of the boy's simplistic rants could be read as Chaplin's rebuttal to those who identify him too closely with such politics. The moments in which the boy works himself up to an oratorical lather are delicately self-mocking and would have been exceptionally funny if Chaplin had handed the role to someone other than his son. That decision, due his son's stiff awkwardness, costs this film a great deal of its effectiveness. Still, it's hard not to like the calm thesis of the film—so expressive of the calm before life's tragedies that Chaplin's silent films had always evinced: that McCarthyism was just a passing childish phase, not to be intimidated by or taken seriously, something at which to laugh.

A Countess from Hong Kong may be Chaplin's most underrated sound film. It's certainly too odd in rhythm and patchy in technique to be counted a success but, based on a script from the 1930s that Chaplin had written for Paulette Goddard, it is refreshingly absent of the didactic qualities of Chaplin's other talkies, a throwback to the more modest goals of Chaplin's earliest cinema. By this point, Chaplin, now in his seventies, seems to have finally weaned himself of his late-in-life taste for political oratory. If the film has any charm, it is in its lack of pretension and its Technicolor reference to a simple filmmaking of the past, a cinema that aimed to be light and airy, but also charming and sophisticated. The few discerning critics who did like it, John Betjeman for example, found it appealing as an antidote, both to Chaplin's recent, strident sound films and the self-seriousness, political activism, and artistic heavy-handedness that characterized much of the cinema at the time it came out. There is something of Chaplin's characteristic boldness in making a film of such slight charm, so fey and delicate in its intents, during the sixties, an era in which films were so often characterized by overt political content or experimental film technique. There are not many films as truculently out of step with their times as is this one.

Interesting and unique as these films are, and intriguing in the way they involve themselves with Chaplin's life story, they are his minor works and represent his talent in decline. For the most part, the rest of this book will concern itself with Chaplin's greatest artistic expression, his silent films starring his alter ego, Charlie.

Two

Charlie's Role-Playing

One of the most delightful, and most celebrated, characteristics of Charlie, Chaplin's fictional silent film alter ego, is his ability to take whatever banal reality he finds himself in and transform it, imaginatively, into a design of his own fancy. Critics tend to point to the Keystone comedy *Dough and Dynamite* as an early example of Chaplin's gift for what has variously been described as gags of "transformation," "transposition," or "metamorphosis." In that film, Charlie is an awful baker but by the time the film is finished he has used his dough, as Gerald Mast notes, "as boxing gloves, bracelets, quicksand, a mallet, a slingshot, a discus, a chair, and something to occupy his roaming hands while flirting with a pretty girl."[1] Everything except what the dough was intended for: the baking of bread.

The real go-to film for this kind of gag, though, is *The Pawnshop*. Chaplin was at the height of his craft when he made this film and, like a few others of Chaplin's pre–feature length films (*The Immigrant* and *A Dog's Life*, for example), it's unusually complete and polished, marked by inventiveness from stem to stern. The hodgepodge of objects to play within the pawnshop setting seems to have particularly inspired Chaplin's metamorphosis gags. The most famous example is the scene in which pawnshop clerk Charlie examines a clock that a man (played by Albert Austin) has brought to the shop in the hopes of pawning it. This is one the most frequently analyzed scenes in any Chaplin film, so much so that Graham Petrie, in his acerbic essay introducing his bibliography of Chaplin studies, refers to the scene's frequent citation in Chaplin studies as an example of the repetitiveness of Chaplin criticism.[2] But it's a hard scene to lay off, as it is such a concise example of Chaplin's skill at transposition and the accumulation of invention of which he's capable in a very short time.

Chaplin passes through an extraordinary number of roles in the course of examining the clock. He grabs a nearby stethoscope and examines it like a doctor, first listening to its heart, then taking its pulse. He picks up an auger and starts to drill into the clock with a neutral, business-like demeanor as though he were a carpenter going about his craft. He pries the clock open as though it were a tuna can, smelling the contents to see if they have gone rancid. He unscrews the mouthpiece of a telephone

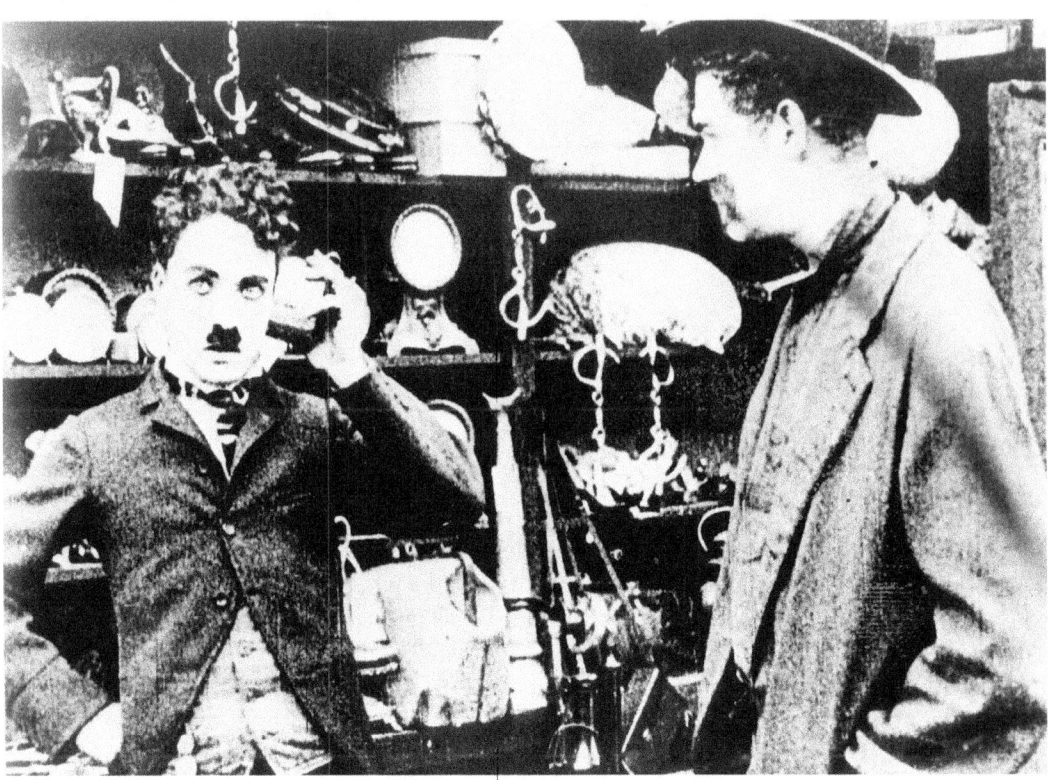

The *Pawnshop* scene in which Charlie engages in a pantomimic frenzy as he examines a customer's (Albert Austin) clock is one of the most studied in Chaplin's entire oeuvre.

and, pretending it's a jeweler's eyeglass, examines the clock as though it were surfaced with gems. He oils the clock as though it were a car engine and extracts parts of it with pliers as though he were a dentist extracting teeth. Stretching out the long coils of the clock's inner matter, he transforms into a haberdasher or interior decorator measuring and snipping bolts of fabric. All this is done with an impeccable deadpan that suggests consummate professional confidence and mastery. Charlie conducts himself as though he's done this kind of thing a thousand times before, as though it were second nature to him, when, in fact, it's apparent that Charlie hasn't the slightest idea how to determine the worth of a clock. Charlie displays only one practical skill, which he exercises to perfection here: how to rile a customer.

This lengthy description doesn't even mention the various little gags that reside in the interstices of all this playacting, for example the way Chaplin twirls his hammer with great finesse, bringing it down, for no reason other than cruel fun, on the hand of the customer, or the way he examines small bits of the clock with his naked eye rather than the one with the "jeweler's eyeglass." Chaplin's rapid-fire wizardry in this scene goes a long way towards explaining why it is no easy matter analyzing his comedy and, in turn, why this scene continues to invite commentary. Chaplin invents with such mercurial speed and precision that it takes enormous effort just to catalogue his effects, much less draw conclusions from them.

Charlie's tendency to playact, to rapidly shift from one role to another with the protean energy of a genie, reflects on his art and thought in a variety of ways. In this chapter, I want to emphasize, in particular, four aspects to Chaplin's gags of metamorphosis that tell us a good deal about the complexity of Charlie's nature and of Chaplin's films in general.

Spirit of Play

First, Charlie's love of role-playing reflects his childlike nature. A great deal of Charlie's attractiveness lies in his unfettered childishness, his way of traipsing through life in a spirit of play. A large proportion of Charlie's transformation gags, those moments where he transposes one reality for another, are due to a childlike exuberance, a sheer enjoyment of life, a desire to playact with any object at hand, to put on a show. In *The Immigrant*, for example, he maddens his competitors in a game of craps with his elaborate pitcher's windup that serves as a prelude to his delivery of the dice. Just throwing dice isn't enough for Charlie. In *City Lights* the formalities of a fancy restaurant remind him of church and so when he is handed a menu he stands up, opens the menu and begins to sing. He needs to make a point, to put on a show.

Sometimes, like a child, he playacts entirely for his own amusement. While sweeping in *The Pawnshop*, for example, Charlie straightens out a long string on the floor and walks along it, pretending he's a high-wire walker, his performance replete with near-falls and a final leap to safety and bows before imaginary applause. He performs a similar feat by means of a long rolled-up carpet in *Behind the Screen*. Charlie will often lark about like this, soaking in imaginary applause on an imaginary stage, in the manner of a hammy child. In *The Pilgrim*, Charlie, an escaped con masquerading as a minister, delivers a distinctly unecclesiastical one-man show on the subject of David and Goliath that leaves his congregation stunned with horror, except for one boy who, it appears, has been entertained at church for the first time in his life. The boy's solitary applause, though, is enough to send Charlie into paroxysms of gratitude in the manner of a star performer reaping plaudits from a wildly enthusiastic audience. He bows with exaggerated gratitude, skips off the stage in glee, and returns over and over again to imaginary calls of "encore." Charlie, like a child, is quick to adapt to the role of adored performer. You can find versions of the same gag when he is introduced in the boxing ring in *The Champion* and after he entertains Edna with his violin in *The Vagabond*.

Behind the Screen is particularly rich in gags of transformation that find their origin in this childlike excess of energy or desire to have fun. In this movie, Charlie is a stagehand working with a film crew (a recurrent scenario in Chaplin's films), and he has been instructed to brush down a bear rug to prepare it for a scene. When he gets to the bear's head, the spirit of fun and playacting takes over him. He sprinkles oil on his hands, rubs them down and gives the bear a deep scalp massage. He draws a comb from his pocket and brushes the bear's head with both the brush he had been using and the comb, a nice imitation of the two-handed dexterity of a barber. He takes the time to draw, with meticulous professional attention, a fine part down the middle of the bear's head with his comb and carefully parts the fur. He takes a nearby rag and throws it over the bear head, pretending it's a hot towel, and finally twists up the rag and flags it at the bear's head a few times in the manner of a barber dismissing his client with a few final cleaning gestures.

This kind of excessive devotion to meaningless detail (usually paired with an indifference to those aspects of a job that do matter) is why Charlie fails at work. Charlie has an excess of energy and ingenuity. However, it does not get channeled into work but rather into imaginative play that draws his energy away from work. Charlie would rather play and playact than work.

Later, in the same film, he will pretend to be a growling, then begging, dog as he competes with co-worker Albert Austin for the leg of mutton Austin has brought to lunch. (Charlie's lunches almost always compare disadvantageously to those of his co-workers.) When Austin, rather insultingly, gives Charlie his left-over bones, as one might a begging dog, Charlie sizes them up and sees they're no good for eating. Dropping to the floor like a child at an adult's party, he assumes the role of a world-class timpanist, using the bones as drumsticks on a number of empty tin plates that the lunching workers have left at their feet. The workers are too dulled by satiety to notice. Charlie is, as usual, mostly entertaining himself—until, that is, he strikes his boss' foot with the bone rather than the plate, making his boss howl in pain, and Austin in laughter.

It's worth noting that Charlie's spirit of play is rarely appreciated by the adult world. With the exception of a few women who are open to Charlie's flirtatiousness, his play annoys others. In this sense, Charlie's playfulness is not just for his own amusement. It has an undercurrent of hostility. Charlie's antics often seem meant to annoy his peers. He's an inveterate clown, and, like a child, prone to hijinks at those moments it's most likely to draw opprobrium down on him. Like a child's, Charlie's playfulness is often offered in a spirit of rebellion, as a refutation to the logic of the adult world. Like a child, Charlie often has to play alone. And like a child, he makes adults pay for his boredom.

So many of Charlie's transformations touch on habits of childhood: hamming it up before an imaginary audience, pretending he or other things are animals, making a clatter in the spirit of music. In the finale of *Behind the Screen,* Charlie finds an opportunity to play the game that little boys have since time immemorial: war. The director of the slapstick comedy movie that stagehand Charlie is working on makes the mistake of asking Charlie to be part of a pie fight scene. This onscreen pie fight, of course, devolves into an off-screen one, a pitched battle on the set between Charlie and other members of the crew, with Charlie on one side of a set wall, the crew members on the other, pies sailing through the door between.

The pie fight incites Charlie's childlike imagination and spirit of play as he begins to conceive of it in terms of emblematic images of World War I. He turns over a table to protect himself from incoming pies and is now peering over the edge of a deep trench. He picks up two wine bottles and, drawing them together, creates the facsimile of binoculars used for reconnaissance; he waves a white flag to communicate surrender. There is no plausible logic to his co-workers playing along with Charlie's game and respecting the white flag, as they do, allowing Charlie to rearm and nail them with another pie. The logic here is comic; Charlie so confuses his co-workers by his play that he stuns them into immobility, allowing him to run circles around them in the manner of a child gone mad. Charlie's play here is not just fun, then, it's also aggressive, a mocking kind of play that lends advantage in battle, and a teasing of others who are too dull to play games and too dull-witted to keep up with his.

Sometimes an event so inspires Charlie with the spirit of play that he will execute several roles in rapid succession. In the course of his son's fight with another child in *The Kid*, for example, Charlie is so excited by the excitement of the event that he portrays (with spot-on accuracy, and all in a matter of a few moments): a ringside audience member taking bets on the match, a boxing manager counseling his boxer in the corner of the ring between rounds, and a ref announcing the end of the fight and proclaiming a victor. It's an elaboration of an earlier gag, from *The Cure*, in which Charlie, watching a man get a vigorous massage, pretends to be the ref at a wrestling match and then, when he gets his own massage, pretends to be a wrestler himself.

Charlie recalls, in these moments, the improvisational theater of childhood, where we created scenarios which were always in transformation, as were our roles in those scenarios. Charlie has brought this habit up into the adult world and in doing so casts his vote for childhood play as more fun and meaningful than adult play, by which we can assume he means that adult habit of assuming one role, taking it very seriously and sticking to it like glue. All the telltale signs of Romanticism are evident in Chaplin's childlike love of metamorphosis: the emphasis on the imagination rather than concrete world, the transcendence of art, the wisdom of the child.

Charlie's Willful Re-Arrangement of the World

A second aspect of Charlie's character that the transformation gags emphasize (and one that reflects the way Charlie holds a variety of opposing tendencies in counterbalance) is that for all his insignificance, maybe *because* of that insignificance, Charlie stubbornly imposes his will on the world, makes it serve his purposes and work according to the way he alone sees fit. It has often been remarked that Charlie is incapable of using the tools of whatever trade in which he finds himself for their intended purpose, but almost always invents marvelous uses for them that accord to his own imaginative designs. In *Work*, Charlie takes time off from his job as painter's assistant to woo a young maid. While he woos her, he affects the posture of an idle man of leisure, though of course he only has the trappings of a house painter at his disposal. As he affects a lordly spirit of leisure, he cleans his nails with his trowel, files the nails with an enormous iron file used for sharpening knives, and brushes them clean with a huge paintbrush, creating, in sum, a kind of Alice in Wonderland file and nail kit of his own device. In *A Burlesque on Carmen* he creates a host of personal uses for his military equipment: His crested helmet is a brush, his poignard a back scratcher, his sword a pool cue.

There's a kind of quiet rebellion going on here. Charlie likes to rearrange the world according to his purposes. The world generally has little use for Charlie; all right, then he will have no use for the world as it is, but rather as he would like it to be. In *A Night Out*, Charlie, drunk, uses the doffed hat of a man dining at a table next to his as a spittoon. Exiting the restaurant, he uses a decorative fountain as his personal sink, splashing water on his underarms, transforming his dinner napkin into a bath towel, and tearing off a huge frond from a plant in the restaurant's fountain design and using its stem as a toothbrush. Later, still drunk, he checks into a hotel but would clearly prefer it to be a bar. His foot instinctively searches for the non-existent foot rail at the check-in desk and he chugs down the ink in the ink well, mistaking it for a shot glass.

Charlie is drunk here, but drunken Charlie is only a few degrees more willful than sober Charlie. His behavior here conforms perfectly with Charlie's general insistence on the right to redefine his surroundings according to his own terms.

There is an oppositional structure to many of Chaplin's transformation gags. Instruments of labor become instruments of play. Instruments of war serve tame domestic purposes. Sometimes Chaplin seems like a Surrealist experimenting with the world, juxtaposing contrarieties in the search for new meanings. In *A Night Out*, the drunk Charlie gently tucks his pants and suspenders into bed and then stretches out on the floor beside the bed. Chaplin loves, in scenes like this, to treat inanimate objects as though they are alive and in others, conversely, to treat humans as if they are inanimate objects.

No gags speak to Chaplin's war with the world more than those in which he manipulates living humans into mechanical devices made for his own convenience. Charlie finds many uses for other people. He likes, especially early in his career, to swing his leg over their laps when he sits down, in the manner of a leg rest. If they bend over, he will sit down on them like a chair or lean on them as if they were a railing. If he is passing a person who is bent over within a narrow passage, he will gently grab their behind and employ it like a turnstile through which he passes. He uses men's beards to dry his tears, clean his mouth after eating, dry his hands after washing, as a blotter for his pen, and as leashes with which to lead them. He uses any human appendage as flint for his matches, preferring bare feet, ears, bottoms and the crown of bald men's heads. The latter he also finds useful as mirrors. If women's stomachs protrude he uses them as shelves to rest his elbow on. He finds fallen unconscious bodies useful as platforms that provide greater elevation or bridges over messy territory. When bossy men gesticulate, he hangs his hat and coat on their outraised arms. He finds exposed tongues useful when he wants to affix a stamp to a letter.

These moments of transformation are creative but also hostile. They represent Charlie, who has nothing in the material world, fighting with the one weapon he does have: an acute imagination. In this realm he can get the best of people, and recreate them according to his ideas and needs. When, in *Work*, Charlie's boss hands Charlie his coat to be hung up, as though Charlie were his lackey, Charlie hands him back a coin as though he were a coat-check person giving a token. Playacting is Charlie's way of contending with the indignities of the world.

Charlie's need to recreate the world according to his personal imaginative enterprise, like his childlike love of playacting, also points to the inherent Romanticism of Chaplin's cinema. Charlie rejects a world of utilitarianism for a higher world, summoned by imagination, and infused with charming humor and, often, suggestions of beauty. Many critics see Charlie's stubborn tendency to use the world as he will as an extension of his inherently aristocratic nature, but of course, when Charlie acts like an elegant swell, he's also only playacting. That's just one of the many roles he adopts, albeit his favorite or default one. The real Charlie makes the world change because it doesn't suit him, because it doesn't have much time for a piece of scruff like him. And when, in rejecting this world for his imaginative one, he makes that imaginative one so much more lively and poetic, so charming and attractive, he strikes a blow for the spirit of imagination, for the power of art and theater. Charlie is, in the end, not an aristocrat, even in spirit. His pride and obstinacy is that of the artist. He is an adherent to a sacred world that transcends our own and which he is, wizard-like, uniquely capable of summoning. Charlie stubbornly insists on the relevance of play, of playacting, of imagination, of cleverness, charm and beauty, that is to say, of art, in a world that only believes in that which is practically useful, the utilitarian.

Charlie's Ease in the World

A good number of Chaplin's transformation gags point to a third, signal aspect of Charlie's nature: his extreme comfort in this world. Charlie has the ability, despite his poverty, to summon, via imagination, creature comforts that allow him to live with great domestic ease, a kind of comfort we would think only possible for those with much greater resources. Take for example one of his most famous sequences, the one in *The Gold Rush* in which Charlie cooks his boot so that he and his mining partner, Big Jim McKay, can have a Thanksgiving dinner. The scene is famous, first, because of Chaplin's ability to successfully mime a Thanksgiving dinner via such meager fare, for example when he removes the body of the shoe from its sole and nails as though he were filleting a fish, or when he winds the shoestrings on his fork as though he were expertly devouring pasta. But the scene is also a charming study in how little it takes to satisfy Charlie, his ability to substitute imagination for want.

Charlie insists that this dinner follow the formula of a Thanksgiving dinner even if he has to act his way through it. He mimics the holiday chef nicely, as he prepares the boots, prodding the boot which he's boiling for tenderness, signifying to Big Jim, with satisfaction and eager anticipation, when it is tender, cleaning (absurdly) a plate of a previously undetected smudge before he lays the boot on it, as though readying a platter for a cherished Sunday roast.

During the dinner Chaplin cuts between Charlie and Big Jim and, in doing so, presents us with two alternatives as to how to deal with straitened circumstances. Big Jim slogs through the dinner, as we would, in somber horror, chewing his bites with a slow, grim determination, barely suppressing his nausea. Charlie, on the other hand, is the picture of holiday satisfaction. He attacks his meal with a bustling air, twirling his shoelace pasta and distributing tacks from the shoe on his plate like so many clovers or spices. He licks the nails clean as though they were chicken bones. After dinner, wearing that post-feast expression of dazed satiety that Chaplin specializes in (which he couldn't possibly be really experiencing after *this* meal), Charlie offers Jim a left-over, bent nail to be tugged at in the manner of the turkey wishbone after dinner. That the nail could not possibly break like a bone doesn't bother Charlie. When Jim turns his offer down, Charlie tries, in one of Chaplin's typically tiny throwaway gestures, to break the nail in half himself, before tossing it away, as it was not conforming to his fantasy. His expression doesn't let on for a second that the nail is an impossible substitute for the genuine article. His gaze remains frozen in that dull expression of post-dinner contentment. After dinner, he indulges in the satisfying burps with which Charlie always concludes his dinner. Not for a moment has Charlie let on that he hasn't engaged in a typical holiday feast.

Many of Chaplin's most beloved scenes are those where Charlie creates a little domestic paradise out of nothing, playacts his way to total comfort. Despite their poverty, Charlie and his son, in *The Kid,* live with a contentedness far beyond their means, due to Charlie's ingenuity in transforming environments. A hanging teakettle becomes a baby bottle, a wicker chair with a hole carved out and a spittoon underneath a potty seat. When summoned to the breakfast table by his son who has been making pancakes for the two of them, Charlie, who has been lounging in bed, pokes his head through a fortuitous hole in his blanket and the blanket suddenly transforms into an elegant caftan. He slips on his ratty old shoes as though they were fine slippers and arrives at the table in an impressive approximation of the elegant lord of the manor. This is Charlie's art in a nutshell, an aristocratic use of disheveled objects, a sense of noble leisure among the worst squalor.

One of my favorite details in Charlie and the kid's domestic routine is that Charlie has rigged their pay-as-you-go heater so that the coin put into it returns immediately to the owner. The unconscious nonchalance with which Jackie Coogan effects this action—asking Charlie for the coin, feeding the meter, collecting the coin and returning it to Charlie, all while the two of them continue to ready themselves for dinner—speaks volumes of how tidily Charlie and he are circumventing their poverty, how practiced their routine is. Charlie's home hums with a jerry-rigged efficiency. It's not just the ingenious way in which Charlie creates things out of nothing that makes his little domestic spots so pleasing, but the way he sells those places, the manifest satisfaction of Charlie and the kid as they go about their cozy routine.

There's a parallel moment in *The Rink* when Charlie, arriving at a skating rink, skirts under the ticket window without missing a step, barely seeming even to see the window, with an unconscious, habitual ease that testifies to years of escaping entrance fees. Part of Charlie's comfortable arrangement with life is this kind of streamlining, paring away all inessential obstacles.

Charlie displays, fairly early in his films, a talent for domesticity or playing house. He sets a fine table for Edna in *The Vagabond*, even if his shirt is the table cloth and its bundled-up sleeves napkins. The dinner party for Georgia and her friends in *The Gold Rush* is impeccably prepared—a roast in the oven, holiday decorations and gifts abounding—even if the tablecloth is a newspaper and an intrusive donkey eats one of the napkins that Charlie has so carefully folded. When, in *The Gold Rush*, Charlie wakes to a cabin so cold that long stalactites of icicles hang from the ceiling, he grabs a basket and, casually plucking the icicles as if they were fruit from the tree, harvests the morning's water. And he performs this action with that air that he has of contentedly going about his business, of doing something as if it were a routine that he had established for years (actually it's his and Jim's first morning at the cabin).

The invention is funny—but even *funnier*, because it's also charming, is the Tramp's determination to transform destitution into cozy routine and comfort. There is little that life can throw at him that he doesn't respond to with a calm sense of routine. This is Charlie's pluckiest characteristic and his most Puritan. Charlie is not all dancing and flowers, the mystical clown. He may not like jobs but he's perfectly capable of going about his business. He doesn't need much and he meets want with calm and resilience. His ability to endure life's travails with a Puritan's sturdiness, asceticism and calm routine is one of the least commented-upon aspects of his character.

Even when he doesn't have the luxury of a domicile, Charlie is always working on refining the domestic detail of his life. *A Dog's Life* begins with Charlie sleeping in the dirt of an abandoned junkyard on a cold day, his head resting on a small barrel he's using as a pillow. But he becomes conscious of a draft issuing from a hole in the wall against which his bottom rests. Charlie reflects momentarily before pulling from beneath his shirt some newspaper that he had obviously been using for padding and warmth and stuffs it into the hole. Lying down again, he finds that his hands exposed to the cold are now his problem. Spying an empty industrial cylinder of sorts, he uses it as a hand muff. Now, he can nestle in contentedly. Charlie is always innovating like this, always padding his nest.

In *City Lights,* the newsboys who tease Charlie are so amused by the ragged fabric, presumably the shards of Charlie's undergarments, protruding from a hole in the seat of his pants, that they grab the fabric and rip it out. Charlie indignantly grabs the fabric back, looks at it and immediately sees its potential as a handkerchief. He folds it carefully, blows his nose in it and then tucks it suavely into his suit jacket pocket, a touch of urbane elegance that ignores that this material was once his underwear and that the rest of his clothes are in utter disrepair. Chaplin's films are filled with examples, like this, of Charlie finding creature comforts at the moment when he would be least expected to. In *Shoulder Arms,* Charlie opens his wine bottles and lights his cigarettes by holding them above his trench and letting enemy snipers, respectively, nip off the top of the bottle and ignite the end of the cigarette. Charlie is a master of efficiency but even more of finding the comforting aspects of the bleakest circumstances. In fact, the bleaker the circumstances, the greater the field of play yielded to imagination.

Amazingly, Charlie's attention to creature comforts can be even more fleeting than these small examples. In *The Count,* tailor Eric Campbell fires his assistant Charlie, and then forcefully shows him the door, fast-stepping him out, holding Charlie by the back collar and seat of his pants. Charlie's toes barely touch the floor as he is hustled out the door, but that doesn't stop him from pulling out a cigarette, striking a match on a passing sideboard, and lighting the cigarette before he reaches the door. In *City Lights* the butler throws him out of the house but Charlie has managed to steal some fruit on the way, and as he stumbles on to the pavement he transitions, in a blink of an eye, to the erect posture of a man of leisure taking a walk while peeling a banana. In *The Floorwalker,* Campbell lifts Charlie from the ground while strangling him but Charlie is blasé enough about the whole thing, presumably from years of enduring this kind of abuse, that he takes the time to scratch one leg with another, and then the other leg with his arm.

These gags represent the *reductio ad absurdum* of Charlie's ability to find domestic security in the most straitened circumstances. Charlie cultivates his creature comforts even in moments of violent threat. To be sure, these moments also convey his obstinacy and unwillingness to let someone get the better of him. But they also underline Charlie's immense skill at finding comfort in the eye of a hurricane, his ability to establish comforting routine in the most trying of circumstances. Even in those tense moments when Charlie is stealing food, and is under intense threat of detection, he can't stop himself from also stealing a little sauce or flavoring for his filched food, as in *The Circus* where he interrupts his brazen bite-by-bite theft of a child's treat (while the child is in his father's arms) to spread on it a little jelly he finds in a nearby vendor's stand. Charlie insists on the creature comforts in the most perilous moments of danger. One of the things that mark Charlie as a superior sort, despite his shabby trappings, is his ability to meet adversity with this kind of resolute calm and aesthetic panache. Even under the most dire threats, Charlie insists that he is a man of leisure who is essentially unruffled by his trying circumstances.

In these gags Charlie's insistence on his creature comforts has reached the point of being a kind of challenge to the world. Just try to bother him. This touches on one of the most significant aspects of Charlie' persona. Charlie has very little in the world, in most films next to nothing. But precisely because he has nothing, he is free. Thoreau would have loved Charlie, whose happiness and freedom exist in proportion to how little he needs and how little he has. In film after film, Charlie provides evidence of a fundamental law: It's not easy to disturb a man who has nothing to lose.

Surely one of Chaplin's most emblematic gags, in this vein, has to be the one in *The Kid* where Charlie readies himself for bed in a flophouse. As he undresses, a pickpocket in the cot next to his, who is pretending to sleep, and to whom Charlie's back is turned, searches Charlie's pockets. We have just witnessed Charlie spend his last cent on this flophouse bed and so, when Charlie sees the man's hand rifling through his pocket, he shares a conspiratorial giggle with the audience and continues to go about undressing. This image alone, of Charlie, untroubled, untying his tie while a man picks his pocket, is expressive of the liberating freedom Charlie experiences in the heart of his poverty. Charlie is unassailable because he has nothing. There's a double payoff to Charlie's poverty here: He's not bitten by the mania of protecting his possessions and he is able to tolerate, with equanimity and good humor, the world as it is, to let it go along its comic and corrupt way. When you are not always in a state of protective paranoia, the world can seem a more benign place.

But the second part of the gag is best: The thief discovers in Charlie's pocket a coin of which Charlie had no awareness. Now *this* surprises Charlie and he quickly arrests the man's search and takes back the coin. The man withdraws his arm but Charlie, still up for some fun, impishly grabs the man's arm and returns it to his pockets, hoping that the arm might unearth more booty.

The gag is, in many ways, a celebration of the way life can reward those who least think about their own welfare, the providential grace of unsought rewards. Chaplin seems to suggest here that good things come to those who need little, as opposed to those graspers, like the pickpocket, who hunt things down and come up empty-handed anyway. It echoes a scene in the earlier film *Police* in which Charlie, who we know to be penniless, is robbed. While the robber searches Charlie's back pocket in what we know is futility, Charlie casually reaches into the robber's coat pocket and easily plucks out a coin. In scenes like this, Charlie is rewarded for not seeking fortune. Fortune finds him. Conversely, things often go badly for him when he tries too hard or cares too much about the outcome. Charlie thrives on low expectations and improvisation.

Because Charlie really needs nothing in this world, jail doesn't intimidate him very much. His problems in *Police* begin when he is released from prison, as the title card says, "once again into the cruel, cruel world." And we see in *Modern Times* what a cozy nest he makes of jail, to the point of being very disturbed at having to leave. Even as late as *Monsieur Verdoux*, Chaplin is working variations on the recurrent gag of Charlie's comic willingness to go to jail. In that film the police have finally located Verdoux at a restaurant. Verdoux, feeling his fate closing in on him, decides to give himself up but, comically, has a difficult time getting the attention of the police who are racing around in a dither trying to track him down.

It might even seem that there is a contradiction in Chaplin's films between Charlie's abject fear of police, the way he turns on a dime at the mere glimpse of a police officer, and his characteristic indifference to being arrested. But it's not fear of arrest that makes police so frightening to Charlie. Police, in Chaplin's films, are oppressive, paternal figures who touch on Charlie's innate guilt, a guilt we all carry and which makes the heart of even the innocent beat more rapidly when near a policeman. But when Charlie is actually escorted to prison, he tends to be quite light-hearted, for example in the *City Lights* scene where, his quest to find money for the blind flower girl accomplished, Charlie goes off to jail quite happily, expressing his calm resignation with his trademark gesture of flipping his cigarette backwards over his shoulder and giving it a backward kick with his heel as he's led through the portals of the jail.

Certainly one of the sequences that best inscribes Charlie's great comfort in having nothing is the *Modern Times* one in which he intentionally gets arrested because he misses so much the security and comforts of jail. Charlie decides the most enjoyable way to find his way back to jail is to have a great meal and then not pay for it. Part of the success of the gag is pure wish fulfillment. Charlie eats whatever he wants at a self-serve deli, knowing he will not be paying. But the real humor in the gag is Charlie's immense calm as he eats this meal. Never has anyone feared arrest less. After he's fully sated himself, he strolls leisurely to the cashier, tapping the window of the cafe with prim superiority and summoning a cop from the street as though he were summoning a servant. He takes the time to assure the check-out girl that the meal was good before presenting the cop with the bill. He manages to grab one last creature comfort, a toothpick, as the cop drags him away and to doff his hat to the woman at the counter in one last moment of civility.

As the policeman calls in his collar on a street phone, Charlie, handcuffed to the policeman, turns his attention to a nearby newsstand where he buys a fine cigar, starts to smoke it, and proceeds to hand out candy to several street waifs. The policeman, phone call finished, snatches Charlie's cigar away, but Charlie, as soon as the policeman's attention is diverted again, grabs the cigar back and the cop turns to find him smoking happily again. (This is a common gag in Chaplin. He turns into a kind of octopus, a parody of a grasping toddler, whenever someone tries to lead him away by force.) When the cop yanks the cigar away a second time, Charlie tops off the whole routine with a little party trick for the benefit of the policeman and the newsstand vendor. He blows his last puff of smoke out, pretends to grab the smoke with his hand and compress it into the top of his hat and then opens up his mouth from which the smoke escapes, as if it had traveled through his hat to his mouth. The vendor too gets one final doff of the hat before Charlie disappears into the paddy wagon. The whole gag is a celebration of Charlie's indifference to incarceration, of the inability of the world to confine Charlie, of the independence he maintains despite having nothing, but really *because* he has nothing.

The humor here is in Charlie's calm in a storm, that ability that Fred Karno fostered in his comedians, to be calm and dignified in the midst of chaos they themselves have unleashed. Who but Charlie could care so little about going to jail, who could need so little that he is just as content to be in jail as out of it? For Charlie, one place is as good as another. He's a free man because he carries his contentedness with him; it isn't contingent on job, money, home. And who but Charlie could so thoroughly enjoy himself in the middle of his arrest. This calm enjoyment comes from years of practicing the art of snatching pleasure on the run, of building nests in the middle of storms. This habit makes Charlie something of a philosopher, along the practical lines of Stoicism or Buddhism. Charlie has the gift for creating calm columns of space for himself, for soothing domesticity in the midst of poverty and turmoil. There seem to be no situations so dire that Charlie can't find a comfortable perch within them. "Remember too," Marcus Aurelius wrote, "on every occasion that leads you to vexation to apply this principle: not that this is misfortune, but that to bear it nobly is good fortune." There's something of Charlie's philosophy here. Charlie tends to see opportunity in misfortune, where his imaginative skills are most in need and have their freest play.

Three

Chaplin's Satire

The fourth characteristic of Chaplin's cinema that his transformation gags highlight is his gift for satire. This subject requires its own chapter because Chaplin's sense of satire is so central to his art, such a big part of why we take Chaplin seriously as an artist.

When Charlie playacts a role, he does it with a devastating accuracy that, in the end, makes his playacting something more than gleeful child play, something more like biting parody. David Thomson writes of Chaplin using "mime as a weapon"[1] and Andrew Sarris notes "the wheedlingly maternal pose" Charlie strikes at times in *The Kid*, which, he writes, "derives from a merciless mimicry of motherhood as comic mode of behavior."[2] Both critics emphasize the quiet viciousness inherent in much of Chaplin's satire and role-playing. In an early interview, Chaplin bridled at being called a clown, describing himself as "a mimetic satirist, for I have aimed in all my comedies at burlesquing, satirizing the human race—or at least those human beings whose very existence is an unconscious satire on this world."[3] Chaplin is referring to his favorite target here, those who feel so sure of themselves that they are unaware of the spectacle they make of themselves, those who believe so much in the role they play as to be unwitting participants in their own satire.

The incisiveness of Chaplin's intellect as well as the depth of his skepticism are most apparent in his gift for "merciless mimicry." Thomas Burke felt that Chaplin had "a swifter and acuter eye than any novelist I know" for people's "oddities and their carefully hidden secrets. It is useless to pose before him; he can call your bluff in the moment of being introduced."[4] Chaplin had a penetrating intellect that expressed itself in mime rather than words. Burke was astonished by the exactness with which Chaplin caricaturized London high society: "One by one he produced them before me. Most of them I knew, and while there was not one stroke of exaggeration in any portrait, each one, presenting the person in the person's daily gait, and habit, was an exposure of ludicrous character. They were exquisitely funny … but they were also painfully funny; there was such cold analysis behind them. Latin caricaturists can be brutal, and English can be satirical, but none of them knows how to touch on the vulnerable spot as Charles does."[5]

Burke mentions several key aspects of Chaplin's immense gift for satire here. First, he stresses its calm understatement. Chaplin used the term "burlesque" to describe his satire but critics rarely do, because the term seems inappropriate for satire that is so quietly perceptive, that registers human inanity in such fine, ironic detail. And Burke notes the precision in Chaplin's satire that was so exact as to produce "painful laughter." One of the triumphs of Chaplin's comedy is the way it makes us laugh and cringe at the same time; it's gently comic *and* ruthlessly honest. Burke also stresses the coldness of Chaplin's intellect. Chaplin had, in many ways, a cruel, calculating eye that had to be, at least in part, the result of years of examining the well-to-do and successful from the perspective of the social outcast. Even though, in his later years, he bragged in his autobiography of his friendship with royalty, Chaplin, in his comedy, always remained amused by the trappings of success. Nothing breeds humor more than self-satisfaction. It takes only the slightest expression of pretension, in Chaplin's films, to draw Charlie's ire and often his punishment. The law also applies to Charlie, who, even if he only gets the slightest bit full of himself, draws disaster down upon himself.

Burke, in referring to Latin caricaturists and British satirists, examines Chaplin's satire within larger literary traditions. Chaplin does deserve a place with the world's great wits and satirists. The only difference between him and them is that he expresses his devastating portraits of human pretension in mime rather than words, an approach that has its advantage for, as Burke says, "touching on the vulnerable spot" of his subjects. We're often astounded by how vividly we see our moments of greatest embarrassment, vulnerability, weakness and pretense in Charlie's mimicry. It is in his satire, this wide-ranging study of the myriad nature of human foolishness, that we best apprehend the acuity of Chaplin's intelligence and the depth of his skepticism.

Chaplin's Satire of the Man of Means

Of course Charlie's most recurrent presentation of his self to society represents a parody of a role: that of the distinguished gentleman, the man about town. Chaplin was born to this role, as his father, in his music hall career, specialized in playing elegant swells with a taste for the high life. Chaplin calls himself Sir Cecil Seltzer when he passes himself off as this kind of gentleman in *The Rink*, but has a tendency to lapse into the role unconsciously throughout his films. Charlie's taste for this role touches on one of the essential paradoxes of his character. Charlie is uneducated, a fact that often presents itself, for example, in his alarming lack of table manners and taste for off-color jokes and bodily humor. And yet, he is nearly faultless in his imitation of aristocratic habits. Charlie has the cruel mimetic skills of the gutter snipe. Who sees an aristocratic ass as clearly as a poor man?

One of Chaplin's finest articulations of his parody of the gentleman is his first appearance in *The Kid*, an example both of Charlie's identification with the dandy and his fine skills of mimicry. The title that introduces Charlie, "his morning promenade," also introduces his state of mind, that of a well-to-do man at his leisure, out on his morning constitutional, even though Charlie actually walks through garbage-ridden back alleys. Charlie's carriage, despite his big awkward feet, is regal. He moves with the slow pleasure of a strolling gentleman, flexing his cane, and elegantly smoking a cigarette.

This is Charlie's default role, the one that allows Chaplin, child of the London streets, to send up his betters. Some critics make the mistake of associating Charlie, in his aristocratic manner, with his real self, seeing it as an expression of the dignity of soul despite the poverty of his milieu. But Charlie, in his role of the dandy, is not the real Charlie. Charlie is mocked in his role-playing just as much as anyone else in this film. We see the real Charlie in moments of love, sadness, cockiness, combativeness and empathy. The dandy role is the one Charlie chooses to navigate the hazards of society. Charlie playing that role allows Chaplin to set up countless situations where Charlie must preserve his ludicrous sense of dignity in the midst of embarrassing situations (as the Tramp does here, several times dodging trash thrown out of the windows above), a universal situation that we all respond to since it mirrors the small indignities we all suffer on a daily basis, and deserve when we pretend to be something more than we are.

In that introductory scene from *The Kid,* Chaplin pauses before the camera to deliver a litany of little gestures that finely and economically inscribe the mindset of the elegant man about town. With a heightened sense of his own importance, Charlie elegantly draws a cigarette case (really an abandoned tin container) from his breast pocket and carefully chooses a cigarette from a variety of stubs he's picked off the street. He tamps the cigarette down on his container, that key movement in the miniature dance of lighting a cigarette, and, again with self-conscious elegance, returns the container to his pocket. He removes his gloves with care, finger by finger, as if they were the finest leather molded to the shape of his hands and not the tattered throwaways, missing several fingers, that the insert shot reveals them to be. Chaplin does this all staring straight at the camera with the vacant look of a man engaged in little rituals that have become second nature to him, a man too bored with the world to let his actual attention wander to the banal details of his actions. It's a spot-on imitation, etched in fine, precise detail. Charlie may be just a tramp but he's got the rich man's number. Who is superior to whom here?

Chaplin, as Thomas Burke noted, had a knack for imitating the well-to-do. If I were to pick one impersonation out of the hundreds that sparkle in his film as being most representative of the fine filigree he brings to his imitations, it would be when he assumes the role of husband and "man of the house" in *Police.* In that scene, the police have just collared house-thief Charlie and brought him to the homeowner, Edna. The policemen are holding Charlie by his suit collar as you might a cur by the scruff of his neck. But by this time Edna, who thinks she has talked Charlie into abandoning his criminal ways, pretends to the police that they have accidentally arrested her husband.

In that moment, Charlie's transition from stray cur to man of the household is really something to behold. This was a favorite moment of one very sensitive student of Chaplin, Walter Kerr, and it would be hard to improve on his summary of Charlie's transformation here: "It is at this point that a virtual miracle takes place. With no transitions at all Charlie becomes Edna's husband. Affable, outgoing, utterly at home, digging his hands into his pockets and flexing his knees as though he were master of his own domain and ready to get out the humidor, he is all bourgeois bonhomie, the host par excellence, eager to show his guests about and have them back soon again. No one has ever been more completely the confident man of the house."[6]

Kerr is right about there being no transition. Charlie's transformation from criminal to respectable gent is, if such a thing is possible, as invisible as it is tangible. His muscles start to ripple with a new looseness. He kicks his legs and shakes his arms as if fastidiously arranging the nicely hung suit that he pretends to wear. He brushes off his sleeves with a natty particularity, draws a cigar from his pocket, and hooks his thumbs in his waistcoat, striking the pose of the comfortable, masculine man of the house. Charlie settles into his role the way a change in the atmosphere settles into an environment. And yet the transformation is utterly complete, from mangy cur to affable host in seconds. A lesser comedian would have adopted a gruff, pompous attitude of husbandly outrage. Chaplin, instead, lands on that moment after dinner, when the host—jocular, cigar in hand—leads his subordinates to the pool room. Chaplin is a connoisseur of pretension, recognizing that we never enjoy our power more than in those moments where it is masked by affability, those moments where we seem not to be conscious of our power at all.

It's a testimony to the complexity of Chaplin's art that even Kerr's excellent description omits one of the best details of the transformation. As he warms to the pretense of bourgeois bonhomie Kerr describes, Charlie draws a cigar from his breast pocket and, spitting out its end (in the eye of one of the cops), rudely jostles Edna for a match, slapping her side with the back of his hand and snapping his fingers at her, before a cop saves Edna from her bewilderment by lighting Charlie's match for him. If you're going to play the role of the man of the house, according to Charlie, you're going to have to be rude to your wife, even if she did just save your skin moments before. Charlie can often be disturbingly physical in his flirtatious horseplay with women but he was rarely, in his true identity, demeaning to a woman in this manner. The husband is one of the many conventional masculine roles that Charlie associates with brutish behavior. On the other hand, the gesture *is* typical of Charlie's tendency to presume on people's generosity. Charlie has led a hardscrabble life and when he is provided an advantage he makes full use of it. Charlie's gratitude has a short shelf life, especially in this earlier permutation of his character.

Chaplin's Satires of the Working Man

One can't help but notice that Chaplin has a great gift for mocking figures of authority in these imitations. Putting his betters in their place is one of Charlie's great passions. But he is an equal opportunity satirist and is just as adept at mocking the disadvantaged and the working man. The parody of the hairdresser in the scene mentioned earlier from *Behind the Screen,* where Charlie arranges a bear-rug's hair, is so finely realized that it represents both an ode to the fine art of barbering *and* a parody of the silly finickiness of the barber, the unctuous servility of the man of service.

Similarly, Charlie does a nice imitation of the queasily ingratiating sales clerk when he sells Edna a pair of socks in *Sunnyside,* laying them out on his forearm elegantly, folding them in neat easy flips, looking away with a kind of professional calm and neutrality as he neatly tucks them into their wrapping paper. Of course, the end result of this elegant wrapping process is unconventional. Charlie arranges the socks in tissue as though they were a bouquet of flowers. Charlie's exquisitely rendered professional mien should never be confused with actually knowing how to do the job.

Charlie is always satirizing the professional that he plays, here for example in the unctuous self-satisfaction of the job well done.

In *The Rink*, Charlie does a nice job of imitating the self-conscious artistry of the bartender. He juggles glasses, crisscrossed the bottles from which he pours, cracks eggs and tosses them into the concoction with a single hand. He manages the whole thing as though it were a form of table top ballet, with his arms as the dancers. His face, all the while, is a study in that neutrality that marks the calm savvy of the seasoned professional. It's only upon very close observation of his bartending, however, that we notice, again, Charlie really doesn't know what he's doing. Several things get thrown into the drink that really shouldn't—eggshells, a nearby flower, some coffee from an urn he passes in the kitchen. And most comically, we notice that, though he shakes the drink in the shaker with consummate bartender aplomb, only his body is in movement—the drink remains immobile. It's a virtuosic example of form over content, a child's view of a profession, of what's fun about a job, devoid of any real sense of the job's requirement. Or an aesthete's imitation, interested only in artful form, not in the least in boring function. When Charlie sees a role he sees only a kind of dance, a ritualistic strutting. He is absolutely indifferent to the role's actual purpose.

All of these imitations are noteworthy for their careful study of the artistry of a profession, to the point where they represent something of an homage to that profession, a kind of rendering into dance of the profession. And yet, all at the same time parody the profession, emphasizing the egotism behind the artistry, an egotism all the more comic for being so closely linked to servility. Charlie's as good at mocking the servant as he is the lord. Chaplin is highly sensitive to *all* our posing. It is significant that in his very first appearance to the world in his Tramp attire, in *Kid Auto Races* (it was actually the second film in his Tramp attire, but first released), Charlie is mocking a form of posturing, in this case the inherently comic look people have when they think they are being filmed and try to look natural, nonchalant and suave. The Tramp arrives in the world teasing us for striking poses.

Aesthete that he was, often trumpeting the notion that beauty was the sole purpose of art, Chaplin was nevertheless pretty able at satirizing aesthetes and artists. There is a good deal of mocking of artistic posturing in his films, for example Charlie's spot-on imitation of an art connoisseur early in *City Lights* (when his real goal is to get as many glimpses of a statue of a naked woman as he can). In *The Kid*, Charlie, applying the final touches to an awful caulking job on a window, playacts the great artist, stepping back, cocking his head in scrutiny, and advancing to the window dramatically to make surgically small adjustments to the caulk. There's a great gap between the meanness of the job and the ridiculously grand sense of artistic accomplishment. Similarly, those scenes referenced above, where Charlie soaks in an often nonexistent applause in the manner of a celebrated entertainer, are notable for the gap between reality and fantasy. Those gags also capture, beautifully, the spectacle of artistic egotism preening in a false display of touched and grateful humility. Here again, as in his imitation of a husband, Chaplin shows a Tolstoy-like ability to capture egotism at its moment of greatest disguise, when it masks itself in cordiality or humility.

These satirical moments are immensely important in revealing just how perceptive Chaplin is, how sensitive to the slightest, most understated registering of egotism. There's been a debate, from the moment Chaplin was first described as a "genius," as to just how smart he actually was. Artists and intellectuals trumpeted praise for Chaplin fairly early on and this recognition set off a long-lasting backlash of criticism by those who felt the intellectual celebration of Chaplin ignored the inherently base nature of the medium in which he toiled and his actual intellectual and artistic lack of sophistication. He didn't read much, they pointed out; his spelling was atrocious and he found even writing a letter a hardship. Chaplin didn't help matters by warming to the role of sage and studding his later interviews and films with sometimes fatuous comments characterized by artistic naiveté and intellectual pretension. But this entire debate is rendered irrelevant by any close study of Chaplin's role-playing, which displays a razor-sharp intelligence, expressed via wicked mime. Chaplin creates portrait after portrait worthy of La Rochefoucauld in their incision and subtle understanding of just how self-deluded and pleased with themselves humans can be. In his best films, Chaplin is one of the most subtle and perceptive satirists, one of the most honest voices art has ever known.

Chaplin's Psychology

Chaplin's acute satirical skills grew out of a gift for human psychology, albeit one that expresses itself via mimicry rather than through words. Chaplin is expert at getting at the way people think, spying out their little cover-ups and hidden agendas. And though his satire can be cruelly honest at times, at other times he expresses great sympathy for the little strategies to which humans are reduced in their struggle to maintain their dignity. Charlie's tendency to affect the airs of a distinguished gentleman, for example, is one long sustained joke, sympathetically rendered, that finds its humor in the comic ways humans desperately try to maintain their gravitas in the midst of embarrassing situations. One of the most emblematic gags in Chaplin's films is the "cover-up gag," built around those moments where Charlie puts on an air of dignity rendered ludicrous by the circumstances in which he finds himself.

Examples of this kind of gag abound in Chaplin's cinema. They are the stuff of Charlie's everyday reality. In *The Pilgrim*, Charlie is an escaped con with a fear of cops. At one point he gets involved in a chase that leads him in the direction of a policeman. Not wanting to call attention to himself, Charlie slows down his run, transitions to a little skip, starts to kick out his legs and rub his hands and to trot back and forth. In other words he tries to sell to the cop that he has just decided to engage in some light calisthenics, an idea rendered mildly ludicrous by the fact that he's on a train platform and dressed in the minister's garb he's chosen for disguise.

Similarly, in *A Dog's Life*, when a shopkeeper catches Charlie reaching for a pastry that he aimed to steal, Charlie, in a split-second, changes his arm motion to suggest he was only swatting away a fly. Later in the same film, Charlie rears back to throw a brick through the door of the dancehall from which he has been expelled. But just as he readies his throw, he becomes aware of a policeman's presence and, ludicrously, throws the brick out in the street, encouraging his dog to go chase it, as though it was routine habit for his dog to fetch bricks.

These gags in which Charlie tries to affect an air of normality in absurd circumstances, and under the withering gaze of some figure of authority, are essential in his cinema, touching on Charlie's sense of being out of sorts with the world, of constantly having to pretend to be normal, to fit in. Audiences, however, have never needed to be homeless or criminal themselves to identify with Charlie in these moments. Chaplin understands that we all feel this self-consciousness to a degree, that we all travel through a world that is suspicious of us, hostile to our presence, that we all have little moments of embarrassment, and turn to asinine cover-ups to cope with those embarrassments, cover-ups that even we find comic after the fact. For Charlie these cover-ups are so routine as to represent a kind of second nature.

And Charlie doesn't have to be involved in a crime to engage in this kind of cover-up. In *Easy Street*, Charlie, a policeman on his beat, wants to call for reinforcements on the street phone that connects to the police station, but can't because he's being carefully monitored by the bully who terrorizes the street. The situation allows Chaplin to employ all of his favorite nervous tics—his wandering fidgety hands; his nervous, shifting legs; the ridiculous childlike smile that he flashes in moments of intense nervousness. When he's caught with the phone mouthpiece near his mouth, he pretends to play it like a flute; caught again, he looks through it at the sky as though it were a telescope. Whether he's on the right side or wrong side of the law, Charlie is always under threat, always being stared at suspiciously, always mistrusted.

And we identify with this aspect of his existence. We squirm with him. Charlie embodies our own sense of self-consciousness, our own tendency to hide our actions, our sense that we have to pretend to be normal, that we don't fit in, that others are suspicious of us. You might call him a poet of paranoia except Charlie's sense of persecution is rarely unwarranted. Rather, Chaplin is a poet of man's inhumanity to man. He specializes in our often pathetic means of justifying ourselves to a world hell-bent on rejecting us.

Poor Charlie gets very few moments of unaccosted freedom in his life. In *The Gold Rush*, Georgia discards a half-torn photo of herself. Moments later Charlie comes across it on the barroom floor and picks it up. But, as he picks it up, he realizes a man standing nearby has watched him and is scrutinizing him, wondering what he wants with it. Charlie, enamored of Georgia, wants desperately to hold on to the photograph but realizes he looks a bit pathetic in the eyes of the bystander, as he, Charlie, pockets the picture of a woman who doesn't even know he's alive. For the following twenty seconds or so, Charlie is gripped in conflict. Every time his hand moves to tuck the picture inside his jacket, his eyes meet the man's and he instead lapses into the pretense that the picture is just an oddity that he has come across but of course has no intention of keeping. Of course, he doesn't have to concern himself with this man's opinion; they don't even know each other. But that's part of the comedy of the situation, depicting how wholly unnecessary much of our self-consciousness is. Charlie tries to indifferently toss the picture to the floor, but the photo remains glued to his hand. He can't get it into his coat, he can't get rid of it. For awhile he uses it as a fan, his dignity allowing it that small utilitarian use. Finally, he walks past the man as though passing through a gauntlet, his look of grim determination testifying to a decision to keep the picture even in the face of the man's silent judgment.

Sigmund Freud saw Chaplin's comedy as evidence that "the achievement of artists are intimately bound up with their childhood memories, impressions, repressions and disappointments." Chaplin, Freud writes, "always plays himself as he was in his dismal youth. He cannot get away from those impressions and humiliations of that past period of his life."⁷ Chaplin's cover-up gags represent, to a great extent, a rehashing of the humiliations he experienced when he was the kind of non-entity that brought down suspicion upon itself in the streets of London. Chaplin, for example, spoke of how intimidating he had found waiters when he was poor. We have to be struck, in the context of that remark, by how many scenes Chaplin devised around the particularly repressive air of restaurants, with their stuffy code of conduct and judgmental waiters. The second half of *The Immigrant* is perhaps the most famous example: Charlie dies a thousand deaths under the scrutiny of a bully waiter, played by Eric Campbell. (It was Campbell to whom the role of the disapproving world was most often given to.) Campbell cannot be convinced, no matter how much Charlie affects the air of sophisticated diner, that Charlie deserves a place in his establishment. Chaplin mocks the way we affect airs of indifference and neutrality in our nervous moments in society. Over and over again, Charlie struggles to master the rituals of dining under the oppressive eye, not only of waiters but hosts, fellow diners, women he hopes to impress, anyone who notices that Charlie doesn't have a clue how to conduct himself at the dinner table. But, again, the humor of these gags can't be entirely rooted in Charlie's impoverished past as we don't have to have a similar background to his in order to enjoy these gags. Most of us have made our share of dining *faux pas* and been cowed by the absurd rituals of the upscale restaurant. Enough so, in fact, that we delight, for example, in Charlie's insistence on eating beans with his knife and his inability to trust a fork. Our manners, and our confidence in situations where the standards are exacting, are only marginally stronger than Charlie's.

Chaplin's cover-up gags are good examples of how his satire can be as kind and empathetic as it can be cruel and honest. They reflect Chaplin's acute sense of, and sympathy for, the indignities humans suffer and, even more touchingly, the sad and comic ways they try to cope with these indignities. La Rochefoucauld wrote, "[W]e are never so ridiculous for the qualities we have as for those we pretend to." Chaplin's comedy provides endless variations on this maxim. We are rarely more comic than when we try to hide our insufficiencies from the world or try to be something we aren't. La Rochefoucauld also wrote that "almost all our faults are more pardonable than the means we employ to hide them."⁸ He is often characterized as a misanthrope but there is, in his writings, an acceptance of human flaws that is refreshing and that bespeaks a great affection for humans. He only has problems with people who pretend to have no flaws. The same philosophy lies behind Chaplin's cover-up gags. Our inherent foolishness is never as comical as our pretense that we aren't foolish at all. Chaplin's enemies are the same as La Rochefoucauld's: the pious, the self-assured, those who think they have no faults.

Another example of Chaplin's gift for translating psychology into comedy, of touching on certain essential truths about the way humans operate via Charlie's comedy, is his emphasis, throughout his films, on how humans are often crippled by consciousness and, conversely, how they often perform more ably when they have little time to think. One recurrent gag in Chaplin films is the "gaping chasm gag." In many of his films (*Pay Day*, *City Lights*, *Modern Times*, *The Great Dictator*), Charlie finds himself dangerously close to a yawning precipice of which he is unaware. In *Pay Day* and *City Lights*, it's an elevator shaft that he doesn't see behind him. In *The Great Dictator*, Charlie is blinded and walks out onto a plank that juts out from the roof of a tall building. In *Modern Times*, Charlie, skating blindfolded to impress a girl, skates precariously close to a second floor overhang in a shopping mall where the railing is missing due to repairs.

In these gags, Charlie is fine as long as he is blissfully unaware of his danger. For example, in *Modern Times*, skater Charlie elegantly skirts the line of the precipice several times before he becomes aware of it. It's as though his actions are being guided by the unseen hand of an angel. When Charlie becomes conscious of the precipice, however, his considerable skills with roller skates abandon him: He is no longer capable of the graceful pirouettes we have just seen him perform; now he can barely skate at all. Unable to even stand, he falls into the manic throes typical of a first-time skater. Instead of gracefully skirting the edge of the precipice, his wild thrashings only draw him closer to the abyss from which he's trying to escape.

The gag touches on several psychological laws. First that ignorance is bliss, that we often move with the grace of angels when we are unaware of danger. Secondly, that consciousness is a burden. Often, fully understanding a situation only makes it more difficult for us to deal with that situation. The gag finds its echo in many of Charlie's fight scenes. Given too long to calculate a strategy or deliver a blow in a fight, Charlie's plans often go painfully awry. But if, in defending himself, he has little time to think and is forced to improvise, he's well nigh indestructible.

Similarly, in *The Circus*, Charlie is the comic hit of the circus but only when he doesn't mean to be. When he tries to be funny, he bombs, leading to the wonderful self-reflexive oddity of those scenes in the film where we are presented the spectacle of Charlie Chaplin being taught by others to be funny. Thought is often Charlie's enemy, spontaneous action his greatest ally.

The gag also touches on human perversity: our tendency, when confronted with a danger, to find ourselves inexplicably drawn towards it rather than move away from it. Perversity is an aspect of the human psyche in which Chaplin is something of an expert. Charlie is the embodiment of perverseness. Often it's just at the moment where an irksome boss apologizes to Charlie for earlier cruelties that Charlie decides to leap up and kick him in the chest. It's often just when a girl is falling for Charlie that he will dissolve into spasmodic hijinks guaranteed to destroy any affection she might have for him. It's often Charlie who finds moments of peace intolerable and picks a fight with a co-worker. Charlie often suggests Dostoevsky's underground man in his tendency to favor freedom so much that he's willing to ruin his own chances of success to maintain it.

Itemizing the number of human foibles, frailties and pretensions Chaplin sends up, both cruelly and sympathetically, in his films is as futile as trying to itemize each of the lightning-fast gestures in his physical comedy. I will find many occasions throughout this book to note how the comedy in certain Chaplin gags is drawn from his subtle understanding of human nature. Chaplin's gift for psychology runs throughout his cinema and is one of the aspects of his cinema that gives it the breadth and depth of a great nineteenth-century novel. Some of his perceptions about human nature, like his parody of our ludicrous cover-ups, or his sense of how we are burdened by consciousness, are essential aspects of Charlie's character, revisited in gag after gag. But the films are jam-packed with all sorts of pithy moments that comment intricately on human nature.

The *Immigrant* scene in which a desperately poor Charlie gets stuck paying a restaurant bill that he can't afford because he magnanimously insisted, once too often, on paying the bill he really had no intention of covering, resonates with anyone who has vociferously offered to pick up a check while hoping, in the dark of their soul, they wouldn't have to. We laugh at Charlie affecting the pose of an art connoisseur as he examines the statue of a nude woman in *City Lights* because we've all found circuitous ways to glimpse nudity (and would all look as comical as Charlie does if we were filmed doing so). In *The Gold Rush*, we smile when Charlie gleefully tears his little home to pieces after Georgia has accepted his invitation to a party, because we all know the insane bliss of our first nervous forays into a romantic relationship meeting with success. We laugh when Charlie struts and swaggers after accidentally vanquishing an opponent in a fight, because we are conscious of our own tendency to believe in our successes, even when they are not earned or legitimate. We laugh when Charlie generously gives money to Edna Purviance's character in *The Immigrant*, then surreptitiously steals some of it back because we all know how difficult it is to follow up on good intentions. In *The Circus*, we laugh when we see how thoroughly, and with what suavity, Charlie trounces his competitor for Merna's affections in his daydreams, because we know that we too are often ludicrously impressive in our own daydreams. We feel for Charlie when he has to perform as a clown in *The Circus* moments after he has found out that Merna loves Rex, not him, because we have all had to put on faces of social ease in moments of private despair. We laugh when Charlie flinches dramatically as a policeman merely passes his hand through his hair because of our instinctual fear of policemen. We privately identify with Charlie when he runs away from some fight or bit of chaos that he has instigated, regarding it from afar with a pronounced air of innocence, because we too, at times, have dodged responsibility for the messes we've created. We laugh in recognition when Charlie counts pancakes like so many cards in *The Kid* because we remember how obsessive we, too, were in apportioning treats as children.

One of the ways Chaplin's comedy rises above the common fare is that it is tied, in this manner, to the vagaries of the human soul. Chaplin's films provide their audience one long lesson in self-understanding, one reminder after another to own up to our many foolishnesses and to accept them, by laughing at them. Chaplin was not unusually skilled in putting his observations about human nature into words. Often, in his sound films, his interviews, or his autobiography, when he discusses comic laws or the connection between comedy and psychology, he comes off as a little pompous, the ideas as familiar. But, in the mimicry that his camera catches, Chaplin can reveal us to ourselves in a way that makes us ache with the fineness and precision of his observation. He leaps to the job with the viciousness and enthusiasm of a child bent on mockery, and indifferent to the cruelty of his effect. And he accomplishes the job with an accuracy that has to be, at least in part, honed from his years of privation. Chaplin had plenty of time to study, with a jaundiced eye, those who were better off than he was.

The accuracy of his imitations has to be due in part to Chaplin's essential nature, that lack of humbuggery that his friend Thomas Burke noticed about him. However he conducted himself in his private life, Chaplin was an enormously honest artist in his films and he put that honesty in service to a study of human nature that is impressive in its wide range, often cruelly calling us to task for our pretense, often expressing a heartbreaking sympathy for the little strategies we adopt in defense of our dignity.

One of the reasons I suspect Chaplin critics often tend toward a sociological approach when analyzing Charlie is that it may be easier for us to pity Charlie, to look at him as the disadvantaged sufferer of an unjust economy, than it is to see Charlie as a prod to our own conscience, a satire of our own weaknesses and inequities. Chaplin's aspirations were a great deal more ambitious than political ones. He was an astute psychologist who had a great capacity for representing, via comic satire, a vast panoply of human pretensions. We watch Chaplin for the same reason we read Leo Tolstoy or Thomas Hardy, to study someone gifted with a wealth of perception on human nature and who has a keen sense of our little lies, foibles and foolishnesses. Like Hardy or Tolstoy, Chaplin takes us to task.

Hardy said that the purpose of his poetry was to "mortify the human sense of self-importance," and the same could easily be said of Chaplin's cinema. Chaplin's films make us acutely aware of our poses and pretensions, our playacting and absurd sense of self-importance. There is much to learn from Chaplin if we humbly accept Charlie's guidance rather than pity him from a superior point of view. Charlie is far too universal a figure to be contained within any political view. A bank president or a bum would recognize, in Charlie, the paradoxes and contradictions of his own soul, if I'm correct in assuming that bank presidents fall in love, are jilted, make asses of themselves, and swerve manically from bravery to cowardice, just as Charlie does. There may be something consoling in thinking of Charlie only within a specific economic milieu. It saves us the difficulty of confronting just how thoroughly he has our number.

Social Satire

No discussion of Chaplin's gift for satire is complete without considering the social satire in Chaplin's films. From time to time, often quite successfully, Chaplin would satirize societal structures as well as human nature. Prominent examples are the scene from *The Immigrant* in which Charlie and the other immigrants arriving in America are herded behind ropes like animals, the opening scene from *City Lights* in which Chaplin deftly mocks civic piety, and the famous factory sequences from *Modern Times* where Chaplin mocks industrialization and the division of labor. And, of course, running throughout all of Chaplin's films is a revolt against conventional law and authority that is represented by Charlie's endless warfare with policemen and other figures of authority.

But, as I've suggested in my introduction to this book, we should be careful about generalizing too freely about Chaplin's social satire or vision. The scenes in which he takes on society as a whole tend to be effective but they are also rare. Chaplin's attitude toward social satire is something like his attitude toward arty shots; he does it only when it's just right, which means not too often—particularly in the silent films. There is, for example, no other particularly significant reference to the plight of immigrants in his works aside from the Ellis Island scene in *The Immigrant*. The *Immigrant* scene represents just one of many times Charlie and Edna suffer at the hands of authority figures. It's just that, in this instance, those figures are immigration officials.

As I also noted in my introduction, there is not a really a consistent enough attitude toward the working man, in Chaplin's films with Charlie, to justify Chaplin's reputation (mostly born from episodes in his private life and from an appreciation of the *Modern Times* sequences) as a pseudo–Communist filmmaker. In both *Dough and Dynamite* and *Behind the Screen*, for example, striking workers are cast in a negative light. You might even call Chaplin's attitude towards them reactionary. "How dare you wake us up. We strike," say the workers in one of the title cards from *Behind the Screen*. "Bakers want less work, more money" is the title card in *Dough and Dynamite*. In both films the workers devolve into bomb-carrying thugs who represent an even greater threat to Charlie and Edna than Charlie's cruel boss does.

Even in the supposedly Socialist *Modern Times*, organized labor causes Charlie as much suffering as his bosses do. By accidentally turning from one street into another and finding himself at the head of a Communist workers rally, Charlie is thrown into prison for the first time. Later, when he finally gains the employment by which he hopes to support Paulette Goddard's waif, it's the workers' strike (which is depicted simply as a collection of angry, brutish men) that ends his dreams of success. Workers rights organizations are just another large violent entity with which Charlie has to contend. Even getting the job at the factory is a question of muscling his way past the vast number of men waiting at the factory gate, of cheating his peers, via his dexterity and size. That shot is not characterized by particular sympathy for any worker other than Charlie.

Charlie's biggest concern in *Modern Times* is not the rights of the workers but finding a nice little home for him and his girlfriend. The Tramp has never been so domestic as he is in *Modern Times*, a film in which Chaplin's own increasing desire to settle down found expression in that of the aging Charlie. Graham Greene noted the apolitical nature of the film in his review: "Nor do we find him wondering 'what a Socialist man would do,'" he says of Charlie, "but dreaming of a steady job and the most bourgeois home."[9] Charlie's dream in *Modern Times* is of the property he would share, not with his fellow workers, but with the girl he loves. And yet it is typical of modern Chaplin criticism, addicted as it is to a Social Sciences–oriented approach to film, to describe this touching film about love and the longing for simple warmth and companionship as, in the words of one critic, "an anthem to the plight of the working man trapped in a cold, mechanical age."[10]

At least one problem with that summary is its confluence of Charlie with the "working man." Charlie is a great deal more anarchistic than any run-of-the-mill pseudo–Communist. And he's a great deal more simple-minded. He's not incensed about injustice in the workplace. He just doesn't like jobs in general. A great irony in Chaplin's real-life politics tending towards Communism is that there may not have ever existed in cinema a creature more antithetical to work than Charlie. Moreover, Charlie doesn't get along with the working man any better than he does with management. A quick survey of job situations in Chaplin's films will show you that Charlie's co-workers rival his bosses in their brutality. He probably exchanges more blows with "the working man" than with any other breed of foe in his films.

These political takes on Chaplin's cinema are in part, due to the critical obsession with his biography. Chaplin became more outspoken politically as he warmed, in his middle years, to the role of national sage. Therefore, logic suggests, his films must be political, a dictum that works a great deal better in considering the talkies he made during his more overt political years than it does his great silent films, which are, for the most part, barren of political content. But even the talkies often reflect Chaplin's unwillingness to hold to political doctrine or to take his politics seriously. In *A King in New York*, young Rupert Macabee sometimes expresses Chaplin's opinion, for example when he asks the king whether taking an interest in Karl Marx makes one a Communist. But other times he's mocked for the clichés and vehemence of his political ideas. The film gently ridicules political idealism.

Even Chaplin's attitude towards police in his films is not entirely consistent. *The Kid* finishes with a kindly policeman facilitating Charlie's reunion with Edna and the kid. *Police* criticizes law enforcement, not for being too severe and unjust in their carriage of the law, as so many Chaplin films do, but in being too lax. The police are shown as lazy, effete fellows who would rather enjoy their tea than do their job. They respond to robbery victim Edna's call for help with a leisurely indifference. Like the references to workers in *Dough and Dynamite* and *Behind the Screen*, the attitude toward police here is more consistent with a conservative, law-and-order sentiment than a liberal point of view.

Similarly, Chaplin often satirizes organized religion bitingly in his silent films and yet, in the end, evinces too much sympathy to Christianity to be defined as inherently hostile to religion. Chaplin is, however, an able religious satirist. The opening to *Police* probably represents his best satire of religious sentiment. Charlie, just released from prison, falls into the hands of a street-side minister bent on saving souls. It's one of the more charmingly comic traits of Charlie, that for all his punkish street savvy, he is easily manipulated emotionally and has a ready heart; the preacher has Charlie weeping and bent on a new life in no time. Only later does Charlie discover that the minister has absconded with the wad of cash with which Charlie was discharged. Charlie is still seething over this theft when he is approached by a second minister, an honest one for all we know. But when the second minister repeats the line of the first, "Let me help you get straight," he is awarded the pummeling from Charlie that the first minister had earned.

Later in the film Charlie will find himself basking in the kind of female attention he generally longs for. Edna, having caught him robbing her house, tries to mend his ways. She feeds him, gives him a beer and talks softly to him about the redemption of his soul. Charlie lives for intimate little moments like this one, where women lavish attention on him, and he easily falls under her sway. But when she says, "Let me help you get straight" (the third time Charlie has heard this line), Charlie snaps out of his emotional state, checks all of his pockets to see if they've been picked and returns directly to burgling the house, all of Edna's admonitions now for naught. We rarely see Charlie separate himself from the influence of a pretty woman this easily. But by this time in the film, Charlie has concluded that, even when it comes in the pretty form of Edna, religious sentiment is to be avoided at all cost.

Sunnyside also begins with a pointed attack on religious hypocrisy. The first shot is of the church in the small town in which the film is set. Chaplin irises in on the cross at the top of the church and then cuts, Griffith-like, to a plaque on a wall that reads "Love thy neighbor." As he irises out, we find that the plaque hangs above the bed of Charlie's boss, one of the cruelest and most unforgiving bosses for whom Charlie will ever work.

Chaplin shows a similar resistance to Biblical cliché in the scene from *The Kid* where Edna, citing Matthew, encourages the neighborhood bully to meet violence by tendering his cheek to Charlie, at which point Charlie smashes him over the head with a brick. Both *Easy Street* and *The Pilgrim* focus on the money-making machinery of church services and both make astringent little observations on church services. *Easy Street* comments on the behavioral challenge they represent for a lively spirit like Charlie; *The Pilgrim* notes the fifth of whiskey in the pious church deacon's pocket, the excruciatingly bored child in the congregation, and the dour nature of the church choir and congregation. All of them, except the child, remain immune to Charlie's attempts to enliven the service by interpreting it as a kind of saloon show.

That said, when Chaplin re-cut *The Kid* and took out scenes (many of which, it could be argued, had artistic merit), he left in one of the loonier moments in all of his cinema, a didactic bit of montage, straight out of a Griffith film, in which the shot of the unwed mother leaving the hospital with her child is followed by a still photo of Christ mounting the hill of Golgotha. The idea is a rather explicit expression of ideas that run throughout Chaplin's films with Charlie, his sense, for example, of the holiness of the outsider and the underling (Charlie, children, street curs, and abused women), or the pleasure Charlie takes in wreaking vengeance on the pious, self-righteous conventionally successful. Chaplin's films are those of a conventional post–Renaissance Humanist more than of an atheistic Marxist. He loves to take down organized religion but his cinema often represents, in its broadest sense, an ode to the Sermon on the Mount.

In the end, Chaplin's social vision is subservient to his artistic one. The hallmark of Chaplin's aesthetic style is balance, a balance of comedy and pathos, a balance of virtues in the paradoxical Tramp. And he keeps his social vision in balance as well, mocking workers and bosses alike, mixing liberal and conservative tendencies, satirizing organized religion while at the same prone to a Victorian religious sentiment.

This balance in social commentary is particularly evident in *A Woman of Paris*. Chaplin takes some nice shots at the well-to-do in that film that might seem representative of a populist spirit. For example, after the consummate man of the world Pierre Ravel (Adolphe Menjou) visits the kitchen of the restaurant at which he's dining, in order to check on the details of his meal, the chef remarks, in a bit of class rage, "these perfumed handkerchiefs stink up my kitchen." But it's not just a moment of class rage because, during the kitchen scene, there has been a running gag based on the stink of an exotic bird that the chef is preparing for, and proudly presents to, Pierre. So the chef is mocking Pierre. Chaplin, however, is having fun with the chef and with the concept of fine dining. If anyone is being mocked, it's the French chef who's blind to the irony of his comment about smells.

Later in the dinner, as Henry Bergman's obsequious waiter slavishly prepares Pierre's truffles in champagne sauce, table side, Chaplin interjects a rare didactic title card: "Truffles, a delicacy for pigs and gentlemen." It's interesting, though, that Chaplin films the preparation of the dish with great appreciation for its luxury and the preparer's artistry. Nearby is a man (already identified as a gigolo) who looks at the dish with envy as he sips his thin gruel. Obviously the matron beside whom he sits doesn't treat him as generously as Pierre does Marie. The scene, summed up, seems to say, "Isn't it awful how the rich live and wouldn't you love to have some truffles?"

Moreover, we have to be careful of identifying Chaplin too closely with the populist sentiment in his title card, as the card mocks Pierre, a character who, thanks to Menjou's bright performance, represents a good deal of the life and vitality of this film. Pierre is not conventionally moralistic but he is, in the manner of Maupassant's worldly gentleman, immensely likable, charming, and to be respected for the consistency of his mildly debauched worldly ethic. He's a clever man who often understands Marie better than she does herself. He never loses his sense of humor and we see a good deal of Chaplin's own demeanor and carriage in Menjou's performance. Chaplin doesn't turn a blind eye to his cruel amorality but he doesn't finally judge him either, just as he does not judge Marie for allowing herself to be a kept woman. One of the impressive aspects of this film is the way Chaplin can maintain our respect and empathy for flawed characters. In Chaplin's work, as in Maupassant's, a character can be treated with irony and respect at the same time.

Chaplin also intermingles some social commentary with the scene of Marie's massage. In that scene, the masseuse (played by Chaplin's secretary, Nellie Bly Baker) stares blankly at Marie and her friend Fifi as they chatter away frivolously. The blankness of her stare, the way she has of averting her gaze from time to time, and the way her massage seems to get more vigorous at the moments where the conversation is silliest, all seem to convey the annoyance of the working stiff for the pampered elite. At the same time there is something comic in her irritation and her voyeurism, the intensity with which she tracks their conversation. And she herself is an example of Chaplin's fascination with the cover-up gag, as the humor in the scene in many ways comes from her efforts to regard the two women as closely as she can without being noticed. Chaplin is always on the lookout for the comedy of our little duplicities.

There is a nice balance in this scene, as there is in the one with the chef, as the workers in both scenes express class annoyance, with which we sympathize, but are also gently teased as they do so. Chaplin's political commentaries are always balanced in this way and so avoid stridency. One could even say that these scenes testify to a conservative or quietist strain in Chaplin's films. Chaplin is amused by the predictable nature of the never-ending battle of the classes. He notes the tension between the two sides clearly and comically, but there is little sense of outrage at the situation, rather a sense that it has always been this way and always will be.

But, in the end, Chaplin's social satire in his silent films is infrequent. Chaplin only turns his attention to social entities here and there. These moments do not add up to a coherent political philosophy. And, usually, Chaplin's motivation is not so much to make a social comment as it is to find yet another way to depict Charlie's repression at the hands of the self-righteous. Charlie has no politics, other than an instinctual mistrust of the pious and judgmental (a category which can include striking workers).

If I were to cite my favorite moment in his films that might be taken as one of "political" satire, it would be that often commented-on scene in *Work* when the woman who has hired Charlie and his co-worker (Charles Insley) to paint her house, locks her china in a safe, right under her workers' noses, making it clear how little she trusts them. Charlie, miffed, returns the favor by collecting his and his friends' watches and small change, depositing them in his trouser pocket, and pinning the pocket shut with a safety pin he uses to hold his shirt together. Then, looking appraisingly at the woman, he leans into his friend and shares a few pointed remarks behind his hand, making it clear that he finds her just as unsavory a character as she finds him. Yes, there is some class consciousness here, but that particular social situation is swallowed in Charlie's larger politics, his rebellion against anyone who is certain their virtues and worth outstrip his. Chaplin's cinema is much more ambitious in scope than a cinema of political protest; it's a protest against piety in general.

Four

Beyond Satire: What Charlie Believes In

A Radical Spirit

Charlie's skill at mimicking societal roles has the Shakespearean effect of calling the validity of those roles into questions. Charlie plays our roles so well that he makes us aware that much of what we do is playacting. Charlie's acting points to the illusory nature of much of what we take to be solid in the world. He calls into question the validity of what we call "reality." At the same time, he elevates what he is doing, acting, into something more serious than mere entertainment. Acting is what we all do. Acting touches on the nature of existence, the human tendency, due to our consciousness of death, to be both in and out of the world at the same time, to be invested in the world, but not really there. The stage represents a conscious reflection on the role of acting in our world. The role-playing in which we engage in our daily lives, on the other hand, is unconscious and makes the mistake of seeing those roles as real.

This emphasis on the superficiality of the roles we play in the world is particularly apparent in those scenes where Charlie rapidly shifts identities, like the aforementioned one from *The Kid* in which, in a matter of a minute or so, Charlie does dead-on imitations of a boxing fan, manager and referee. Identities are, for Charlie, something to be picked up and abandoned at the drop of a hat, in the manner of child's play. The ease with which he can inhabit these roles testifies to their superficiality. Charlie can play all roles, hence he believes in none. As Walter Kerr noted in his essays on Chaplin, Charlie dances outside, or in between, the roles of society. He is a failure, not because he cannot find a role in society, but because he cannot find a role to which he cares to commit himself. Charlie seems the most naive person in his films; he is actually the most perceptive. Chaplin, student of Fred Karno, believed devoutly in the straight face. Charlie pretends to care about the roles he plays. He doesn't. He thinks they're funny.

The most significant shift in identity in *The Kid* is the one between different family roles that Charlie plays. At times Charlie does a pitch-perfect imitation of a mother in *The Kid.* When his son John comes home after playing on the streets, Charlie goes on a very maternal hygiene patrol, making sure that Jackie is clean behind the ears, blowing his nose, cleaning each nostril, picking lice from his hair. He cooks up bountiful meals for the child and fusses over him when he is sick, applying mustard poultices, for example, when he has a cough. Other times, Charlie playacts the stern *pater familias*, lording over the breakfast table, insisting on prayer (though the quickest, most pro forma prayer in the history of film), gently but sternly lecturing the child on table manners. Charlie's often just as much a sibling as a parent, cheering his son on in his fight with the bully rather than breaking the fight up, and kicking him away like one might a little brother when the boy leads the police to Charlie. Quite often *he's* even the child; for example, when John (who, parent-like, has made pancakes for him), has to scold a recalcitrant Charlie to get out of bed for breakfast.

It's not easy to summarize what exactly Charlie's relationship is to Jackie Coogan in *The Kid.* Charlie exhibits a protean kind of parenting in this film for which I can find no comparison. Charlie is father, mother, sibling, child—a kind of "all hands on deck" notion of parenting. But it's effective; Charlie is one hell of a loving family member, whatever he is. It's typical of Chaplin's art that he advances a notion of parenting that is as charming as it is radical, that warms us with its familial sentiment while sending up that sentiment, an ode to family that mocks family at the same time. Chaplin linked his indifference to nationalism and patriotism to his lack of experience in any sound societal or familial structure. "I cannot vociferate about national pride," he wrote in his autobiography. "If one is steeped in family tradition, home and garden, a happy childhood, family and friends, I can understand this feeling—but I have not that background."[1] Charlie's treatment of the family in *The Kid* is that of someone who has had no experience within the traditional family structures and so is not swayed by their conventionalities and even finds those conventionalities amusing. One of the reasons the film is so effective is because Chaplin steers clear of parental clichés, not an easy thing to do. There's a radical notion at the heart of this film: that being a loving human is not a matter of playing the role assigned to you but deftly dodging that role, that real human contact exists in the interstices of the roles we play, where we glimpse our real selves.

Charlie, as a parent in *The Kid*, exists outside, or in between, the roles of the family. But it must be emphasized that he still has a real, substantial relationship with Coogan's character. That understanding is sometimes missing, it seems to me, from the writings of critics who emphasize the nihilistic aloofness implied by Charlie's mockery of the roles we play. Walter Kerr's most acute observations about Chaplin were those on his role-playing. He was very sensitive to the rejection of life implied by Charlie's ability to imitate all roles. "The secret of Chaplin, as a character, is that he can be anyone. That is his problem. The secret is a devastating one. For the man who can, with the flick of a finger or the blink of an eyelash, instantly transform himself into absolutely anyone is a man who must, in his heart, remain no one. To be able to play a role … is to see through it. To be able to play them all is to see through them all. But that leaves nothing, no way of life, no permanent commitment in which such a man can possibly believe. Just as Don Juan, loving everyone, can love no one, so Chaplin, impersonating everyone, can have no person."[2]

To "have no person" is a pretty serious charge to level at Charlie, and a curious one considering Chaplin's emphasis on Charlie's physicality, the earthbound nature of Charlie's existence in general. I'll take issue with this idea momentarily. But I would first note that there is much to agree with in Kerr's comments here. It's hard not to see in Chaplin's sense of the fluidity of the self, his sense of what Kerr refers to as the instability of the self, a kind of Modernist view of an unstable world that is not what it seems.

In this quality of his cinema, Chaplin is really of his time. In so many ways, Chaplin is a conservative, retroactive artist. He is Victorian and Dickensian in his emphasis on sentiment in the midst of industrial squalor (his favorite book was *Oliver Twist*). He is conservative in his camerawork, one of the progenitors of classic Hollywood's invisible style. But his sense of the fluidity and insubstantiality of the self is part and parcel of his time and makes those pictures of him and Einstein seem less anachronistic than they sometimes can. It's because of his satiric role-playing that he can, despite his very conservative aesthetic, arrive at a kind of radicalism linked to the modernist currents of his time. The modernist aspect of his dizzyingly free satire must explain, at least in part, the appeal that he has always had, and still does, to avant-garde artists, the European Surrealists of his day, for example, and certain art house directors of our day.

I'm not sure it's emphasized enough just how radical a spirit Chaplin was and how much that spirit is reflected in his work. Certainly he has the reputation for being politically radical, Socialist in his politics, but as I've discussed elsewhere in the book, that political radicalism is not a significant aspect of his best cinema. His radicalism extends beyond the political domain. When, at the press conference for *Monsieur Verdoux* that brought down so much opprobrium on him during the McCarthy era, he was asked whether or not he was a Communist sympathizer, he responded: "I have no political persuasions whatsoever. I've never belonged to any political party in my life, and I have never even voted in my life."[3] After a pause he asked, with amusing understatement, "Does that answer your question?" The public Chaplin was often at his best during his period of political persecution.

Chaplin's confession of how apolitical he was, essentially, reflects something really radical in his makeup, more radical than simple leftist politics. There's something comically naive, but also a little brave, in trumpeting, as he did, during the McCarthy era, his hatred of patriotism and nationalism and his indifference to citizenship in America, in asserting his right, as an artist, as he often did, to be a citizen of the world. Reflect how well that would go over in America at any time, much less the American-centric era in which Chaplin found himself in. How well it would go over now in our own post–9/11 era of rather rigidly enforced patriotism? Other filmmakers, like Hitchcock, did not become American citizens, but they said little about it, rarely broadcasting their ideas as freely as Chaplin did.

Thomas Burke noted that Chaplin often got himself in trouble when he mistook himself for his artistic creation, Charlie. And that's what he did here. He insisted, like Charlie, on his right to exist outside societal structures, something easier done in film than reality. And he claimed this right as an artist, just as Charlie chooses to transform societal roles into well-articulated parody rather than fulfill them in reality. It was this indifference to patriotism and citizenship that raised the ire of the government, as much as it was Chaplin's consorting with Communists or his perceived lack of moral standards.

Whether it was brave or childish, Chaplin's refusal to hold himself accountable to the political structures of the time represents a radical point of view. And that radical point of view is reflected in Charlie's behavior. Charlie is the furthest thing from "engagé." He is perfectly rootless; he lives, essentially, outside reality. In many ways he is a very irresponsible character. Chaplin's cinema is characterized more by a Romantic or spiritual rejection of this world than political engagement in that world. "There are days when contact with any human being makes me physically ill," Chaplin told one interviewer early in his career. "Solitude is the only relief. The dream-world is then the great reality; the real world an illusion."[4] Chaplin was prone to striking these kinds of Romantic poses in the interviews from early in his career, but his comments here are consistent with the nature of his work overall and with the nature of Charlie. Charlie is an anarchist who chooses not to live in this world but in one of his own making, and to not assume one role but to play them all.

The real question to ask in analyzing Chaplin's greatest films is not how engaged were they—the answer is not very much, for all their very acute references to the dehumanizing machinery of modern industry in *Modern Times.* The real question is how anarchistic are they. Just how radical is the Tramp? Does he believe in anything, this expert role player making a mockery of most every position we strike and of the institutions we tend to hold most sacred?

In the passage I quote above, Walter Kerr answers this question rather gloomily. Charlie's ability to be anyone, he says, is a "devastating" "problem," "leaves nothing" for Charlie, "no way of life, no permanent commitment." Charlie "has no person." Now, Kerr was normally somebody sensitive to clichés about Chaplin. He complained, for example, about the incessant comparisons of Charlie to Pan and about the overemphasis on the "pathos" in Chaplin's cinema in Chaplin criticism, but here he falls prey to a standard cliché of Chaplin criticism, that of seeing Charlie as the tragic clown, the wise fool whose tragedy is that he sees the world too honestly to ever be able to partake meaningfully in that world.

Now obviously there's something of the sad clown to Charlie and the tragic nature of his character is developed to great effect in *The Gold Rush* and at the end of *City Lights* (though far less often in the rest of his oeuvre). But, for the most part, Charlie's ability to see through the pretense of society seems as much a gift as it does a "devastating problem." Even Kerr admits that "awareness of instability in some way exhilarated him" and "taught him how to dance."[5] Charlie seems quite content in the midst of his cynicism. Chaplin, for all his love of sentiment, consistently steers clear of morbidity in his films. The Tramp, despite his repeated experiences of unrequited love, is a pretty happy, resilient fellow. What, then, is he so happy about when he believes in so little? What, according to Chaplin, is left when we no longer believe in the roles we play, when we leave off our playacting? What does he feel is authentic in life?

Creature Comforts

Chaplin's films do not provide any obvious answers to those questions. Even when his silent comedies with Charlie became more serious, Chaplin was careful to avoid large-scale, didactic comments on life. And in his talkies when, to his films' detriment, he started to speechify more largely on the state of humankind, his ideas were modest in scale and didn't propose a comprehensive view of the human condition.

But if his films don't offer any pat answers as to the meaning of life, they do express an appreciation of life. "I am never too shocked at the bad things that happen, and am agreeably surprised at the good," he writes in his autobiography.[6] He was a cynic whose cynicism did not get in the way of a certain predisposition to happiness. He belongs to that group of artists that stretches from Ovid to Maupassant, thoroughly amused cynics who are as characterized by their mockery of life as they are by their delight in it. Chaplin's films are often cynical, bitingly so, but they are never bitter. They reflect a rich appreciation for life.

Chaplin's impoverished childhood seems to have left him with a strong appreciation for the basic necessities of life, the kind of things that people who have always been comfortable might take for granted. He was in many ways a materialist. He was careful to never posit, at least overtly, a faith that depended on much more than the pleasures of the earth. Like Chekhov, another miserably poor child who became a great realist artist, Chaplin never lost a sense, born of bitter experience, of the importance of physical health and comfort to happiness. As cynical as he is in his biting satire, his unending mockery of the roles we play, he still is something of an optimist. It takes so little for Charlie to be happy: a warm meal, a roof over his head, a little bit of warmth and companionship. Because the comforts of life evade Charlie, he treasures them all the more when he has them and Chaplin's films are often celebrations of these comforts, even the most meager of physical pleasures. A smoking cigar on a sidewalk, a filched treat or drink, even an imaginary dinner—they are all occasions for celebration to Charlie. In this manner, Chaplin's films are often reflections on the sheer pleasure of existing.

And it's one of Charlie's great talents that, despite his poverty, he exhibits such a great talent for the creature comforts. As I discussed in the chapter on Charlie's role-playing, Charlie is expert at carving out little homey spaces in the midst of his poverty, of turning hovels into transient paradises. And every once in a while, he arrives at a short period of domestic bliss: his few minutes of cohabitation with Edna in *The Vagabond*, the days before his New Year's Eve party in *The Gold Rush*, his few nights of companionship with the waif in *Modern Times*, and his greatest accomplishment of all, several years of cozy poverty with "the kid." Charlie has a certain expertise in bringing a little cleanness and order to a disheveled space, often only for a moment or two, or via a couple of creative little touches that marginally increase his comfort. His domesticity is not so much a reflection, on Chaplin's part, of a larger faith in societal structures, but rather an expression of a gift for keeping the darkness of existence at bay, for creating meager, but cozy, shelters in the storm. Chaplin's films are often celebrations of little moments of concrete warmth and sensation, small respites from the misery of life.

Play and Companionship

But sensual pleasures and creature comforts are not Charlie's only source of pleasure and meaning and, in the end, Chaplin cannot be adequately summed up as materialist. Charlie is a playful fellow and his spirit of play points to other ways in which Charlie finds meaning, certain things he believes in. You might say that there is an Existential quality to Charlie's love of play. As even Kerr concedes, Charlie is more exhilarated than dismayed by his rejection of society's roles. Seeing through our lies and charades doesn't seem to bother Charlie; in fact, he seems to find it quite enjoyable. Charlie is a testimonial to the exhilarating effects of honesty. He dances with pleasure as he mocks us. And though he effectively discounts most everything we find meaningful, his mockery of our conventional beliefs is its own meaning, a *sui generis* thing, a striking out or nose-thumbing at meaningless that, in itself, is meaningful. Charlie carves out little spaces in the darkness; he laughs at the darkness. Neither of these approaches to life tries to discover its meaning. Both simply try to confront that meaninglessness with humor, confidence, pride, honesty, or, in Hemingway's terms, "cleanly." And in both cases—his artful hovels, his artful satires—Charlie, like a good existentialist, brings his own meaning into a world in which, perhaps, there is none.

But there is too much Romanticism in Chaplin's films, too much latent Christianity (for all his satire on organized religion) for him to ever qualify as a fully fledged Existentialist. Charlie's talent for play suggests something else he believes in, something that tends towards the transcendent, that is, art. Charlie doesn't believe in the roles of the world but he loves to play them anyway, to analyze them, break them down, render them in refined, essential versions. Charlie is perpetually surprised, and disappointed, when his expert imitations of people, his little funny shows, are met with disapprobation, as they usually are, by those who are blind to his creativity. Charlie takes pride in his work and his work is to render the world to itself in the form of a charming, comic poem. Charlie believes in art, in ordered, well-structured interpretations of the world, staged for our amusement and edification. He believes in charm and humor, especially when they are artfully arranged. This tendency argues against the notion of Charlie as a pure Existentialist, as it points to a profound interest in essential forms that transcend and judge reality, a sense of taste and aesthetics that we see echoed in so many other aspects of Charlie's life: his love of flowers, his musical nature, his warm response to the grace of women.

Charlie's love of play also points to something absolutely at odds with Kerr's notion that Charlie's inveterate role-playing "leaves nothing, no way of life, no permanent commitment," and that is Charlie's love of companionship. From his first films on, Charlie likes to horse around with others—early on, more in the fashion of a child or a dog, out of fierce competiveness and with an unmanaged, chaotic, destructive energy. But as Charlie ages, his friendships deepen. As early as an Essanay film like *The Bank*, Charlie demonstrates a tendency towards "permanent commitment." By the time of *The Immigrant* we start to see Charlie's capacity for a real relationship with Edna, one which is informed charmingly on screen by their real-life relationship, particularly in the end of the film where they flirt engagingly for the camera. By the time of his feature films, Chaplin has become adept at depicting Charlie's capacity for real relationships convincingly, never more so than in *The Kid*. The four great feature films, *The Circus*, *The Gold Rush*, *City Lights* and *Modern Times*, are all studies in companionship, empathy and love.

In the early films Charlie is, like any young man, disturbed by the mere physical proximity of women, electrified by their sexuality. But as he ages, what he feels for women broadens from an expression of pure sexuality to a longing for companionship. Increasingly, women become something more than just sexual triggers, though a hair-trigger responsive sexuality remains with the Tramp to the end. Increasingly it's simply the chance to be with a woman that sets Charlie off into his moments of destructive frenzy, not just the electric stimulus provided by a glimpse of their derrieres. And they become associated with other things the Tramp finds that he likes, that were part of his DNA before he was even conscious of them: charm, humor, grace, elegance, beauty, flowers, art. In women he finds something that corresponds to his gift for playacting (that has been there from the earliest films), a consciousness of something of greater value than that of the utilitarian world of men and industry. Women introduce Charlie to his own latent spirituality.

This warmth of character and latent spirituality is what Kerr seems to lose sight of when he suggests there is no Charlie when he is not playing a role. Actually, there is a great swath of reality that exists outside of the roles that Charlie demolishes. In fact, the things that Charlie most appreciates, like art and love, require the honesty that comes from escaping role-playing. Relationships with women are real to Charlie and they call out a real, non-ironic response from him. Not believing in any of societal roles *does* leave him without a societal role but it does *not* "leave nothing for Charlie." One of the most significant theses of Chaplin's films is that escaping roles leads to actual living, to living authentically. Living authentically is never easy because it requires a constant, mocking attention to the pretentious poses we strike, a cleansing honesty towards, and sense of humor about, ourselves. We have always to be on guard for an ever-encroaching vanity that throttles the genuinely human.

Charlie *does* have a way of life outside of the roles he plays in the genuine relationships he enjoys with the kid and with the women he loves. He even manages some sustained relationships with men along the way, with Big Jim, for example, in *The Gold Rush*, with Henry Bergman's clown in *The Circus*, with his drunk rich friend, in *City Lights*, though there is usually more tension in Charlie's relationship with men. If they're dominant males, like Big Jim, he's always a little frightened of them; if they're gentler than him, like Bergman's clown, he can't stop himself from bullying them. There's always an edge of competitiveness in his relationship with men that is stilled in his relationship with women and children.

This is not to say that love, and Charlie's amorous nature, are never mocked in Chaplin's films. Chaplin often teases Charlie for his moony attitude towards women and Charlie has a habit of making an ass of himself when he strikes romantic poses. As I will discuss in more detail in my chapter on Chaplin's impeccable sense of balance, one of the signal gags of Chaplin's cinema is the one in which Charlie hams it up as a romantic suitor and is punished for his pretense by some small indignity, for example, in *City Lights*, when he strikes a Romeo-like pose under the blind girl's window and a cat knocks a flower pot on his head. Gags like these reinforce the idea, so prevalent in Chaplin's films, that genuine behavior, genuine emotion, is hard to come by. It's our nature to strike poses. When genuine behavior does come, it tends to surprise us, to escape by itself from our narcissism. And it disappears easily, withering under too much self-consciousness or, more specifically, self-satisfaction. No human action is ever undiluted by egotism and self-consciousness, because we are the one creature that is conscious of ourselves, that is always, in a sense, filming ourselves.

But there are moments of love and emotion in Chaplin's films that are not subject to irony. There is no irony in the close-up of Charlie and John's kisses when they are reunited in *The Kid;* or in the *Gold Rush* scene where Charlie tears his room to pieces in insane happiness because Georgia and her friends have promised to dine with him on New Year's Eve; or in the scene, later in the film, on New Year's Eve, when Charlie gazes sadly out the door, realizing the girls never actually planned to come to his party; or in the ending of *Sunnyside* when Charlie touches Edna all over, as if to confirm that she is really all his; or in the shot of Charlie looking at the flower girl in *City Lights* wearing an expression that has intrigued viewers for decades—a look of combined sadness, humor, wisdom, fear and disappointment. These scenes are registered with a simple, limpid clarity. They bring to mind Arthur Miller's praise of *Bicycle Thief* (a film inspired by Chaplin): "[I]t is as if the soul of man had been filmed." They remind us of the essential duality of Chaplin's cinema, which is characterized by a hilariously vicious cynicism shot through with expressions of a simple, abject idealism.

In these scenes Chaplin seeks to convey the power of love and empathy. That too puts him somewhere far from the Existentialists, with whom he otherwise often seems aligned. Sartre saw love as an escape, not as a glimpse of the authentic. Chaplin, to my mind, is more akin to certain 19th century quasi, or religious, Existentialists, like Tolstoy. Tolstoy, in a work like "The Death of Ivan Ilych," shows himself to be, like Chaplin, a prodigious satirist, mocking and calling into question nearly the entirety of what we define as a normal, successful life. Ivan is allotted only a very few moments of honest living, when on his deathbed, with only a few hours left to live, he realizes that he should have lived entirely differently than he did, not for professional success and the esteem of others, but in a spirit of pity and forgiveness. The moment of awareness comes with an exhilarating feeling of relief, a sensation of walls dropping away from him on all sides, but Tolstoy, rather mercilessly, only allows Ivan a few hours of this feeling before he dies. In fact, Ivan is not even allowed to express his new sense of understanding to his family. He wants to say "Forgive me" but only, to the confusion of his family, manages to say "Forgo."

This kind of story is close to the spirit of Chaplin's films. Chaplin, though obviously in a much more comical vein, describes a similarly artificial world, relieved by a similarly few vivid moments of authentic experience. And those moments are brought on, as they are in Tolstoy's works, by a deep and painful consciousness of love, a consciousness so hard to come by that it comes only in brief glimpses.

Ironically, given how much Charlie's relationship with women dominates his cinema, the one film in which Chaplin most fully delineates a relationship between Charlie and another is the one film in which a woman is not his principal companion, *The Kid.* Chaplin wrote in his autobiography of the difficulty of creating a sustained romance for Charlie, given how implausible it was that a woman would seriously return his affections. A loving relationship with a child presented no such problems. In this film Charlie is actually able to live with his companion (and not just in fantasy) and so Chaplin had the luxury of scene after scene where he could delineate their relationship in loving detail. And the film is very instructive on the issue of whether Charlie, who sticks to no role, is an anarchist. In *The Kid,* as I've emphasized, Charlie refuses to play conventional parental roles, any consistent family role, and yet the film represents the artful embodiment of love and companionship. Its key to success is that it defines a relationship that is *not* given to cliché, that exists outside the realm of role-playing.

Charlie's freedom from roles doesn't leave him outside the world, it just places him in the most real world. Charlie lives authentically, more often than anyone else in his films at least. He steers clear of roles and cliché. It's a lot easier to do in cinema than real life, as Chaplin found when he tried to claim Charlie's freedoms in real life. But Chaplin's cinema argues there are areas of our life that are closest to the authentic. Food, for example. A good meal on the table is nothing to be sneezed at. Companionship. Another essential need, and, in Chaplin's cinema, celebrated as often as it is satirized. The experience of love and beauty. Charlie's early sexual intensity develops, over the long course of his films, into a broader appreciation of all things feminine and leads him, eventually, to a taste for the aesthetic, summarized most often by his attraction to flowers (which, it should be noted, pops up pretty early in his films). And of course Charles's predilection for the aesthetic had always been there in his taste for playacting, in his tendency to turn a fight into a dance, a job into a dream. Charlie believes in love and art and he is never happier than when he can combine the two, as when he dances with the nymphs in *Sunnyside*, performs the dance of the rolls for Georgia and her friends in *The Gold Rush*, dances at the top of the pole for Merna in *The Circus*, or artfully prepares a meal for a young woman in any number of films.

A Cult of Feeling

Harold Clurman writes that "Chaplin's politics—insofar as they exist at all—are 'poetics.' His approach to political affairs is intuitive, emotional, almost, one might say a matter of aesthetics."[7] Clurman's point is certainly borne out by Chaplin's own reflections on his cinema. "The highest object in life is the pursuit of the beautiful," Chaplin wrote in a 1936 article.[8] And from the few notes he left during the making of *Monsieur Verdoux*, some ten years later: "the most complete concept of meaning is beauty."[9] These comments represent Chaplin's largest-scale assessment of the meaning of his films. He was, otherwise, generally loath to expound on their significance.

Later in life, when he was often at his most curmudgeonly about the current culture and cinema, he berated both for their lack of aesthetics. "We have ... lost our appreciation of aesthetics," he wrote in his autobiography. "Our living sense has been blunted by profit, power and monopoly."[10] He felt that the current cinema, with its increasing love of special effects, echoed this decline in aesthetics: "Aesthetics have gone into things like space and science—those beautiful airships: utility at its height. No artist could compete with that."[11]

In his autobiography, Chaplin recounts that his friend, the historian and philosopher Will Durant, asked him what his concept of the beautiful was. Chaplin's response was "an omnipresence of death and loveliness, a smiling sadness that we discern in nature and all things."[12] This notion of a "smiling sadness" also aligns Chaplin with the Romantic concept of the sublime, the idea that the most intense joy or awareness lie, as Tennyson wrote, in "the midmost heart of grief," an idea, of course, which is just a recapitulation of the Judeo-Christian notion that suffering and wisdom go hand in hand.

Chaplin's definition of the beautiful also brings to mind the final image of the Tramp in *City Lights*, a moment that, in many ways, caps off the Tramp's fifteen-year evolution from punky satirist to feeling man. In this moment we are happy that the Tramp has rediscovered the woman he loves, that he can witness the fruits of his charity in her cured vision, that he can finally be rewarded for his kindness in the manner of a medieval knight who finally sheds his disguise. We are happy too that she has rediscovered her benefactor, as we know she has been anxiously awaiting his reappearance. But we are, of course, sad for her, that the man who took care of her falls so short of her fantasy expectations. We're sad for both of them because it's nearly impossible to see the kind of relationship they might embark on. We're saddest for Charlie because he loves this girl with a childlike adulation that, for all the kindness in her eyes in the final shots of her, seems unlikely to be reciprocated.

That this image has been seen by so many critics as the most emblematic or expressive of Chaplin's art, and that it matches so precisely the definition of beauty he offered Durant, suggests an impressive unity of theory and practice. "I first thought of him in terms of satire," Chaplin said of Charlie in 1931. "But he persists in growing more and more human and getting perhaps a little nearer to the heart of things."[13] For all of Chaplin's emphasis on bodily function, on the squalor and beauty of the material world, Chaplin's end-game is this feeling of "smiling sadness." This represents the "heart" of his cinema.

But note also that scenes like the sublime moment that finishes *City Lights* represent only a fraction of a filmography that for the most part resists excessive expressions of sentiment, that more often mocks sentiment than indulges in it. As in the ending of Tolstoy's *Death of Ivan Ilych* we are, at the end of *City Lights*, given only a glimpse of revelation. We harbor deep uncertainties about Charlie's fate as the film concludes. If there is an idealism in Chaplin's film, a cult of beauty, it is one that is intermelled with, and dependent on, a great sense of sadness and cynicism.

Chaplin often emphasized that he didn't like to traffic in ideas, or ideals, the latter of which he described as "dangerous playthings and for the most part false." He was careful, in reflecting on the meaning of his films, to only speak of their emotions. He often compared film to music. As we have seen, he felt that film, like music, "starts not from an idea but from an emotion." In his autobiography he recalls Rachmaninoff scolding him for his religious disbelief and for confusing religion with dogma. "How can you have art without religion?" he asked Chaplin. "My concept of religion is a belief in dogma—and art is a feeling more than a belief," the naive Chaplin recalls responding. "So is religion," said Rachmaninoff.[14] Chaplin conceded that point in the conversation, and forevermore it would seem. For Chaplin, religion and art are the same thing; both pursue sacred feeling.

In seeking to describe what feeling Chaplin tries to capture, what his notion of beauty is, we probably have more to go on than just his evocation of "smiling beauty." Thomas Burke, noting the inherently childlike nature of the Tramp, wrote that every Chaplin film "asks help for the young and the wounded."[15] Chaplin described his films as having always emphasized "pity and understanding—I've always been cognizant of that. I think pity is a great attribute. Civilization—without it—we would have no civilization."[16]

Chaplin often turns to the words "pity" and "understanding" in trying to express what emotions his films aim to evoke or what effect they aim to have on the audience. In his notes on *Monsieur Verdoux*, he wrote that "it is more important to understand crime than to condemn it."[17] And in an interview from 1925 he said, "As far as I have a philosophy, it inclines to not asking too much of the unfortunates who bewilder this crusty old planet with their antics. A little gentle skepticism makes for toleration and for kindliness. It's easy to judge. It's not so easy to understand. And I take it art exists to further understanding."[18] The bulk of Chaplin's art mocks us, but its ultimate aim is to soften us. "It is a phenomenon of life, thank God, that when a thing is overstated it becomes ridiculous. This is the salvation of a man's soul," he told Philip Scheuer.[19] Chaplin had an immense faith in the beneficent effects of satire, its potential for humanizing. Satire humbles us, knocks us down, makes us less judgmental, opens our heart. There is a surprising unity of purpose in Chaplin's cruel satire and his moments of sad pathos; the goal is the same—to cultivate pity and understanding, to make us less sure of ourselves, less puffed up with pride. His most sensitive critics have always noted the gentling effects of Chaplin's cold satire. Alexander Woollcott described Chaplin as "the bearer of healing laughter" such "as the world had never known."[20] J.B. Priestley described him as "at heart a genial and gentle anarchist and the laughter he provokes only clears and sweetens the air."[21] Both critics emphasize the healthful nature of Chaplin's satire, the way it cleanses and ennobles rather than demeans.

When Chaplin discussed the feeling he tried to engender in his films, he was willing to express ideals that he never would allow himself when speaking strictly about his films' "ideas." In the same interview in which he spoke of skepticism making for toleration, he asserted that the audience is predisposed to enjoy this feeling of gentle chastisement. "What is more, I believe that if you edge the audience towards that understanding, not by means of their heads, but through the feelings, you will be giving them genuine entertainment. And that's what they want."[22] This is a strongly idealistic statement. Chaplin sees a companionship between art that moves people to empathy and art that is popular, successful, and entertaining. His comments here suggest a faith in a self-improving faculty in his audience, a desire to be taught. But he emphasizes that they can only be taught via elevated feelings, not thought, a principal dictum of his film philosophy that he certainly lost sight of in his later sound films.

This is not the only time Chaplin, in a way, posited a view of the universe that is essentially benevolent, that moves naturally in the direction of pity and empathy. "My faith is in the unknown," he wrote in his autobiography, "in all that we do not understand by reason; I believe that what is beyond our comprehension is a simple fact in other dimensions, and that in the realm of the unknown there is an infinite power of good."[23] This is about as far as he ever got in delineating his system of belief, and perhaps further than he even should have gone, flirting as he is here with platitudes. But it should be emphasized that Chaplin, in many ways an arch-cynic, could entertain ideas of a benevolent universe. But note that his belief is shrouded in the unknown. He only gets this assertive in his faith when he is talking about something he can't, in the end, grasp. And note that it can't be registered in ideas, only in feelings, as in music. Most of his comments about humankind in general have a (sometimes pompous) Schopenhauer-influenced, sad cynicism to them. But he was more idealistic when he came to human feeling. There he is unwaveringly optimistic in his detection, in the make-up of man, and the universe, of a subtle but powerfully evident sway towards empathy.

Chaplin, then, for all his materialism (which should never be lost sight of; no mystic aesthete he), is essentially a Romantic, albeit of a rather practical, earthbound variety. He believes it is via feeling, not thought, that we experience our widest sense of ourselves. If he is an Existentialist, he is one of the Christian kind, like Tolstoy, who paired a New Testament faith in the heart with a modernist cynicism towards most all systems of belief. But one thing is certain: Charlie is no mere anarchist, dancing entirely outside the forms of existence. He's just like the rest of us, a bifurcated creature, a human, the creature Reinhold Niebuhr compared to a tower, rooted to the ground but with the ability to scan its world. We are, according to this way of thinking, both inside and outside our world. There is, to Chaplin's thinking, no logic to our existence, only paradox and irony. "There's a universal law of paradox," Chaplin told an interviewer in 1967, "and all that I do is more or less paradoxical—though not consciously. I used to have a saying: 'This will get them woozy!' I rather enjoyed getting them woozy."[24]

Charlie gets us "woozy" partly because of Chaplin's rapid-fire comedy routines, but also because we never can quite make out where Charlie stands. Charlie is never completely inside a role and Chaplin would argue it's a fool's errand to be. Humans, mortal creatures that they are, have to be detached from whatever they are doing if they don't want to be an unconscious cliché, to become the role they play. Hence the need for art, and in Charlie's case, artful satire. Satire is a purifying agent; it keeps us honest, helps us escape our clichés, hounds out the vanity that has such a lasting grip on us, makes us a little less high on ourselves and, thus, a little more tolerant of others.

Just because Charlie mocks us so exhaustively and discounts all the roles we play in society doesn't mean he has no place in the world. Charlie may find people comical but he loves life: He likes to eat, drink, chase women. And he likes to play; he likes companionship, provided the companion is willing to climb down from his or her high horse and not strike pious poses. There's a softness to Charlie's satire (that isn't accounted for by those who see him as a wicked Pan) and a sturdy upbeat resilience (not accounted for by those who see him as a tragic harlequin). Yes he taunts us mercilessly, but it's only because he knows we'll be happier if we drop our pretenses. Like a child or a dog, he's quite sure we want to play more freely than we do.

To live like this requires constant vigilance, a sense of self-satire as acute as Charlie's. But the reward of that kind of self-monitoring is that the clouds of our narcissism can clear long enough for us to experience those moments of greatest authenticity, those moments of "smiling sadness," that Chaplin registers in such simple, unpretentious glory. One of the keys to Chaplin's success is that he is so devastatingly cynical and childishly idealistic at the same time. And his films don't marry those two polar opposites in some lukewarm blend. He is intensely cynical and idealistic at the same time. Charlie is no more a randy goat than he is purely an ethereal sprite. Like all of us, he's both.

Five

Chaplin and the Intimacy of the Camera

For the next four chapters, I'd like to turn my attention to Chaplin's skills as a filmmaker, to the formal virtues of his cinema. Chaplin, despite his preference for a static camera, is one of the most cinematic directors in film history, a pioneer in understanding the nature of the film camera. The most cinematic aspect of his films is their intimacy. If Chaplin was not given to expressive camera angles, swooping camera movement and extravagant large-scale compositions—all practices that loudly announce the artistic qualities of cinema—he was ahead of the game in understanding how well the camera recorded the smallest, quietest gesture, the near-invisible detail, in his understanding of the camera as a revelatory instrument that deepens our awareness of our world.

The greatest argument for the essentially cinematic nature of Chaplin's films is that, though they replicate some of the straightforward presentation of theater, his best gags and films could never be replicated on the stage. They are too fine in gesture. They necessitate an intimate relationship with the audience that can only be found in film. And as Chaplin got better at understanding how sensitive an apparatus the camera was, he quieted his gags even more, trusting an audience that was watching closely to work even harder at spying bits that were smaller and quieter than those of other filmmakers.

I'm not just talking about quieter gags but slower ones as well. Dan Kamin notes that one can detect even in Chaplin's first directorial efforts at Keystone that "the pace suddenly slows up. Director Chaplin allows the actor Chaplin the breathing space to explore the possibilities of each scene [and] the various gags develop in a leisurely fashion."[1] The leisure of Chaplin's cinema goes hand in hand with its quiet. Chaplin slows cinematic time down. He does more with less. The slower the pace, the more time he has to work ingenious variations off a single idea, to dig deep in one spot, to decorate his ideas with curlicues of fine detail.

While Chaplin spent a lot of money on his films, it wasn't on great sets. As Mast

It is striking how often photographers caught an expression of anxiety on Chaplin's face when he was filming. Dressed as he is here, in Charlie's outfit, the expression takes us aback, as it is so out of keeping with Charlie's nature.

writes, "[T]he money that Chaplin spent on his films did not show in the usual way that money shows in films. As opposed to costumes, extras, and ornate sets in a DeMille or Griffith extravaganza, the money went into the quality of the filmed material, not its quantities. He invested money in time, not space."[2] Chaplin cashed in money for time. He provided himself the shooting time and the extravagant number of takes that allowed him to polish his routines with exact precision. You could also say he invested in space as well as time, but microscopic space rather than macroscopic. His leisurely approach to filmmaking allowed him to increasingly hone in on finer and finer gags, material that you could miss with the blink of the eye.

Chaplin's sensitivity to the camera has to be due in large part to his unusual filmmaking style. He is famous for shooting epic amounts of footage but using very little of that in the final product. He shot, for example, the same amount of footage for his Mutual two-reeler *The Immigrant* that D.W. Griffith did for his three-hour and twenty-minute epic *Intolerance*. Chaplin's method would be economically unfeasible now, but it was even then. He was able to shoot so freely only because of his enormous personal wealth and because of the independence that wealth brought him.

Critics have often cited Chaplin's perfectionism in this regard as evidence of his high standards and artistic seriousness. But as documentarian Kevin Brownlow notes, laughingly, in his documentary *The Lost Chaplin*, it could just as easily be read as incompetence. Chaplin would arrive on a set with the vast part of his film unplanned. He would work it out as he went along, often making cast and crew wait for hours, at great expense, and then doing take after take until he got it right, often ditching a day's work or a week's work after he saw failure in the footage he shot. It has to be one of the most inefficient methods of filmmaking Hollywood has ever seen.

Brownlow, in his documentary, says that Chaplin never referred to early shooting methods in his published writings on his career and posits the idea that this is because Chaplin was embarrassed by the fact that he didn't really know what he was doing. That's not entirely true. In his autobiography Chaplin refers to the "charming alfresco spirit" of his Keystone films: "[T]hat was a delight—a challenge to one's creativeness. It was so free and easy—no literature, no writers—we just had a notion around which we built gags, then made up the story as we went along."[3] And that, of course, accurately describes his shooting method after Keystone as well. And his interviews are peppered with references to his improvisational technique. Chaplin's good friend Douglas Fairbanks noted that Chaplin never worked out his ideas in advance: "He takes an idea, a theme, and works it out by himself as he goes along. He's a remnant of an aristocrat ... reel after reel without subtitles—action!"[4] Fairbanks attributes an aristocratic attitude to Chaplin's method, a devil-may-care sense of artistic freedom. And though some of that artistic bravado and "charming alfresco spirit" was somewhat diminished by the grim perfectionism that became the hallmark of his filmmaking, the breezy improvisational approach to filmmaking that he and Fairbanks describe here remained a vital aspect of his filmic genius. In these instances, Chaplin seems rightfully proud of, not embarrassed by, his improvisational methods.

Brownlow is right, though, when he notes that Chaplin's naiveté in filmmaking was the key to his success, as Chaplin arrived, however clumsily, at a method that was purely cinematic. He wrote with his camera and the film was minimally impacted by pre-production plans that might have depended more on words and literary approaches to film. As Chaplin said, "no literature, no writers," and as Fairbanks emphasized, "no subtitles." Chaplin's method was entirely filmic and dependent on an intense relationship with the camera.

One of the first things Chaplin did when he signed with Essanay studios was insist on a printer that would allow him to examine positive rushes. Up till then, cutting at Essanay had always been done from negatives. Chaplin's method was to shoot, see how it looked, shoot again. The camera told him what was successful, what wasn't. "I study the screen closely," he said in an interview as early as 1915, "and I am firmly convinced that everyone in the industry should do likewise. There are many things we can learn from it, even though we think we have perfected ourselves in our own line of the great industry."[5]

Chaplin subordinated himself to the camera. This intimate relationship with, and sensitivity to, the camera is the key ingredient of his cinema and the thing that most explains why it is inherently filmic, as cinematic as any cinema with freewheeling camera movement and angles. He went to school on the camera, and arrived, before anyone else (and still to a measure rarely matched in filmmaking today), at an understanding of how sensitive the camera is, how much it picks up, how superior it is to the naked eye in noticing things and retaining information, how it could not only record but teach, show us things that we miss. He often noted that scenes recorded entirely differently than how he experienced them. "I've come to the conclusion," he said in explaining that phenomenon, "that it was the camera. You only see half of one's self that's photographed. There's a shutter that comes in between every frame that's black. And it may catch you between these vibrations. That's my own explanation. It's very fascinating, that you might just be out of sync with that spiritual thing, whatever it is."[6] In the almost mystical respect he accords the camera, Chaplin sounds here a little like French filmmaker Robert Bresson, who revered Chaplin, and who described the camera as "a prodigious heaven-sent machine."[7] "Divination," Bresson writes, "how can one not associate that name with the two sublime machines I use for my work? Camera and tape recorder carry me far away from the intelligence which complicates everything."

Both Bresson and Chaplin, different as their cinemas were from one another, emphasize that the camera sees more than the eye sees and that it can teach the eye to see more. The camera, Bresson writes, "catches not only physical movements that are inapprehensible by pencil, brush or pen, but also certain states of soul recognizable by indices which it alone can reveal."[8] This is very close to what Chaplin is trying to describe in his sense of "that spiritual thing in the camera." "Where words leave off, gestures begin," Chaplin told one interviewer. "The final motions of the soul are speechless…. Think of the murderer anxiously scratching himself as he looks at the jury. Think of a mother kissing the wee hand of the child she holds in her arms. And how the camera helps us over all that."[9] The camera is expert at registering small, often seemingly inconsequential gestures, that in the end are revelatory of "certain states of the soul." In Chaplin's sensitivity to these gestures we detect his skills as both a mime and a film director. He is sensitive to those "tells" by which the soul reveals itself and understands that the most loaded communications occur through the smallest and most unaware gestures, the very kind of gesture the camera is designed to detect.

Critics have been closest to understanding what it is that Chaplin does in his films when they reflect on this intimate relationship to the camera. "Chaplin's 'picture sense' is unerring," wrote Walter Vosges in 1927, "and he gauges his work, the light and shade of it, the value of a raised eyebrow, the significance of the faint tremor of a lip, in a way unsurpassed by any other man in the moving pictures."[10] Richard Schickel noted, eighty years later, that the clock gag in *The Pawnshop* could never take place on the stage: "The intimacy of the camera, its ability to reveal the pun in, as it were, the wink of its closely peering eye, permits the joke to work."[11] Andre Bazin writes that, thanks to the camera, "the evolution of the comic effect" in a Chaplin gag does "not need boosting … on the contrary now it can be refined down to the utmost degree; thus the machinery is kept to a minimum, so that it becomes a high-precision mechanism capable of responding instantly to the most delicate of springs."[12]

All of these comments emphasize the efficiency of Chaplin's cinema, its way of getting the most out of the least. And it's the camera, with its intimacy, its closely peering eye, that allows Chaplin to get the most out of the minimum, to refine his filmmaking, to arrive at such delicacy of effect. His minimalism is his great cinematic achievement. He's the anti-stylist. Instead of moving his camera, he keeps it still. Instead of rapid editing, long takes. Stasis instead of showy mobility. "Dig deep where you are," wrote Bresson, "don't slip off elsewhere. Double, triple bottom to things." Bresson wrote dismissively of "slow films in which everyone is galloping and gesticulating," of "the immobility of X's films whose camera runs, flies," and, conversely, he writes appreciatively of "swift films in which people hardly stir," an accurate description of some of Chaplin's most marvelous scenes, those for example where Charlie moves us to laughter through near immobility and a purely neutral gaze. Excessive style often results in waste, a quiet aesthetic in discovery. "Be sure," Bresson writes, "of having used to the full all that is communicated by immobility and silence."[13]

Bresson is, of course, one of film's greatest iconoclasts, at odds, it sometimes seems, with almost all of cinema, which he felt had been perverted by stage technique and commercialism. I've often thought it was ironic that this director, the most puritanical and exacting when it came to cinema and the need for cinema to separate itself from the stage, would be as appreciative of Chaplin as he was, considering that Chaplin is often criticized for not being cinematic enough, too stagey. He's not the only avant-garde artist to appreciate Chaplin. From the outset of his career, Chaplin has always managed the difficult trick of appealing to the masses *and* the avant-garde. The Surrealists took to him in the 1920s and to this day it is almost amusing how the most austere and exacting directorial students of cinema, directors like Bresson, Tarkovsky, Pasolini, Straub, directors who reject so much of commercial cinema, revered Chaplin.

It's not surprising that Chaplin would have such strong correspondences to the Catholic Bresson, in particular, one of film's most spiritual directors. Certainly Charlie's nature provides Chaplin's films with a spiritual element. The Tramp is an elegant dreamer, trapped in a clumsy, awkward form, the embodiment of the Judeo-Christian person, a creature who has a profound acquaintance with a better realm than he is able to realize on this planet, except in temporary fits of genius. But there is spirituality inherent in Chaplin's film technique as well. His camera is on the hunt for something unseen. And his filmmaking style is sometimes something on a par with prayer more than spectacle, a style that aims to slow down time, awaken perception, to make manifest the near-invisible, to alert us to the quietest details of existence and to the camera's marvelous ability to detect those details.

An Art of Small Gestures

To gain an understanding of Chaplin's film technique, one of the most useful moments is the *Gold Rush* saloon scene where Charlie first falls under Georgia's spell. When Charlie, by hazard, finds himself in close physical proximity to her in the crowd, his body stiffens and his face becomes immobile. Only his eyes move, barely—two or three quick, intense glances towards Georgia that, with his stiff posture and tense expression of neutrality, convey a body bent on not revealing itself. It's a situation we've all been in, a moment of hidden voyeurism, where we are intensely conscious of someone, but careful not to reveal that interest. The moment is effective, in part, due to an aspect of Chaplin's art that I discuss later in this book, his excellent understanding of human nature. He's good at catching, via the Tramp's behavior, little bits of behavior with which we are very familiar, in this case those little moments where we comically try to hide our feelings, where we pretend to be indifferent to things that actually engage us deeply.

But what interests me in this scene, at this point, is its stillness and quiet. Chaplin conveys most of what he wants through sheer immobility. The only movements he makes are the two surreptitious glances he steals. Otherwise his body is motionless, his gaze directionless. And, in many ways, the scene is funniest when his eyes aren't even moving, when he stares off to space, because *we* know, even though he's not moving a muscle at this point, how much he's thinking about this girl. This is an example of the maximum of emotion conveyed by the minimum means. It's a touching scene, building our sympathy for the Tramp via a universally experienced moment of painful shyness. And it's all expressed through a shot of near-immobility and the kind of fine glancing detail that is so small and intimate it could only happen in the cinema. It's a scene in which the meaning exists in the glint of an eye, a quiet moment that only the film camera can magnify. This is what Bresson means by having "used to the full all that is communicated by immobility and silence."

Chaplin is often able to get his idea across without even the slight eye movement that we see in the scene with Georgia, by means of a blank expression. One of my favorite recurrent gags in Chaplin's films is that in which Charlie is being yelled at by a man, usually a boss or co-worker. While the man screams at Charlie, Charlie looks at him with an absolutely neutral expression that doesn't suggest he is moved or angered by what he says. His face doesn't express anything. Sometimes he seems to actually be listening to what the man says, as though he may be acknowledging his points. Other times he seems just to be scrutinizing the contours of the man's face. But, after watching a few Chaplin films, we learn that the neutral expression with which Charlie confronts other men's abuse often conceals mounting violence and that Charlie will, after a few seconds of what seems meek submission, spasmodically slap the man who's yelling at him or leap up and kick him in the chest. We learn, by watching Chaplin's films, to detect nascent emotion in his neutral expressions, to see in his scrutiny of his enemy, not a genuine interest in what his enemy is saying, but a "tell," a sign of nearly invisible but mounting anger. This is an art of inference. We read an invisible emotion by a slight physical action, and an action that does not even conventionally relate to that emotion.

The same thing happens often when Charlie is around women. A passing beauty will immobilize Charlie, as Georgia does in *The Gold Rush*. But, again, as we get to know Charlie better, we learn that there is a proportional relationship between a calm, neutral expression and a seething interior landscape. Charlie goes all quiet, often, when he is most excited. (One might say the reverse is true as well, that when Charlie is sailing like a sprite in the middle of a fight, he's in a state of calm and freedom.) As in his moments with angry men, Charlie, around a beautiful woman, always threatens to explode insanely. Of course in the case of a woman, he is more likely to devolve into a series of nervous twitches and absurdly self-destructive show-off gestures, rather than violence, at least violence to the woman; more than a few men come to injury by finding themselves near Charlie in the midst of his love throes.

Chaplin is a virtuoso of the neutral expression and puts that expression to a variety of uses. Often, in the midst of some absurd moment, he looks out at us with a blank expression that doesn't necessarily explain itself. Sometimes he seems to be asking us to share his mockery at a scene, other times his surprise. And of course Charlie often adopts the neutral serious expression of a professional in his various imitations of a man at work. When he is doing his imitation of a bartender in *The*

Rink or a hairdresser in *Behind the Screen*, an essential aspect of the imitation is the imitation of the grave, in-control mien of the consummate professional going about his artistry. Here his neutral expression represents a satire of our self-seriousness, an understanding of how our deadpan subtly betrays our self-consciousness and egotism.

These are just a few examples of how Chaplin can evoke humor out of a nearly immobile, expressionless face, how he can "[use] to the full all that is communicated by immobility and silence." He was helped in this art of neutrality by eyes that engage our attention. Stan Laurel, who worked with Chaplin in Fred Karno's troupe of comedians that toured America, wrote, "Chaplin had those eyes that absolutely forced you to look at them. He had the damnedest way of looking at an audience. He had the damnedest way of looking at *you*, on stage. I don't think anyone has ever written about those eyes of his…. That's a part of his great success—eyes that make you believe him in whatever he does."[14]

It's hard to be too scientific in talking about the effect of Chaplin's eyes. Like the eyes of other great actors, for example Gary Cooper and Marlene Dietrich, they had a kind of watery, luminous brilliance that light plays off beautifully. It is difficult to explain why certain actors' eyes light up on the screen more than others. The great actors seemed to be blessed with deeper reservoirs of water and light in their orbs. But Laurel's comment that they were "the damnedest eyes" and "seemed to stare right through you" suggest something about the intensity of Chaplin's commitment to selling a gag. Chaplin seems to exist in his gag more fully than other comedians, and when he looks out at us, even with a neutral expression, he rivets our attention. One of the mysterious aspects of Chaplin's pantomime is that, even in the midst of a neutral expression, Chaplin's eyes seem to grab us by the lapels and say "Look at me, something's coming." Kyp Harness also notes the "seriousness" of Chaplin's eyes, the way they have of riveting our attention by their commitment to the gag, though in the end he sees their power resting, as well, in the complexity of the emotions they convey: "Chaplin's eyes, searing, dark, emotional, glow like coals at the heart of every piece of celluloid he appears on. There seems something in the depths of them, even in the midst of gaiety, which is deadly serious, and sad."[15]

It's worth considering again Bresson's admiration for Chaplin when we recall that Bresson once defined cinema as an art form of hands and eyes. Bresson meant several things by this, all relevant to Chaplin's cinema. First, that cinema should aim to express itself visually rather than verbally; second, that humans are most expressive via their hands and their eyes. Hands and eyes are so expressive that we can't always control them; they work on their own, expressing what we intend to conceal. And so they have great potential in visual communication, often offering a counter note to words being expressed, the suggestion of a truth undermining a lie, a truth that trumps language. Many of Chaplin's gags are built on a related principle, where the body expresses one thing while his eyes or hands manically convey the opposite. Sometimes Charlie's hands break free from the rest of the body like two lunatics from an asylum, following their own agenda which Charlie seems helpless to dictate.

Finally, by saying cinema is an art form of eyes and hands, Bresson is saying that cinema is, by nature, an intimate art form best managed by a minimalist touch. If we are going to notice eyes and hands, if they are going to express themselves, we are going to have to be close to the figures expressing themselves; there will have to be some quiet and intimacy to the scene. And the image will need to be still if we are going to be able to read those eyes and hands.

Charlie's hands and fingers often have a life of their own in his moments of heartbreak. In *The Tramp*, for example, Charlie's face is lost in thought when he realizes that Edna loves another man, yet another example of Chaplin working his magic via a neutral expression, but his hands range nervously around his soiled jacket and the kitchen chair before him. He unconsciously peels a scrap of paint from the chair and flicks it away, his face registering not the slightest consciousness of his action. One of Chaplin's talents in conveying emotion is his attention to intimate detail like this, little movements that testify as quietly as possible to the soul's disorder. Charlie's fingers often stray to his lips in moments of intense feeling. In *The Bank*, as he eavesdrops on Edna and hears her disdain his offer of love, Charlie's hand is elegantly poised before his face in an almost dancerly pose, his fingers gently working at his lower lip in a gesture that anticipates the final moment of *City Lights* where Charlie, holding a flower, nervously bites his fingers as he stares into the eyes of the flower girl who finally recognizes him.

Perhaps the greatest example of Chaplin's cinema being one of hands and eyes is the final sequence of *City Lights* (which I will analyze in greater detail in that section of the book having to do with Chaplin's musical approach to cinema). To be fully appreciated, this scene must be read by means of the multiple hand gestures and subtle expressions of both Chaplin and Virginia Cherrill. But another scene in Chaplin's work that reminds of Bresson's dictum on eyes and hands is the scene in *A Dog's Life* where he substitutes his hands for those of an unconscious man (Albert Austin), turning the man into a kind of sleeping marionette. The man is sitting at a restaurant table in a curtained booth, opposite his partner (the brutish Eric Campbell). They have just stolen Charlie's money, and Charlie aims to get it back. Charlie, hiding behind the curtain behind Austin, strikes Austin in the head, knocking him out. But Austin remains seated, unconsciously staring ahead. Chaplin slips his arms underneath the man's now slack arms (Austin's forearms are hidden by the table) and begins to animate the man through his own arm gestures. (He aims to knock Campbell out too in a moment.) Amazingly, Austin comes back to life entirely through the fluttering animacy of Chaplin's arms.

What Chaplin's arms accomplish here is quite impressive. First, they very effectively convey life to the unconscious man. As usual when Chaplin worked on these kinds of visual stunts, the *trompe l'oeil* is impeccable. Chaplin's arms seem to be Austin's, Austin seems to be conscious. But more importantly Charlie's arms go off on a dance of their own, mesmerizing in its rapidity, delicacy and abandon. Here we are, again, at the utmost extreme of the kind of fine, intimate delicacy that cinema is capable of. Most everything in this scene has gone static to provide a still stage for this miniature dance. In that sense, the scene is the cousin of the famous *Gold Rush* "dance of the bread rolls" scene where Chaplin's hands also are the stars. But though the dance of the rolls is the more charming scene, the *Dog's Life* hand dance is just as virtuosic and characterized by even more rapid accumulation of fine detail. The effect is extremely delicate, like watching somebody doing origami, as the hands express in rapid succession a myriad of creative detail.

The rapidly fluttering hands work on two levels during their dance. On the one hand they do an impressive job in conveying to Campbell that Austin is actually conscious. Chaplin hooks his thumbs behind Austin's vest and wags his fingers. He puts his finger to Austin's lip and cups his ear with his other hand, as though Austin were conveying to Campbell that they must be stealthy. He drums on the table, rubs his hands, asks (with palms out) for his share of the stolen money and then counts it with Chaplin's trademark card shuffle technique. He straightens Austin's tie and smooths his moustache. He pulls out Austin's hankie and wipes clean his moustache (though he has trouble finding the pocket in Austin's jacket to which he should return the hankie and finishes by foolishly tucking it behind his back collar). He shakes Campbell's hand after he gets his cut of the money.

But at the same time, Charlie has some fun with his pantomime, pushing its limits, enjoying his own virtuosity and often making gestures that are meant for the audience, not Campbell. When Campbell looks away he sneaks Austin's beer over the shoulder and enjoys it himself (another example of how adept Charlie is at sneaking food and liquor even in the most trying situations). After he shakes hands with Campbell, his hand collapses in fatigue. It exaggeratedly shakes off the pain and then his other hand jokingly pulls each finger back into place, a gag meant for our amusement. He often goes further than he needs to in his charade. After wiping Austin's face with his handkerchief, he absurdly goes on to wipe clean the table and even the rim of Austin's beer mug as if he had just segued into the role of officious waiter. Here Charlie is not just trying to pull off his pantomime but exercising his virtuosity in mimicry.

The success of the entire gag rests on the sheer accumulation of Chaplin's invention here as well as his communicating to us on two levels: the first, his pitch-perfect imitation of Austin's arms; the second, his little side-jokes to us. The scene lasts less than two minutes but in that time there is an extraordinary wealth of small comic detail. And its success is not due only to Chaplin's comic invention. Its effectiveness is also dependent on the static quality of the rest of the image which frames the dance. It's Chaplin's hands, these mercurial sprites, that we attend to alone.

Many of Chaplin's comic gags are built around hands and eyes. One of his favorite routines is when Charlie tries to sneak something under the scrutiny of the oppressive gaze of some heavy, for example, the street scene when he tries to sneak a call to the police on the police phone while epic bully Eric Campbell gazes at him menacingly in *Easy Street* or in the superbly timed *Dog's Life* scene where he sneaks cakes from a food stand under the vigilant scrutiny of the stand owner (Sydney Chaplin). In these gags the three coordinates are the angry man's eyes, Charlie's nervous hands, and Charlie's careful eyes which alternate between feverish activity when he tries to accomplish his goal and hilariously blasé neutrality whenever he is close to being caught.

In the *Dog's Life* sequence, which is one of Chaplin's most virtuosic, we might add another component to these three, Charlie's mouth: In one of his excellent imitations of a dog wolfing down food, Charlie disposes of the biscuits with ravenous efficiency. The general effect is of a plain background (one of those uninspired Chaplin sets) with several small feverish areas of motion: Chaplin's eyes, hands, and mouth. One is put in mind of other arts that are characterized by fine miniature work, like illuminated manuscripts from the late Middle Ages, the greatest pleasure of which is often in examining up close and at your leisure the almost microscopically fine coloring or textural details hidden in the corners and background of the work. It may be telling that, consummate professional that Sydney Chaplin is, he can't match Chaplin in the subtlety of his gestures or eye-play in the scene. Sydney's comedy is characterized by the loud double-takes and eye-blinking characteristic of the music hall or cheap silent comedy.

Dan Kamin, himself a mime, examines Chaplin's mimetic skills with great attention in his book *The Comedy of Charlie Chaplin*. He points out that Chaplin is unique even among mimes in the clockwork precision of his acting, his ability to quickly strike a pose in the midst of action, to still his body for the split second necessary to provide a clear, articulate image. In Chaplin's comedy, Kamin notes, there is "a peculiar quality of stillness in the midst of motion. Watching Chaplin move is almost like watching a flip book; one sees the stillness and motion at the same time." Kamin notes that Chaplin's talent for creating memorable photos and his talent for freeze gags, such as the one in *The Cure* where every time the curtains of his dressing room are opened, Charlie, in his swimsuit, strikes an new absurd pose, are "natural outgrowths of an extremely crisp movement style that gives him a puppet-like quality."[16]

You can see this mixture of feverish movement and photographic stillness in both the fake arms sequence and the food stand scenes from *A Dog's Life* that I describe above. In the fake arms sequence, Chaplin's hands never stop moving; they flap around like elegant, nervous butterflies. But along the way they make microsecond stops for crisp articulate little gestures and gags, straightening Austin's tie, cleaning his moustache, counting his money. In the food stand scene, Chaplin's eyes and mouth alternate between feverish activity and hilariously still repose.

These are notable examples of Chaplin inscribing his ideas on the smallest scale but, really, an appreciation, or cult, of the small gesture runs throughout the entirety of his films. The Tramp, as we know, is an irrepressible creature filled with energy that rarely finds sufficient expression in normal conduits. At a job for example, Charlie erupts in all sorts of inutile movements. Wherever the Tramp goes he is a swirl of excess energy, characterized by unnecessary gestures that he tosses off here and there, like so many sparks that are gone before we can register them.

If I were to point to one film as an example of Chaplin's love of throwaway gestures it might be *The Pawnshop*. Chaplin was at the top of his form in this film, which has been critically celebrated from its first appearance. Throughout, the Tramp's body erupts with little jokes and gestures that express his great ease and confidence. Picking up a ladder, he peers through its rungs at Rand and mimes an ape in a zoo. A brief sparring with Rand devolves, on Charlie's part, into a few jazz dance moves that express his disdain for even bothering to fight in the first place. When a histrionic customer soliloquizes dramatically while pawning his dead wife's ring, Charlie, gloriously unmoved by the melodrama, quietly draws his hammer closer and tests it in the air a few times, with an eye towards ending the melodrama. When customer Eric Campbell lays his bowler hat on the floor, Charlie twice pretends to step on it as he walks by, freezing his foot above the hat until Campbell rises in alarm, then nimbly stepping past the hat, all the while not letting on that he has noticed either Campbell *or* the hat.

These are tiny, throwaway bits and gags, tangential to the central actions at hand. But in many ways these decorative flourishes, in the margins of the film, are the glory of Chaplin's cinema, the little details that make us breathless because they happen so often and so fleetingly that we can't keep track of them. It's not lush sets or extravagant camera angles that give Chaplin's films their density and cinematic richness, but these decorative flourishes, many of which are accomplished on the most microscopic level. Chaplin's greatest work overwhelms the audience in its accumulation of these tiny gags. We have, in watching these sequences, the sense that we can't quite take them in or keep track of what we are seeing. And so we watch them again and again as we might repeatedly listen to a musical recording. Like other great works of art, they cannot be appreciated in one viewing. They are meant to be seen more than once. Chaplin's cinema invites scrutiny. In fact, it's devised so that close scrutiny only intensifies your appreciation of its clever embellishments, as it might the fine detail of Gothic tracery.

The early critic of the popular arts, Gilbert Seldes, felt compelled after seeing *The Pawnshop* in 1924 "to write down exactly what happened."[17] He wanted to convey to his readers just how much Chaplin had accomplished in the twenty minutes or so of the film and he felt the need, for himself, to revisit what he had seen, to try to gain control of it. Seldes, in his often anthologized essay, records some three or four pages of recollections from the film but doesn't even come close to recording all the telling detail of the film and, to my mind, leaves out many of the best gags. The piece is an interesting study, as so much early film criticism is, in faulty recall. But it also points to the near-impossibility of containing Chaplin's protean comedy in words.

Seldes was among the first of many critics who have been confounded by Chaplin's art, who have run themselves ragged trying to track down his elusive charm or tied themselves up in knots trying to describe in voluminous descriptive passages what Chaplin managed to etch in the air in a few seconds. Nothing speaks to Chaplin's art more than the critical dumbfoundedness it leaves in its wake. Chaplin condenses complex ideas into gestures of such fine delicacy that often only the camera, with its fine, exacting eye, can fully capture what he does. But it's in toiling on the microscopic level of Chaplin's films that we best discover his genius, not an easy task and one reason, I suspect, that entertaining biographies of Chaplin's colorful life outnumber solid analysis of his filmic technique.

In teaching *The Kid*, I like to check in with my students to see which gags they got and which slipped past them after one viewing. Some jokes they nearly all get. Some are fifty-fifty. But almost no students, after one viewing, note a beautifully inscribed gag late in the film. The evil head of the orphanage has come to remove Charlie's adopted son from his charge. Such is his disdain for the plebeian Charlie that he won't even speak to Charlie, addressing all of his questions via an assistant. "Ask him where the kid is," the man says to his sidekick. Charlie gestures to the child with a dawning sense of being insulted. "Ask him if he has any belongings," the orphanage director barks. Charlie, increasingly annoyed at being treated so disrespectfully, tries to respond directly to the orphanage director, but the director's sidekick makes it clear that Charlie is to direct his answers to him, the assistant, not to his boss. Charlie, angry now, says "tell him it's none of his business." This insult from an underling sets the orphanage director off on a blistering tirade that he directs, this time, right to Charlie's face. Charlie weathers this storm of angry words with calm neutrality. After the orphanage director has had his angry say, Charlie calmly turns to the man's assistant and cups his ear with his hand as though to say, "What did he say?"

It's a nifty gag in which Charlie tidily hoists a bully on his own petard, and by a single, small gesture. And it's a cleanly delineated gag. Sometimes Chaplin doesn't calibrate his gags correctly and the audience misses them, but the clues are crisp and apparent here; it's no fault of Chaplin's if we miss it. How to explain, then, that so many people do miss it on the first viewing? Well, part of the problem is that we have to be paying attention to get it. Chaplin's movies, like all silent film, require an active viewer; that is one of the things that makes this hoary old melodramatic cinema, in a way, a more sophisticated and demanding kind of filmmaking than that which followed it. Silent film asks its audience to read the screen carefully, to be a more active viewer than they would need to be in the sound era.

And Chaplin's particular brand of silent cinema ratchets up the demands on the audience. The gag here goes by quickly and is communicated by small gestures. And it's just one of a cascade of small jokes that Chaplin builds around the orphanage director's visit. Chaplin's protean creativity is another thing that make his films hard to take in. It's just very difficult for a viewer to capture all that Chaplin works into a scene. His gags require attention, are small in scale and arrive in rapid succession. This dense fabric of comedy and meaning is the triumph of his art. And, again, that triumph has to do with working in miniature and taking advantage of film's enormous capacity for intimacy, not in moving his camera about and striking bold compositions.

Chaplin and Acting

Chaplin's sensitivity to cinema's capacity for intimacy, his appreciation for how much the camera sees, his emphasis on small, intimate gestures and small but powerful physical detail, all contributed to his valuing of a quiet, naturalistic acting technique. Adolphe Menjou remembered that, on the set of *A Woman of Paris*, Chaplin had "one wonderful, unforgettable line that he kept repeating over and over throughout the picture. 'Don't sell it!' he would say. 'Remember, they're peeking at you.'"[18] This piece of advice reflects Chaplin's understanding of the intimacy of the camera's gaze. The fact that Charlie often looks out at us and consults us in the midst of a gag also tells us how conscious Chaplin is of our presence, how close he feels to us in the midst of his comedy. Chaplin's comedy is based on the notion that the audience is just behind him, looking over his shoulder, peeping at him. It's scaled for this kind of intimate relationship. He not only capitalized on the movie camera's capacity to capture the intimate but on the way it fostered a new, more intimate relationship with an audience.

Chaplin used a vocabulary very similar to that which Menjou quoted when he directed his son Sydney in a theater production in L.A. "You must not act, you ... must ... not ... act," Chaplin emphasized to his son. "Give the audience the feeling that they are looking through a keyhole." Even on the stage, then, he advised his actors to quiet their technique by thinking of their audience peeking on them, attending to their quietest gestures. He advised his son to minimize his gestures, noting that "gestures are not to be seen. And I'm a gesture man. It's hard to keep them down." Half of Chaplin's art was his exquisite gestures, the other half scaling them down for the cinema. Even when directing on the stage, he longed to consult a camera. "Thank God I can see myself on the camera the next day," he also said when directing Sydney.

He felt at sea on the stage, without a camera to tell him how he should pitch his performance.[19]

Chaplin had confidence in the camera's power to detect the quietest detail and also understood, conversely, how easily the camera was overwhelmed by excessive technique. "I would see my action on the screen and I'd say God, I'm like a windmill, throwing my arms all round the place and I'd know that was wrong. Then I'd come the following day and have the thing right," he said in one interview.[20] The camera taught Chaplin to quiet his gestures. Critics have often commented on the naturalistic quality of Chaplin's acting. Walter Vosges wrote that Chaplin has "something of the Japanese and American Indian abhorrence of unrestrained emotionalism. It seems indecent to him."[21] Ernst Lubitsch's biographer, Scott Eyman, notes that Chaplin's *A Woman of Paris* "gave Lubitsch an all-important attitude: dry, sardonic, emotionally cool, with the actors invariably giving quiet, uninflected performances."[22] Chaplin had a great gift for striking an equilibrium in his comedy. He trafficked in expressive gesture but pitched those gestures to the measurements of the camera. Not only did he not overwhelm his audience, he tended to draw them in by specializing in gestures that required his audience to scrutinize the text, lean into the frame. His acting wasn't just quiet, it was often near-invisible.

The quiet and subtlety of Chaplin's acting technique is not attributable to the demands of cinema alone. Fred Karno had taught his traveling performers the importance of the straight face, of keeping a center of absurd calm at times of chaos. Part of Chaplin's success was in following the old dictum of not laughing at your own joke. "When I dip my fingers in a fingerbowl and wipe them on an old man's beard, I do it as if were normal behavior. So they still laugh at me."[23] This is something he spoke of often in his interviews, of doing the absurd things that Charlie did with a straight face, never stepping on your audience's laughter.

But what he learned as a filmmaker was that the camera had a particular appreciation for the straight face in comedy. The camera gets right up close to that straight face, allowing Chaplin to work miracles of subtlety with it. A quick sideways glance at a woman reflects his lust if he narrows his eyes with a little leer, but childlike adulation if his stiff face contrasts with quick, nervous glances; a glint in his eye while suffering abuse from some man reflects a nascent, gathering force of retribution; a furrowing of his eyebrows as he looks at the audience invites us to share his confusion; a widening of his eyes as he looks at us invites us to share his surprise. What Chaplin learned was that this new medium that focused on the eyes and the hands was a particularly apt medium for his brand of comedy, built as it was around the subtlest of expressions, an art of eye movement.

Chaplin, then, was always looking for a naturalistic feel to his actors. Restraint, he said, was the thing he most prized in his actors. He had much of his greatest success with non-professional actors. Chaplin's tremendous rapport with Jackie Coogan in *The Kid* is the best example. But most of Chaplin's leading ladies were more or less non-professionals, as emphasized by Chaplin using their real-life names in his films. Chaplin needed a great actor far less than he needed someone with whom he could develop a strong rapport, hence his habit of using actresses with whom he was romantically involved.

One of the most repeated observations about Chaplin is that he would instruct his actors by acting out every role in a scene himself (just as his mother, veteran of the stage, used to do for him when she would tell him stories as a child). It is often said that Chaplin would have liked to play every role in the film himself. He never really saw his comedy as being about anyone but himself. Everything that happened was dictated by his particular sense of comedy and his particular comic timing. He surrounded himself with competent comic sidemen but no one really shines in Chaplin's films but Chaplin. And, later, in his sound films, he wasn't really able to take advantage of the character actors he worked with. *The Great Dictator*, for example, does not make particularly great use out of a stable of outstanding character actors. Billy Gilbert, Henry Daniell, Reginald Gardiner, Maurice Moscovich, Jack Oakie—these are all Hollywood greats but you'd be advised to look elsewhere than Chaplin's film for their best work. Chaplin's talent was not for drawing performances from established personalities. "What he really wanted," wrote David Robinson, "was an actor who was a kind of empty vessel, a conduit for his ideas, bodies through whom he could convey his own performance."[24]

Robinson cites the performance of Chaplin's secretary, Nelly Bly Baker, as the stone-faced masseuse in *A Woman of Paris* as a particularly fortuitous example of Chaplin using a non-professional actor as a conduit for his ideas. And he's right; her performance is a pitch-perfect imitation of Chaplin's commitment to deadpan neutrality. The masseuse, in the scene, gives Marie a massage while Marie banters with her frivolous socialite friend. The masseuse keeps her opinions to herself but we sense her disdain for the two women anyway, and it's a testimony to Chaplin's ability to fascinate us through immobility that she becomes the principal visual interest. She keeps a straight face but her eyes dart about, tracking the women when they don't know she's looking at them. She looks away at certain moments as though trying to contain her irritation and massages a little more vigorously when the chatter gets particularly catty, but she never violates the essential neutrality of the scene, yet another example of a successful Chaplin scene that is dependent almost entirely on eyes and hands for its expression.

What's really interesting in this scene is how much Baker channels and resembles Chaplin in this scene. We can see his facial expressions in hers, sense his direction in her comic timing. It's as though the spirit of Chaplin was animating her. The scene represents an example of an actress doing exactly what Chaplin tells her to and of the scene succeeding marvelously because she did, something that is going to happen more easily with non-professional actors who are more pliant, less likely than seasoned professionals to balk at their every moment being dictated.

We see these moments throughout some of Chaplin's greatest work. Chaplin practically makes love to himself in the final moments of *City Lights*, so clearly can we see Chaplin's direction in Virginia Cherrill's delicate gestures. We see a host of Chaplin's favorite "elegant swell" gestures in Adolphe Menjou's man of the world, Pierre, in *A Woman of Paris*. After all, Menjou is just filling out the performance that we've seen Charlie enact many times when he pretends to be an aristocratic gentleman. In *The Kid*, Jackie Coogan seemed to have been a particularly sensitive conduit to Chaplin's comic vision, often offering a kind of miniature version of Chaplin, for example when he kicks his legs and indulges in a host of Chaplin-like nervous tics under the scrutiny of a cop.

Even as late as *A Countess from Hong Kong*, we can see evidence of the way Chaplin tried to get his actors to imitate his comedy. That film operates at its best in those moments when the actors best imitate Chaplin's comic gestures and rhythm, for example in the many farce scenes in which Marlon Brando and Sophia Loren have to run about, opening and closing doors and hiding stowaway Loren. In these scenes we see many of the stunts and sense much of the rhythm that characterized the chase scenes from Chaplin's silent comedies. Watching those scenes confirms what we know from accounts of the production of that movie, that Chaplin got along much better with Loren than Brando, as Loren partakes in the whooshing slapstick with a great deal more childlike abandon and Chaplinesque resonance than Brando does. One of the film's brightest moments is when Chaplin's son Sydney, who by now was exhibiting a much greater flair for acting than he had when he was in *Limelight*, performs, at the ocean liner's bar, a kind of imitative homage to Chaplin's old routines of filching drinks from unsuspecting neighbors at the bar.

There is a tendency to think of Chaplin as a poor director of actors, an obsessive tyrant who drove these players to exhaustion trying to get them to enact some little gesture of which he alone was capable. There's some truth to this reputation. Later in his career, it's not clear how often he is doing retakes because they are really necessary or because he had arrived at the obsessive habits and demands of a prima donna. Film historian Kenneth Brownlow recalled accompanying Gloria Swanson to the *A Countess from Hong Kong* set on a day when Chaplin was struggling to communicate an idea to Brando, something that by all accounts happened often in the making of that film. Brownlow recalls Swanson observing, "You can see why actors find him difficult. This is a simple scene, and he's making much ado about nothing."[25]

Certainly, Chaplin's insistence that actors mimic his approach to a scene was out of step with the inwardly inspired school of method acting that was flourishing at the time *A Countess from Hong Kong* was being made, a school of which Brando was the most famous representative. Still, *A Woman of Paris*, *The Kid*, and *City Lights* are films that testify to Chaplin's talent in leading actors to top-notch performances by getting them to channel *his* comic timing and expressiveness. I'm a great fan of many Adolphe Menjou films but I've never seen him better than he is *A Woman of Paris*, never seen him able to convey his cheerily corrupt man of the world persona as crisply as he does in that film, via a host of cleanly articulated details, all reminiscent of Chaplin's own comic take on "the man of the world." *A Countess from Hong Kong* is obviously a failed film in many ways (though perhaps less so than critics have made out) but when it's good, it's precisely in those moments where the actors get ahold of Chaplin's gift for farce and slapstick, when they subordinate themselves to his vision and even his own crisp, articulate gestures. Chaplin's approach to actors might have been that of a control fiend but it was the right one for his cinema. His actors have always been best when they saw the world through his eyes.

Chaplin is not unusual in his propensity for actors who are less schooled in technique. Directors from the studio era and the art film alike have bloviated to the point of cliché about asking actors to lose their technique. Hitchcock moaned endlessly of the difficulty of getting actors to dial back their technique and simply register the neutral look he sought in a scene. He fought with a variety of actors—Charles Laughton, Paul Newman, Gregory Peck—who he felt were always intruding their technique into his vision. In the 1950s, he and most of the other better studio-era directors spoke quite disdainfully of method actors who, they felt, had a philosophy of acting that was antithetical to the quiet understatement of the best studio acting. The best actors, in their mind, were unaffected, like Gary Cooper and John Wayne, or held something back from the camera like Marlene Dietrich and Humphrey Bogart. They decried method acting as they decried extravagant camera angles and composition as self-serious and showy, far removed from the invisible classical technique they most venerated.

Directors from the world of the art film have often expressed themselves similarly. A cornerstone of Robert Bresson's aesthetic was his mission to make actors lose their technique. So insistent was he on their neutrality that he referred to them as models rather than actors. He badgered them to the point where they offered the semi-automaton performances he sought. In his mind, once he had stripped them of their technique, his camera (a kind of emotional Geiger counter) could record their unconscious gestures, little flashes in their eyes and nervous gestures in their hands that even they were not conscious of. The camera could spy out what they were hiding. Something very similar happens in Chaplin's comedy where he often counted on the camera to discover fortuitous comic effects that sprang from his improvisations and which he didn't know what to make sense of till he had seen them on the camera.

Vittorio De Sica was another of Chaplin's most ardent admirers and, in his lyrical mixture of hard realities and pathos, a great nominee for being the truest heir to Chaplin's cinema. He was led to neo-realism by the same impulses that guided Chaplin as a director. De Sica too had a very clear idea of what he wanted from each of his actors and, like Chaplin, would act out all the roles in a scene, male or female. Like Chaplin, he found that non-professional actors were an easier conduit for his ideas, that his image of how the scene should play out registered more vividly when he used amateur actors.

Film acting defies easy definition. Those, like myself, who tend to emphasize the power of the quiet gesture would do well to consider Orson Welles' comments on James Cagney. Cagney always played to the rafters, Welles noted, and his performances are among the greatest of the studio era. Still, the history of much of the best in film is inextricably linked with a softening of gesture, an introduction of casual technique, the weaving in of non-professional actors, and in some cases the handing over of the entire film to them. There is no corresponding history of the success of the untutored on the stage. Success there requires technique. Film often thrives on a lack of technique. Chaplin, from a very early stage of cinema on, had an eye for the unvarnished and authentic on the screen. His films can be described as naturalistic, not only because they are grubby and set in milieus of poverty, but because he takes advantage of the objective eye of the camera to attend to the subtlest detail of the reality he films.

Six

The Concrete and the Suggestive

Elimination from Accumulation

Chaplin's style is quiet in more ways than one. As we have seen, he was alert to the sensitivity of the camera, how little emphasis was needed to amplify a gesture on the screen. He was also careful not to inundate his audience with more information than was needed. One of the most cinematic and influential aspects of his cinema is his gift for what David Robinson has referred to as "just selection."[1] He had a gift for winnowing his films down to essential scenes, and his scenes to essential details. "Elimination from accumulation is the process of finding what you want," he wrote in his autobiography.[2] Critics have often marveled at the scenes that he was willing to leave out of his films: the ingenious seven-minute gag where the Tramp tries to forces a stick down a sewer grate in *City Lights*, for example, or the clever reverse sequence involving an axe in *Behind the Screen*.

Chaplin exercised the same "elimination from accumulation" within his gags, often reducing a key scene or moment to a single visual idea. Chaplin, who jumped into filmmaking without a screenplay, became adept at finding ways of communicating that were purely visual and at distilling complex ideas into simple gestures and objects. Robinson praises Chaplin's "ability to reveal the inner workings of the mind and heart through external signs."[3] In *The Immigrant*, to cite one famous example, Charlie is delighted to find Edna at the dingy restaurant. He had met her and her mother on the boat to America and fallen in love with her. He is as delighted as a child to see her, the way Charlie always is when he falls into company with a pretty woman. He hugs her, ushers her over to his table, clutches her hand in his and holds it to her face. Only then does he see that she is clutching a black-lined handkerchief. His face and Edna's fall to sorrowful expression as he realizes she's grieving over her mother's death. The handkerchief has two virtues here; it is economical in expression and it is purely visual. It took little time and no recourse to words. It is purely cinematic, not literary, in nature.

Chaplin got increasingly proficient in this kind of "just selection" as he developed as a filmmaker. *The Vagabond,* for example, opens with an interior shot of the swinging doors of a saloon. Then we see, in the open area beneath the doors, Charlie's famous oversized feet approaching, before the doors swing open and Charlie is fully introduced. It's a niftily conceived shot, a shorthand way of introducing Charlie, that capitalizes on our knowledge of, and affection for, Charlie and for his trademark big feet—a minimal approach with a large comic effect.

Similarly, in *City Lights,* Chaplin introduces Charlie the night he and his rich friend paint the town red, by plying his camera through a packed and active dance floor, weaving between the dancers until it arrives at a close-up of two huge tapping feet: Charlie's, in dress versions of his ridiculously oversized shoes. Only then does the camera tilt up and show us the entire Charlie, drunk and mesmerized by the dancing women. It's the same gimmick as the opening shot from *The Vagabond,* cuing Charlie's presence by his most obvious feature alone, and appealing to our affection for the Tramp via the pathetic feature by which we are most familiar with him. But Chaplin hardly ever repeats a gag wholesale and here there is a second joke. Who ever thought the Tramp could find his way to dress versions of his ridiculously oversized shoes? Dress versions of a bum's shoes? Not really possible. It's really just a little self-reflexive joke outside of the confines of the story, a little nod to the Tramp's iconic status.

Chaplin often expresses significant emotions via Charlie's relationship with small, seemingly insignificant objects. In *The Bank,* Charlie doesn't just leave a flower and a note for Edna, he kisses the note and smells the flower, over and over in fact, until he gets confused and starts to smell the note as if it were a flower. He lays the flower across her typewriter and the note beside it but, before he leaves, picks up the note and dusts it off with his jacket sleeve, as though it were a fine vase. When he lays the flower back on the desk, he carefully arranges it as though he were rearranging furniture trying to arrive at the perfect *feng shui.* He caresses the flower with his fingers, raises the fingers to his lips and addresses two kisses via his fingers, one to the flowers and another, touchingly, absurdly, to a single key on the typewriter. Chaplin is something of an alchemist here, taking the mundane (a typewriter key) and making it, somehow, an incarnation of both the delicacy of Edna's body and Charlie's love. Charlie animates the world around him with his love.

Chaplin is reminiscent here of another silent film great, Greta Garbo, who was also able to work magic with incidental concrete objects, for example, in that famous scene from *Queen Christina* where she tours the inn room with which she has been so happily ensconced with John Gilbert for several days but now must leave. As she prepares to separate from her lover, Garbo walks about the room, caressing nearly every item in it, veritably making love to the room as she tries to commit each of its details to memory. The credit to this scene goes to Rouben Mamoulian, a director who, like Chaplin, knew about the symbolic value of seemingly insignificant props, and to Garbo, who, like Chaplin was by nature a silent film actor, who knew how to speak to things before she knew how to speak on film.

But Chaplin does not have to work with an object as traditionally associated with love as a flower to create an emotional effect. In *Sunnyside,* he has great fun delineating Charlie's emotions via the front gate through which he passes when he comes to court Edna at her home. The first time Charlie comes to court, the gate is wide open. Charlie, however, does not step through. He's too spirited and too much in the throes of love to make such a conventional entrance. Instead he leaps over the fence next to the gate, closing the gate behind him. He doesn't use the entrance but closes the gate as if he had. Charlie likes absurd nonsense like this.

Later in the film, during a dream sequence, Chaplin, with his taste for unity, returns to the same gag, but with a variation. Charlie visits Edna's house a second time. This time the gate is closed as Charlie approaches. He repeats his previous action, leaping over the fence, but this time, absurdly, opening the gate behind him. There's great structure to the gag. Charlie closed an open gate after he jumped over the fence the first time; he opens a closed gate after he jumps over the fence this time. His actions are also typical of his bravado. Charlie always has the energy for this kind of game and loves to rearrange the world according to his own whim: hopping over gates when the door is open to him, opening a gate when it should stay closed. Making conventional use of a gate is all well and good for some, but not Charlie. Moreover, he is in love and love makes Charlie spirited, creative, and playful.

All the more pathetic, then, is Charlie's dejected departure from Edna's house once he has spied her through the window with her new suitor. Charlie turns tail and trudges out of the yard, not only walking through the gate entrance like a normal person, but closing it behind him with a servile attention to rules that we know is anathema to the real Charlie. In this manner, Chaplin manages to touchingly (and comically) convey Charlie's grief. And how? Through his relationship to a gate.

Critics often turn to Chaplin's *A Woman of Paris* for examples of his unique ability to show rather than tell, his gift for distilling information and emotion into elegant concretes. Russian poet Vladimr Mayakovsky praised *A Woman of Paris* for its "organization of simple little facts" that are laden with the "greatest emotional saturation," also an apt description for the examples of "just selection" from Chaplin's films with Charlie that I've discussed above.[4] Ernst Lubitsch was particularly struck by the inferential nature of the film and by Chaplin's ability to draw powerful emotion from small details and mere suggestiveness. He took the film as his filmic bible and his Hollywood films are peppered with specific references to it. Lubitsch's assistant Henry Blanke said that seeing *A Woman of Paris* "influenced Lubitsch's entire life from then on ... [F]rom being very spectacular with crowds ... he became very simple."[5]

When a writer who was a particular nemesis of Lubitsch, and knew how much he loved *A Woman of Paris*, egged him on by saying the film was just an ordinary story, a distressed Lubitsch responded, "But the treatment. The treatment."[6] Lubitsch's point was that the genius of the film and of the kind of aesthetic that he, Lubitsch, came to believe in devoutly, was not in the originality of the story but in the clever translation of that story into the medium of film. Like the best of the silent filmmakers, like the best of the studio era filmmakers in general, Chaplin prized simplicity. He didn't traffic in highly plotted stories or complex thoughts. The great Hollywood filmmakers, Chaplin above all, emphasized "treating" a story, making it interesting, via fine visual and plastic ideas, curlicues of decoration. Robert Mitchum recalled asking Howard Hawks what the story of *El Dorado* was when he signed up to do the picture. "Oh—no story, Bob," responded Hawks.[7] For Hawks, too, the key to making a great picture was not the story but what you did with a story.

A Woman of Paris is a top-notch classical Hollywood film, an excellent "treatment" of a familiar story, filled with examples of "just selection," as Robinson puts it, or with the "simple little facts" providing immense emotional payoffs to which Mayakovsky refers. Adolphe Menjou, in his autobiography, recounted one example of "just selection" in an anecdote that is widely cited in Chaplin studies. According to Menjou, Chaplin wanted to strike upon a concise visual means for conveying that Menjou's character, Pierre Revel, was Marie's long-term lover upon his first entrance into her apartment. He thought of having Pierre light up a pipe that was stored in her apartment but then thought Menjou was more elegant than the pipe-smoking type. He thought of Marie's maid bringing him slippers but that didn't jive with his having arrived to take her out for the evening. Finally, he arrived at the idea that Pierre, having helped himself to a drink, realizes he has forgotten his pocket handkerchief. He walks into Edna's bedroom. She is making herself up there and pays him no heed as he opens a drawer to a dressing cabinet, pulls out a gentleman's handkerchief and folds it into his pocket.

We like this kind of scene, as we do so many scenes in Lubitsch, not only for its efficiency, but for its elegance and charm, its clever innovation. It does the job but does it with panache. As Menjou noted, "little touches like this gave the picture a flavor that was new to picture making." Moments like this might be described as having the Chaplin touch, a touch as light and elegant as Lubitsch's.

If you watch the scene to which Menjou refers, though, you realize he has, maybe for the sake of a good anecdote, overemphasized the one detail of the handkerchief. Actually, Pierre's pulling the handkerchief out of the drawer is just the last of a host of visual clues that Chaplin provides to tell us quickly and efficiently that Pierre is keeping Marie. In this scene, Menjou's Pierre, arriving at Marie's apartment, quite unceremoniously leaves his jacket on a chair and his hat on a side table. He takes a quick look at the wine available in a carafe on a table but finds it wanting and instead delves into Marie's private supply in a liquor cabinet. While he is opening the bottle and helping himself to a glass, Marie enters the room and passes him by without even looking at him. When, on her second pass through the room, their eyes meet, they stop to exchange an affectionate but perfunctory kiss. Edna barely stops for the kiss and her expression remains unchanged during it. She continues to go about her housework while Pierre pours himself, and samples, a glass of wine. Only then does he realize his need for a handkerchief. But the nature of their relationship is quite clear already: Marie is a kept woman and has been for such duration that their life has reached the state of comfortable, almost marriage-like routine. Pierre's pulling out of the handkerchief from the dresser in her bedroom emphasizes, in particular, the intimacy of their relationship, but it's only the last of a host of finely etched details that convey, in just a few moments, the nature of their relationship.

We have the sense here of experiencing the directorial equivalent of Chaplin's comedic talent. Chaplin the comedian can, in the blink of an eye, toss off a half-dozen sparks of comic and visual information and the same is true of Chaplin the director. His films are notable for the kind of rapid accumulation of finely registered detail we see in the scene depicting Pierre's arrival at Marie's apartment.

A Woman of Paris is packed with lovely little concretes, far too many to exhaust within the context of this brief study. Pierre's father's death, for example, is tidily communicated by a close-up of a still smoking pipe near his slumped body near the fireplace, the visual clue that tells us he is not, as we assumed till that moment, only asleep.

Six. The Concrete and the Suggestive

When Marie visits Pierre at his hovel in Paris, Chaplin communicates Pierre's discomfort via a napkin with a hole in it that he is forced to offer Marie when they have tea together. Pierre folds the napkin in such a way as to obscure the defect, but Marie unfolds the napkin to put it on her lap, exposing the napkin's distress. Fortunately, though, she still doesn't notice the hole. Pierre nervously eyes the napkin for the rest of their conversation and at the first opportunity, when she announces her departure, whooshes the napkin back to the kitchen.

This is the kind of small detail with large emotional "saturation" that Mayakovsky referred to, a simple but concrete means of making us feel, rather deeply, both Pierre's embarrassment over his financial distress and his tension throughout the tea. This tension is Chaplin's means of deftly providing an undercurrent of discomfort to what is otherwise a wonderful occasion for Jean, the rediscovery of his lost love.

Marie is embarrassed when Pierre later comes to visit her: A maid, rummaging through drawers near them, accidentally drops a man's collar on the floor. Pierre had been staring uncomprehendingly at the luxury of Marie's apartment. The moment he sees the collar, he understands the source of her wealth. Even here, though, nothing in his face registers his new awareness. Chaplin understood that people often don't let on, in the slightest, what they are thinking. Simply showing Pierre see the collar suffices. Marie sees that Pierre has noticed the man's collar but she too betrays no emotions whatsoever, though we know she's devastated. This kind of neutrality in expression is one of the hallmarks of the film. Several times Chaplin manages to absorb our attention, or to move us, by having his actors hide, rather than dramatize, their feelings, the dramatic equivalent of Charlie's great comic neutrality, his ability to get laughs via his mockingly unemotional expressions.

Throughout *A Woman of Paris* Chaplin goes to visuals when other directors would go to title cards. When Marie tells Pierre that she would like "marriage, babies and a man's respect," Pierre, who is looking out the window at that moment, calls her attention to an impoverished family crossing the street several floors below, the woman struggling to corral several stray children while walking behind a bored and indifferent husband. When she asks Pierre, "What do I get out of life?" Pierre teasingly fondles her necklace. At an elegant Parisian restaurant, Marie notes a striking young man at a table with a wealthy old matron. "Who is that man?" she asks Pierre. Pierre only smiles. Chaplin asks us to read his films, not his title cards.

There is an extraordinarily quiet moment in *A Woman of Paris* that typifies the subtlety of this film and of Chaplin's directorial style in general. Pierre has taken Marie's friend Paulette to a fancy restaurant. Since Marie's former lover Jean has arrived in town, Marie has balked at being a kept woman and Pierre is auditioning her replacement. Pierre and Paulette are having a good time and Menjou's eyes twinkle with the merriment that is his signature trait and one of the most attractive aspects of this film. Until, that is, Paulette pulls out her lipstick and does a little at-the-table cosmetic adjustment. Menjou's expression changes at this little gaucherie that Marie would never be guilty of, but his expression changes only a small bit, not enough to betray annoyance even, just enough to register a deflation of merriment. In the remaining few shots of the two together, Menjou's face is more remote and he surprises Paulette when, as they leave the restaurant, he sends her home in a cab.

The emotions I describe here are more apparent in description than they are on the screen. I had to rewind the film to confirm the connection between the makeup moment and sending her off in the cab, so quiet is the registering of cause and effect. And of course Chaplin refused to help us along with a title card. Here we see the same art that we do in the comedies of Charlie, an art of subtlety and miniature that demands close attention of the audience.

But of course Chaplin was as much Griffith as he was Lubitsch, more Dickens than Franz Lehar, so he didn't only employ his gift for economy of expression in moments of subtle elegance. It was left to Lubitsch to weave entire films, like *Trouble in Paradise*, out of this kind of elegant charm. Great as *A Woman of Paris* is, its elegant melodrama is not fully representative of Chaplin's aesthetic. Chaplin would often put his gift for the concrete in service of a more old-fashioned, Victorian melodrama, for example in a film like *City Lights* where a flower is so weighted with meaning in regards to Charlie and the blind girl's relationship. In that film his purpose in concentrating on a single object is not elegant suggestiveness, *a la* Lubitsch, but a richness of pathos conveyed via one simple, traditional symbol. He sounds much more like the son of Griffith than the father of Lubitsch when he describes costuming Paulette Goddard in *Modern Times:* "I wanted the most beautiful patch [for her dress] in the world, something a poor girl must have searched weeks for. Perhaps, she hunted a dozen bags for it."[8]

Here we see a few aspects of Chaplin's particular art: his emphasis on expressing himself visually and through the smallest object, his telescoping a great many ideas into a single object, and the importance of objects, not just for their elegant suggestiveness, *à la* Lubitsch, but for their emotive power, *à la* Griffith or the Victorian cameo. Nevertheless, what links the handkerchief scene from *A Woman of Paris*, the flower scenes in *City Lights* and the girl's patch in *Modern Times* is a talent for, as Gerald Mast says, "the delineation of character, emotion and thought through Charlie's relation to tangible, physical objects."[9]

Ellipticism

But Chaplin's gift for efficient, suggestive and elegant visual communication is more wide-ranging than simply finding objects in which to distill his meaning. He is not only adept at distilling and reducing but at omitting. He is a master of ellipsis and developed, over the course of his career, a talent that often seems to define the greatest of filmmakers, that of knowing what to leave out.

Hitchcock, when trying to summarize the essence of what he saw as sound film technique, would often turn to the opening sequence of Chaplin's *The Pilgrim* as an example. In the first shots of the film, a police officer posts a notice of reward for an escaped convict. The picture on the notice is of Charlie. In the second scene of the film, a man in a swimsuit, fresh from a dip, heads to a bush behind which he lifts up, in some confusion, a man's prison garb. In the third scene of the film, Charlie appears on the platform of a train station, walking towards the camera in a minister's outfit.

For Hitchcock this was the definition of the efficient, purely visual filmmaking he sought to emulate. Chaplin has conveyed that Charlie has escaped from prison and stolen a minister's clothing in three wordless images that comprise a half-minute of time and done so without showing us any extraneous information that would slow the film down, like the minister swimming or Chaplin stalking him. As Chaplin wrote in his autobiography, "[T]ime-saving in films is still the basic virtue.... [B]ecause economy of movement is important you don't want an actor to walk any unnecessary distance unless there is a special reason, for walking is not dramatic."[10]

But we admire this scene for more than its efficiency. We are tickled by its cleverness, its sleight of hand. When Charlie appears on the tracks, audiences cackle with appreciation. It's a clever introduction to our hero and one that expresses his wiliness even before he has done anything. We know Charlie and how he operates. And Chaplin puts that knowledge to work; Charlie doesn't have to do a thing but show up. It's a masterpiece of efficiency. Not only does Chaplin infer an action that he has not had to show, he gains a laugh by reference to something (Charlie's mischievous nature) that he hasn't had to demonstrate.

Chaplin is expert at setting up, in this manner, a certain number of coordinates that the audience needs to draw together to figure out the joke. The joke itself is purely inferential, a thing of nothing. In *The Kid*, for example, Charlie makes his first appearance walking down a garbage-strewn back alley, affecting, as usual, his gentlemanly behavior despite his surroundings. At one point he dodges garbage tossed from a window. Moments later he finds an abandoned baby bundled up near the wall of a tenement. Now he casts his eye upwards. Here we have to read his mind. There is no title card to help us come to the realization that Charlie thinks the baby was tossed out with the garbage. We laugh here, not only because we have figured out what he is thinking, but because the thought itself is comic. It's typical of Charlie's naiveté, his tendency toward literal-mindedness, that he would entertain the possibility that the kid was dropped with the trash. And there may be a small bit of social commentary here as well, a mordant reference to how cheap life is in the areas of town that Charlie inhabits.

Granted, this is not a hard joke to get. But it is, nevertheless, typical of Chaplin's tendency to give you the coordinates (garbage tossed out a window, baby on ground, upward glance) and let you piece the joke together. And, as easy as the joke is to get, there is a tangible response in an audience to this kind of gag, a kind of audible chuckle that says, "Oh, I get it." Kevin Brownlow noticed when screening his documentary *The Unknown Chaplin* that Chaplin's gags did not make BBC officials laugh until he put them on a big screen. Chaplin's films play better on a big screen because, like all silent films, they need to be puzzled out visually and that is more easily done on a big screen where you can see the smallest and often most important communication, the kind expressed through hands and eyes. But Chaplin works better on a big screen for another reason as well: the group dynamic of the audience. There's a kind of delight in the laughter of an audience viewing a Chaplin film that expresses the audience's sense of having figured out the film's gags, and this laughter is infectious. Chaplin keeps his intertitles to a minimum, leaving us a good deal of room to participate in the film.

Another example of Chaplin's gentle ellipticism in *The Kid* occurs when Charlie, after trying to palm off the child on several other people, resigns himself to the fact that he will have to tend to the child himself. He sits down on a curb, with the child in his arms, and notices a sewer grate to his right. He lifts up the grate to investigate, looks at the child and then back at the grate nervously before closing it and finally beginning to minister to the child's needs, as he will for the rest of the film. But we caught the meaning of that little gesture with the grate: Charlie gave fleeting thought to dumping the kid in the sewer.

Again, it's not hard to read the signs. But it's the kind of scene that gets an audience talking back to the screen (and they still do). In showing Chaplin films, I often notice students explaining, to the friends they sit with, what they have just figured out in reading Chaplin's visual clues. They feel the need to express what they have seen, because Chaplin has given him the pleasure of figuring it out for themselves, left just the little bit of room to exercise their deductive skills. They want to announce the fruits of their findings in these moments, the success of their small burst of mental energy.

This is of course the great beauty of silent film and why certain film purists still consider it the golden age of cinema. At its best, silent film forces us to watch closely, puzzle things out, participate in the characters' lives. The silent film and studio-era director Allan Dwan praised D.W. Griffith (probably Chaplin's greatest influence) for his ability to get us to read his actors' minds. "When you can make an actor sit dead still and think of something and have the audience know what he's thinking, you've got a hit," said Dwan, perfectly describing Chaplin's deft mixture of deadpan and suggestiveness here as well as Griffith's art. "If an actor can do that, he's a great actor and that's what Griffith's girls learned to do. These little movements they made and the silences that followed—you know what they were thinking, what their problem was and your heart went out to them."[11] Little gestures followed by silences is also not a bad description of many of Chaplin's best elliptical sequences. Chaplin, too, deepened his audience's relationship to Charlie by making them puzzle out his thoughts, enter into and sympathize with his singular apprehension of the world.

Not that the exact nature of Charlie's thoughts is always easy to puzzle out. There's a scene in *Pay Day* when, having just been paid his week's wages, Charlie stashes a substantial portion of the money in the lining of his hat so that he won't have to hand the rest over to his rather formidable battle-axe of a wife. The rest he pockets. Shortly thereafter, a beautiful woman sashays by. Charlie stares at her long and hard, one of those quiet, neutral expressions of the type I discussed earlier, that, by its very inexpressiveness, draws our greater scrutiny. His face is emotionless but, typically, his cane twirls excitedly, always a sign of inward agitation, often of a sexual nature. He then reaches into his pocket and adds an extra bill to his hat lining. We don't know exactly how Charlie plans to spend those extra funds but we do know, generally, that the passing woman has just upped his romantic ambitions for the night. This is exactly the technique that Dwan meant when describing Griffith's films. Charlie maintains a deadpan expression while we try to figure out what he's thinking. Chaplin puts us to work and we enjoy the job. "That's the great trick in any enterprise that looks for public acceptance," Dwan said, "make the public work. If you do all the work for them, they sit there bored to death."[12]

And the thoughts that we puzzle out aren't always Charlie's. There's a marvelous moment in *Sunnyside* when Charlie's country girlfriend (Edna Purviance) has come to the general store at which Charlie works but can't remember what she meant to buy. Charlie, trying to be helpful, offers several possibilities (butter, a toothbrush, a razor), none of which jogs her memory. Finally he brings out a hunk of cheese that is, apparently, somewhat redolent, as Charlie is jolted by its odor. Edna, at this point, is not even looking at Charlie or realizing that he is offering her the cheese, but the smell of the cheese does the trick anyway. She suddenly remembers that she meant to buy socks.

Chaplin's powers of suggestiveness were often inspired, as in the gag above, by his love of the indecorous. He found off-screen space, for example, very useful for subtly conveying those things he was not supposed to show. In *The Kid*, when Charlie brings the child back to his neighborhood, he shows it to a few of the rather careworn women who populate his district. One asks Charlie's the child's name. Charlie's expression registers that he hasn't given the idea of naming the baby a moment's thought. In his typically abrupt manner, he quickly enters the nearest building with the child and exits moments later smoothing the child's blankets. "John," he says.

The humor here is first in the ellipsis. We have to deduce Charlie's actions in the house: He quickly checked the child's sex and then arrived at an appropriate name. (This by the way is another gag often missed by students on a first viewing.) It's also comical that Charlie is proudly parading a baby as his before he's even contemplated its sex, much less its name. The humor of the elliptical gag is also intensified by how quickly Charlie accomplishes the action. No baby name books for Charlie. He discovers the child's sex and arrives at a corresponding name in a matter of seconds. Charlie doesn't know the first thing about children or parenthood but he will be a quick learner.

City Lights, too, has an elliptical gag built around an indecorous off-screen action. Charlie is in the locker room before his boxing match, already wearing his gloves. He whispers in another boxer's ear and this man points off screen. Charlie nods, thanks him and heads off screen. We presume he's looking for a restroom. Charlie returns to ask the man to remove his (Charlie's) gloves. Here Chaplin decorates his joke. Now Charlie seems like a child, devoid of foresight and helpless enough to need assistance in relieving himself. We laugh too at the way Charlie typically subverts gender expectations, turning a tough guy boxer into a solicitous mom. When we track Charlie to his destination off screen, however, we find that he's only visiting a drinking fountain. Here's Chaplin third joke in the small gag: He's teasing us for making off-color assumptions.

One of Chaplin's more interesting uses of off-screen space is in a deleted scene from *Shoulder Arms*: Charlie comes home to an abusive wife, one we never see. We are first alerted to her presence by that time-honored engine of wifely abuse, the rolling pin that comes flying from off-screen and hits Charlie in the head. Charlie's a hen-pecked husband in this scene (probably one of the reasons the scene was cut; the role doesn't suit Charlie's persona in the end) and he goes about making dinner and doing the laundry, but nervously, and under the constant scrutiny of the off-screen shrike, who every now and then expresses her displeasure by tossing dangerous objects at him. We register her physical presence only by these objects that come flying at Charlie from the right side of the screen.

The scene is typical of Chaplin's particular brand of cinematic innovation. It's a conservative shot, with a fixed camera and long take, but one that takes advantage of off-screen space to suggest and infer, that cleverly builds itself around the lacunae in our knowledge. It's a hoary old comic gag, the abusive wife, rendered, paradoxically, with fine, delicate suggestiveness. The most comical moment occurs when Charlie, hanging out the wet laundry, pulls from a hamper an absurdly immense nightgown and equally gargantuan bloomers that suggest Charlie's wife is of elephantine proportions. One of the benefits of elliptical gags is that a filmmaker is allowed to exaggerate the comedy without falling into the trap of broad, vulgar physical comedy. The intended effect is softened here and becomes more gently amusing because it exists only in our imagination. No human being was actually insulted in the making of this scene and we are saved from the unpleasant spectacle of a woman of Fatty Arbuckle proportions, the very kind of image that marks the more vulgar Keystone films and Chaplin's own earlier efforts.

A Woman of Paris is packed with elliptical moments. Many of the moments that I discussed earlier, as examples of "just selection" serve as examples of ellipticism as well. If Chaplin leaves us to read his action rather than his intertitles, to puzzle out what his actors are doing via physical props, he is engaging in elliptical gags. But certain gags build themselves more specifically around missing information. The prurient nature of the story in this film provides, for example, several opportunities for off-screen gags as well. During the scene in which Marie is visited by her masseuse, for example, Chaplin frustrates the viewer by exiling Marie's body to the off-screen space below the frame and fixing his camera, instead, on the muscular efforts of the masseuse. At one point, the masseuse sweeps away, with a broad gesture, the sheet that had been covering Marie's off-screen body. The camera remains on the masseuse as she slathers her hands in oil and engages in an intense full tissue massage along the length of Marie's body, Chaplin's way of making us, for a short while, reflect, rather intently, on the texture and contours of the body that lies just outside of our visual grasp.

There is another piece of rather clever off-screen titillation at the bohemian party: The guests have devised a novel striptease in which a woman wrapped head to toe in one long bolt of fabric gets turned on a revolving platter like a record on a turntable, while one of the guests holds the end of the bolt of fabric, thus slowly removing her wrap. Chaplin films the woman from the waist down as her revolving ankles and legs are unveiled, then cuts to the crowd, registering her final unveiling via the reaction shots of an extremely animate and expressive audience, arranged in multiple layers and with intertwined limbs and contorted poses reminiscent of an Italian Mannerist painting. One woman scrutinizes the striptease lasciviously through her monocle. Another man looks so simultaneously shocked and pleased that a woman sitting behind him covers his eyes and angers him. The twirling woman's nudity is conveyed via these little vignettes which translate the scene's action indirectly and, in so doing, pique our imagination. We see only fleeting glances of her bare legs and shoulders as, the striptease accomplished, she dashes naked from the room.

Chaplin finishes this scene with a deft gag. Early in the party, when Paulette is on the phone with Marie, inviting her to the party, an anonymous drunk stands in the background behind a desk, yawning and doing a pretty good imitation of a Chaplin drunk. He's only background information until he passes out and slithers down behind the desk. We forget about him during the striptease. Later, the naked woman, having just fled the crowd, pokes her head out from behind a curtain to provide one last tease. The drunk, whom we have completely forgotten, as he was only on the screen for a few seconds, many minutes ago, now stands up from behind the desk where he had fallen, and which is just behind the woman. He is treated to the view of the naked woman that everyone at the party (and in the cinema) desires. Seeing the woman, he passes out a second time, this time from shock.

This gag is expressive of Chaplin's gift both for inference and for clever arrangement of seemingly disparate coordinates. This is the kind of scene that gets old fogeys nostalgic about how sex was handled in the past. But of course this scene is effective, not because of its more refined morality, but because of its more refined aesthetic. The great gift of the Code in Hollywood was many elliptical gags like this one, stylish and clever sleight of hand that elegantly inferred nudity by a few fragmented images and, in this case, via the gaze of onlookers whose expressions we interpret and whose minds we read.

The elliptical nature of Chaplin's cinema is another reason Robert Bresson venerated him. This same art of omission is at the heart of Bresson's cinema as well. "Draw the attention of the public (as we say that a chimney draws)," writes Bresson, echoing the aesthetic of the French Symbolist poets, who also believed that you draw a reader's interest by what you leave out of your poem, keep unexpressed, by little gaps of information that draw interest like the chimney draws the flame. "Translate the invisible wind," Bresson also writes, "by the water it sculpts in passing."[13] Chaplin's art is an art of small gestures but also one of invisibility, of illusionism. Often the key aspect of his gag is what is left out, the theft of clothes at the outset of *The Pilgrim*, the train in the famous station scene from *A Woman of Paris*, Charlie's thoughts as the attractive woman passes in *Pay Day*.

It's probably not surprising that, gifted mime that he was, Chaplin seemed to have an innate understanding of cinema's capacity for suggestiveness, its potential for implying meaning. Chaplin's gift for elliptical expression has to be seen as one of the most significant features of his cinema. It influenced not only the Hollywood classical aesthetic that believed so devoutly in showing rather than telling, in conveying meaning via quiet actions that had to be carefully read, but an artier cinema, like Bresson's, that prized elliptical technique for its poetic grace and subtlety and the challenge it posed to the viewer. This two-pronged influence of Chaplin on both the studio and the art house film, dating from the very outset of his popularity, is one of the unique aspects of Chaplin's cinema. His ellipticism is at the heart of that universal appeal.

Ellipsis of Sound

That Chaplin's creativity was piqued by the challenge of conveying what was not there, by suggesting things or working around an ellipsis, is evidenced by how many gags he works around sound in his silent films, for example the scene in *The Count* where he has to combat Eric Campbell's loud soup slurping in order to continue flirting with Edna, and in *Sunnyside* where he mistakes various timbres of goat calls for a poorly tuned piano, and in *The Vagabond* where he keeps surprising Edna with increases in volume when he serenades her with his violin.

For a large chunk of *Police*, Chaplin sets himself the paradoxical goal of communicating the terror of sound in a silent film, as Charlie and a fellow robber, Wesley Ruggles, tiptoe through the house they are robbing in the middle of the night. Charlie finds his way to many explosive sounds in this film: He accidentally sits on piano keys (twice); he topples a display table of china by accidentally hooking it with his cane; an alarm clock that he aims to steal goes off in his pants. Chaplin provides visuals for each of these sounds but what really sells their effect is Charlie's acrobatic response to them. Two of Chaplin's great skills were for going from speed to immobility in a split second and, conversely, going from frightened stillness to cartoonish, manic animacy just as fast. It was the latter talent he tapped in conveying loud noise in silent cinema. It's often the abrupt explosion of movement, the crazed zigzag run in response, the literal blur of Charlie's limbs that sells the sounds he wants to convey.

But other times his means of conveying sound are more subtle. One of my favorite sound gags in Chaplin films is the moment in *The Immigrant* when Charlie discovers a badly needed coin on the floor beside the table where he dines. Charlie has realized he hasn't the money to pay his bill, and he has also just seen a customer brutally beaten for the same offense. We've watched his anxiety accumulate for several moments. All the while, a piano and violin duet plays in the background of the image, framed by the doorway beside Charlie's table. Finally, Charlie, legs crossed, and turned aside from the table at which he sits, with one hand resting on his lap, lays his head on his other hand and looks to the floor in resigned despair.

Providentially, at this moment a waiter drops a coin on the floor next to Charlie and walks off without noticing. Charlie doesn't see the coin right away, does a double take when he does see it, and then, though his legs are still crossed, brings his foot down on the coin with a resounding thump, his legs seeming to have acted on their own cognition even before Charlie's awareness caught up with them. The explosive nature of Charlie's stomp on the coin is registered in "visual sound" as the musicians behind Charlie jump in their seats, stop playing and turn to Charlie who, fortunately, still has his legs crossed and is in a fairly decorous position. Charlie claps politely, as though the enormous thump of his foot had merely been his means of expressing his enthusiasm for their music. The "noise" here is comical, not only because of the way it is implied by the surprised musicians, but because their reaction is so strong as to register massive volume, which, in turn, comically underlines Charlie's desperation. The "sound" here comically expresses just how astonished and relieved Charlie is, just how instantaneous, explosive and unplanned that stomp was. It's the sound, that of course is not really there, that provides the "hallelujah" moment of the scene.

One of Charlie's most famous gags also involves inferred sound. It's the scene where Charlie first meets the flower girl in *City Lights*. Charlie is crossing a busy street when he sees a traffic cop. As he always does when he sees a policeman, Charlie scurries in the opposite direction with an instinctive rapidity. The traffic is so thick, though, that he cannot reach the curb he seeks without passing by the cop, so he simply enters the back seat of a parked car by one door and exits to the curb via another. As he closes the car door behind him, the blind flower girl, assuming he is the owner of the car, asks if he would like to buy a flower. Charlie warms to the mistaken role of well-to-do citizen and buys the flower, affecting his best "lord of the manor" attitude. In the course of purchasing the flower he learns that the girl is blind and arrives at profound feelings for her. He'd like to spend more time with her but, as she is fetching his change, the actual owner of the car, a quite well-to-do gentleman, passes Charlie by, gets into the car from which Charlie exited, slams the door shut and drives away. The flower girl, hearing the car door slam again, assumes Charlie has left and meant her to keep the change. Charlie, even though he could badly use the change, does not want to disabuse the girl of her mistaken impression of him and very carefully tiptoes away.

The gag is emblematic of Chaplin's cinema. It's an example of Chaplin finding purely visual means for communicating his information, in this case, the mistaken identity that will be the crux of the film, and visual means that are notable for their efficiency, simplicity, and elegance. It's the sound of the car door that leads to the girl mistaking Charlie for a wealthy man, a role he will play for the girl for the rest of the film. And it's the sound of the door that makes her conclude that Charlie has tipped her generously. Of course, neither of these sounds can actually be heard.

The scene typifies Chaplin's subtle, elliptical nature. It's built around several ellipses. Chaplin has to imply sound and to imply the thoughts of both the blind girl and Charlie. We work hard at reading the scene and experience several of those "Oh, I get it" moments. It's a gag to be figured out and its success in great measure lies in how delighted we are by what we've figured out. And we not only enjoy figuring out the gag, we also delight in its cleverness and ingenuity, as we might in a small but clever puzzle. We enjoy putting the coordinates together but we also appreciate the elegance of the coordinates themselves, how deftly managed they are. It's a scene that is characterized by a mathematical grace and precision and yet poetically dances around a subtle gap of information.

Seven

Chaplin's Filmmaking Skills

A Classical Aesthetic: Unity

In the 1960s and 1970s there was a vogue for the films of Buster Keaton and a correspondent deflation in the critical appreciation for Chaplin. Films in this period were influenced by the gamesmanship and hijinks of contemporary European art films, particularly those of the French New Wave. There was a good deal of showing off in cinematic technique at this time and, perhaps, a sense that the classical style of the studio era, with its goal of seamless editing and invisible camerawork, had had its day.

So Keaton, whose films were so much more outlandish and experimental than Chaplin's, and whose films were characterized by large stunts and ideas that seemed more inherently filmic than Chaplin's, gained ascendance. Keaton made films with ocean liners and trains. How could they be anything but filmic? Chaplin's films seemed stagey by comparison. His aesthetic was conservative. Often his camera remained fixed from a single perspective and from the same distance. Chaplin's editing is often spare, recreating the kind of experience of time we might have in viewing Chaplin on the stage. Keaton used the physical world like his playfield. His films were carved from the substance of reality. Chaplin's seemed antique and artificial, particularly in the later sound films where his set design, never his forté, didn't keep up with technological developments and so relegated him to a kind of old-fashioned silent film world preserved in aspic.

But Chaplin's films are in fact cinematic, only in a quieter way. His filmmaking is characterized by a classical aesthetic. He has, for example, the classicist's taste for unity. His quiet style—his tendency to keep the action in one place for a long while, to shoot it from a single point of view, and to shoot in long takes that allow the action to unravel unimpeded by edits or camera movement—all reflect a natural bent for unity. Part of the success of a film like *The Pawnshop* is that Chaplin so thoroughly explores all the comic possibilities of a single place or single comic scenario. He likes to dig deeply in one spot. His method of filmmaking was to arrive at a scenario and then improvise as many ideas as he could from that scenario. Many of his best sequences, like the dining sequence from *The Immigrant* and the boxing sequence from *City Lights*, owe their success to his natural tendency towards unity of place and time, his natural proclivity to improvise on a single subject and discover a wealth of ideas.

As Chaplin developed as a filmmaker, his sense of unity became more sophisticated. In a famous quote from his autobiography, he notes that, from *A Dog's Life* on, he began "to think of comedy in structural sense, and to become conscious of its architectural form. Each sequence implied the next sequence, all of them relating to the whole." In this manner, he gave his films a pace and saved them from a danger comedies often run into, of just being a series of sketches. "If a gag interfered with the logic of events," he wrote, "no matter how funny it was, I would not use it."[1] Hence, the legendary ratio of footage used versus footage shot and the deletion of scenes that would have been the pride of many a lesser filmmaker.

Though Chaplin didn't always arrive at *A Dog's Life*'s near-perfect sense of unity, his later films are characterized by this kind of thoughtful arrangement of scenes, by gags that, as Kyp Harness says, "are woven" through his films "like a necklace of gems."[2] The great feature films—*The Kid, The Gold Rush, The Circus, City Lights*—all, to some degree, owe their success to Chaplin's careful weighing of the purpose of each scene. In these films, much more so than his earlier ones, comedy is subsumed to the purposes of narrative. But even before the features, we can see a stronger sense of unity in many of his Mutual and First National films. Not only *A Dog's Life*, but *The Pawnshop, Easy Street, Shoulder Arms, The Idle Class, The Count* and *The Pilgrim*. All of these films have the sense of being whole unto themselves. Some, like *The Pawnshop*, owe their sense of unity to their setting in a single place. Others owe it to a concentration on a single subject matter, religion in *The Pilgrim* and war in *Shoulder Arms*, for example. The first half of *Idle Class* is characterized by tight, D.W. Griffith–like editing that holds its separate plot strands together before they unite at the party in the second half.

Nevertheless, we shouldn't overemphasize Chaplin's gift of unity. Despite his willingness to let go of scenes if they were not just right—to kill, as Faulkner said, all his babies—we still scratch our heads at some of his editorial decisions. Was it the right idea to leave out, from *City Lights*, that whimsical scene with the stick and the sewer grate, so typical of the Tramp's accidental charm, and yet keep the scenes where Charlie swallows a whistle and mistakes confetti for spaghetti, two puns (one aural, the other visual) that are among the few moments that slow that film's lovely forward movement? Why delete the church scene in *The Kid* where the young bride's marriage to an older man is summarized, in grand silent film tradition, by a close-up of his heel grinding down a rose fallen from her bridal bouquet, or the scene where the stained glass window behind the unwed mother who watches the wedding creates the illusion of a halo above her head? If, as Chaplin said, he found these scenes dated, by which he must have meant melodramatic, why keep the bit of didactic montage where he cuts from the unwed mother leaving the foundling hospital with her baby to an image of Jesus mounting the hill of Golgotha?

Chaplin obsessed to the point of depression over these films and, no doubt, had trouble seeing the forest for the trees. But for the most part, he got better and better, as he developed as a filmmaker, at weaving together his scenes, linking them nicely at the joints, and leaving out scenes that got in the way of this natural, organic unfolding of events. Take a look at how nicely one gag leads to another at the outset of *The Circus:* the ingenuity of the pickpocket gag, the filching of the baby's treat; the funhouse mirror scene, the wax statue *trompe l'oeil* outside the funhouse. These are all virtuosic gags, each worthy of its own fame, but they are all woven together dexterously and seem to exist, not for themselves, but for the part they play in the sequence of events that culminates in Charlie charging into the circus tent, ten minutes into the film, as the rightful story of the film begins. As good as these gags are, they are all subsumed to the musical thrust of the film's introduction.

Meanwhile, that bent for unity that expressed itself early on in a taste for simple long takes and fixed camera angles continued to express itself in his later films, only with even more precision and rhythmic care. For example, in the boxing scene from *City Lights,* Chaplin draws an infinite number of comic possibilities from the spectacle of a boxing match, an event he had visited in earlier films, but never with this much precision and variety. In that sequence, one of his greatest, the camera tracks the action a little more than it had in his early days but, for the most part, shoots the match from a single fixed perspective. And yet this is one of his most triumphant sequences. The boxing match from *The Champion,* though often carefully choreographed, can't compete with the one from *City Lights* in its ingenuity or in the organization of complex detail. The latter is played out like a carefully orchestrated piece of music, with repeating refrains, but each time with new variations and experiments, and gags that are mapped out with the precision and variability of an algebraic equation. The camera remains fixed; the gags that it registers have become mind-bendingly complex. One of the paradoxes of Chaplin's cinema is that his films improved in their unity and their complexity at the same time. He had a gift for getting the most from the least.

Cinematic Restraint

Those sequences that Chaplin edited out of *The Kid* when he reissued the film in the early '70s tell us some things about his work. First, the shots he took out had nothing to do with Charlie, who Chaplin knew was the main attraction of his films. The lukewarm public reaction to the beautifully styled *A Woman of Paris* confirmed that. If a shot didn't help deepen our relationship to Charlie, Chaplin looked at it very suspiciously. Several of the shots that he removed from *The Kid* are also highly melodramatic and remind us that Chaplin was wary of saccharine expression of emotions. And then several of the shots, like the church scenes described above, are somewhat showy in technique. These edits emphasize how much Chaplin was on the lookout for extraneous bits of excessive artistry, which he felt were antithetical to the clean unity of his work.

All of Chaplin's forays into cinematic expressiveness, whether they be elaborate compositions, compositions on a large scale, lighting effects, special effects, or expressive shots, are characterized by several features. First they are used minimally. Chaplin had a conservative aesthetic and only turned to grand gestures when he was sure they were absolutely called for. Secondly, they are characterized by flawless execution that matches the obsessive perfectionism we see in his comic performances. In many ways the greatest defense to the argument that Chaplin did not have Keaton's cinematic talents is how perfectly Chaplin pulled off Keaton-like experimental cinematic stunts the few times he turned his attention to them. Third, these more expressive shots are woven very carefully into the naturalistic texture of the film so that they don't stand out too loudly as a stunt or detract from Chaplin's greater concerns, such as the development of the story or the delineation of Charlie's nature. Chaplin's conservative shot selection is due, in no small part, to his devotion to his works' unity.

Ironically, Chaplin was Hollywood's first great independent artist. He had the money to make any kind of film he wanted, to be as artsy and self-indulgent as he wanted. But he fully subscribed to a fundamental law of what was fast becoming the aesthetic of the studio era: the idea that the best style was the least obvious one. The camera should never announce itself, either through strange angles or excessive movement. Editing should be invisible. Loud shots should be few and only employed when they are most appropriate and can accomplish the maximum effect. Special effects should be doled out sparingly and then very lightly and in such a way as *not* to interfere with naturalist effect. Films should be solid aesthetic objects but reach a wide audience as well. A film should be tasteful and understated, not loud and obvious.

This is the classical ethos of the studio era film. Keep your ego and your technique in check. In many ways, it was Chaplin who pioneered this aesthetic, as evidenced by all the studio-era filmmakers who cited his films as sacred text when trying to express their ideal in filmmaking. It is interesting that the two times Chaplin worked with another director of some renown, the collaboration was not successful and, in both cases, the director was a great deal artier in his shots than Chaplin would be. The only time Chaplin produced the work of another director was a film directed by Josef von Sternberg called *The Seagull*. According to von Sternberg, it was only shown one time, in one theater, before Chaplin withdrew it. Filmmaker John Grierson claimed to have seen the film, describing it as a "beautiful and empty affair—possibly the most beautiful I have ever seen—of net patterns, sea patterns and hair in the wind." "When a director dies," Grierson noted acerbically, "he becomes a photographer," a notion with which Chaplin and just about every other Hollywood auteur would have concurred.[3] Later, looking for some technical guidance, Chaplin hired future auteur Robert Aldrich as his assistant director on *Limelight*; the French filmmaker Eugene Lourie remembers that Aldrich "always wanted more artistic shots. Chaplin did not think in 'artistic' images when he was shooting."[4]

Grierson's idea that "when a filmmaker dies he becomes a photographer" succinctly conveys the attitude of the classical studio filmmaker, an attitude to which Chaplin, for all of his financial freedom, subscribed absolutely. "I suppose I ignore the 'modern techniques,'" he said to Ella Winter in an interview in 1957. "I don't like camera trickery—that's for technicians or track layers.... It's too simple to shoot through a nostril or the fireplace."[5] This is a kind of standard statement of the Hollywood pro, particularly abundant towards the end of the studio era, when the old artisans were confronted by a new cinema that was influenced by arty European fare. In fact, you'll find Chaplin's exact words echoed in the complaints of other studio-era filmmakers late in their careers, as if they had all been commiserating at the same parties. "Don't worry about the camera angle," Mervyn LeRoy said, "don't shoot up somebody's nose."[6] "I never set up the camera to astonish," said Billy Wilder. "In France they call it *epater le bourgeoisie,* to astonish the middle classes. 'Boy, do I have a setup: going to shoot through the fireplace with the flames in the foreground.'"[7] Chaplin was particularly prone to these statements late in his career when his sound films were under constant fire for being stagey, archaic and uncinematic, charges that are, ironically, far more accurate when leveled against those later films than they are of Chaplin's silent fare starring Charlie.

For the old Hollywood pros, exhibiting technique was akin to showing off. Great filmmakers hid their style. "I never heard anybody walk out of the theater and say, 'Wasn't that a great camera angle.' Never," said Mervyn LeRoy.[8] This attitude might make us laugh today when shot analysis is all too common and films are rated highly for their expressive aesthetic, but it was a religion for Hollywood pros to keep their artistic style to themselves. There is a great humility to these directors, who saw a film's success as proportionate to the invisibility of its technique. Studio era filmmakers tended to subscribe to Ovid's aesthetic, as expressed in his description of Pygmalion's statue: "such art his art concealed." Chaplin did too. As Richard Schickel notes, Chaplin had "no interest in films of 'crowd splendor' … or in Eisensteinian montage or in the expressionism that was Germany's great contribution to the intellectual stir surrounding film in the twenties."[9] He was only interested in technique that served to translate clearly Charlie's comedy and his pathos.

Chaplin's Cinematic Skills

But even as we consider the significance of Chaplin's quieter aesthetic, we should note that he could be quite expressive with a camera when he chose to be. There is ample evidence in his films of an artist who could create images on a large scale and with elaborate *mise-en-scène*. In the end, Chaplin opts for a more conservative cinematic technique, but it is important to note that it is a matter of choice, not necessity.

In *The Comic Mind,* a book that is nearly forty years old now but which still represents one of the richest and most cogent summaries of Chaplin's art, Gerald Mast cites several examples of Chaplin's cinematic proficiency, "for those who think he could not manage a camera." He mentions, for example, the "house of mirrors" shots from *The Circus,* where Charlie's image is multiplied to the point where we can no longer locate the original Charlie in the image, shots that are as beautiful in their kaleidoscope complexity as they are mesmerizing in their mathematical precision; the shot in *Modern Times,* downward from high above, of the chicken dinner which waiter Charlie lifts high above a floor of dancers and which floats above the dancers like a boat on a turbulent sea; the scene in *Monsieur Verdoux,* where Verdoux, in the center of the image, cons a vulnerable widow on the telephone via a wealth of romantic clichés, while an impressionistic young woman in the foreground of the image melts to Verdoux's insincere but effective pitter-patter. "In each of these scenes," Mast writes, "the camera has found precisely the right angle to communicate the pictorial, intellectual, and emotional view of the shot."[10]

Chaplin considered the arrangement of his shots carefully. Camera placement, he writes in his autobiography, "articulates a scene." It "represents cinematic inflection," "the basis of cinematic style." He notes that the slightest mistake in placing the camera too close to, or far from, the action can disturb a gag. In his autobiography, he identifies one scene in particular as an example of the expressiveness of camera placement, the one in *The Rink* where Charlie, having set off a melee among the skaters at an ice rink, disappears from the scene only to be spied later, sitting in the distance, eyeing his chaotic handiwork innocently from afar. "The small figure of the Tramp in the distance," writes Chaplin, "was much funnier than he would have been in close-up." Chaplin felt that every scene calls for its own logic in camera placement. This instance proved, Chaplin wrote, that, contrary to conventional wisdom, in some cases a far shot is more emphatic than a close-up.[11]

Chaplin had a great gift for the way in which, in this manner, the delineation of space in the set-up of a shot could intensify the humor of a scene. Take, as another example, the scene early in *Police* where Charlie is chasing a minister whom he suspects of being a fraud. Charlie is so engrossed in this chase that, when it carries him by a policeman, Charlie does not even experience his regular default fear of cops. Instead, he breaks stride in his run just long enough to kick the cop in the chest so that he might continue to chase the man. The cop of course picks up the chase and all three figures disappear around a street corner far in the depth of the screen.

In the next shot, the camera is placed far down the sidewalk onto which the minister, Charlie and the policeman will soon turn. We are looking, from afar, at the corner around which they will come. The shot is set up so that the characters will have to run a great distance directly towards the camera. First the minister races by our camera. Charlie, in pursuit, pauses just before the camera, finally giving up the chase. The depth of the long sidewalk down which he has just run is visible over his shoulder. Charlie, not prone to long-term memory, seems to think the chase is over, but we remember the cop and look nervously over his shoulder, waiting for the cop to come around the distant corner. The camera has been placed in such a way as to make us anticipate the policeman's arrival in the image. Charlie, in the foreground, mutters some angry oaths at the escaped minister, turns around and begins to ascend back up the sidewalk with his trademark comic walk. He gets about halfway up the sidewalk when the cop sprints around the corner. Charlie turns and flees precipitously. The chase is on again.

The humor of the gag is, in part, in its timing. We count down the seconds before the cop's appearance. He arrives with the inevitability of a percussive beat in a musical score. But there is humor also in the camera set-up, which provides us a little bit of dramatic irony. We have the opportunity to *visually* reflect on the impending peril that Charlie has forgotten. We look at the corner of the building, waiting for the cop to come around it. Knowing something is going to occur before Charlie does makes it funnier when it does. There is a kind of comic neutrality to the camera as it sits there, with the filming equivalent of a straight face, waiting for the inevitable. Charlie thinks the hubbub is over; the camera knows better. Great mime that Chaplin was, moments like these remind us that he knew how arrive at humor via the visual layout of the scene, that he understood how to tell filmic jokes as well as entertain us with his stage-trained pantomime.

Large-Scale Composition

There are certainly more examples of cinematic prowess sprinkled through Chaplin's films than the few scenes that Mast mentions. For example, Chaplin often composed on a large scale, in a Keaton-like manner. The line of over a thousand gold miners climbing the snowy tundra in the early shots of *Gold Rush*; the famous shots of Charlie passing through the enormous cogs of machinery in *Modern Times*; the final shot of *The Circus*, in which Charlie, abandoned by the circus, sits alone in the center of a large dirt circle that marks the spot where the circus once sat; the scene in *Pay Day* where dozens of workers shift rapidly from lazy inanimacy to busy efficiency in the blink of an eye, when their boss passes by—these are only a few of the many shots in Chaplin's oeuvre that attest to his ability to paint on a large scale.

The far shot, in *Work*, in distant silhouette, of the diminutive Charlie pulling a massive, heavily loaded wagon up a hill, anticipates Ingmar Bergman's later arty silhouettes of distant figures on the horizon in *The Seventh Seal*, and represents one of those moments in Chaplin's films where the image is so strong that it almost begs for a political interpretation.

The rooftop shots of Charlie in *The Kid*, when Charlie chases the car conveying the kid to the orphanage, are particularly Keatonesque in their large scale and meticulous structure and timing. One shot in this sequence features Chaplin on the roof and his matching coordinate, a truck barreling down a street, several floors down and several blocks away. The continuity of the shots in this sequence, as well as the effectiveness of the final stunt, with Chaplin jumping from a rooftop into the moving car, is on a par with anything Keaton accomplished.

The *Woman of Paris* scene in which Jean Millet's body is carried away also composes itself on a large scale, and across three planes of information. A large, animate crowd gathers around the fountain where Jean's body has been found. The body is carried up a staircase in the back upper right of the frame. Marie, in the front lower left of the frame, spies the body across the crowd and faints. The crowd that had been turned to the body in the back upper right, now surges towards her in the lower left as she falls into Pierre's arms, giving the whole scene a rich diagonal movement from the back upper right to the front lower left.

Chaplin is particularly good at creating little vignettes in the midst of crowds in this manner. In *Modern Times*, when the police disperse the Communist rally in which Charlie has accidentally found himself, great crowds of people move in all directions—left, right, forward and backward—leaving Charlie alone in the center of the image, running in circles madly like a frightened mouse that has just been frightened from its hiding place.

In *The Gold Rush*, Charlie, a weary traveler, steps in from the frigid cold to a warm and crowded saloon. The shot is from behind Charlie's back as we watch him perusing the saloon crowd in front of him. Just then a tune is struck up and the crowd abandons Charlie for the dance floor. As in the scene from *Modern Times*, Charlie is left alone, this time silhouetted in the foreground of the image, watching the crowd that has surged forward deep into the frame. The effect of the scene in *Modern Times* is one of comic panic. Here the effect is one of lonely pathos.

The shot composition throughout this sequence is top-notch, and on a large scale. It's shot from behind Charlie's back, with all the animate action of the saloon set before him, and with a John Ford–like sense of composition-in-depth. And the action before Charlie is broken down into several attractive components. The dancers dance on the left. To the right, miners assemble around a bar that, as in Ford's films, recedes into the background, further emphasizing the depth of the image. In the rear of the saloon is a balcony that overlooks the dance floor, creating a second tier of animated human movement. The balcony is, in turn, segmented into two halves, where two different groups of men and women carouse. Each section of the balcony is backlit by open doorways that highlight their movement. An overhead light captures the smoke of the saloon rising to the ceiling around these upstairs revelers.

But Charlie rests outside all this activity, a silhouette in the foreground, watching all this activity from afar and gently tapping his hand on his thigh in a private attempt to be part of the gaiety. In short, this is a nicely composed image on a large scale and with great depth and finely wrought detail. And yet the image is powerful most of all, not just because of its excellent compositional virtues, but because of the sad idea that all that activity communicates: Charlie excommunicated by society.

The Gold Rush is also the occasion for another striking composition, one of the most attractively set-up shots in Chaplin's entire oeuvre. The shot occurs on New Year's Eve when Georgia and her friends have not shown up for Charlie's New Year's Eve party and he now realizes that their seeming affection was a cruel hoax. Charlie sadly wanders into town and arrives at the tavern where he watches, through a frosted window, the holiday festivities in its warm interior. Chaplin neatly divides his image in half: The left half is comprised of the window, lit from within and revealing the happy, dancing celebrants—another example of nicely composed composition in depth. The right half, comprised of the exterior wall of the saloon in the dark of the street, is entirely dark. The window on the left is, itself, neatly divided into four panes, so that the overall effect of the shot is one of tidy symmetry, frames within frames, four frames within the left half of an already neatly divided frame.

Charlie is divided too. Dressed in dark clothes, most of his body is lost in the darkness of the right half of the frame. Only the front surface of his body, turned to the window, is illuminated by the light from inside, and only his face is flooded with light. It's a striking image of loneliness that has about it a self-reflexivity, as if Charlie were himself peering at a movie. Chaplin, with his gift for simplicity and clarity, strips the image down to Charlie's sad face and the interior festivities. It's a shot of exquisite balance, and not just because of its frames with frames, but also because it balances a close-up with a far shot, stasis with activity, sadness with celebration.

All of these scenes testify to Chaplin's gift, particularly late in his silent film career, for elegant shot composition and for composition on a large scale, and also to his insistence that his most expressive and attractive shots subordinate themselves to the larger purpose of his film, whether that be amplifying the humor of a gag or making us feel more deeply the plight of Charlie. More often than not, art-for-art's-sake shots tended to end up on Chaplin's cutting room floor.

Moving His Camera

Despite his preference for a static camera, there are also many instances in which Chaplin is adept at building gags around a moving camera. *The Rink*, *The Vagabond*, *The Circus* and *Modern Times* all have gags recorded from the point of view of a backward tracking camera borne by a vehicle.

In a famous gag from *Modern Times*, Charlie picks up a red warning flag that has fallen from a truck with an extended load in its back. Charlie waves the red flag at the truck to get the driver's attention and then chases after the truck. Meanwhile, unbeknownst to Charlie, a parade of Communists rallying for workers' rights has turned the corner behind him at just this moment and he finds himself at the head of the parade, waving a red flag and looking like the ringleader or mascot of the rally.

Like the scene in which Charlie enters the saloon in *The Gold Rush*, Chaplin chooses to shoot this scene, head on, from the front to back of the screen. Our point of view is from the truck, just behind the flag, as it falls to the ground. The camera then tracks backward with the moving truck as we watch Charlie pick up the flag in the receding distance. The next shot is of Charlie, again face on, though from closer up. Chaplin abandons the point of view of the truck bed. The camera is now situated in the space just before Charlie. Charlie heads directly towards the camera with the flag. Again, the camera tracks backward as Charlie moves toward us, waving the flag just as the men turning the corner form a parade behind him.

This sequence, characterized by reverse tracking and a camera set-up that has Charlie staring directly at the camera, is much better at getting across the plausibility of the joke than it would have been if Chaplin had shot it, more conventionally, from a third-person camera and off to the side of the action. Charlie, looking at us, never sees the crowd. Our view of him, face-on, also improves the humor of the gag, as we get to enjoy the comic irony of watching the people gather behind Charlie's back without his knowing it, transforming him into a comic, unknowing version of Lady Liberty leading the people in Delacroix's homage to the French Revolution.

Chaplin had an affection for this kind of tracking shot from inside a vehicle, looking back on a road. He films Charlie and the pickpocket running from the police in *The Circus* in this manner, with the two of them running directly towards a camera that films them, face on, from the back of a moving vehicle with which they keep pace. And there is a similar shot in *The Vagabond* in which Chaplin films men chasing Edna and Charlie from inside the moving gypsy caravan Charlie has stolen from the men. The men are filmed face-on as they chase the van and are nicely framed by the open door at the back of the wagon.

This shot also pays off comically: The leader of the pursuing gypsies (Eric Campbell) has just about caught up to the wagon when Edna, leaning out of its back doorway, strikes him over the head with a log. We watch Campbell fall, as we did Charlie picking up the flag in *Modern Times*, from a receding distance, because the camera shoots from the perspective of the moving vehicle.

The scene has a fine Keaton-like sense of choreography. Two seconds after Campbell falls, three of his men, unable to halt their acceleration, trip over him. Immediately after that, two more men fall over the four already down, and, immediately after them, two old gypsy crones who have been bringing up the rear fall onto the heap of bodies as well. In all, eight bodies are downed in what is, in the end, a nicely choreographed accumulation of bodies in the distance. The humor of the gag is obviously in the well-timed waves of bodies falling. But it's also in the point of view of the camera. Watching this all transpire from the point of view of a receding camera, moving away from the action, makes the debacle more comic. Not only are the gypsies falling all over themselves, but quickly falling out of sight, their foolishness matched by their inconsequence. And all this business is neatly framed by the doorway of the receding wagon.

The sequence is a more accomplished redux of the closing shots of *The Rink*, where Charlie, on skates, hooks his cane to a vehicle and rolls away from his pursuers. There too we view the pursuers in first-person perspective from the vehicle that tracks away from them and, there too, Campbell falls, setting off a barrage of well-timed falling bodies, though the falls are not as delineated in waves as they are in *The Vagabond*.

Trompe l'Oeil

Another aspect of Chaplin's cinema that testifies to its cinematic inventiveness is his taste for elaborate visual puns and *"trompe l'oeils."* In *Shoulder Arms*, for example, the sequence in which Charlie, spying behind enemy lines, masquerades as a tree is rendered flawlessly. Only when he moves is the illusion of a real tree lost. Similarly, in the golf sequence from *The Idle Class*, the surface of a water trap is so covered with mossy residue that it perfectly masquerades as solid ground. Charlie and a fellow golfer argue over whose ball rests on this "ground." Charlie gives way, the other golfer steps forward to set up his shot and promptly drops into the water. Again, careful scrutiny of this false landscape before the fall does not reveal a single tell before the gag accomplishes itself; the visual trick is not undermined by the slightest undulation on the surface of the water.

In these cases the visual gag was characterized by extraordinary realism in its effect. Other times, Chaplin's visual gags are fanciful and elaborately staged visual conceits. In *A Dog's Life*, for example, Charlie is not allowed to bring his dog into the dance hall, so he absurdly hides the dog in the back of his capacious pants. The dog's tail slips through a hole in Chaplin's trousers and it seems, much to the delight of the dance hall patrons, that Charlie is gifted with a wagging tail, an illusion quite suitable to Charlie's nature. Whereas the *trompe l'oeils* in *Shoulder Arms* and *Idle Class* aimed for perfect verisimilitude, this one goes for an outlandish, cartoonish effect and one that is so expressive of Charlie's nature as to carry metaphorical import as well.

Despite his inherently understated classical style and his taste for naturalism in image and acting, it is in these visual gags that Chaplin is most surreal and stylized, most willing to leave reality behind. In a sequence excised from *Shoulder Arms*, Chaplin shoots Charlie's visit to the doctor in silhouette through the translucent window of the doctor's office. The shadowplay allows Chaplin to depict a variety of outlandish, cartoonish doctor-patient moments. Charlie is seen, in silhouette, to swallow both a foot-long tongue depressor and the pliers used to fish the depressor out. The doctor also retrieves the pliers via a fishing line dangled down Charlie's throat. The tongue depressor is hiccupped out.

In *The Circus*, Charlie escapes the detection of the police at the funhouse by blending into the exterior of the funhouse, which is decorated by mechanized moving automatons. Chaplin's imitation of an automaton is impressive here, particularly in the way that he sells his jerky movement by perfectly mimicking the small, jiggling effect the automatons make as they come to a halt. But the large-scale image of the funhouse exterior is just as memorable. Charlie is only one of four automatons, each moving with metronome-like regularity. His movements are also timed to those of the policeman who stands in the foreground at the funhouse gate. Every time the policeman turns to look in Charlie's direction, Charlie's nascent attempts at escape are foiled and he has to resume his clockwork movements. The overall effect is of a large-scale, elaborate mousetrap, a building-sized mechanical toy with all sorts of eye-capturing visual intrigue, a testimony to Chaplin's gift for *trompe l'oeils* and for large-scale composition. We have here, again, a sense of having momentarily left reality and slipped into a cartoonish dream world, albeit one composed of the natural elements of the films we are watching.

Other times, though, Chaplin's puns are less elaborate, more slight, incidental and whimsical, growing organically out of the action of the film. In the opening segment from *City Lights,* Charlie is in trouble with the local citizenry for clambering around their recently unveiled piece of (hideous) civic sculpture. Charlie, leaning forward to politely respond to their complaints, puts his face right before the splayed hand of one of the statue's figures, creating the effect of thumbing his nose at the people he's trying to placate.

Some of Chaplin's visual gags are based on misleading information, scenes where he sets up a decoy view of reality and then surprises us with what's really going. In *City Lights*, Charlie is angry that he has almost fallen down an open subterranean elevator shaft and, in the manner of an affronted gentleman, scolds a construction worker who is ascending on the shaft from underground. Only when the shaft arrives fully at ground level does Charlie realize he is chewing out a giant of a man. He quickly tips his hat and slips away.

The Idle Class features one of Chaplin's most famous misleading *trompe l'oeils*: Charlie, shot from behind, seems to be hunched and weeping over the letter from his wife that he has just received and which informed him that she has left him because of his drinking. In fact, we find, as he turns towards the camera, that he is actually suavely shaking a cocktail mixer. Similar, and equally famous, is the introduction of the Tramp in *The Immigrant*: He is again shot from behind and seems to be vomiting over the side of the ship. When he pulls his heaving upper torso back up from over the side of the ship and turns around, he is holding a fish on a line that he has just hauled in.

Many of Chaplin's visual puns are built around surprising uses of the human body, for example in the famous *Dog's Life* scene in which Chaplin substitutes his arms for those of a seated, unconscious man and, in doing so, reanimates him. This gag is echoed by one in *Idle Class*: Charlie, reading a newspaper, sits next to a man on a public bench when a pickpocket creeps behind the bench and insinuates his arm through the back of the bench into the pocket of Charlie's neighbor. The origins of the arm, however, are obscured by the newspaper Charlie reads, and so it seems to stretch from Charlie's shoulder. Even Charlie, who witnesses the event, is momentarily confused by what seems to be his own arm reaching out to steal the man's wallet on its own initiative, without consulting him.

Of course, what is arguably the most charming scene in all of Chaplin's films, Charlie's dance of the rolls in *The Gold Rush*, is a *trompe l'oeil.* This little illusion was one of Chaplin's favorite party tricks, and he performed it often at social events—but never as he did on film, with his face and collar lit up to add to the illusion that his head is the natural extension of the dancing rolls and in such a way as to accentuate every charming glint in Chaplin's eyes.

One of my favorite bodily visual puns in Chaplin's films occurs in *The Idle Class*, during the scene in which Charlie's aristocratic character (he plays two roles in this film) finds that though he is otherwise impeccably decked out in full tails and top hat, he has forgotten to put on his pants and is half undressed in public. Chaplin remedies the situation by dropping to a crouch, covering himself in front with a newspaper, and scooting on his feet, almost as though he were riding a small tricycle. With the tails of his coat behind him and his newspaper outstretched in front of him, his lower torso is completely covered and so he is able to motor around in the costume of an elegant dwarf, very much redolent of Toulouse-Lautrec. Chaplin moves with such velocity (while never sacrificing perfect elegant posture) that he seems to have a small engine under his newspaper. His obscured means of propulsion creates the comic effect of a small parade float, a kind of fast-moving Toulouse-Lautrec on wheels.

Chaplin's taste for these visual puns is one of the most distinctive aspects of his cinema. It's a very idiosyncratic taste and one that is not echoed in the films of many others. Why? Well, first off, it's a cumbersome habit. Scenes like the doctor's office visit in *Shoulder Arms* or the dog tail scene in *Dog's Life* require a lot of elaborate set-up—and all this work for a single visual payoff. They stand out rather loudly and don't necessarily contribute to the unity of the film, no doubt one of the reasons that Chaplin excised the doctor visit from *Shoulder Arms*. He may have also decided that the effect of that scene was too outsized, that its cartoonish nature conflicted with the naturalism of the rest of the film.

And these gags sometimes misfire. In *City Lights* a bald man at a costume party wears a crown of sun rays that renders the top of his head identical to a mounded dessert concoction served on a nearby platter. Needless to say, Charlie at one point tries to dig into the man's head with knife and fork. But neither the dessert nor the costume is particularly familiar and the scene feels forced and unlikely. Chaplin seems to strain for humor here, to create a connection that couldn't really exist. A good *trompe l'oeil* should be a slight exaggeration of something we might actually see in the world.

It isn't uncommon for great silent film directors to misfire in the effort to communicate visual puns. Hitchcock often told the story of how he tried, in *Blackmail*, to create a light effect that would result in the shadow of a clichéd villainous moustache being cast on a character who, at that moment, was entertaining evil designs. No one, he was saddened to find, noticed the effect. Experiences like that led Hitchcock to make films that are characterized by large, clear design. That clarity of design is one of the reasons his films remain more accessible to modern audiences than other directors from the classical era. Chaplin and Hitchcock both went to school on silent film, always questioning themselves as to how to get their ideas across visually. Curiously, whereas this experience led Hitchcock to larger bolder designs which couldn't be misunderstood, it led Chaplin to become more and more expert at expressing himself on a microscopic level, more adept at knowing what it took to make sure his small designs and gestures registered with his audience, even when the visual joke was buried deep in his image.

Even when Chaplin's visual puns do work, they tend not to be guffaw-producing. Gilbert Adair put his finger on the nature of these gags when he wrote, "Like those of Jacques Tati, [Chaplin's] gags are brilliantly contrived but often simply too lovely, too clever, to be laughed at."[12] The charm of these gags is more fey and quizzical than other types of Chaplin gags. Their purpose is to delight more than provoke laughter.

But their effect is, nevertheless, durable. After watching a lot of Chaplin or Tati films, we start to notice these visual puns in the world around us, those little moments of accidental absurdity when, for example, we see one person's mouth open here but a noise from elsewhere, or see the effect of an action (say dirt coming up from a man digging in a hole) but not its cause (the man himself). The purpose of these gags is to exercise our sense of absurdity and to alert us to the comedy of the everyday world, the way visual puns arrange themselves for us all the time if we look at the world with a lively interest and in a spirit of amusement.

Filmmakers tend to avoid these kinds of gags because they are so purely visual. They don't advance the plot. They are part and parcel of a kind of filmmaking that values leisure and is willing to stop for digressions. They are the product of a non-literary cinema, one that conceives itself via the camera, not the screenplay. Chaplin, with his tendency to make his films on the spot, without the aid of a detailed script, saw a film as a series of visual gambits. These visual puns represent a kind of cartoon made of real-life material. And they again remind us of how strange it is that Chaplin's oeuvre has often been denigrated for a lack of cinematic sophistication. These are all essentially filmic moments, puns that could only be arrived at in cinema, in fact an entirely new kind of visual humor born with cinema. Even the puns that have to do with his pantomime, like the count pretending to be a dwarf, only work because they are designed to be shot from a particular camera angle that hides their mechanics. That stunt could not have been pulled off on the stage. And these gags are not done in slapdash manner. Chaplin had his failures in the visual pun category but mostly because he aimed so high. The successful sequences, like the tree gag and doctor gag in *Shoulder Arms*, are meticulously worked out, flawless, and required a great deal of preparatory work, the former in terms of a costume that would be flexible enough to provide movement and yet so flawlessly mask as a tree, the latter in terms of the hidden machinery that made the impossible physics of the scene so plausible.

Even though Chaplin's taste for *trompe l'oeils* does not find a great many echoes in subsequent filmmaking, he had a devotee in French comic filmmaker Jacques Tati. Tati, like Chaplin, mixed the populism inherent in physical comedy with a challenging technique that has made him, again like Chaplin, popular with general audiences and film cognoscenti as well. His films are even more replete with these visual gags, many obviously inspired by Chaplin. Like Chaplin, Tati loves gags built around people popping up from holes that, thanks to the compression inherent in far shots, are invisible to viewers. The *sui generis* feel of Tati's films, I think, is a testimony to how rare it is to find sensibilities, like Tati's and Chaplin's, that are so un-literary and so visual. Neither Tati nor Chaplin sees the screen as a vehicle for a story but rather as a frame with which to play visual games. (Of course, Tati's greatest film is titled *Playtime*.)

Tati explores film's capacity for visual puns even further than Chaplin. His films are chock full of these visual puns and some are awe-inspiring in their scope, as in the *Mon Oncle* scene where M. and Mme. Arpel, both looking out their respective small round windows on the upper floor of their house, create the illusion that the house is an enormous face with two rolling eyes. Tati is very comparable to Lubitsch in the way that he took a Chaplin tendency (in Lubitsch's case, it was the elegance inherent in Chaplin's inferential style, in Tati's the taste for visual puns) and carried the habit even further than Chaplin had, making it a cornerstone of his cinema.

Editing

Along with his indifference to set decor, Chaplin's editing has probably come under the most criticism. He was famous for not caring about continuity and often commented, particularly in the era of his talkies, when his cinematic talents were under fire, that if the audience were bored enough to notice errors in continuity, the scene they were watching was a loss anyway. Asked if he thought editing was important, Chaplin responded yes, "but simple cutting. Trick cutting doesn't interest me because I'm so interested in the human equation, and not in photographing a stone or a drop of blood falling on it."[13] Chaplin had no interest in Eisenteinian montage or symbolism. His editing was subsumed in the registering of his comedy. That doesn't, however, mean it is non-existent.

In fact, by the time he had reached his prime, Chaplin was capable of great fluidity in editing. There are, of course, different kinds of continuity errors. Chaplin was most vulnerable to errors that involved costume and prop. The most famous example is in *City Lights*: In the final scene, the shots of Virginia Cherrill from Charlie's perspective show him, in the foreground of the image, holding a flower to the side, while the close-ups of him from her perspective show him holding the flower to his face. Many critics have noted that this example bolsters Chaplin's argument that the importance of continuity is overrated, as this is one of the most studied and appreciated scenes in Chaplin's films, its continuity problems hardly making a dent in its powerful effect. You can find continuity errors like this throughout Chaplin's films and for the most part Chaplin is right, we don't really notice them easily; and once we do, they don't have much of a negative effect on our appreciation of the scene, particularly those from his glory days.

But if he was sloppy about costume continuity, the spatial consistency in Chaplin's editing is often superb. Anyone who thinks Chaplin couldn't edit would be advised to take a close look at the climactic chase scene in *The Adventurer*, which I will analyze more closely in my chapter on Chaplin's sense of rhythm. This sequence represents an example of virtuosic editing. It's a fight and chase scene, carried on in several different spots: a front porch, a foyer, an upstairs landing, a balcony. The highly rhythmic and perfectly timed comedy requires pinpoint match cuts between the different rooms. In fact, the editing becomes part of the joke, with Chaplin jumping off the balcony several times, one shot concluding with his body plummeting to the bottom of the screen, the next with it dropping from the top. Other Mutual comedies also devise gags around ideas that require great fluidity in editing together different rooms, for example the scene in *The Cure* where the drunk Charlie is spun out of a revolving door like a top and tears through the sanatorium like a comic tornado, spinning upstairs, down hallways and into his room, creating havoc along his path.

But even in more static sequences, the kind that have earned Chaplin the reputation for being stagey, there is evidence of expert editing that is entirely appropriate to the goals of the piece. For example, the famous restaurant scene that comprises the second half of The *Immigrant* is one of Chaplin's most static set pieces. The camera always faces the action from the point of view of the audience. Charlie, seated at his table, faces us. Many of the shots within this sequence run for a good length. And Chaplin only sets up five different shots in the entire scene: a distant shot that allows us to watch a man who did not fully pay his check in the foreground while keeping an eye on Chaplin in the back of the scene; a medium shot that covers the horizontal span of two tables, each of which flanks a door used by Eric Campbell's threatening waiter; a closer medium shot of the door and just Chaplin's table; a closer shot of Chaplin and Edna at their table; a still closer shot used to convey the quietest of Chaplin's facial detail.

But Chaplin moves quite dexterously between these five shots, each of which is chosen according to the gag it will record. One of Chaplin's great talents was in understanding just what it takes to make sure the audience "gets" his gags, without drawing the audience so painfully close to the action as to hit them over the head with them. His films are noteworthy for both their subtlety and clarity. And so we get a very close shot when we need to read Chaplin's eyes. The shot that includes the doorway (through which we also spy the restaurant's orchestra) and the twin tables is tailored exactly to the dimensions of the full-body gags that will revolve around Chaplin trying to snatch a stray coin from the floor. This is not editing that is notable for its angles or movement but for its gradation and sensitivity to dimension. It doesn't explore the room a great deal but it encases the gags, large and small, with pinpoint precision.

For all the commentary on the famous dance of the rolls in *The Gold Rush*, it is striking how little commentary there is on the scene's exquisite lighting, which highlights only the delicate play of Chaplin's hands and eyes, a typical example of how Chaplin the director is often overshadowed by Chaplin the performer.

It may be editing like this that made French avant-garde filmmaker Jean Marie Straub say, "People think Eisenstein was the best editor because he had some theories about it. But the greatest and most precise editor was Chaplin."[14] Chaplin's forte in editing was not expressiveness or didactic ideas, *a la* Eisenstein, it was *precision*: precision in mapping out his spatial consistency very carefully, precision in measuring what frame was needed for what gag.

"It's true that Chaplin's editing is very sparing," Mast writes. "He allows scenes to play themselves out for minutes but this is extremely effective editing for Chaplin because the scenes remain hypnotic regardless of their length."[15] In other words, if the sequence is as effective as the second half of *The Immigrant* is, then the editing has been just fine. It has made way for, not interfered in, what is important in the scene. He is a long-take filmmaker, someone who respected the gathering momentum of time, the way a gag could be played out inventively when not interrupted by edits.

There is, of course, a school of criticism that favors long-take cinema, most notably that of Andre Bazin. These critics like the long take for the way it preserves integrity of space, fosters choreographic invention and respects the observer by not guiding his vision each step of the way, as though he were a child. Chaplin's films are characterized by all these virtues, but particularly the last one. His films unroll with a temporal and spatial continuity that allows us to look around the world he has provided and, to a degree, discover for ourselves the jokes and visual games he has distributed there.

Lighting

Chaplin's films are also characterized by a variety of interesting lighting effects, something we've already seen in the saloon scenes from *The Gold Rush* and the famous silhouette from *Work* commented on earlier in this chapter. Chaplin liked the silhouette effect and the shot from *Work* finds its match, in many ways, in the final image of *Modern Times* where Charlie and Paulette Goddard's waif are shot in silhouette against the lighter road down which they travel. The effect gives the couple a cartoonish effect, removing them from reality and underlining the mythic nature of this moment in which Charlie walks off the screen for the last time with, finally, the woman companion he's been seeking for some twenty-five years firmly in hand.

Charlie is a great dreamer and his dreams often seemed to call forth Chaplin's most lyrical lighting effects. The dance with the nymphs in *Sunnyside,* for example, can be frozen at just about any spot in the sequence into a lovely still. That dream sequence, shot on a graceful pastoral incline, has a lush, blurry, Rococo quality. The shots are bathed in a diaphanous light that both illuminates and penetrates the lovely nymphs' white veils and seems to highlight every leaf on the tree branches used as framing devices in the foreground while relegating the massive sumptuous trees in the back to a soft, diffused featheriness, like the trees in a painting by Boucher or Fragonard.

Charlie's dream of the party with girls on New Year's Eve is lit so as to accentuate surface light, highlighting all the things that most matter to the Tramp in this dream of Eros and celebration: the women's flesh, their decorative caps, the festive decorations around the apartment. When Charlie entertains the women with his famous dance of the rolls, Chaplin darkens the lighting, flooding only Chaplin's face and hands with light, creating the impression of an enormous head on two dancing legs. As important as the dancing rolls in conveying the illusion of a little dancing woman, Chaplin's eyes provide the imaginary figure with her animacy.

There are also moments in Charlie's waking reality that are beautifully lit. Chaplin was proud of the *Gold Rush* scene in which Charlie tears up his cabin in jubilation after Georgia and the girls have accepted his invitation to a New Year's Eve party. He cited the lighting in this scene as expressive of something that could not be duplicated on the stage. "Too many producers are on the wrong tack thinking that this medium is connected with the curtain stage instead of being something new," he told Robert Nichols in 1925. "Think of that bit in *The Gold Rush* where I tear the pillow to pieces and the feathers dance white in the black screen. Impossible on the stage! I enjoyed it more than anything I did in that film. There I extended myself to the full."

It's interesting that, in this film that is Chaplin's most poignant and laden with pathos, it is this small comic scene that he most treasured. And his comments here tell us that he was conscious, in his filmmaking, both of using light meaningfully and of arriving at images that were purely cinematic, that he valued a scene for its abstract rendering, or pure representation of, movement, in this case, white forms dancing on a black screen. And yet as dazzling as this image is, it's unlikely that most viewers would first note it for its lighting, so effective is the scene's humor and its commentary on Charlie's jubilant, childlike nature. The lighting here is appropriately expressive but also quiet in its effect.

A Woman of Paris is chock-full of excellent lighting effects, reminding us that, if Chaplin had made other films that didn't center on Charlie, his cinematic artfulness might well have been more pronounced. Jean and Marie's fathers, who conspire to block their children's marriage, are each introduced by large, oppressive shadows that precede their actual physical presence, one of the few examples of Expressionist lighting in Chaplin's films, obviously more available to him in a drama than in Charlie's comedies. Charlie's non-stop contention with men, and fathers in particular, in Chaplin's comedies are echoed in this drama, particularly in the way the film places the blame for the young lovers' tragedy at the fathers' feet.

Chaplin does dabble with Expressionist shadow effect in a few of his comedies—in *Police*, for example, when Charlie and his burglary accomplice (Wesley Ruggles) approach the house they will rob. Chaplin introduces them first by ghoulish shadows that precede them. The effect here is a strange fusion of gothic and comic, mostly a chance for Chaplin to render, in shadow puppetry, some of Charlie's trademark gestures, like the one where his hat seems to pop off his head of its own volition. It's the cousin to the shadow puppetry scene cut from *Shoulder Arms* and there's probably an argument for it being cut from this work as well, as it seems, in tone and image, to be out of sync with the rest of the comedy, as Expressionist shadows are, in general, with comedy.

A Woman of Paris is also replete with well-lit vignettes in the manner of D.W. Griffith, like the one early in the film of Jean's dead father by the fireplace, a lovely little study in chiaroscuro. Just a few key ingredients are highlighted: the fireplace before which he dies; his face lit up by the fire; the smoking pipe on the floor, the little detail that communicates to his son that he is dead, not sleeping.

Throughout the film, Chaplin also artfully employs the same device Orson Welles would carry over from the silent film era and into his films. When scenes begin or end on static vignettes, Chaplin does not just cut or dissolve to or from those scenes. He slowly turns up the illumination at the beginning of the scene or slowly turns it down at the end. In this manner he begins and finishes scenes more ceremonially and also highlights certain aspects of the image with key lights just before the more general lights go on or just after they go down.

For example, the shot of Marie weeping over Jean's dead body opens in near dark, with one light illuminating the feather on her cap, a symbol of the wealth and social frivolity that, in the end, separated her from him. Accenting the feather also draws attention to the focus of the scene, the spatial point where her face rests on his body. Chaplin holds his lighting only for a few seconds, then illuminates the image more generally. These little opening and closing bits of chiaroscuro are very brief and meant to frame scenes with a fine, gentle edging.

Tricks of the Trade

Chaplin's command over the cinematic medium is also evidenced by how neatly he handles special effects. His sound films are sometimes faulted for his clumsy use of rear projection (*Limelight* is particularly abundant in examples) but in his prime he made quite effective use of it, for example in the driving sequences in *City Lights*, where Chaplin sells the rear projection of the city far more successfully than did most Hollywood directors.

He was also particularly adept at the art of trick dissolves, for example the many dissolves that take Charlie back and forth between reality and his dreams. Chaplin's dissolves are almost always points of interest in his films rather than just comic technical stunts. First, they are technically proficient, usually carried out with unusual precision and elegance, like those *trompe l'oeils* that we looked at, the success of which hinged on their verisimilitude. When Chaplin played around with any cinematic effect he often did so to the point of perfecting it. Chaplin's dissolves are also interesting and persuasive because he builds touching comic ideas around them and adorns them with fine visual details. All of Chaplin's dissolves are just a little different from one another and all cleverly integrated into the film.

In *The Circus,* Charlie steps out of his seated body to administer a fantasy beating to Rex, the trapeze artist and his competitor for Merna's affection. The effect is faultless. Chaplin dissolves elegantly both in Charlie's exit and his return to his body. And the double imaging of Charlie is persuasive, as Chaplin films the action from a distant enough perspective that we aren't reflecting too much on the trick nature of the shot. The seated Charlie on the right side of the image rests before a partition that frames him and separates him from the action of which he dreams, thus lending the scene a nice compositional virtue and also visually suggesting the act of dreaming, while maintaining a naturalist unity of space. The shot has sound compositional values in general. Open curtains create a triangular space in the very back of the image that provides a background for Charlie's imaginary bout with Rex. The diagonal lines of a circus wagon and steamer trunk on the left are set up to recede diagonally in such a way as to point to the scene of action as well. In this manner, Charlie's dream fighter steps into a ready-made arena.

Chaplin also uses his space creatively during his dissolves in *Shoulder Arms*. In the scene where Charlie dreams of America, he stands guard next to a barracks that fills the left half of the screen. As Charlie begins to daydream, the barracks dissolves into a street scene of New York, dividing the screen handsomely in half: New York on the left, uniformed Charlie on the right. As the dream on the left transitions to Charlie's daydream of a bartender mixing a drink, Chaplin repurposes the shot, now fitting the image under the reappeared roof of the barracks, so that the bartender seems to be ensconced in the trenches with Charlie.

Chaplin's dissolves are often effective because they come in stages that gentle the transition. Chaplin moves to dreamland in several stages in *The Kid*. First, flowers festoon his neighborhood as Charlie sleeps on the stoop of his tenement building; then dancing angels appear, heavenly versions of his neighbors. Only now does Charlie wake up, no dissolve necessary in moving his body to dream state. The dissolves that mark this return to reality are particularly touching. The winged Charlie of the dream, having been shot out of the sky by an angel-policeman, has landed on the ground in an elegant sprawl, suggestive at once of Renaissance renderings of the fallen Icarus and the crucified Christ. Charlie's son, also an angel in his dream, embraces Charlie with the fine intimate gestures that have marked his and Charlie's relationship throughout the film. He puts his cheek on Charlie's, runs his hand through his hair. And then, sadly, the boy dissolves away, just as he has disappeared in real life at this point in the film. The angel-policeman now approaches and lifts Charlie's body in an effort to rouse him. In a dissolve, he becomes the real-life policeman Charlie has been at odds with throughout the film, Charlie becomes his wingless self and the slum loses all of its flowery decor and returns to its bleak state. In both the opening and closing of this dream sequence, multiple dissolves are layered, simulating the effect of slowly falling into, and out of, a dream. This gentle layering of dissolves is in keeping with the sad mood of this moment in the film where Charlie thinks he has lost his son forever.

The dissolves in *Sunnyside*'s nymph dream sequence are used very similarly. There too the world transforms around Charlie. As he dozes under a bridge, four lovely young dancing nymphs appear on the bridge. Charlie need only wake to a new reality. And in this scene too, the dissolve back to reality finishes with Charlie being roughly handled by his earthly tormentors. In Charlie's dream the nymphs lift him back onto the bridge, which he has fallen off of, with a garland of flowers. As Chaplin dissolves to reality, Charlie finds that a grappling hook, wielded by his nasty boss and hooked to his bottom, is the engine of his ascent.

Another hoary trick of the trade that Chaplin puts to particularly good use is the wire that lifts him off the ground, providing the ethereal Charlie with the illusion of flight. There are a couple of reasons Chaplin is able to put such an old and stagey device to such good cinematic use. First, he often uses the artificial wire quite minimally, as in the boxing scene in *City Lights* where the attached line allows him only to lift himself a little further off the ground than a human actually could when Charlie dives into the body of his boxing opponent. The attached line provides just enough of an effect to make Charlie seem a little more superhuman than his opponent, but not enough to really call attention to itself. Charlie's movements have a plausible, natural quality.

Also, Chaplin is, by nature, so gravity-defying to begin with, that he is able to blend his flying stunts seamlessly into his earthbound dance. *The Kid*'s flying sequences are wonderful not just because of the novelty of the stunt but because of the way Chaplin moves so effortlessly from walk to flight and vice versa. Because he was a dancer by nature, Chaplin could take advantage of this stagey effect in a graceful way that transcended its general use as a prop. If anyone could convey flying in a naturalistic fashion, it's Chaplin. Also, given Charlie's dreamy nature, the stunt of flying has a dramatic reason for existing in Chaplin's films. Charlie's dreaminess is close to his essence. The illusion of flight has a purpose in Chaplin's films; it gives expression to Charlie's longings. This too prevents the use of wires from being seen as a mere stunt.

And to this day I can think of no other director who has made as good a use as Chaplin of reverse action, a staple comic effect of the most tedious and unimaginative comedy. Before I saw Chaplin do it, I didn't think it was possible to use reverse action in a meaningful way. However, one of the most virtuosic scenes in the entirety of Chaplin's oeuvre is due to a reverse action effect, the one in *Pay Day* where workers at ground level toss bricks up to Charlie who, standing on scaffold one story up, arranges them in stacks along the wall before which he works.

Charlie executes this task with a dancer's virtuosity. Turning his back to the men so that he can stack the bricks against the wall more efficiently, he catches the bricks, from behind, in his right hand, his left hand, in both hands at the same time, on the back of his heel, on the toe of his shoe, in the crux of the back of his leg, on his backside (which he delicately proffers as a shelf), under his arms, under his chin, on top of bricks he has already caught and perhaps most amazingly by squeezing the brick between his thighs. Of course these actions could not occur in reality. But what's amazing about the scene is how accurately Chaplin has simulated forward moving time via backward time. And the use of reverse action is meaningful. It's not just a stunt but used to arrive at an elegance of movement not available to humans in real time. Chaplin found a cinematic dance available to him only via the effect of reverse action. Most first-time viewers are unaware that the scene is done in reverse action until they have had time to reflect on it—and then only because the scene stupefies our logic, not because we detect an awkwardness in its action. And even when we realize the scene is actually shot in reverse, the effect is not spoiled, so complete is the accomplishment of the illusion.

Chaplin shot a similar scene for *Behind the Screen* but discarded it in the end. There Charlie is a film set prop man who repeatedly passes by a costume epic being filmed. The director of the epic is demonstrating, to an actor, how to wield an axe by hoisting it up and letting it fall to the ground, where the axe buries its head in the ground. Charlie keeps passing at this point of instruction, and the axe repeatedly falls inches from his feet, though Charlie is unaware of his proximity to danger. The effect is perfect and we marvel at how Chaplin repeatedly put his foot in danger of being severed by the obviously real and quite heavy axe until we realized that this was all done in backward motion. As with the sequence from *Pay Day*, we are not likely to realize this from the footage itself, so complete is the illusion. Kevin Brownlow's documentary *Unknown Chaplin* shows how Chaplin worked the gag by walking in reverse, then reversing the film shot to look like he is walking forward. In watching this footage of him executing this stunt, we see the difficulty of getting everyone to mimic their actions in reverse in timing to Chaplin's movements. It's an eerily effective stunt, and suggests that Chaplin, had he desired to, could have been a premier innovator in the genre of cinematic comic stunts, *a la* Buster Keaton.

Sound

It's also significant that, even though Chaplin resisted sound in films and only made two films with Charlie that are built around sound to some degree (*City Lights* and *Modern Times*), he approached that technology with a sense of innovation and originality as well. Any study of Chaplin has to celebrate the irony of Chaplin, one of the greatest of the silent film directors, having struck on two of the most innovative uses of sound in film history.

The first is from the opening scene of his first film in the sound era, *City Lights*, which concerns the unveiling of a new civic memorial. A portly politician (Henry Bergman) gives what we recognize to be a prototypical political speech, all clichés and unctuousness. Of course what makes the scene so creative is that this speech is rendered not in words, but in a series of carefully arranged kazoo squawks that convey a very clear idea of how annoyingly predictable the speech is. When the politician yields the dais to a woman who we recognize as the prototypical matronly civic do-gooder, the kazoo sounds rise in pitch and we are able to just as clearly make out a different brand of empty cliché, that of the self-pleased society matron.

The sequence is a wonderful send-up of empty civic discourse. Chaplin would execute a parallel gag in *The Great Dictator* when the dictator Hinkle speaks in a mock German nonsense language that gets across the point that political rhetoric is more concerned with manipulating emotions through tone than actually expressing meaning through words. But, of course, the speeches in *City Lights*, coming as they do in Chaplin's first film after the talkie revolution, represent a statement on that era as well. Chaplin began his career in talkies with a deft dismissal of the significance of words.

Just as good is the scene in *Modern Times* where the world would, for the first time, hear Charlie Chaplin's voice in one of his films. Charlie is a singing waiter thrust on stage without the words for the song he had planned to perform, "Titina," a popular song of the day. Charlie is forced to make up the words on the spot and arrives at a lovely nonsensical language that merges several tongues, though French and Italian especially. The words represent a charming comic gibberish, but Charlie is able to convey the meaning of the song through pantomime. It's a mildly lascivious piece that recounts a wealthy man cruising in his immense automobile and propositioning a young beautiful woman. Again, Chaplin takes advantage of the possibilities of a watershed moment in his cinema for an ironic effect. And again he uses a pioneering moment in his use of sound to mock the significance of words. The ironies are numerous. The world, waiting to hear Chaplin speak, hears only gibberish. The Tramp will only speak once in Chaplin's films and that one time makes no sense. And, as in *City Lights*, Chaplin lights on a conceit that makes a very persuasive argument against the significance of words, striking one last blow for silent cinema. The words amount to a collection of sounds serving only to attest to the superiority of mime. Chaplin gives and Chaplin takes away. The Tramp remains silent even after he has spoken.

All of these accomplishments in striking composition and *mise-en-scène*, large scale composition, shots built around a moving camera, wildly inventive *trompe l'oeils* and visual puns, editing, lighting and sound effect, testify to a director who had a mastery over the cinematic medium and not someone who merely used the camera to film effects that, though marvelous, were those of the stage. Chaplin's cinema is characterized by a visual flair that is as impressive in itself as it is in the rarity to which he put it to use. Chaplin did like technique, and was good at it, but only when it was called for and only when he was supremely confident of its effect. Chaplin was a classical director and the hallmark of his cinema was, as Leo McCarey noted, "good taste."

Eight

Chaplin's Sense of Balance

Charlie Chaplin's cinema has been underrated as a seminal style of filmmaking that, along with the films of Griffith, defined the aesthetic of the classical Hollywood studio era film. Andre Bazin felt that the greatest virtue of the studio era film was its "equilibrium." The studio era film is characterized by a classical aesthetic that prizes, above all, balance. This balance is manifest in the studio era film's form as well as its content. We see it in the studio film's faultless match cuts and its harmonious compositions arranged, like a Greek sculpture, around groups of three. We see it in its use of mirrors to balance frames and its composition of frames within frames. And we see it in the emotional equilibrium of its greatest practitioners, in Capra's blend of populist idealism and cynical politics, in the way John Ford mixes a sunny mythic idealism with a saddle-worn, dusty pictorial realism, in Hitchcock's mixture of the romantic and the sinister.

Of all the great Hollywood directors, Chaplin had the most subtle and complex sense of balance. The most famous example of this, and the most important in recognizing the seriousness of his filmmaking, is his deft balance of pathos and comedy. What separates him from all other comedians is his ability to move his audience deeply as well as amuse them, often at the same time. Howard Hawks complained that filmmakers and critics alike underestimated the seriousness of comedy. "The critics don't know anything about comedies. They don't know what to write so they don't write anything about it," he told students at the American Film Institute in 1976. "Study Chaplin," he concluded, "Everything that he made was a tragedy, but he made it funny."[1]

Of course all of the greatest comedians mix some pathos into their comedy but in no other comic body of work do we find anything to rival, in depth of emotion, the moment when, for example, Charlie's son is taken from him in *The Kid*, or when Charlie is abandoned by Georgia on New Year's Eve in *The Gold Rush,* or when the blind girl, her sight restored, finally lays eyes on the little Tramp who has been her benefactor in *City Lights*. These are some of the most emotional moments, not only in film comedy, but in all of cinema. Chaplin aimed high for a comedian. Gerald Mast wrote of *The Kid* that "the strategy of the whole middle section of the film is to develop the meaning of the word 'love.'"[2] Woody Allen felt that Chaplin "said more about love than so many purportedly serious investigations of the subject in books or films." Usually, when filmmakers aim to be moving or sentimental, Allen noted, "you want to wring their necks," but when Chaplin moves us, as he did in *City Lights*, he arrives at "a finer achievement, a deeper achievement than all of the moments in Keaton's film."[3] I think Allen's comments are key to understanding Chaplin's greatness, stressing the difficulty of pulling off moments of pure emotion. Invoking pathos in an audience is a difficult thing to do with validity in any art form and in any time, as the vast number of awful "feel good" films from any era of Hollywood (including ours) illustrates.

John Ford is, in many ways, an apt parallel to Chaplin. He too had a strong streak of sentimentality and his films have many saccharine moments. But when he succeeds, he accomplishes something that few filmmakers can: He makes goodness manifest. I'm a great fan of directors like Welles and Hitchcock but, in a sense, that ilk of directors has it easier than directors like Chaplin and Ford, at least when it comes to modern audiences. Welles and Hitchcock have an expressive style that wins modern audiences easily. Chaplin and Ford have a quieter, classical style. And Welles and Hitchcock traffic in all sorts of complex and sinister ideas fascinating to the modernist spirit. Chaplin and Ford toiled in a more antique terrain. Both of them looked backward, at least in part, towards the sentimentalism of D.W. Griffith and the Victorian era. When they failed, they could look stale and old-fashioned. But when they succeeded, they did so with great cleansing doses of pure sentiment.

Of course Chaplin is not Ford. Ford, at his best, conveys the sturdy goodness of man, the best of the American Puritan. Chaplin's films express a deep empathy for humans. As I discussed earlier in the book, Chaplin often stressed that the final goal of his films was to awaken his audience's sense of empathy, exercise their sense of pity. But pity is dangerous material to work with, the line between pathos and bathos being particularly fine. One of Chaplin's great talents was his ability to convey empathy without grating on us or making us feel emotionally manipulated. He doesn't turn on the faucet of emotions blithely; rather, he thinks of clever ways to draw out our emotions.

First, as we have seen, Chaplin takes advantage of the silent film medium to find all sorts of clever visual ways to express emotion. He doesn't just tell us to feel; he charms us with a host of physical detail that incarnates the feeling, those "simple little facts," that Mayakovsky wrote of, which lead "to the greatest emotional saturation," for example in that scene from *The Bank* where Charlie's love for Edna is expressed in his tomfoolery with a note, flower and typewriter. Or he translates his love scenes into "dances" of eyes and hands as in the ending of *City Lights*. What Chaplin doesn't do is demand our feelings via explicit title cards or obvious, melodramatic poses. He finds subtle ways to express emotion, via the concretes of cinema. And he asks us to work some, to scrutinize his images to arrive at their meaning.

And Chaplin shows the same reluctance to repeat himself in melodrama that he does in comedy. One of Chaplin's hallmarks as a comedian is to constantly rework and revitalize his gags. He may return to old ideas, but then he always does something new with them. The same is true of his appeal to pathos. Each of the touching moments in Chaplin's films is its own thing.

For example, Charlie is sad to have lost Edna to another man in *The Tramp* and finishes the film by heading down the road sadly. But suddenly he stops and all of his limbs seem, of their own accord, to jump about spasmodically. Soon he has shaken off his despair and fallen back into his joyful Tramp trot, the crisis passed. A year later, Chaplin reprises that moment in *The Vagabond*. Edna has left Charlie for yet another fellow and Charlie is seen slouching at the roadside camp he had briefly shared with Edna. Then his resilient body takes over as it did in *The Tramp*. His legs start to kick freely, he rubs his hands together, he briefly falls into the Tramp's skipping walk. But the bravado dies as quickly as it returned and he is left in despair.

These scenes reflect how Chaplin was loath to go after the same emotional effect twice. Chaplin varied his moments of pathos, making them a little different in each film. The most repeated moment of intense pathos in Chaplin's films is that one where Charlie, often eavesdropping or spying from some distance, finds out that the woman he loves does not return his affections. But this moment is tailored differently in each film. For example, Chaplin probably never milked Charlie's suffering as much as he did in the two shots from *The Gold Rush* that occur just after Charlie realizes that Georgia was only toying with his affection: the one at the doorway of Charlie's cabin where Charlie wakes to find that no one has shown for his New Year's Eve Party, and the one outside the saloon window where he stares at the New Year's Eve celebrations within, from which he is excluded. Both of these shots are held for a long time and in close-up. They are so powerful in their rendering of Charlie in still pensiveness as to threaten to efface the identity of the Tramp and replace it with a countenance that belongs only to Chaplin, not Charlie.

But the scene in *The Circus* in which Charlie learns the woman he loves does not return his affections is entirely a different matter. Here, Chaplin doesn't hold the reaction shots as long as he did in *The Gold Rush*. The dynamics and context of the scene are different as well. Charlie, the biggest comedy act the circus has, is called into the ring moments after finding that the girl doesn't return his love. In this instance, Chaplin encases his pathos in a situation with which we are all familiar: having to pretend to the world all is fine moments after personal heartbreak. The scene also contributes to the unity of the film, which from the outset has examined the paradox of sad clowns and the touching heroism of pretending to be happy.

This scene from *The Circus* also points to another way in which Chaplin successfully drives home his moments of pathos: by taking care, in his scenes of emotion, to arrive at a situation that has universal resonance. When Charlie first sets eyes on Georgia in *The Gold Rush*, she seems to be interested in him. She smiles at him and approaches him, her arms open to him invitingly. Charlie smiles nervously in response, steps towards her, proffers his arm as well and begins to doff his hat. Only when she sails by him does he realize she has been interacting with a man standing behind him. It's through little social embarrassments like these, ones that Chaplin knows we have all experienced, that he deepens our sense of pity for the Tramp. He doesn't just turn on the spigots of emotion; he reflects on the ways we might most deeply commiserate with Charlie, see ourselves in his suffering. Chaplin is something of an expert at the psychology of suffering and he puts that expertise to use in drawing out our feeling for Charlie.

But perhaps the greatest key to Chaplin's effectiveness in conveying emotion is how rarely he did it. It is remarkable how little Chaplin turned to emotion before his

This publicity shot from *The Circus* shows how much Charlie's pathos had become a selling point by this point in his career.

feature films. Films with strong sentimental content like *The Bank, The Tramp, The Vagabond*, and *Sunnyside* are the exception more than the rule. And for all the movies like these, where Charlie's heart is broken, there is another, like *The Immigrant, A Dog's Life, Behind the Screen* and *Modern Times,* in which Charlie's relationship with a woman is marked by a simple, requited affection. Chaplin continually softened the character of the Tramp and became increasingly dexterous at managing his character so that his audience was taken with his charm. But scenes in which Chaplin overtly elicits our emotion are far and few between. It's interesting that Chaplin is famed for his pathos when, in the long run, there is so little of it in his films. It puts one in mind of the art history chestnut that the greatest colorists were those, like Rembrandt, who used color sparingly. Chaplin's moment of pathos in his films stand out so distinctly because they are so few, because he prepares for them carefully and employs them sparingly.

Even in the feature films for which Chaplin is most famous and which most turn to emotion for effect (*The Kid, The Gold Rush, City Lights*), Chaplin is reluctant to milk the tear ducts too often. In *The Gold Rush,* Chaplin probably went furthest in developing Charlie's tragic outsider status. But he seems to have feared that he had gone too far into the Tramp's dark side. His next two films, *The Circus* and *City Lights,* both are characterized by a lighter tone. *City Lights,* with a restraint characteristic of classic Hollywood at its very best, saves its emotional punch for the very last scene.

Chaplin's approach to pathos in *The Kid* is also spare and well-calculated. The scene, for example, in which the child is stolen from Charlie in *The Kid* is a rather flagrant appeal to the audience's emotions, with the child holding his hands out to the camera and screaming "I want my father" and match cuts of Charlie, restrained by heavies, staring into the camera in tortured impotence. But this scene doesn't arrive until almost fifty minutes of a sixty-seven minute film have passed. Leading up to this scene is lighthearted, but scrupulous, character development, for example the long scene in which Charlie and the kid sit down to a pancake breakfast, an extended sequence filled with myriad detail that develops and testifies to Charlie and the kid's relationship. Viewers of this scene typically cite a host of memorable details: the kid rousing Charlie out of bed like an angry mother; Charlie's hole-ridden blanket that serves also as his morning robe; Charlie meticulously counting each pancake as he might a deck of cards to make sure they each have the same amount for the breakfast; Charlie's comically perfunctory prayer before the meal. Chaplin carefully develops the close bond between Charlie and the boy in this scene and a myriad of others like it. It is scenes like this that Mast has in mind when he says the middle of the film aims to define love. Chaplin, by dint of careful forethought and meticulous detail, avoids the cardinal sin of emotional filmmaking, demanding emotion of your audience before you've earned it.

Similarly, in *The Gold Rush,* Chaplin films, in an unusually dramatic close-up, that moment where Charlie, alone and abandoned by Georgia, stands by the open door of his shack, listening from afar as the people in town sing "Auld Lang Syne" on New Year's Eve, his face soaked with a light that captures every nuance of his fatigue and despair. It's probably Charlie's saddest moment in all of Chaplin's films. But this highly expressive shot is effective, not just because it so poignantly expresses Charlie's despair, but because of the four-minute scene that preceded it, documenting in fine detail Charlie's meticulous preparations for, and childlike anticipation of, his party.

And it's successful because of the even earlier sequence in which Charlie tears his room to shreds because he is so delighted that Georgia has accepted his invitation to a party. It's because Chaplin has laid the groundwork in earlier scenes like these that he can make as strong an appeal to emotion at the doorway as he does. Chaplin only turns to the large gesture after a hundred small ones have made it possible.

Many a less successful melodrama, old or new, ask us to feel emotions, maybe even cue music to make us feel emotions, but they fail to get that emotional response from us because they haven't put in the hard work of developing the relationship. These films usually compensate for their laziness with great oceans of music in the vein of Wagner or Vaughan-Williams. How many commercial melodramas, for example, start off with the death of a loved one, replete with tears and intense emotional music, forgetting only to do the one necessary thing: make us care beforehand about the person who died. This is one of those areas in which one can make it clear to students that Chaplin's films, which can seem so rickety and antique to their modern eye, outstrip, in complexity and careful structure, larger, glossier fare that they perceive as more polished, advanced cinema.

Letting the Air Out of Pathos

Moreover, Chaplin is always very scrupulous in questioning Charlie's empathy, never letting it become maudlin. One of his saving graces is that for every one of his famously sublime moments, there are a hundred or so where he mocks the sublime. He is saved from his taste for sentiment by how good he is at mocking it. Some of his most emblematic and recurrent gags are those in which he pulls the rug out on a moment of sublime emotion. Even as his films became freer in their emotion, Chaplin never lost his taste for taking the mickey out of Charlie's moments of deeply felt emotion. As Mast describes it, "he creates a moment of pathos and then lets the air out of it with a joke."[4]

For example, in *A Dog's Life* Edna, playing a hapless saloon girl, sings a plaintive song that sets off a contagion of weeping in her dance hall audience; even Charlie falls victim. But Charlie is unable to lapse too deeply into his melancholia, to really indulge it, because his neighbor keeps spitting in his face during his own expostulations of grief. In *The Pawnshop*, a pawnshop customer moves Charlie to tears with his hard-luck story. But here again the emotion of the moment is undercut by Charlie, who had been snacking before his crying jag, spraying a storm of cracker debris on the customer as he blubbers.

This kind of highly physical response to a moment of sublime emotion is typical in Chaplin's films, which, as critics have often noted, have an almost Brechtian tendency to emphasize the most sordid necessities of the body. Chaplin loved to intrude into a moment of great emotion with a moment of crass physicality. Some of Chaplin's most famous recurrent gags are built around vomiting, urinating, burping, the slurping and spewing of food, spitting, obesity, nose-blowing, obscene gestures, animal droppings and foul smells (foot odor, bad breath and smelly cheese being his favorite choices here). And of course his cinema exhibits something close to an obsession with the sexual and ironical significance of the human bottom. The first of the many controversies Chaplin experienced in his fame was the clamor that surrounded the sordidness of his films, and even the modern-day viewer is surprised by the frankness of Chaplin's films, for example Charlie's experiences with cocaine (*Modern Times*) and heroin (*Easy Street*), or Chaplin's many references to homosexuality. Chaplin's jokes can be surprisingly explicit, such as that moment in *The Tramp* where Charlie, mistaking a bull for a cow, contemplates milking its penis, or the one in *City Lights* where Charlie shocks a crowd of people by sitting on the face of one of the figures of a venerated civic statue.

Chaplin's coarseness is an essential ingredient to his art, one that is important to reflect on in studying his gift for balance. His earthiness testifies to a realism and materialism, an acute consciousness of physical man, that grounds his idealism and taste for melodrama. It is the great antidote to his penchant for the lyrical. I don't think it's an exaggeration to suggest that there is something Shakespearean in the vast scale, from vulgar to sublime, in Chaplin's cinema, the sheer expanse of human nature that he covers, his ability to be both unbelievably crass and cynical and airily sublime and idealistic, sometimes even at the same time.

Even as late as *A Countess from Hong Kong*, we are struck by Chaplin's insistence on off-color gags involving vomiting overboard (a perennial favorite throughout his oeuvre) and bathroom smells. And as Chaplin became more saccharine and didactic in his later films, prone here and there, as in his speech that concludes *The Great Dictator*, to optimistic bromides, he remained a devout materialist. He was refreshingly immune, throughout his entire life, to spiritual schemes or all inclusive doctrinal systems and tended to trumpet those virtues that had to do with simply living well: love, friendship, enjoyment of the appetites. As Calvero says to Thereza in *Limelight*, "There is no meaning, only desire."

It is Chaplin's materialism, his constant attention to Charlie's large feet of clay, that saves his love scenes from insipid melodrama and gives them their ironic complexity. Sometimes, for example, Charlie, in falling for a woman, is so impressed with his ardor that he falls into pretentiously amorous poses. And in these moments Chaplin loves to punish him for his melodrama.

After meeting Edna on the boat in *The Immigrant*, for example, Charlie, exiting the dining room, pauses at the door and casts his body and face in a posture of poetic reverence, only to be shaken from the pose by an eruptive burp, yet another example of poetic ecstasy racked by physical necessity. In *City Lights*, besotted with love for the flower girl he has just met, Charlie finds a spot near a fountain from which to gaze lovingly at her. But he is shaken from his reveries when the blind girl unknowingly empties a bucket of water in his face. Later, in the same film, he strikes a Romeo-below-the-balcony pose under the flower girl's window, only to be rewarded by a pot, dislodged by an alley cat, that crashes on his head. Charlie regards Edna surreptitiously from a short distance while she eats her lunch in at the worksite in *Pay Day*. Here too he wears on his face the poetic rapture of a legendary suitor, swooning in the depth of his passion, only to be snapped from his rapture by the smell of the cheese she accidentally places under his nose. In *The Bank*, Charlie, after depositing his love note and flower on Edna's desk, turns around before he exits the office, blows a kiss, dramatically holding out his arm in his best lovelorn harlequin manner, turns and walks right into the closed door of the office with such force that he is knocked on his backside. At the end of *Easy Street*, when Charlie is reunited with Edna, he throws his body back in glorious apprehension of embracing her, extends an arm dramatically towards her, clasps both of his hands over his heart, and, striding dramatically towards her, falls into a manhole.

There is nothing that Chaplin takes as seriously as Charlie's feelings for women. A cult of women is central to Chaplin's film ethic. But Chaplin is unwilling to excessively idealize even this hallowed subject. What Walter Kerr says of the love scenes from *City Lights* is true of most every love scene in Chaplin's films: "No love scene is played without functioning simultaneously as humor, which means that a potentially sentimental situation has been scrubbed clean with the sturdy brush of irony."[5] Charlie's Romantic reveries are almost always interrupted by the rude insistence of the real world.

In *The Tramp*, Chaplin effects a particularly seamless transition from sad to comic in the scene in which Charlie has learned that Edna loves another man. This is a genuinely moving scene, one of Chaplin's earliest exercises in pathos and the only one I can think of where Charlie actually weeps at the moment of heartbreak. Chaplin inscribes the scene with that careful attention to intimate gesture and physical detail I describe earlier in the book, with Charlie's hands straying all about the room as if everything he touched were somehow expressive of the woman he loves. He picks up Edna's hat, for example, and strokes it gently.

The depth of his emotion, though, is checked some when, with back to us, he blows his nose in the hat. As Charlie exits, he blows his nose in the door curtain as well. This is typical Chaplin; we start with tears but we finish with nose-blowing. In Chaplin's films, the body often mocks the soul like this. Chaplin makes it clear that no one, Charlie included, can breathe in the pure air of these moments of elevation for long, that moments of elevation themselves are inherently comical, expressive, usually, less of sincere feeling than intense self-consciousness and its consequent playacting. As in his dreams, Charlie tries to soar on the wings of passion, but it's usually only a matter of seconds before his body brings him back down to earth with a thud.

These gags are important ones for Chaplin. They mark a line between sincere love and posturing. As I discussed earlier, Chaplin, despite his cynicism, believes in a few things that he takes pains to celebrate in his films: love, companionship, the reality and power of human empathy. But, to his credit, he holds those few things to an exacting standard and calls out Charlie when his honest emotions are inflated into posturing, when self-consciousness distorts genuine feeling. Then Charlie is the proper object of satire. Chaplin is a great poet of love but an equally proficient satirist of love. In fact, the former skill is dependent on the latter.

This gag, in which a pose is struck, then mocked, runs throughout Chaplin's cinema, not just in scenes of romantic love. Chaplin, for example, had a particular sensitivity to the clichés of intense friendship. Twice in *City Lights* Charlie tries to counsel his suicidal friend to choose life over death. In both scenes, Charlie is so moved by his own sentiments that he finishes by striking the dramatic pose of a soap-box orator, and both times his ostentation is rewarded with swift humiliation. The first time his suicidal friend, trying to drown himself, accidentally ties a rope, to which a rock is attached, to the sermonizing Charlie rather than to himself and Charlie is dragged into the river, his oratorical index finger still in the air as he flies into the water. Later,

Charlie has coaxed a revolver from his friend's hand. Again, the index finger is in the air, again his face awash in an expression of sublime piety, so moved is he by his own speech, when the gun accidentally goes off and Charlie's sanctimony is undercut by an acrobatic leap to the couch where he buries his head, his derriere wagging ingloriously in the air.

Sometimes Charlie himself is the one who mocks piety, for example in those scenes where Chaplin so expertly sends up male postures of sportsmanship and magnanimity. But more often it's Charlie who is the victim of Chaplin's sharp sense of human pretense. After having been "saved" by Salvation Army volunteer Edna in *Easy Street*, Charlie walks out of the church with his eyes piously raised to the sky, his childlike notion of how a convert would act, only to trip on the stairs on the way out. In one of the more famous scenes from *Easy Street*, Charlie defeats the neighborhood bully by holding the bully's face close to the gas fumes of a street lamp that the bully has, in his rampage, bent to the ground. It's a classic bit of Chaplin playacting, where Charlie, while defeating the bully, assumes the posture of a dentist administering gas to a patient. Afterwards, seeing how impressed everyone is by his accomplishment, Charlie falls into the masculine swagger he sometimes adopts in moments of triumph. He stands back on his heels, hitches up his belt, bends his legs in the manner of an athlete limbering up, and decides to conclude his victory with a smoke. Finally, with a gesture of confident masculine bravado, he lights his match on the same street lamp, forgetting that gas is escaping from it. The explosion lands him on his rear end.

Similarly, in *Work*, the family for whom Charlie is doing some painting asks him to look at their gas stove which they are having trouble lighting. Charlie warms to the task, affecting his best "wise, aged handyman" persona, puffing on his pipe as he scrutinizes the oven, tapping its ashes out on nearby surfaces (including the couple's breakfast plates and the husband's head). Finally he lights a match and, to everybody's wonderment, the stove starts up easily. He then walks away from the impressed couple towards the front of the screen and the camera. Now he's playacting as the successful tradesman, having easily dispatched a problem for clients who are not blessed with his practical skills. He has the same cocky gait and blasé expression that he wears in *Easy Street*. He adjusts his tie, spits with workman-like disdain on the floor, and then is promptly blown out of the kitchen by the exploding stove.

These gags, in which Chaplin lets the air out of his pathos, testify to Chaplin's acute sense of our egotism, an egotism born from inescapable self-consciousness. There is no moment of love, triumph, camaraderie, generosity, or revelation that is not corrupted to some degree by self-congratulation. Our actual moments of sincere goodness are short-lived and quickly curdle in the rank atmosphere of our self-consciousness. It makes perfect sense that Chaplin's comedy has always resonated so successfully in France because it partakes in a kind of bitingly cynical tradition, a strain that runs from Montaigne to La Rochefoucauld to Maupassant and that emphasizes especially the egotism inherent even in our greatest acts of goodness (and, concomitantly, the refreshing nature of honest rogues). "Self-love is clever than the cleverest man in the world," writes La Rochefoucauld.[6] We are often least conscious of our base motives at those moments where we perceive ourselves to be particularly selfless or generous. We are often at our most foolish at those very moments when we are most impressed with ourselves. La Rochefoucauld's adage could serve as the title for that genre of gags where Charlie is too sold on his goodness and is subsequently punished for his self-satisfaction. Charlie's genius is that of the street cur, able at outwitting constables and sausage stand owners. Romance, chivalry, abiding friendship, revelation, triumph—these are the stuff of dreams, as the world, in all its sordid reality, never tires of reminding him.

Criticisms that Chaplin overplayed emotion in his films have never been able to gain traction because his moments of emotion and idealism are more than compensated for by his films' widely prevailing cynicism and realism. Chaplin was capable of a simple, warm idealism but one that never lost sight of reality. Charlie has, at times, the heart of a god and the spirit of an angel but, unfortunately, both of those aspects of him are encased within the confines of an all too real body and physical reality. In a 1920 publicity interview, Chaplin did manage, despite an unctuous tone that often marred his larger reflections on art (an unctuousness that he instinctively avoided in his best films), to rather felicitously express his view of humankind. "The human race," he said, "I prefer to think of as the underworld of the gods. When the gods go slumming they visit the earth. You see, my respect for the human race is not 100 percent. My antics on the screen to you are no doubt ridiculous. Well, the antics of men—even in their most serious and what they choose to call their most sublime occupations—are just as ridiculous to the gods." This comment is not a bad summary of the view of the world expressed in Chaplin's films, a place visited by divinity, but for the most part crudely comical.

The Fey and the Base: Chaplin's Dreams

The many dreams Charlie has in Chaplin's films are another way for Chaplin to play with the balance between our grand aspirations and our mundane reality. These dreams are a lovely aspect of Chaplin's films. They represent a stopping point in his films, otherwise characterized by a Dickensian realism, where he can exercise his lyrical talents and treat the Tramp to a light, airy, highly poeticized world that is tailored to his liking. They are good examples of Chaplin's range, his easy movement from the fey to the base. And they express the great balance in the character of the Tramp, who has the soul of the poet buried deep in the body of a rude mechanic. Chaplin's dreams express how we all straddle worlds of ethereal beauty and sordid reality. And they lend his film's a touching Romanticism, commenting on the sublime nature of even the rudest of us and of the tragic destiny of humans to envision dreams that they can't realize, to exceed their grasp with their reach.

But Chaplin not only strikes a balance between Charlie's dreams and his reality. The dreams themselves are a balance of ideal and realistic effects. Charlie's loveliest dreams are shot through with moments of counterbalancing realism. In his dreams Charlie is harried by the same forces that dog him in real life. The dreams never provide perfect respite. Even in the lovely, lyrical dance with the nymphs in *Sunnyside,* he falls on a cactus and dances as much out of pain as pleasure. When he dreams of saving Edna on her runaway horse in *The Idle Class,* he first chooses a nearby donkey as his vehicle of pursuit and finds that he's actually moving slower than he would be if he just ran after her. (The donkey is something of a *bête noir* to Charlie, as further attested by the malevolent one in *The Circus* always bent on taking a bite out of Charlie's hide.) Charlie does not get any final rest, not even in his dreams. The same forces that provide him with worries on earth do so in his dreams as well. And this is typical of how dreams really are. The most luxurious dream has its sinister undertones.

Often Charlie's dreams strike a subtle, carefully calibrated balance between a lovely ethereal vision of an ideal world and, at the same time, a parody of that world, a parody of idealism in general. The dream in *Sunnyside,* for example, is among Chaplin's most gorgeous. The blurred far shots of lithe, fetching nymphs in their Grecian robes against a background of lush foliage on a slanting hillside represents a lovely homage to the "*fete galante*" paintings of the 18th century. The dream is a lovely evocation of grace and lyricism, shot through with a gentle eroticism, true to its Rococo influences. But it's also something of a parody of high art and bogus visions of nirvana. Charlie's overdramatic imitations of the nymphs' graceful moves amount to a gentle parody of the pretentious elevation of ballet and some of the Anna Pavlova moves popular at the time. When he tries to join the nymphs' dance, he does so with his own brand of over-the-top bounciness that (in a mix known only to Chaplin) intertwines childlike glee and subterranean sexual aggressiveness. When he falls on a cactus, the pain leads him to even more spasmodic movements that he tries to disguise with recognizable dance features, at one point putting his hands out sideways and trying to translate his confusion into an Egyptian shuffle of sorts. The entirety of the dream is Charlie trying to elevate himself to an ideal ethereal state but, in doing so, degrading that state to his own joyously chaotic level.

Charlie's daydream of domestic bliss in *Modern Times* is at once an ode to, and parody of, the bliss of setting up home. The house of Charlie's dreams is so cozily appointed, the meal (as in so many scenes in Chaplin's films) so hearty, and our affection for him and his vagabond girlfriend so deep, that the dream is genuinely touching. We would like these two ragamuffins to enjoy such a paradise. But Chaplin includes parodying elements that remove the dream so far from reality as to mock it. Charlie plucks an orange from a tree that hangs outside his window as he arrives at the table for breakfast. He calls a cow to his door as though it were a dog, sets an empty pitcher under it and waits for the cow to milk itself as he bides his time munching fat grapes from a vine that hangs over his doorway. The dream is a mock idyll, at once a touching evocation of Charlie's longing for domesticity and deep feeling for the girl and, at the same time, a biting commentary on the bourgeois dream of "the home." It's a particular aspect of Chaplin's art, this ability to move and mock simultaneously. The dream is lovely but also absurd.

And there are small details that are discordant with the otherwise idealized nature of the dream. After discarding his orange, Charlie dries his hand on the dining room curtains. The meal Goddard cooks consists only of one, immense steak that the two dig into like a couple of junkyard dogs, without even removing their portion to their respective, carefully set plates. These details touch us because they illustrate how far Charlie is from making this dream a reality. His dreams mix childish illusion with crude reality. This kind of home is foreign terrain to a Tramp like Charlie, and always will be.

The elaborate dream that finishes *The Kid* is another parody of a bogus, conventional paradise and it, too, touchingly comments on the limitation of Charlie's notion of paradise. It's one of the strangest dreams in Chaplin's films. From the film's debut it has been a controversial aspect of the film. Even in its day, critics were repelled by its cheap, cardboard staginess and hoary vaudeville aspects; modern viewers are even more baffled by it. It is highly inconsistent with the rest of the film and it probably should be conceded that it impairs the film's unity. For those who appreciate it, though, its cheapness is its point. "What amused me was its limitedness, its meagerness," wrote the perceptive Frances Hackett of *New Republic* when the film came out, "It was like a simple man's version of the Big Change, made up from the few properties with which a simple man would be likely to be acquainted. The lack of inventiveness seemed to me to be its best point.... It was the simplified heaven of the antic sprite whom Chaplin has created and whose inner whimsicality is here so amusingly indulged."[7] The dream of heaven in *The Kid* is another parody of heaven, the purpose of which is to point out that there really is no heaven. Circumscribed by the meager talents of Charlie's mythic imagination, it's partially a melancholy comment on how our dreams are hemmed in by our small lives and consciousness. In the end it touches us in its reflection of just how modest the Tramp's notion of heaven is.

Chaplin's happy endings are often just thinly disguised dreams that, like Charlie's dreams, both indulge and mock the ideal. *A Dog's Life*, for example, finishes with an ending that is introduced by the title card "when dreams come true," a beatific vision of happy marriage in rural retreat that anticipates the one in *Modern Times*. Here again Chaplin pulls off that lovely alchemy by which he can create a world that is idyllic, touching, and poetic while at the same time mocking that world, emphasizing that it is only a dream, and perhaps a puerile one at that. The scene opens with Charlie farming in a large, plowed field. (Chaplin seems to have found his way to an actual farm for this shot.) The enormity of the field with its many deep furrows stretching back into the distance is contrasted with the minuscule precision of Charlie's labor. Charlie, straddling one of these immense furrows, stops every foot or so to drill a single hole with his finger, then drops a single seed into that hole. Happy as he is in his idyllic farm life at the end of this film, his farming method is absurdly childlike and impractical, emphasizing that this kind of happy ending represents far-fetched fantasy.

Easy Street finishes with one of these mock idylls as well. In the final scene, the once debauched and out-of-control neighborhood has been transformed into a one-block paradise that is very reminiscent of the Bowery paradise in *The Kid*. The block is dominated by "The New Mission," the kind of religious revival establishment usually sent up in Chaplin's films. The very fact that Chaplin allows organized religion to dominate as much as it does in this final scene alerts us to the element of parody in it. Charlie wears the costume of his nemesis, the police officer, another reversal of the standard in Chaplin's films. And instead of treating Charlie like dirt, everyone tips their hat to him. The bully is now a tamed husband who moves his wife to the inside of the sidewalk to shield her from the buffeting of passing traffic. It is a surrealist paradise where everything is the opposite of the way things really are, an inverse dream of Charlie's reality, a fantasy sustainable (and of interest to us) only for the last few minutes of the film. It's Chaplin's mockery of the fantasy of a law-abiding world. In endings like these, Chaplin is quasi-modernist, offering a happy ending but in a tongue-in-cheek way, giving the audience what they want and rounding off a film nicely, but at the same time mocking our (and the Tramp's) expectations as well.

Chaplin also displays, via Charlie's dreams, a good feel for what dreams reveal about us. The dream in *The Idle Class*, for example, is a wonderful little study in how little it takes to engender the most grandiose fantasies, in the human capacity for building castles in the air. Charlie sees Edna ride by on her horse. He is immediately lovestruck and lapses into a daydream in which he saves her from a runaway horse, weds her before a stained glass window, and sits in domestic tranquility on the front steps of yet another idyllic cottage, bouncing a baby on his knee, Edna's head resting on his shoulder—and all this within about 20 seconds of seeing her. The dream is both a touching and biting commentary on the human imagination that can construct such elaborate and poetic fantasies so rapidly, that can, in seconds, stand vast structures on the head of a pin.

Charlie is often so absurdly successful in his dreams that they become a touching comment on human egotism, how abjectly we celebrate ourselves in our dreams, to a point that we would be embarrassed to admit to in our waking lives. Part of what makes the dream in *The Gold Rush* so touching is how appreciative the girls (who in reality have barely given Charlie a passing thought) are of Charlie and all the details of his party: his party favors, his little gags, his eloquent toast, and above all his famous dance of the rolls, which earns him a ceremonial kiss from Edna. It's one of Chaplin's most memorable scenes because rarely does Charlie experience such a thorough social triumph. Of course, it's all a dream.

Charlie's daydream in *The Circus* where Charlie knocks out his suitor is another lovely little study in how ludicrously successful we are in our dreams. In his dream, Charlie's victory over his competitor is absolute. He kicks him in the seat of the pants and knocks off his top hat before he decks him. His opponent down, he turns his back to him and, dog-like, kicks dirt all over him. He finishes by snapping his fingers at him before adjusting the crease in his hat and walking away with great dignity. In reality, of course, he does nothing. In his dream, though, he is suave as can be.

Similarly, in Charlie's dream in *The Bank*, he operates with the skill and confidence of a superhero, laying low a vast number of adversaries while defending Edna (who has rejected him in waking life) and winning her affection. The dream concludes with Edna cherishing the flowers from Charlie that, in reality, she spurned. She leans into Charlie and he caresses her hair. Chaplin hadn't mastered the dissolve that he uses so poetically in later films to move Charlie in and out of dreams. Here he irises in to conclude the dream and irises out to show the sleeping Charlie, the bank janitor, who in reality is only caressing a mop. This dream unites the two key ingredients of Chaplin's dreams, first to ponder the balance between our imaginative highs and real-life lows and to emphasize the dream as a reprieve from reality, a place where things occur as they should but rarely do in real life.

Nine

Balance in the Character of Charlie

We see evidence of Chaplin's natural gift for balance in the character of Charlie. Film after film, Chaplin was able to layer his understanding of this alter ego, and by the time of the talkies, he had created one of the most complex and carefully delineated characters, not only in film, but in the history of art and literature. One of the keys to Charlie is his consistency. Chaplin knew who Charlie was and he was careful always to stay true to his character. As Kevin Brownlow points out in *Unknown Chaplin,* Chaplin edited out a very entertaining sequence in *The Cure,* where Charlie plays traffic cop to a wheelchair traffic jam in a sanatorium, because the gag required an authoritarian side that he didn't feel was consistent with Charlie. Just as Chaplin refused to use scores of excellent gags if he felt they impaired the unity of his films, so he excised gags that he felt weren't true to the unity of Charlie's character. Charlie developed as Chaplin developed and Charlie's softening in nature reflects, no doubt, Chaplin's own parallel increasing age and maturity. The two aged together. Over the years, Chaplin evolved a very careful understanding of who the Tramp was, and he was careful to not let him do gags outside the natural circumference of his character.

This constant reflecting on Charlie's character over twenty years and many films led to a character of great depth and complexity. The Tramp is a multifarious creature, holding a vast array of opposing qualities in delicate balance. Many of these characteristics are explored in greater detail in other parts of the book. But the following is an attempt at something of a summary list.

The Tramp can be gentle as a lamb (particularly with the right sort, i.e., children, women and dogs) and yet, as I'll discuss below, at other times an absolute sadist, raining blow after blow on his enemies, even after he's been victorious in battle. He swerves manically from brazen confidence to deer-like jumpiness. He's a born victim but, given the opportunity, an expert torturer. He is by nature weak, craven and fearful but in the right circumstances can scrap like a junkyard dog and be almost insurmountable in a street brawl. He displays the guerrilla tactics of the most hardened street fighter and yet at other times is hopelessly childlike, effeminate and ineffectual in his confrontations with violence. He can be aggressively masculine at times and at others so flirtatiously feminine that the men with whom he competes seem uncertain about his sexual orientation. He can be heroic and cowardly, often within the same scene, his cowardice a way of life, his heroism surprising even himself when he is pushed too far or when someone he really cares about is threatened.

Charlie can be chivalrous and display an almost virginal ardor in his loyalty to some women. At other times, he can barely stop himself from leaping on women in moments of sexual arousal and shows a roué's ability to charm women via his playful wit and innuendo. He is often childlike and sexually charged at the same moment. He can be unbelievably delicate in his approach to women but has a great taste for the coarsest humor.

In the great tradition of clowns, Charlie will often affect happiness when we know him to be inwardly sad. He can be generous to the point of giving everything he owns, but more often is electrically charged by the prospect of money (in much the same way he is by women and, earlier in the films, liquor) and usually shows no moral restraints in the way he gains money. He exhibits mystical tendencies in his vulnerability to dreams and the raptures of love but is even more determinedly materialistic in his appetites, his love of booze, food, sex, money and a good smoke. He is easily moved to tears and seduced by hard luck stories, and yet can be alarmingly unempathetic, often indifferent, even to the dignity of the handicapped, and capable of using people in distress as furniture, for example in the many scenes where he finds fallen bodies convenient as bridges or steps.

Charlie is at once a man of great insignificance and yet, with the array of vaudeville and gymnastics tricks at this disposal, the coolest guy in the film, bouncing a smoking cigarette off his heel with a backward kick as he heads into jail or lighting a match on the collar of a passing man. He moves effortlessly from low comedy to elegant ballet; the greatest scenes in Chaplin's films are delicately choreographed scenes of rough, broad comedy. His essential costume and persona is one of awkwardness. He walks and looks funny. And yet he is the person in the film who has the greatest balletic grace, often prone to dances that are ingenious balances of miscues and sublime artistry.

He is by nature a vagabond, and even something of an anarchist, but his dreams are of the most conventional domesticity, a rambling man who carries a little idyllic home in his heart. He lives in abject poverty but with such ingenuity that he finds more comfort in poverty than others do in the heart of luxury. He can be daft and literal-minded, particularly in following the dictates of a job, but subtle as a fox when pursuing his own interests. He is comically void of etiquette, particularly in dining situations, but at the same time characterized by an inflated sense of dignity and carries himself like a British lord, disdainful of others' low manners. No one respects him but he has a very high opinion of himself. Last, but not least, he is often capable of the greatest moral acts and yet exhibits himself, over and over again, to be a rogue, a thief, a criminal, a scoundrel.

I'm sure this is not a complete list of the opposites that Chaplin unites. We have to marvel at the sheer number of balanced opposites in Charlie's character. Chaplin worked at Charlie's character till he had seemingly amassed all the contradictory vastness of the human species within it. This ambitious summary of human nature is one of the things that makes us take Chaplin seriously as an artist, despite the fact that he worked in the entertainment industry, and at the time of its primitive origins. Chaplin makes one think of Tolstoy in his ability to record, from a cool, ironic distance, and with fine, precise detail, a panoply of universal human characteristics, both bad and good. And indeed, Tolstoy had a similar ability to imaginatively inhabit a wide variety of roles. How to explain that the ascetic, often misogynist Tolstoy could, for example, convey so well the tortured yearnings of a young girl at her first ball?

The way in which Charlie balances so many opposing traits also testifies to the essential Manichaeism of Chaplin's world view. Critics are often befuddled by Charlie hosting so many qualities, seeing an implausibility in his multiple nature. How can one character be so many things?, they ask. Dan Kamin, for example, writes that

> a case can be made that Charlie is not really a coherent character at all, but a hollow device that serves a different purpose with each appearance. Chaplin conjures a golem from a mask of a face, an expressive costume, and complex, stylized movements. The character seems to have depth, to suffer, to have a soul—but he is in the end a glittering shell that expresses his creator, whose ideas, ultimately could not be contained in his familiar outline.[1]

There is a modernist attraction among many Chaplin critics to the notion of Charlie as a floating signifier of sorts, a thing of nothingness. Charlie is, in this manner of thinking, a kind of modern Merlin, a protean wizard conjuring different personalities to teach us different lessons.

But what I really think motivates this thinking is an unwillingness to tolerate Chaplin's hard view of humans as essentially contradictory, paradoxical creatures—creatures who are, as Reinhold Niebuhr describes them, problems to themselves. What I like least about this way of thinking about Charlie is that it strips him of his most essential quality: his humanness. Charlie moves us because he *is* so real, so human, so much as we are. He unites the same contradictions that torture us. He swivels manically from good to bad without ever resolving the two, just as we do. Chaplin has an essentially open view of human nature. He sees humans as both bad and good, often at the same time. He does not try to tie up humans into an orderly equation. We are what we are, and what we are Chaplin often finds laughable, amusing, sad and tragic.

Here again Chaplin is reminiscent of that mordant strain of French humanism that likes humanity enough to not pretend that it is more than it is, that shows humans as capable of goodness but a goodness that also often curdles quickly with egoistic self-consciousness or is contradicted almost immediately by poor behavior. The opposing tendencies that define Charlie are the universal contradictions, or paradoxes, of the human soul. We are all capable of great heroism and great cowardice, great empathy and great cruelty, and like Charlie, we are capable of exercising these opposing qualities within very close proximity to each other, sometimes at the same time. How even to separate our two sides? Our majestic sense of the infinite, for example, feeds our monstrous and destructive egos; our sense of our criminality leads us to redemptive humility. These are just two of the curious paradoxical relationships between good and bad in us that are explored in great detail in Chaplin's films.

Chaplin's films are dosed with a good deal of original sin, set on a planet, as he said, where gods might go when they feel like slumming. We are, like Charlie, froward in our morals. But we also may be, as Charlie is, pleasant enough as we are. Chaplin takes pleasure in the robust tomfoolery of humans. In his films, as in La Rochefoucauld's maxims and Maupassant's stories, the hero is the honest rogue, the enemy the self-righteous prig. For all of Charlie's dreaming, and despite his own strong Romantic tendencies, Chaplin has a good deal of the Naturalist to him. He is a cruel ironist with an extraordinarily exacting eye who took it as his art to examine humankind in all its dimensions and who liked his subject of study enough never to make it something other than it was.

Charlie: The Saint and the Sinner

The most important set of balanced characteristics in the Tramp is his mixture of essential decency and inescapable malignancy. He can be a saint—friend to abandoned children, dogs and women—but he is mostly a sinner. Charlie's goodness exists side by side with a good deal of debauchery. It grows out of a rich, rank healthy loam of real humanity. What makes his moments of goodness so plausible is how deeply ingrained we know his criminality to be.

In *The Kid*, for example, one of Chaplin's most heart-rending films, Charlie's extraordinary goodness—his devotion to the kid, his heroism in defending the kid—is palatable to us because Charlie is otherwise still something of a punk who, despite his reservoirs of deep emotion, displays glimpses of alarming criminality. When he first discovers the lost baby in that film, he tries to palm it off on several other people, tries to abandon it himself and even momentarily contemplates dropping it into the sewer. Even in those heartwarming scenes in which Chaplin builds a relationship between Charlie and the boy, we can't help but notice certain examples of Charlie's selfishness, for example that the boy is the one making breakfast for Charlie, who reads a newspaper in bed. Charlie raises the boy to a life of crime. In one of the film's most memorable moments (both cruel and touching, again a specialized Chaplin mix), Charlie literally kicks away his child, as though he were a stray dog, as he (Charlie) flees from a cop who has linked the two as partners in Charlie's window-breaking/repairing scam.

Charlie can be an awful parent in *The Kid*. When he finds that the boy is in a fight with a neighborhood bully, he responds in the manner of a conventional parent, running to save his child. But when he gets to the fight and finds that his son is winning, he immediately joins the crowd, laying odds with the other spectators as though he were ringside at a boxing match. When the bully's brother shows up and informs Charlie that if Charlie's son beats up his brother, he, the bully's brother, will beat up Charlie, Charlie abandons even further the laws of decent parenting. Taking advantage of one of the few moments where his son is at a disadvantage in the fight and has fallen to the ground, Charlie plants his foot on his own son's chest, while raising the bully's arm in the air, in the manner of a ref calling a match, taking pains, via an array of ingratiating gestures, also to convey to the bully's brother what a fine young man his brother is. It's these moments of less than ideal parenting and intransigent selfishness that give Charlie's moments of decency with the kid depth and shading. Goodness doesn't come easily or naturally to the Tramp and is all the more meaningful, therefore, when it does appear.

Chaplin's films are studded with extraordinary acts of cruelty and amorality on Charlie's part. Not only is Charlie often bad, he's often really bad. In *His New Profession,* Charlie steals a crippled beggar's sign that reads "Help I'm a Cripple" and places it on the stomach of the sleeping, wheelchair-bound man he's taking care of. He grabs the first coin deposited in the cup and heads directly to a bar. In *The Floorwalker,* he comes across a palsied man and places a stringed instrument under his shaking hand to make music. In *The Circus,* he surreptitiously steals and then devours the pastry of a babe in arms. In *Police,* he accidentally strikes his burglary partner with a mallet, then claps in time as the man dances in pain. In *Sunnyside,* he absentmindedly prods an oversized woman gardening, mistaking her for one of the cattle he is tending. In the same movie, he is so anxious to court Edna by himself that he induces her younger "idiot brother" to play blind man's bluff, then leads him out of the house and deposits him on the road nearby where the blinded boy is left to avoid speeding cars. When Charlie is later hounded from Edna's house by her father, he passes the boy on the road, still dodging cars. Charlie delivers one superfluous kick to the boy's bottom for good measure as he exits the scene.

The tough Charlie is of course more apparent in his early films. Over time, Chaplin gradually softened Charlie, transforming him from a scrappy but likable punk to a carefully calibrated mixture of profound goodness and moral recalcitrance. The earlier films are simpler; Charlie's contrariness is less diluted with emotion and depth of character. By the time of the sound era, Chaplin had weighted the Tramp with so much goodness and emotion that, in his last silent features, he ran the danger of making him too soft, and thus betraying his invigoratingly punkish youth. However, the scoundrel in Charlie never disappears. The examples of amorality mentioned above from *The Kid* and *The Circus,* both later and more sentimental Chaplin films, attest to a tough roguishness embedded in Charlie's soul that his increasing kindness doesn't come near to dislodging. In the end, the balance in Charlie's character is more sublime in these later films and he is, despite our affection for his punkish youth, a richer character in the later films.

One film that could challenge that thesis, though, is *The Pawnshop,* a go-to film for anyone wanting to see the earlier, more belligerent Charlie. Here Charlie is so confident, so relaxed, so cantankerous, so full of devilish energy that it presents a persuasive argument for the case that Charlie's character was at its best in these earlier films, before he got so sweet-tempered. The film is notable for Chaplin's ease and confidence at this point in his career and the way that ease and confidence expresses itself in Charlie's indomitable punkishness. I can think of no film where Charlie seems so full of himself, spoils so for a fight. And the film is loaded with examples of just how awful Charlie can be. When a man arrives at the pawnshop with a melancholy story about why he wants to pawn his wedding ring, Charlie instinctively reaches for a nearby mallet, one of Chaplin's briefest but most efficient (and vicious) expressions of his disdain for melodrama. As the man delivers his story with stentorian drama, Charlie mocks him in a variety of ways, all of which involve pawned articles (another example of Chaplin's inherent sense of unity). He takes the man's photo with a nearby camera when the man strikes a dramatic pose. He pretends a telephone is a stethoscope to measure the beat of his pounding heart. When the man point to his dead wife up in the sky, Charlie looks up with his binoculars. Chaplin can be cruel in his mockery of emotion. It should be pointed out, though, that the man turns out to be a con and his story a sham, so Charlie's instincts are sound.

Meanwhile, throughout the film, Charlie wages playful but decidedly aggressive warfare with his co-worker (John Rand). There are almost no tactics too low for Charlie in his fight with Rand. At one point he has pummeled Rand so successfully that Rand has been reduced to a kind of unconscious mannequin which Charlie nevertheless continues to attack with an energy that shows no signs of abating. As he readies his arm to rain his umpteenth blow upon Rand, Charlie hears his boss' daughter (Edna Purviance) coming into the room. Charlie immediately drops to the floor, feigning mortal injury. Edna sees him flinching and shielding himself from the imagined blows of Rand, who stands tottering on his feet, still at the edge of consciousness. Edna falls for the con and, as she alternately soothes Charlie and scolds Rand, Charlie takes the time to furtively and appreciatively size up her behind.

Charlie can be a conscienceless fellow. Many of his gags, like this one, revolve around his lightning-quick ability to shift blame to others or to get them to take the fall. He employs any means to win a fight. When his co-worker in *The Bank* (Billy Armstrong) puts up his dukes to fight, Charlie makes it clear that he's eager to take up his challenge. But first, he notes, he must take off his hat and coat, which he does, handing them to the unsuspecting Armstrong. Armstrong's arms now occupied, Charlie knocks him silly. Armstrong is so dazed that Charlie takes advantage of his stupor to get him to hold his coat again, which Charlie then puts on as if being helped by a servant. He signifies that Armstrong's doing a fine job before he walks away.

Charlie often has his greatest fun with his enemies once he's rendered them incapacitated. He exhibits an almost limitless capacity for cruelty in his fights with Rand in *The Pawnshop*. In the scene that precedes Edna's arrival, Charlie has gained dominance in the fight—but Charlie is rarely satisfied with simple victory. Once he dominates a fight, he enjoys himself to the fullest. Here he has Rand in a head-lock and delivers one uppercut after another to his chin. This continues for so long that, tired of the view, he moves Rand, still in the headlock, to another part of the room, and continues the pummeling there. Tiring of that particular form of punishment, he bends Rand back over a desk and rains blow after blow down on his head, before climbing to his chest and vigorously strangling him. He has just stood up the now vacant Rand on his feet and readied him for blows from a new angle, his fifth iteration of punishment, when Edna arrives.

There are moments in Chaplin's films where Charlie so revels in his moments of dominance that he arrives at a kind of connoisseurship of cruelty. In *A Woman*, Charlie has found one of his competitors for a woman's affection in a vulnerable position. The man is blindfolded, having been playing a game of blind man's bluff with a girl who has since absconded with his wallet. Charlie has suffered some indignities at the hands of this man and sees his opportunity for revenge. Charlie hooks the man by the neck with his cane, grabs the beer the man is holding and leads him to the nearest body of water, all the while pretending to be the woman the man pursues.

But Charlie doesn't just dump him in the water. When Charlie has someone this completely at a disadvantage, he tends to calculate the punishment carefully. Here, he's quite choosy in picking the spot where he will deposit the man in the water. Victim in tow, he visits three water-side spots, taking pains to choose just the right one. He rubs his chin in the manner of an artist trying to figure out where to set his easel. At one point he measures the water with his cane, determining the water is too shallow before seeking another spot. When he finally picks a spot, he weighs the bottle he plans to smash over the man's head for its heft and deliberately rolls up his sleeve. Only then does he deliver the blow that sends the man into the pond.

Charlie is something of a gourmand when he has a chance to really trounce an adversary. No blind fury for him. This kind of physical punishment is a kind of rare pleasure to be savored with epicurean discretion. At times, Charlie is not just bad, he's viciously amoral, artistic in his cruelty.

Charlie's Appetites: Food

One of the ways Chaplin holds Charlie's character in balance is to emphasize, repeatedly, his essential materialism. Despite Charlie's dreamy nature, the majority of Chaplin's films emphasize not only the strong pull of Charlie's appetites but often their absolute mastery over his will. Four physical pleasures in particular rivet Charlie's attention: women's bodies, food, liquor and money. A huge proportion of Chaplin's gags focus on Charlie's helplessness around these objects of desire, all of which at times exercise a hypnotic effect on him, rendering him unconscious and conscienceless, a semi-automaton in the service of his id. With his emphasis on Charlie's appetites, not to mention his emphasis on physicality as a whole (via the recurrent gags in his films that involve all of the most rudimentary bodily functions), Chaplin stresses the blood and sinew of Charlie. Charlie may, at times, prance like an ethereal sprite but we just as often find him braying like a donkey. I deal with his powerful and instinctive responses to women in the chapter "Charlie and Women" but here I will reflect on the other three passions, food, money and liquor. All of them are vitally important to Charlie and to Chaplin in balancing Charlie's saintly tendencies.

Charlie's relationship to food is so intense that it practically calls for its own individual study. To study Charlie in general is to study a man on the quest for food. Many of Chaplin's gags have to do with sneaking food under the suspecting eye of a policemen or merchant, like the famous *Dog's Life* scene where he manages to make a tray of pastries disappear one by one under the suspicious eye of a vendor (played by his brother Sydney).

And Charlie's quest for food cuts close to the essential nature of his personality, for example his street dog–like existence on the outskirts of civilization, scrounging for an existence, or his childlike desire to brook no authority in the satisfaction of his appetites. Food, like sex, drink and money, exercises a hypnotic effect on Charlie, often stripping him of his will and morals and leaving him competing with the bottom dregs of society for survival, stealing candy from a baby in *The Circus*, for example, or begging like a dog for a bone in *Behind the Screen*. One of Charlie's comic skills is to bolt food down in the ravenous, open-throated manner of a hungry dog, so accustomed has he become to these moments where he must hastily consume food on the run.

I can't think of any other comic filmmaker, or any other filmmaker for that matter, for whom food is such a vital part of his cinema: the chase for food, the hunger for it, the delight in it. Chaplin's films are redolent with the smell of food, odors both blissful (a vendor's hot dog, a cut of meat roasting on a fire) or rancid (stinky cheese, lunchtime burps, co-workers' bad breath). Chaplin even stresses the sound of food in his many gags built around slurping soup. Chaplin's films are thick with the presence of food and Charlie is constantly haunted by the desire for it. It's always just around the corner, just outside of reach, savorous in its odor but ungraspable, like the hot dog he tries unsuccessfully to filch at the outset of *A Dog's Life*. How many times does Charlie have a desired treat in his hand but have to drop it before he can eat it as he returns to his eternal flight from some policeman or other figure of authority?

Charlie even dreams of food, as in *The Gold Rush* where he tends, with professional aplomb, to a roast turning on a spit, or the dream in *Modern Times* which concludes with Charlie and Paulette Goddard tearing into a terrifically huge cut of steak. Rarely does Charlie eat so well in reality. The food Charlie gets in "real life" is snarfed down in a hurry, on the run, or it's purely imaginary, like the Thanksgiving dinner in *The Gold Rush*.

Still, as limited as his means are, Charlie does, from time to time, manage to enjoy a good meal. In fact, one of Chaplin's particular talents was in mimicking the abject contentment, the pleasureful inertia we experience after a filling meal. One of Chaplin's earliest and most acute enthusiasts, the critic Minnie Maddern Fiske, noted Charlie's comical renderings of those moments when, belly full, Charlie sits at the table with an "air of sad repletion [and] a glazed eye from which all intelligence has withdrawn, inwardly, to brood over the internal satisfaction of digestive process."[2]

Chaplin can be a poet of satiety, an expert at depicting the physical bliss introduced by a full meal. After his mammoth breakfast with his son in *The Kid*, for example, Charlie reclines in his chair, which he has turned from the table. His elbow on the table as he sits back, he smokes and looks out at the camera with that dazed look of unconscious satisfaction that Fiske describes so well, his tongue working at a bit of food lodged in his teeth. He burps satisfyingly and takes a deep breath. He huddles a little and rubs his arms as though he were just a little chilled now that his body has turned all its resources of heat to digestion. He grants his son's request to go outside with a half-conscious calm, as though his brain were only half-operative. Chaplin's fond of depicting a parallel moment in his scenes of drunkenness, when the drunk Charlie stews happily in a state of near catatonia. Chaplin cherishes these few moments where the normally hyper-vigilant, peripatetic Charlie slows down and can, for awhile, enjoy the inertia introduced by a sated appetite.

Chaplin's attitude towards food highlights his difference from other comic filmmakers and perhaps points to the greater seriousness of his work. Other comedians are fundamentally too comfortable in the world to care about food as much as Chaplin does. Chaplin's emphasis on food is no small matter. It reflects how precarious Charlie's hold on the world is. Chaplin's preoccupation with food obviously stems from the poverty he experienced as a child. And it's a preoccupation that never wanes. As late as *Modern Times* we are still witnessing Charlie's enormous appetite and lust for a good meal, for example in the scene where he fills himself up at a deli because he wants to be arrested and has no intention of paying the bill. The pleasure Charlie takes in essential creature comforts—a full meal, a warm bed, a snatched drink, a good smoke—reflect Chaplin's insistent materialism, the materialism of a man who never forgot the lessons of poverty. Chaplin's respect for material pleasure is also reflected in his attitude towards money, sex and liquor. Chaplin never preaches against any of these panaceas in his films, and frequently emphasizes their soothing, redemptive effects on Charlie's tough little existence.

Early on in Chaplin's films, food exists as a comic gambit. Charlie is always on the make for a good meal. In the later films, eating takes on a more sacred, ritualized quality just as, in his later films, Charlie's lust for women transforms more into love and a desire for friendship and affection. His love of food evolves into a love of companionship over food.

Some of the most moving scenes in Chaplin's cinema involve the preparation of food for others, particularly the women he loves. Preparing food is a significant part of Charlie's courtship ritual. One of the characteristics we discover in Charlie, when he quiets his role-playing and reveals himself, is an inherently maternal nature. Charlie loves to take care of the people he likes. And he loves a good sit-down dinner with friends, even if the dinner is imaginary, as the Thanksgiving dinner is in *The Gold Rush*.

Charlie's later attitude towards food and meals is a gentler expression of Chaplin's materialism but it's still materialism. When Charlie strikes the pose of the great lover, as we have seen, Chaplin usually submits him to some little humiliation, a burp, a trip, a pot falling on his head. When he makes a woman a meal, on the other hand, he is on the right track. To feed someone is to love them in Chaplin's films. That is such an essential law of Chaplin's cinema that it is prevalent throughout his talkies, where in films like *Limelight, Monsieur Verdoux* and *A Countess from Hong Kong*, key scenes revolve around the male lead feeding the stray waif who has fallen into his charge. Even when it comes to love, Chaplin never loses sight of the importance of human appetite.

Money

Charlie's attitude towards money also represents a good example of how Chaplin deftly balances the pros and cons of Charlie's character. Charlie can be surprisingly generous with money. When he's offered payoffs by those who supplant him in Edna's affection, both in *The Tramp* and *The Vagabond*, Charlie makes a point of turning down the money with a mildly affronted but quiet dignity. Charlie is not without standards. He won't be bought off by the man who bests him in his pursuit for a woman's affections. He reflects only a moment before turning all of his gambling winnings over to Edna and her mother in *The Immigrant*. And in *City Lights*, Charlie reduces himself to pauper status, forwarding every penny he has to the flower girl so that she might cure her blindness.

Moreover, as I discuss in my chapter on Charlie's role-playing, a part of Charlie's charm is his essential indifference to money. Charlie is the embodiment of the adage that if you have nothing, you have nothing to lose. Charlie happily destroys his chances at most every job he has because he prizes freedom more than money. And his ability to create comfortable domestic situations out of the most penurious conditions seems part of a philosophy on Charlie's part that argues that happiness can be achieved in the most modest circumstances—that it even *thrives* in those situations.

That said, Charlie's default nature is not one of generosity. Generally we find Charlie as much on the make for a little cash as he is for a drink or a bit of food. There are a great many bits in Chaplin's films that emphasize that Charlie not only likes money, but has a passion for it. When Charlie comes across the embezzlers' bag of money that he hopes to appropriate in *The Floorwalker*, he responds with a series of gestures normally reserved for religious devotion or lovemaking. He kisses the money, raises his head rapturously to the sky, places his hand over his heart. In acting out for the viewer how happy he is to have the money, Charlie does a little impromptu dance that results in him miming a happy dive into the bag of money as though he were plunging into a swimming pool.

Charlie's lust for money, like his lust for food, is one of the habits that cut to the quick of his character. Charlie, poor as a church mouse, is always thinking about money, always on the make for a few coins. He is, by daily habit, often by profession, a con man and a thief. In two different films, *The Pilgrim* and *Easy Street*, he even tries to steal the money from church coffers. In Charlie's particular moral hierarchy, neglected women are a far worthier subject of charity than organized religion, which, actually, seems to sit high on the list of worthy targets of larceny. But even attractive women are not to be trusted entirely when it comes to money. After Charlie returns the burgled goods to Edna in *Police*, Edna rewards by offering him a coin. Charlie, at first, resists her charity but ends up pocketing the coin—not, though, before he's had a chance to bite it to test its authenticity, yet another example of Chaplin undercutting noble sentiment with an action dictated by the reality of material needs.

In fact, money is one of those things (like free liquor or a woman's behind) that rivets Charlie's attention no matter what he is doing. In *Easy Street,* Charlie's attention is drawn to the collection box from the moment he walks into the church mission in exactly the same manner as his attention is drawn to the little statue of a naked woman from the moment he walks into the house he has been contracted to paint in *Work*. Sex and money are two things that hypnotize Charlie, render him nearly unconscious.

The collection box gag is developed beautifully in *The Pilgrim*'s scenes where escaped convict Charlie impersonates a minister and is forced to preside over a church service. The offering box scenes from these two films represents a good lesson in how much more complexity Chaplin could bring to ideas that he reprised in later films. Whereas in *Easy Street,* Charlie nervously eyes the coffer, sometimes expressing his tension in nervous gestures, like rubbing his hat or petting the box as it passes by; in *The Pilgrim,* Chaplin comes up with about a dozen quietly comic points of contact between Charlie and the collection boxes.

Charlie is very nervous in this scene as he tries to pass himself off as a minister. The twelve members of the church choir remind him of a trial jury. And he does not have the slightest idea how to conduct a church service. But as soon as he spots the collection boxes, he settles into his official role. His eyes are riveted to the boxes being passed around by two deacons, one on each side of the congregation. From his pulpit spot he barks orders at the deacon (Mack Swain), pointing out to him which parishioners have not coughed up an offering. He watches the two men collect the offerings with such intensity that he doesn't even realize that he is shocking the choir by lapsing into his conventional barroom behavior: lighting a cigarette, posting his foot on a rail, and whistling to the hymn they are singing as though it were a saloon ditty.

When his two assistants move towards an exit with the filled coffers in hand, Charlie, who had till now been leaning comfortably on his dais listening to the choir, starts to chase after them. He quickly realizes, though, that his spasmodic movements reveal his greed and so suddenly slows down and calms himself, speaking to the assistants with an overelaborate calm and joviality, politely asking them to return the boxes to him. He weighs them both carefully as they are handed over to him, casting a dirty look at the side of the congregation he feels has been less forthcoming in funds.

Later, after he has completed the one-man theater version of the fight between David and Goliath that constitutes his best effort at a sermon, Charlie dances around the altar bowing dramatically in the manner of a great stage diva to imagined applause (in fact only one small child is clapping, the rest of the congregation sits in stunned silence). But even while engaged in this hamminess, he notices out of the corner of his eye that the deacons are, again, removing the coffers through a door to the back of the church. Without interrupting the balletic strides of his diva-like bows, he chases after them into the back room, reemerging with both offering boxes in his hands, as though they were large bouquets of flowers offered after a performance, using them to add even more flourish to his absurdly theatrical bows.

Many of Chaplin's gags revolve around this kind of invisible link that Chaplin establishes between money and Charlie, the way he is super-sensitized to its presence, drawn to it hypnotically. In that same scene from *The Floorwalker* where Charlie dives into the bag of money, he drops a small bundle of cash on the ground while counting the money. He makes a gesture to pick it up but then shrugs, deciding it represents such a small percentage of his stash that he needn't bother, and kicks it under a table. Only a second passes, though, before he reverses that decision and madly scrambles under the table, reclaiming the bundle in the same way a dying man in a desert might desperately retrieve a few drops of fallen water. Chaplin devises many gags like this, where Charlie will try to separate himself from cash, but can't complete the action, as if the cash were connected invisibly to his body or as if his body has other ideas than his mind and acts on its own to physically reclaim what Charlie's mind has intellectually abandoned.

In *Pay Day*, for example, Charlie's battle-ax wife, meeting him at the end of his shift, knows that he has not forked over all of his week's earnings. She has seen him, in fact, hide several bills within the inside band of his hat. She grabs his hat to retrieve the bills but in the split second that her attention is concentrated on his hat, Charlie retrieves the bills he had already given her from her open purse. Charlie may not get money often but when he does, it's not easy to wrest it from him. Charlie gets more protean and uncontrollable around money, just as he does around liquor, food and women. He seems to grow another arm that makes sure that a certain unaccounted percentage makes its way back to him in his transactions.

Chaplin balances Charlie's character by showing that he can, at times, be quite charitable and selfless, but more often is devoted to money, to the point of thievery and amorality. But such is the delicacy of Chaplin's art that he is even able to convey Charlie's tug of war between his selfishness and selflessness in a single scene. One of Chaplin's favorite gags is to show how money seems to stick to Charlie's palms, how hard it is to detach himself from money, even in his moments of generosity.

For example, in *The Immigrant*, after hearing from a weeping Edna that her mother has been robbed, it takes Charlie all of ten seconds to decide to hand over the bulk of his cash to the women. But actually parting with the cash is more difficult. As for most of us, generous actions for Charlie are more difficult than generous impulses. At first he forwards his entire roll of cash to Edna, but she is looking away and doesn't notice his offering. Charlie quickly reconsiders his generosity. He unwraps a bill for himself, secretly stashing the rest in Edna's pocket. Again he reconsiders, dexterously picking her pocket of the bundle of cash and drawing another bill for himself. He returns the wad of cash to her pocket but reconsiders a third time, generosity getting the best of him, and returns the second bill to her pocket.

This is a prime example of Chaplin's delicate sense of balance, Charlie both rewarding and stealing from the woman at the same time. Charlie has the capacity to be angelic and a scoundrel in the same moment. The gag also testifies to Chaplin's gift for psychology, his knack for boosting the effect of his gag by creating a situation we can all identify with, in this case, our own corner-cutting in acts of generosity or philanthropy. In doing so, Chaplin saves the gesture from simple bathos, instead turning Charlie's moment of philanthropy into a moment that comments comically on the turgidity of the human impulse towards charity and the paradoxes of human nature.

Similarly, in *City Lights* Charlie hands over hard-earned money to the flower girl to pay for her rent and an operation to return her sight, taking care to reserve only a single bill for himself. The girl is so grateful that she grabs his hand with both of hers and smothers it with kisses. The effect of this kiss on Charlie is palpable. Charlie is extraordinarily sensitive to the vibrations of feminine affection. Any time a woman responds favorably to Charlie's attention, the effect is like an electric current running through his body. In this case, as soon as the girl kisses Charlie's hand, his face transforms from a comic expression of self-satisfied altruism to one of shock and confusion. His free hand, as though acting of its own volition, capitulates on the paralyzed Charlie's behalf, fishing the remaining bill out of his pocket and sticking it in the girl's hand. Given the right circumstances, Charlie's generosity to a young woman can be absolute.

Earlier in *City Lights*, there's a lovely little moment along the same lines, one of those blink-and-you-miss-it moments in Chaplin's films that, accumulated, represent the triumph of his art. Charlie has rediscovered his beloved flower girl and rushes up to his rich friend to get some money so that he may buy flowers from the girl. His friend, drunk, as he always is when he hangs out with Charlie, proffers a massive wad of bills. Charlie plucks one bill and scampers off. But, looking back, he hesitates, mid-scamper. That's a good deal of cash still left in his friend's hand. We sense, again, that same magnetic attraction between Charlie and money, his nearly physical inability to walk away from it. And, again, we note that even the rapture of love doesn't entirely blind his calculating eye. So Charlie returns, plucks a second bill from his friend's hands and dashes away again. But, again, he casts a glance back, still finding it difficult to leave such an opportunity behind. Here he is held suspended in a scamper that no longer moves forward or backward, like the flight of a hummingbird or an object held aloft by opposing currents, in this case greed and love. Finally, love wins; with one last longing look at the cash, Charlie breaks free from his suspended flight and takes off. But that moment of suspension is classic Charlie and classic Chaplin, a moment of combined charity and greed, love tinged with a habitual greed and tendency to larceny. This is what Kerr means when he writes that Chaplin always takes care, in this film, to clean his sentimental scenes with "the sturdy brush of irony."

Chaplin works a lovely variation on this recurrent gag in which Charlie battles with his own selfishness in *A Woman of Paris*. It's one of those many scenes in the film that seem like it could be right out of one of Chaplin's comedies, where the only difference is that an actor is imitating Chaplin rather than Chaplin doing the gag himself. Marie, tired of being a kept woman, throws the pearls that Pierre has given her into the street to make clear to him that she no longer cares for his money. Moments later, she spies, from the same window, a bum finding the necklace and bearing it away. Marie can't get Pierre to retrieve the necklace and so is reduced to the indignity of chasing the bum in her high heels and fashionable garb and grabbing the pearls from him, presenting the comic image of wealthy society woman robbing a penniless man of the streets. He works a variation on the same gag in *City Lights* when Charlie, driving his rich friend's great car, and looking to the world like a man of means, comes to an abrupt halt and darts towards the pavement to steal a smoldering cigar butt from the grasp of another poor hobo, thus presenting the image of a wealthy man stealing a cigar butt from a bum.

Marie chasing the necklace that she had so nobly discarded moments earlier is trademark Chaplin, typical of his tendency to undermine grand gestures and reminiscent of those gags where Charlie too finds it hard to follow up on his supposed indifference to money. It's a fairly significant moment in that film too, as it reflects a cynicism towards one's leading lady that is not typical of the silent film melodrama of the time. Most filmmakers would not be willing to cede that much moral territory in their leading lady. It's reflective of Chaplin's sophistication and artfulness that moments like this don't impinge at all on our empathy for Marie. She's even rather comically cute as she, in the manner of a spoiled child, steals the necklace back but sheepishly leaves the hobo some money in recompense for his loss. This scene typifies the cynicism and determined materialism of Chaplin's cinema, his Maupassant-like ability to create likable characters who have, nevertheless, feet of clay, who in fact are likable precisely *because* they have weaknesses, because they are not implausibly or melodramatically virtuous.

Liquor

Charlie, despite moments of generosity, is an appetitive, materialistic creature, a product of the streets. This is borne out by his devout attention to alcohol. Again we have to note that Charlie's character evolves over the course of Chaplin's films. He drinks much more as a young man. Many of the gags that earned Chaplin repute when he toiled in Fred Karno's traveling band of music hall performers, many of the gags, in fact, that landed him a job in Hollywood in the first place, centered on his expert imitation of drunkenness, born from years of examining the many drunks in his South London neighborhoods, particularly his father, a dipsomaniac who died of liver failure. And so many of Chaplin's early films feature gags built around drunkenness. Certain films, like *A Night Out* and *One A.M.*, find their entire *raison d'etre* in gags sprung from Chaplin's imitation of drunkenness. Many of Chaplin's drinking scenes are among his best. Charlie's attention to drink is a vital expression of his character throughout all of his films. When Charlie drinks, he does so with a kind of refreshing disrespect for authority and all-out commitment to punkishness. There's a refreshing decadence to Charlie's character, embodied in his drinking gags, that runs counter to his saintlier characteristics.

Liquor, too, is one of those things, like a naked statue, a woman's bottom, a pastry, a wad of cash that rivets Charlie's attention, robs him of mind and conscience. Many of Chaplin's gags involving liquor operate under the same principle as his gags involving sex and money: They establish a comically strong, invisible tether between Charlie and his object of devotion. In that scene from *Police*, for example, where robbery victim Edna tries to get Charlie to see the error of his ways, Charlie is the picture of repentance and remorse as Edna streams words of redemption into his ear. At one moment she moves his glass of beer aside as she makes a vehement point and Charlie's humble downward countenance is immediately alerted. He looks up just long enough to quickly bring the glass back to its original spot and then, just as quickly, returns to hanging his head in shame. The scene is reminiscent of those from *The Pilgrim* in which Charlie conducts a sermon while always maintaining a bead on the collection coffers. There are distinct limits as to how much of his attention Charlie can commit to virtue. His eyes tend never to lose sight of their true object of desire.

That liquor plays a significant role in Charlie's life is evident in *The Cure* when he checks into a spa bearing a large trunk that turns out to contain no clothes, only a traveling bar of sorts. When offered a glass of the spa's famous healing waters, he spits it out and rushes to drown its flavor in a bottle of hard liquor. The famous gag from *The Idle Class*, in which Chaplin tricks the audience into thinking he is convulsed in weeping over his lost wife when in actuality he is shaking a cocktail, typifies the general attitude in Chaplin's films that there is little that ranks above drinking in importance. Marriage doesn't seem to represent much of a contest for the pleasures mixed drinks provide here, just as religion doesn't deter Charlie's greed in *Easy Street* and *The Pilgrim*. Later that same character in *The Idle Class* (Charlie plays two characters in the film, his normal Tramp self and a twin aristocrat) dresses for a costume party and goes nearly insane when he realizes that he has encased himself in a knight costume, replete with medieval helmet and visor, before he's had his final drink for the road. The humor of the scene resides in the comic frenzy to which he is reduced by his attempts to escape his iron trap, at one point slamming a door on his head to jar his helmet loose, all for the sake of one last stirrup cup.

That a lust for liquor runs in Charlie's veins is evident in the way that he is constantly on the make for a drink, as he is for a bite to eat. As the scene from *Police* shows, Charlie will keep a surreptitious lookout for drinks even in the midst of lovemaking. Charlie is never too involved in a fight to grab an available drink and down it before returning to the battle. Charlie perpetually cadges drinks, grabs them off passing trays at parties and bars, steals them from neighbors at bars, exchanges smaller glasses for bigger ones when waiters pour his drinks, or tips the waiters elbows so they fill the glass more than they intended. He often bumps into other people at parties in such a way as to make their drink pour into, and refill, his empty glass. Many of Chaplin's best drinking gags involving Charlie downing hard liquor with alarming rapidity, behind the backs of, or under the imperfect surveillance of, suspicious bartenders. When offered liquor freely, for example in those rare moments where he poses as a respectable citizen at a cocktail party, Charlie abandons all social decorum and sets about the task of downing as much booze as he can with the precision of a laborer carefully completing a job.

In *The Adventurer*, Charlie shocks the butler who has presented him with a tray upon which sit a small glass, a bottle of whiskey and a soda bottle. Charlie inspects the glass, but finds it wanting in size. He takes the soda bottle and administers it directly to the bottle of whiskey, keeping the bottle and returning the glass. In an afterthought he flicks his ashes into the glass before dismissing the butler. Later in the same film, the butler will bear a tray with five glasses of wine on it. Charlie checks the staircase to make sure his hostess is out of view before rapidly pouring all the glasses into one and gulping it down.

When a butler in *The Count* wheels a liquor trolley out to where Charlie is flirting with Edna on a bench, Charlie removes all five bottles from the cart and places them on the ground before him and Edna. He briefly inspects the bottle of soda water before deciding to let that remain on the cart. When the waiter offers Charlie a glass, Charlie points to the bottles at his feet to indicate that he's fine with what he has, politely tipping his hat at the butler to dismiss him.

One aspect of drunkenness that is a particular specialty for Chaplin is that moment of drunkenness where the drinker has reached a point of sated oblivion. Hogarth, another British chronicler of impoverished street life, had a particular flair for representing this stage of the drinking evolution as well. As I mentioned earlier, Chaplin is similarly fond of expressing satiety in eating, often depicting Charlie after a meal with a vacant gaze on his face, his mind shut down, his body happily floating on a string of burps. Chaplin specializes in deadpan and the catatonic stage of drunkenness that he favors allows him to maintain an expression of utter neutrality while his body continues to find its way ingeniously to trouble. At this late stage of drunkenness in which he specializes, consciousness has more or less closed up shop and the field is left open for the body to roam in unchecked mischief. Gone is the nervous flutter and chaotic guerrilla warfare that characterizes Charlie's daytime mischief. Catatonically drunk, Charlie is slower and more cruel, less nervous and freer to do what he wants.

Take the restaurant scene in *A Night Out* in which a plastered Charlie annoys a dandy sitting at the next table. Charlie, in his state of drunken stupefaction, tortures this man in several ways. Reeling backwards as he tries to sit down, Charlie's cane seeks purchase on the man's top hat, knocking it to the floor. Settling into his chair with an air of great exhaustion, he rests, with a sigh of relief, his leg on the man's lap, as though the man were an ottoman. (One of Charlie's favored means of aggression, drunk or sober, is to use humans as furniture; and they don't have to be enemies. Later he will try to use Edna as a chair when she bends down to unlock a door.) When the dandy puts his hat on the floor, Charlie uses it as a spittoon.

This provokes the dandy to give Charlie a sound verbal thrashing. Up to this point, Charlie, lost in his oblivion, seems not to have noticed the man he tortures, but now that the dandy has scolded him, he has Charlie's undivided attention. Charlie's look of drunken cordiality dissolves into a kind of fatigued, immobile expression, reflective of profound inebriation but also nascent anger. He leans back in his chair, takes full account of the man, as though he were trying to focus his image, and then very purposefully lifts his cane and knocks the man's top hat off his head. The man's hat is the perfect target because each time he had primly reproved Charlie, he had followed his admonishment with a smarmy tipping of his hat. Charlie hadn't really retained consciousness of the man's admonishments, but the tipping of the hat had stuck in his craw.

As the dandy and Charlie square off chin to chin, Chaplin makes my favorite gesture of the scene. Chaplin has a habit, that I discuss in my section on Chaplin's lampooning of male posturing, of removing his suit jacket halfway down his back in moments of drunken aggression. The gesture is a sign that he's ready to fight, but only a sign. In the end, it's really Chaplin's satire of the way men posture when drunk, parading their aggression like a bird or a dog might, with no real intention of following though. It's one of the ways Chaplin has fun with men's peacock nature. Here, though, Charlie is too drunk to accomplish even this action. All he can manage here is a kind of cursory, fatigued outward flapping of his lapels. The dandy doesn't notice the gesture, only we do, and only because we recognize it as a kind of thumbnail reference to a familiar gag, a bit of minimalist self-reflexivity on Chaplin's part. Charlie's not only too drunk to fight here, he's too drunk even to engage in his typical mockery of fighting. Charlie drunk is Chaplin's humor slowed down to a crawl, Charlie, but jelled in aspic. The humor here is also in how little Charlie cares about, or is even conscious of, his actions. In these scenes, he creates chaos while barely taking stock of what he's doing, in the manner of a great artist who, all the while wearing a bland expression, tosses off a work of great virtuosity with seeming effortlessness.

There is some complexity involved in analyzing Charlie and drinking. First off, many of Chaplin's drinking films, like *One A.M.* and *The Cure*, involve a character who is not entirely recognizable as Charlie. These characters are partly comprised of leftovers from the aristocratic sot of Chaplin's music hall days. Secondly, as the Tramp evolves he drinks less. By the time of *City Lights*, things have changed so dramatically that Charlie actually wrinkles his nose at the drink offered him by his drunk, rich friend, one of the moments that most testifies to Chaplin's desire to soften the Tramp in his later years. This tendency has to be, at least in part, a reflection of Chaplin's consciousness that his public was increasingly finding his morals wanting. But perhaps it also reflects a simple gentling in Chaplin's character as he got older, a lack of interest in playing a cocky youth.

Nevertheless, inebriation and intoxication remain central to Charlie's persona right up to the end of his films, even in his teetotalling years. Charlie may evince distaste for alcohol at the outset of *City Lights* but he is still drunk for a good portion of the rest of the film. Chaplin still delights in a drunk Charlie in that film, which is to say a more chaotic, less moral Charlie, for example in that moment when, drunk and sexually aroused by watching so many beautiful women dancing, Charlie leaps on a poor unsuspecting matron and spins her off on a chaotic dance.

Charlie becomes more passive in the ways that he arrives at inebriation in the later films. The rich friend insists he drink in *City Lights*. In *Modern Times*, he accidentally drinks ale at the shopping mall and unknowingly imbibes cocaine in prison. But in all these scenes it's the crazy id of the old Charlie that resurfaces. Charlie rediscovers his old fighting skills under the influence of cocaine. And we relish the *Modern Times* gag where Charlie is discovered, passed out and hidden under a collection of fabrics, by a customer who mistakes his shirt tails for a piece of material she might buy, the night after his debauchery at the shopping mall. Charlie may soften as the years go by but he never passes too much time sober. He evinces, up to the end of his films, a gift for intoxication. Even in his later, more saintly guise, Charlie still has his Bacchic habits.

Ten

Charlie and Women

In the following three chapters, I will examine the fictional world that Chaplin creates via the ongoing story of Charlie. One unifying principle that is helpful in getting hold of all of Chaplin's films starring Charlie is to think of them all as representations of one continuous war, a war in which Charlie has very specific allies and enemies. That Charlie's life convenes as naturally as it does to the metaphor of a war may point to the Existential nature of Chaplin's films. Charlie is under constant stress. He knows no final rest or peace. Whatever peace or happiness he experiences tends to be temporary and enjoyed within a much larger context of fear and privation. Charlie's enemies in this war are almost entirely men, aside from a few stuffy society matrons. These men come in several forms: husbands and fathers who thwart his efforts at romance, policemen who constantly harass him for his vagrancy, and bosses and co-workers who are perpetually annoyed by his incompetence at most every job he takes on and by his natural tendency to play rather than work.

The allies are far and few between, as Charlie has a good deal of the Existential loner about him, a quality which Chaplin emphasized in those films where, whether Charlie has found temporary companionship or not, he finishes by walking alone down a road that disappears into the depth of the screen. But Charlie does find some friends along his way. Three particular allies in his struggle with men are women (particularly pretty and poor young women), children and dogs. Charlie relates to all three because they are, like him, powerless sorts, lacking in wealth, respect or social standing. Charlie's particular comic persona draws a good deal from Chaplin's observations of children and dogs. And Charlie has a pronounced feminine side as well, from which he also draws humor and which predisposes him to be more comfortable around women than men.

In many ways, there is no more important element to Chaplin's comedy, or Charlie's persona, than Charlie's attitude towards women. It's Charlie's relationships with women that gives Chaplin's greatest films their depth and emotional resonance, the charm and seriousness that separates Chaplin from conventional comic fare. You can more or less date the moment when critics started to take Chaplin seriously as an artist to the time when Edna Purviance, with whom Charlie was involved in a relationship at the time, began to appear in his films. The films that critics tend to point to as landmarks in the development of Charlie's character (*The Tramp, The Bank, The Vagabond, The Immigrant*) are those in which Charlie cares for a woman or suffers at her hands. With the exception of *The Kid*, all of his crowning accomplishments in feature-length film involve a sweet and sad love story.

There are, of course, many great Chaplin films that don't center exclusively on a love story. *The Pawnshop* and *The Pilgrim* are top-tier Chaplins that are not dependent on Charlie's relationship to a woman for their success. But even those films have moments of sweetness between Charlie and Edna that draw out clever and touching aspects in Charlie's character. For the most part, no matter how far you go back in Chaplin's oeuvre, the film's likelihood of providing that which we most look for in Chaplin's films increases if Charlie is pursuing women. Women introduce Charlie to qualities that have been missing in his life of constant street warfare with male figures of authority. They awaken an interest in flowers, the gentler passions, morality, beauty and art. They soften Charlie, drawing out idealistic, chivalric qualities in him, characteristics of loyalty, kindness and devotion that are at odds with his otherwise mer-

Charlie is much more of a rogue and roué in his earlier films than in his later ones (here in *The Masquerader* with two unidentified players). Like many men, he mellows with age.

ciless contention with the world. They represent a salvation from the barren, Hobbesian, male-dominated world of professionalism, work, competition, violence and brutality. I don't think it's stated quite strongly enough how anti-male Chaplin's cinema is. More or less abandoned by his father, and warmed for his entire life by memories of a much closer relationship with his mother, Chaplin had a twin genius for satirizing men and poeticizing women.

Charlie's Eros

Charlie, of course, was not always the lovelorn harlequin that he became in the last silent features. In many ways, his development in regards to women over the years matches that of many men: Almost belligerently sexual early on, he softens in his attitude to women as time goes by. Increasingly, dreams of home and domestic bliss crowd his thoughts until we arrive at what is ostensibly the last film of the Tramp, *Modern Times*. More than any other Chaplin film, it represents an ode to domesticity.

Early on, however, Charlie is aggressively on the make with women. He coolly appraises their behinds, crowds them on park benches, flirts aggressively with them, making himself so at home with them that he often throws a leg over their laps. Sometimes he gets so lost in his excited flirtations that he borders on physical abuse. In those early films, Charlie uses his cane to draw women to him, lift their skirts and, with feigned unawareness, tap them on the behind.

It's no coincidence that Chaplin's early films are characterized by both a more sexually aggressive Charlie and more swordplay with his cane. Charlie's cane acts as a kind of barometer of his sexual energy. Often the sight of a woman's behind will reduce Charlie to mute immobility except for his cane, which spins more wildly, just one of the many ways in which Chaplin balances neutral expressions with animate bodily movement. Tentacle-like, Charlie's cane strikes out wildly. It seems to move of its own power and with cunning, serpentine alacrity. It's an aerial id of sorts and will only slow in its sport with the advance of the years.

Charlie's cane is a psychoanalyst's dream come true, a disembodied phallus of sorts that seems to pursue its own agenda with women, acting in utter disregard of Charlie's conscious intent. At least that's how Charlie would have it seem. In *Getting Acquainted*, Charlie, using his cane hand to doff his hat, also manages to lift Mabel Normand's skirt, just one of dozens of moments in Chaplin's films where his cane helps Charlie find his way to a view of a woman's leg. Charlie affects surprise at what he's done, giggles a bit, then taps his cane on its handle, as though it were its head, and scolds it for its misbehavior. That his irritation with the cane is not real is suggested by the reconciliatory kiss he gives it moments later. Charlie's cane is his means for entry into territory where he is otherwise not allowed.

To say that women are important to Charlie, or that he is attracted to them, is an understatement. One of the recurrent gags in Chaplin's cinema is the way the mere presence of a woman will stop Charlie dead in his tracks. The humor in these gags is in the contrast between Charlie's animacy before the woman arrives, his immobility after, his intense concern with whatever matter is at hand before, his absolute indifference after. Often an attractive woman need only flash a bit of ankle, walk by him in a revealing outfit, or provide a glimpse of her bottom and Charlie will drop whatever

he is doing and follow her in a kind of trance as though his mind had shut down and his body assumed full control of his actions.

One of the most perfectly timed small gags in *The Kid* occurs near the end in Charlie's strange dream, that odd little moral allegory concerning sin and temptation. A demonic figure has just cursed Charlie with lust and instructed a young girl angel (played by the girl who would become Chaplin's second wife, Lita Grey) to "vamp" the vulnerable Charlie. The gag is typical of Chaplin in the way it works through slow accumulation. Slow accumulation also accurately describes the way Charlie's eros tends to operate. Women stun him and then, when he finally collects himself, he tends to explode in energy.

The young girl sidles up to Charlie, who had been innocently playing a lyre, and whispers into his ear. Chaplin, typically, inscribes Charlie's response to her flirtations in the tiniest gestures. His eyebrows rise in intrigue and his hand strums the lyre a little more furiously. Both details testify to that way Chaplin has of capitalizing on cinema's ability to register the quietest of details and his tendency, accordingly, to speak to us via his hands and eyes.

Charlie's cane seemed to reach out directly from his id. He'd use it to abuse men and tease women. The cane is more integral to the earlier films when Charlie was something of a cad.

But, of course, Charlie has not been visited by lust for very long as of yet, so he doesn't quite understand the feelings which the young angel awakens in him. She lifts her skirt for him, revealing her ankle, and *that* gets his attention. He drops his lyre and follows her obediently. She stops near a building and casts flirtatious glances at Charlie before disappearing around the corner. But Charlie is still slow on the uptake. He turns and looks at the audience, as Charlie often does in moments of sexual confusion. This feeling is obviously new to him. She calls his attention again from around the corner and he turns back to her but, still, only stares at her in confusion.

However, when she extends, by itself, her bare ankle from behind the building, Charlie's response is immediate, eruptive: He makes a beeline towards the very spot where the ankle presented itself, and more literally than you might think, as Chaplin is attached to wires that allow him to fly with extraordinary speed and velocity to that spot. The stunt allows Chaplin to create an image of sexual response that is actually stronger and more immediate than regular, ambulatory humans are capable of. Charlie's libido is no small thing. Women have a powerfully disruptive effect on his consciousness. The humor is also, of course, in the timing. Charlie, just awakening to the nature of lust, takes a while to gather his wits but when he does, his reaction is superhumanly spasmodic. The comedy is in the slow build-up of the gag and its lightning-fast payoff.

A similarly comic moment occurs in *The Count*. Charlie is at a costume party, talking with his girlfriend, when a woman in a revealing costume pauses near him. Her presence has a riveting effect on Charlie. His posture intensifies, his expression becomes laughably vague and he finds it increasingly difficult to maintain his banter with his girl. He steals surreptitious looks at the attractive woman, her behind in particular. When she walks away, though, and he gets a long look at that backside in action, all attempts to fight his impulse disappear. Charlie parts from his girlfriend with an outrageously cursory "see you later" tip of his head and follows the scantily glad girl up the stairs and out of the room. The woman's physical attractiveness robs Charlie of all will, decency and consciousness. Chaplin seems to be emphasizing how dormant an organ the male brain is during moments of lust. The next few scenes find Charlie following her like a duckling might its mother, from a distance, but wherever she goes, from room to room, inside the mansion to outside and back inside again, his mind is entirely absent, his movements purely instinctual.

Explosions of Sexual Excitement

Charlie's reaction to women is often like this, not just intense, but insane, not just instant but spasmodic. Some of the greatest moments in Chaplin's films are those when a woman returns his favor, perhaps only in the slightest way, and sends him into paroxysms of chaotic glee, during which no nearby object or bystander is safe from assault. In *The Floorwalker,* for example, department store manager Charlie follows a woman with engaging ankles to the shoe department where he helps her try on shoes. Charlie often contrives situations where he can help women with their shoes. This allows him to get closer to his beloved ankles and to tickle their feet, one of his favorite methods of winning women over. Charlie gets so giggly and excited as he tickles the woman's toes that he can't contain himself and, in nervous abandon, shoves the shoe attendant, serving a customer next to him, off his stool. Charlie then leaps, *à la* Douglas Fairbanks, onto a tall ladder that runs on grooves along the wall of shoes. He flies off on the ladder in search of the pretty customer's shoes, one leg extended in mock balletic arabesque pose. When the other shoe salesman chases after him, Charlie socks him in the face and reverses the ladder, sailing back to his lovely customer, her shoes in hand, leg still extended in flirtatious ecstasy.

In such moments, Charlie doesn't mean to be cruel to innocent bystanders, such as the shoe salesman here. It's just that his amorous emotions are so explosive that there are bound to be victims of friendly fire. Of all of Charlie's eruptions when visited by Eros, my favorite is in *The Count* when that woman that Charlie follows around finally returns Charlie's affection, smiling at him. There's really no explaining the logic of Charlie's actions in these moments. When a woman returns his favor, he falls prey to emotions he can't contain and so acts wildly, irrationally. Here the flirtation occurs at an elegant party, just in front of a fancy buffet table upon which rests, among other things, a roast turkey and an elaborate cake structured like the Taj Mahal. Couples dance nearby.

The woman's smile first reduces Charlie to his standard childish giggles and body contortions. Charlie tends to diminish in years when he flirts. Then Charlie does what he often does when he wants to impress a lady: amuse her with tricks. Here of course Charlie's cane (always a barometer of sexual pressure) comes into play. He turns his cane into a pretend sword and starts to skewer the turkey as though it were an opponent in a fencing match. It's not really a logical maneuver in terms of impressing a woman, but in moments like these Charlie is doing more improvising than thinking. Lifting the enormous turkey into the air on the edge of his "sword," Charlie unaccountably smashes it over the head of the liveried servant serving just behind the table. Again, there's no accounting for why Charlie must punish others when he's besotted. He's just drunk with energy that he does not know what to do with.

The woman doesn't help matters when she chooses that moment to adjust her shoe, bending over slightly and treating Charlie to a generous view of her behind. This triggers an even more explosive burst of energy in Charlie. It's a tie between women's ankles and their bottoms as to which most sets Charlie off. Now he paces back and forth in a kind of repressed panic, throttling his cane as though he were strangling it, before approaching the cake, which he begins to attack with fierce baseball swings, using his cane as a bat, exploding the sculpture and sending messy chunks of heavily frosted cake cascading across the dance floor, several of which fortuitously strike the men the film has already identified as hostile to Charlie. He turns back to the woman every now and then with his childlike expressions of flirtation. (She's more stunned than responsive by now.) New surges of energy return him to the cake, upon which he continues to rain blows, great explosions of baseballs swings. Charlie's sexual attraction for women is volcanic, its effect epic. You don't want to be around Charlie when he has a fit of eros.

Of course, Charlie's sexuality changes over the course of Chaplin's films. Dan Kamin has astutely noted that "as Chaplin's sex life became the subject of tabloid headlines, his screen character became less sexually aggressive."[1] Of course, Charlie ages for over twenty years in his films and it only makes sense that, over the years, his sexuality would gentle and his attitude to women deepen. Still, the opposition between the sexually charged early Charlie and the virginal late Charlie can be overstated. As early as *The Bank* in 1915, we see the heartbroken dreamer and as late as *Modern Times* he's in high–Satyr mode, using his mechanic's wrenches to suggest a faun's goat ears and chasing women whose outfits with buttons on their breasts and backsides suggest to him, in his work-induced madness, screws that need to be riveted.

In fact, one of Chaplin's latest films, *City Lights,* has one of Chaplin's best renderings of Charlie's spasmodic fits of eros. Charlie and his wealthy benefactor are celebrating New Year's Eve. An inebriated Charlie sits at a table by a dance floor watching the dancers with a look of intense concentration, while keeping beat with his hand on the table. A young woman parks herself just before Charlie. She's so excited by the prospect of the dance that she begins to gyrate wildly as she waits for her boyfriend to join her, shaking her hips in a dance for which Charlie alone has a front row seat. Charlie stares at her intensely but is careful not to betray his agitation. He has that look, that Chaplin so cherished, of concentrated neutrality, the one drunks get when they are trying to hold it together, one of those many moments in his films where he contrasts an external neutrality with an incipient, internal agitation. The only detail that betrays his excitement is the way that his hand, which was tapping the table, freezes in mid-air as soon as the young woman starts to gyrate.

Of course, when Charlie goes immobile like this, it often means storms are brewing within, the mind shutting down, the body gearing up for action. The woman is swirled off to the dance floor by her beau and Charlie looks away a little, as though he were coming up for air; temptation has been averted. When his gaze returns to the dance floor, however, another woman now stands before him. She too is waiting for her dance partner. This woman, however, is much more matronly than the first and certainly not given to any gyrations or seductive movements. She's simply holding out her arms for her silver-haired partner, who approaches from behind Charlie. But it's too late; the pump has been primed. As soon as the drunken Charlie sets eyes on the poor woman he pounces, spinning her off crazily onto the dance floor, her husband in pursuit. The humor of the gag resides, as it so often does in Chaplin's films, in the lag of Charlie's reaction. The older Charlie still has a libido, even if his timing is a little off.

Charlie even retains, in his later films, some of his ability to wittily charm women in the manner of an experienced rake, for example, in the scene from *The Kid* where he flirts with the woman whose window he is fixing. But increasingly, Charlie becomes less a conventional comic study in amoral male behavior and more a complex representation of a kind of male sexuality that veers wildly from aggressiveness to shyness, from lasciviousness to innocence, that at one point seems hardened and cynical and at others quite naive and childish, sometimes driven by sexual desire, other times by fantasies of domestic bliss. In the end, Charlie is characterized by a multifarious sexuality that has something to say about the contradictions, paradoxes and inconsistencies in all men's attitude to women.

Charlie and Inanimate Women

Chaplin also registers Charlie's highly sexualized nature in scenes where Charlie comes across representations of scantily clad women. In *A Woman,* for example, Charlie (hiding from an angry father upstairs in the father's house) comes across a woman's dress on a headless mannequin. The idea occurs to him that he can escape by donning the outfit and appearing as a woman. Chaplin turns the removal of the dress from the mannequin into a gentle seduction. He looks away discreetly from the mannequin as he undresses it, with a look of nervous and excited *but respectful* affection. He is an ardent but still ginger lover. As he removes the last article of clothing, he puts his fingers to his lips, urging his mute companion to calm and discretion.

This gag is actually a little atypical in that Charlie seems to play the role of the confident, accomplished lover. But there are few roles beyond the scope of Charlie's mimicry and we should never confuse Chaplin with the roles he plays. More typically, when Charlie comes across the image of a naked woman, it staggers him with confusion and draws out virginal aspects of his nature. The opening shot of *His New Profession* is an unusually close-up shot of Charlie stumbling across a picture of a bathing beauty while reading *The Police Gazette*. Till that moment he had been bored by the magazine, stifling a yawn. But as soon as his eyes rest on the picture, his comportment changes. He knits his brows as though he's come upon something troubling. He meets the gaze of the audience with a look of vague reflection. He's not so much looking at us as looking *out* at us as he gathers his thoughts. He holds the picture back from some distance as though it were a work of art, or something he's trying to puzzle out. He tries to go back to reading the *Gazette* but is constantly drawn back to the picture of the girl. Finally, his lips curl in the slightest smile and he steals a surreptitious glance of complicity at the audience. Scenes like this suggest an innocence to Charlie even in his aggressive, highly sexed incarnation of the early films. He reacts to sex in a manner that is half virginal nervousness, half giggly childishness. He may be interested in sex but he's nervous about it also and, like a child, thinks it's funny.

More commonly in Chaplin's films, Charlie has comic encounters with statues of nude women, a gag we see played out in *His New Job, A Jitney Elopement, Behind the Screen, Work* and *City Lights*. In *Behind the Screen*, in which Charlie is a movie studio prop man, he realizes that a statue of a male nude rests at such an angle that it seems to be scrutinizing a nearby statue of a female nude. Affecting the gestures of a man saving his buddy from trouble, Charlie moves the statue to another part of the room.

Chaplin's most developed use of the statue gag may be in *Work* where Charlie, a painter's assistant, finds his attention drawn to a small decorative statue of a naked woman. Throughout the first twelve minutes of the film Charlie's attention is riveted to the statue. He steals dozens of surreptitious glances at it as he goes about his job and often picks it up to examine it, usually having to put it down again with false nonchalance when his boss or employer comes by. He pretends not to care much about the statue when others are in the room but finds any excuse to gravitate back to it, at one point striking his match against its base. There seems to be an invisible tether between Charlie and the object of his desire here just as there is between Charlie and the women he follows around robotically in other films.

Free, at one point, to inspect the statue at leisure, Charlie removes a small shade, with fringe tassels, from a nearby lamp and puts it on the statue, transforming the carved nude into Polynesian beauty in a grass skirt. Charlie moves the statue to make it dance a little and then sneaks a peak under the skirt, guiltily smiling at the camera after he does so. Sexual situations often intensify Charlie's self-consciousness before the audience. At moments of greatest privacy he's reminded that we are out there. Here again we see that same mixture of infantilism and lasciviousness. Charlie flirts with the woman in *The Count* like a child, at one moment writhing in giggly ecstasy, the next knocking things down to impress her. Here his sexuality mingles with the games of a child.

Chaplin reprised the statue gag years later in *City Lights* when Charlie, wandering the city streets, happens on a full-sized statue of a naked woman in the window display of an art dealer. Charlie obviously wants to stare his eyeballs out at it but is too self-conscious to do so. The scene is shot from inside the store through the window, from behind the statue, looking out at Charlie, with the business of the city street behind him. As in *Work*, Charlie initially feigns indifference, pretending to look only at a statue of a rearing horse next to the nude, while, as in the scene from *Work*, stealing as many glances at the nude as he can. Tiring of this method, he assumes the appraising manner of an art connoisseur, so that he may drink in the statue at his ease. He cocks his head, moves backward and forward to see it from different distances, and makes vague gestures with his hands that suggest he is somehow examining its proportions.

Both of these gags are gentle satires of our own surreptitiousness when faced with erotic images in public, but they are also expressive of Charlie's particular obsession with women's bodies, his comic, near–physical inability to shake the thought of a woman's body. They are also expressions of innocence as well as lasciviousness. Charlie's reactions to the statue are more typical of a child than a man, someone for whom sex is still new, confusing and mysterious. Alive or in representations, women tend to stop Charlie dead in his tracks, to cross all his wires in confusion.

Charlie's Femininity

We know Charlie can be as tough as a scrap-yard dog. But another aspect of his uniquely balanced nature is how that toughness co-exists with strongly feminine tendencies that separate him from his more conventionally masculine comic peers. One of the curious aspects of Charlie's nature is that, despite what is often a frenzied sexuality, and though he is sometimes sexually aggressive towards women, women don't fear him much. In fact they are quite comfortable with his flirtations and often enjoy his company. One of the reasons women are comfortable with Charlie is that there is, in the end, very little masculine bravado or intimidation to him. Charlie's very outfit represents a kind of reversal of the male physical ideal. His small suit jacket accentuates the smallness of his shoulders, his baggy pants and big shoes his bottom heaviness. He is a pyramid that finds its base on the ground whereas the male ideal aims for a well-chiseled triangle that finds its widest horizontal in the shoulder.

Dan Kamin breaks down nicely some of Charlie's feminine characteristics, for example, his tendency to rest his hands high up on his hips or his tendency to touch others so often and so appreciatively.[2] David Thomson notes, "[T]he delicacy of Chaplin's own features, the Italianate daintiness of his gestures, and above all, the mooning after misty emotional contentment are feminine characteristics as conceived by an exquisite man."[3] Indeed, he notes, "Chaplin's persona is often very close to eighteenth-century sentimentality: a beautifully mannered dreamer who has trained himself into the emotional sensibility that will sometimes shame a woman with its refinement."

Thompson might be referring to those scenes in Chaplin's films, for example, where he lovingly arranges a note and flower for Edna in *The Bank,* or more famously in his dinner preparations for Georgia and her gang in *The Gold Rush,* where we see Charlie put more aesthetic care and loving detail into his approach to women than, it turns out, they deserve.

It is noteworthy, not only that Chaplin has distinct feminine characteristics, but how boldly he exploits them, and not just in those films like *Masquerade* or *A Woman,* where he literally dresses in the costume of a woman. Chaplin's comedy is distinct in the ease and confidence with which he plays with his feminine side. There's very little masculine insecurity to the Tramp. Even when he does play the tough guy, it's mostly an act, almost a parody of masculine habits and aggressiveness. Charlie is only a visitor to the world of men.

One of the things we like about Charlie in *The Kid* is the way he warms to the role of mother. Take the scene where, with a warm dinner heating on the stove, Charlie sits the kid on his lap and gives him a cleanliness inspection. He checks his hands for grime, dabs his neck clean with his own spit, and inspects his hair for nits. He blows the child's nose and, in a gesture repeated from earlier films, winds his handkerchief into a fine point that allows him to delicately clean each nostril.

In fact, the scene is a reprisal of one in *The Vagabond,* when Charlie cleans up the poor uneducated girl he has saved from vicious gypsies. Charlie cleans Edna up in much the same way that he will the kid, including the nostril bit, though here he uses a sock as his washcloth. But he goes even further in this scene. Playacting as Edna's hairdresser, he helps her comb and pin up her hair (sacrificing a pin with which he held up his pants). He also prepares dinner for her, turning a big tub upside down for a table, spreading his shirt over it for a tablecloth and tying the sleeves up in neat bundles that will serve as napkins.

Charlie often takes pleasure in, and demonstrates a great flair for, domestic tasks like these. He bustles around in the makeshift homes that he repeatedly creates out of nothing in his films with the competent air of a practiced housewife. *The Kid* is filled with all sorts of fine makeshift domestic details, like the potty chair Charlie devises out of an old bamboo kitchen chair and the milk bottle from an old tea kettle, both inventions for the infant he brings home. In the films where he cohabits with men, Charlie often assumes the role of domestic caretaker. He is happy to bustle in the kitchen and get meals on the table for Mack Swain in *The Gold Rush* and Tom Wilson in *Sunnyside.* His meals are eccentric but also ingenious, for example the way he fashions a Thanksgiving dinner out of his old boot in *The Gold Rush* and the way he gets a chicken to lay its egg directly onto the skillet in *Sunnyside.*

One of the things that makes *The Gold Rush*'s New Year's Eve sequence (when Charlie hosts a party to which nobody comes) so moving is that Chaplin takes the time to show us how much care Charlie has put into his dinner party for the young women he expects. Here again he moves around his cabin with the consummate efficiency, self-satisfaction and skill of a seasoned host, with the air of someone who has mastered the domestic arts. The cabin is festooned with decorative garlands, and an adorned Christmas tree sits in the corner. The table is elegantly set (the tablecloth a newspaper this time) with place settings, candles and place cards. Charlie is dressed to the nines (for him) and fully prepared for his evening's entertainment. Moments before his guests' expected arrival he moves about his place with quiet deliberation and confident pleasure as he marinates a roast in the oven and looks to the final details of his preparations. He very ceremoniously removes presents from the tree and places them on the table, a present for each guest. He places a wrapped New Year's Eve cracker in each glass.

This scene is a good example of the subtlety of Chaplin's approach to pathos. Charlie's sadness when the girls don't arrive touches us, not just because the little man looks so sad, but because we have seen the delicacy and thoughtfulness of the kindnesses he had in store for them. This is what Thomson means when he writes of an "emotional sensibility that will sometimes shame a woman with its refinement."

Despite his default status as a vagrant, Charlie relishes domesticity and, especially as the years go by, harbors a dream of domestic paradise (as we see in the dreams of domestic bliss in both *Sunnyside* and *Modern Times*). But again we do not want to overstate the difference between Chaplin's early and late films. Charlie, from early on, likes to spend time with women and to do womanly things with them. As early as *A Woman* we see Charlie happily ensconced between Edna and her mother having afternoon tea. He loves to share the kitchen with the objects of his affection, making donuts and washing dishes with Edna in *The Pawnshop* and making a cake with her in *The Pilgrim*. Charlie likes not only to be with women, but to be in their worlds, to do the things women traditionally did: cook, set up house, have tea, mother. He prefers the domestic arts to masculine industry.

Charlie is at his happiest with women. He likes to be with them, to socialize with them in large groups. He likes to be one of them. It's striking how often Charlie finds himself with not just one but with a whole bevy of women, as for example when he flirts with an entire harem of scantily clad young cave women in *His Prehistoric Past*. Charlie lives for these moments where he can lose himself in a sea of femininity and is often at his most playful and entertaining when he has an audience of women, as for instance in *Those Love Pangs* where Charlie, blessed with two female companions at the cinema, sits with his arms around both while entertaining them with a story that he acts out with his legs. In his dreams it's often just Charlie alone with a number of young women, for example in the dream of *Sunnyside* in which he dances ecstatically with four nymphs or the dream from *The Gold Rush* where he entertains four for dinner.

Of course there's an element of male fantasy in a dream in which you are surrounded by women and there's certainly an erotic air to the dream of *Sunnyside* with its scantily clad sylvan nymphs. But those dreams seem to be as much about the saving grace of feminine company as they are about women's erotic charms. In these dreams Charlie thrills, with a childlike glee, to the mere companionship of women.

In the *Gold Rush* dream, for example, all of Chaplin's considerable mime skills go into conveying how much Charlie likes being with these women. With his barely restrained glee and carefully maintained table manners, he puts one in mind of a young girl experiencing the greatest tea party of her life. The nymphs in the *Sunnyside* dream occasion Charlie's most emphatic expression of pure, childlike happiness: his famous skip, with knees bent out, arms akimbo. Both dreams represent celebrations not just of women but of women's company. Being with women frees Charlie from the masculine requirements that don't come naturally to him and which dog and confuse him in the world of police, employment and conventional courtship, with its fathers and brothers and husbands. With woman alone, he's free to be a child, free to indulge his feminine interests as much as he wants. With women he's safe, home.

Charlie's Affection for Women

Some of the scenes in which we get our best sense of the sheer delight Charlie takes in women are those where he is reunited with the woman he loves after a long separation. These scenes are singular to Chaplin. Here, Charlie expresses a glee that is childish in its abandon and feminine in its warmth, a kind of affection that, in its exuberance, sometimes seems outside the normal parameters of masculine courtship.

For example, in *Sunnyside*, Charlie wakes from a dream in which he has lost Edna to the rich city slicker (Tom Terris) who is staying at the store-inn where Charlie works. When Charlie wakes up and realizes, to his great relief, that this tragic scenario was only a dream and that Edna is still his, he is jubilant. His first chore upon waking is to carry Terris' luggage to the car, and as he does so, Edna walks into the inn. As soon as Charlie sees Edna, he drops all the luggage and runs to her. He doesn't so much hug her as clothes-line her from behind, knocking her hat over her face and nearly strangling her with his hold on her from behind, as he buries kisses into her neck.

Spying the hated Terris from the corner of his eye, while he holds Edna, Charlie instinctively threatens him with a forearm, as though Terris were at that moment trying to steal Edna from him, though of course Terris has no idea what's going on, no idea that he competed with Charlie for Edna's favor in Charlie's dreams. Charlie lifts Edna's hand before Terris' face to display her engagement ring (Edna also doesn't know what's going on), shoves him and then, as though Terris were begging for a fight, falls into his best imitation of a dancing pugilist. Terris, bewildered by Charlie's behavior, just wants to make his way to his car.

As Terris leaves town, Charlie runs after the car, holding Edna's hand, dragging her along and skipping with trademark childish jubilation, the skip that he falls into when women return his affection. The film finishes with Charlie, the car gone, turning to Edna, rearing his arms back and giving her another hug. He kicks one leg back as he embraces her, a gesture that gives his posture a more feminine quality than Edna's; Charlie is always a bit of a dancer in his moments of elation.

Chaplin had a gift, in this manner, for physically expressing the sheer bliss of having someone to love. He's able to express this glee so effectively because his gestures are different than the typical male suitor's. They're unguarded. Clutching someone from behind, holding hands and skipping, kicking a leg back in a hug—these are gestures that mix childishness and femininity with masculine appreciation. Charlie doesn't stop to consider whether he is being dignified or masculine. He just erupts with happiness.

One of the most striking aspects of these scenes in which Charlie showers his beloved with affection is how expressive Charlie's hands are. During Charlie's speech in the dream from *Gold Rush*, for example, his hands seems to have a life of their own as they stray all over Georgia's hand and arm, which he holds during the speech. It's one of those moments that Chaplin specializes in, where his body expresses itself separately from his mind. Absorbed in his speech, Charlie does not seem conscious of the fact that his hands are engaged in this gentle dance up and down Georgia's arm. Charlie's doing his best to say some charming and dignified words, but his hands are expressive of uncontainable elation.

When Charlie is reunited with Edna at the restaurant in *The Immigrant* it's his hands that best express his delight. He rubs them together in glee, clasps them to his chest in delight, covers her hands in his and draws them to his chest as he looks at her with explosive happiness. When they tuck into their meal together, he squeezes her arm to communicate how happy he is that she is there. Many of these gestures are repeated in the scenes from *Modern Times* where Charlie is reunited with Paulette after his stints in jail. Charlie's hands constantly flit over his objects of devotion, not in sexual longing (that's more the domain of his cane and his eyes), but in expression of affection, as if he were touching them to make sure they are real, or out of a superabundance of joy. Chaplin is something of a poet of reunion. He specializes in those moments, early in relationships, where lovers are astonished by how happy they are just to be in each other's presence.

Charlie's relationship with the child in *The Kid* is characterized also by this striking physicality. I find that modern audiences are still struck by the intimacy that exists between Charlie and the boy, the way he kisses his toes when the child is a baby, the long mouth-to-mouth kisses of the father and son when they are reunited after the orphanage has tried to steal the child away. Audiences spy an openness and intimacy in Charlie's relation to the child that is not typical of male-child relationships in cinema. Charlie's love is lavish, physical, and generous.

Chaplin's films are filled with moments when Charlie is simply brimming with happiness in the company of women. In these scenes he expresses the simple, universal pleasure of being in love. There is a certain plausibility to women responding favorably to the scruffy Charlie despite his obvious deficiencies in wealth, masculinity and sophistication. He's not cagey; he wears his emotions on his sleeve. From his earliest, spasmodic stirrings of sexual attraction, to his blissful dances in homage to partnership and domesticity, Charlie is an open book. He couldn't hide his feelings if he tried. When it comes to expressions of affection, no woman will ever find Charlie wanting.

Ecstatic Love Scenes

As I discussed above, one of the great triumphs of Chaplin's films are those scenes where Charlie, charged by the slightest bit of erotic urging, goes absolutely crazy, turning into a destructive force and wreaking havoc on all nearby. These scenes are comic and ecstatic evocations of how sensitively he vibrates to the physical presence of women. But there are equally glorious scenes in which Charlie goes insane, not out of erotic excitement, but from the elation of love. Here, the energy boost comes from the dizzying prospect that a woman might care for him, simply from the prospect of female companionship. Not surprisingly, we see the sexual ecstasy more in the early films, the love ecstasy more in the latter.

One of the greatest scenes in all of Chaplin's films has to be the one from *The Gold Rush* that follows Georgia's acceptance, on her and her friend's part, to Charlie's New Year's Eve party. (They are only pulling Charlie's leg and have no intention of showing up, but Charlie doesn't know that.) Charlie sends the women off with a dignified farewell and then, reentering his little shack, goes bananas. In a matter of a few moments, he kicks over his dining room table, swings like an ape from his rafters, jumps on his bed, and punches out a huge bag of flour, sending sheets of white powder flying across the room. He leaps to the ground, grabs a pillow and, punching it madly, demolishes it, creating a cascade of feathers as well. He does a handstand on the bed, then, after falling from the headstand onto the floor, grabs another pillow and sends a second shower of shimmering feathers into the air. The entire sequence, astonishingly, transpires in twenty seconds and finishes with the flour-bedecked Charlie staring at the camera in vacant contentment as he sits on the floor, feathers swirling about him. He exhales deeply, sending several of the feathers stuck to his face flying into the air.

Chaplin, here, takes the energy inherent in the first throes of love and transforms it into a tangible kineticism. He creates a visual explosion of love. The way the feathers catch the light in this scene give it a finely detailed, shimmering effect. As we have seen, this made the scene one of Chaplin's favorites in the film, the one where he felt he was able "extend myself to the full," creating "a sort of visual music."[4]

What's most characteristic about this scene is its abandon, its boundless glee, the way in which Charlie goes nuts in his excitement over women. It's the most intense and visual expression of the anarchic glee a person feels mounting in their heart at the prospect of requited love that I've ever seen in film. What other character would let himself go this far, be this uncool? And of course Charlie pays for that lack of cool, when Georgia returns, seeking a glove she left behind, and sees the wreckage her small expression of affection has occasioned. And the scene, unlike earlier ones in which Charlie's manic behavior is cued by a woman's sexuality, has an innocent cast. It's not, like those earlier scenes, an expression of the impossible-to-brook power of the male id. It's an ode to pure nascent love, male longing for and capacity to love.

In these scenes in which Charlie is driven crazy by love, as in the more sexually charged eros fits more characteristic of his earlier films, we see that same strange logic in Charlie's character that translates a surcharge of feelings for women into good-natured abuse of others. In *The Circus*, for example, when Charlie mistakenly concludes that Merna loves him, he erupts into paroxysms of destructive elation. He skips up and down his dressing room with the childish prance we are all familiar with, but which becomes particularly manic and dance-like when he is inflamed by love. When his good friend, the clown (Henry Bergman), comes in to see what's happening, Charlie illogically leaps into the air, kicking him in the chest and knocking him down. Exiting the room like a tornado, he throws a sheaf of papers at the clown. As he exits his tent he sails by a donkey and its trainers. He smacks the donkey on its behind, causing the donkey to buck wildly and sending its caretakers ducking for cover.

The scene is evidence of Chaplin's skills as a filmmaker. He doesn't just trust to his mimetic skills to portray his excitement. He finds plastic means to express that excitement; he fills the screen with kinetic visual activity, as he did in the scene from *The Gold Rush* where he fills the air with feathers. Hundreds of shimmering feathers there, a sheaf of papers and bodies flying, both man and beast, here. Charlie's like a tornado in moments of amorous ecstasy, wrecking havoc wherever he goes. Chaplin translates Charlie's ecstasy into visual excitement, into tangible chaos.

The scenes in which Charlie expresses, through chaotic and destructive antics, the immensity of his feeling of love are among the greatest in Chaplin's cinema. They are dances, or celebrations, of love, wild expressions of the purity of Charlie's heart.

But of course they have a universal echo as well. Charlie here expresses, in chaotic dance, feelings everyone knows of burgeoning and requited love. Charlie knows no immoderacy in his love, one of the aspects of his character that, in the end, often wins women to him. This total, childlike abandonment to love is not typical of the way men court in movies. And it's this abandonment to love that will make the scenes in which Charlie's heart is broken, or in which he is abandoned, so moving. Chaplin's scenes of pathos are persuasive in proportion to how exhilarating these scenes of elation are. These scenes of love excitement are also among the most visually dynamic scenes in Chaplin's films. There's a tidy unity of form and content in them. Charlie's wild emotions are translated into the pure sensation of cinema: kinetic energy and visual explosion.

Chivalrous Charlie

The intense adrenalin rush that Charlie experiences under the slightest provocation from a woman can also have heroic consequences. Charlie is never more successful in battle than when he is fighting in defense of a woman he cares for. He turns into a combination of Sir Galahad and whirling dervish, taking all that energy that we have seen explode in the scenes analyzed above and concentrating it into fixed purpose. An attractive woman intensifies Charlie's strength in much the same way a can of spinach does Popeye's. When defending a woman, Charlie's sexual energy has a constructive outlet, as opposed to those moments where his sexual energy prompts him to attack innocent bystanders.

What's comical about the scenes in which Charlie defends a woman is how ruthlessly efficient he is. Whereas most of his fight scenes are chaotic, with ups and downs, Charlie sometimes in the ascent and other times beaten mercilessly, in the scenes where he defends women his success is so absolute as to amount to a parody of male action films. In *The Cure*, Charlie saves Edna from two drunken assailants without breaking a sweat. He hooks one by the ankle with his cane, sending him to the floor, steps on him to get to the second assailant, kicks this second man in the rear end to get his attention, then, hooking him by the neck with his cane, sends him flying headfirst into a wall. When the second man rises and takes a swing at Charlie, Charlie simultaneously dodges the blow, spins around and, with a backward kick to the man's rear end, sends him to the ground with his peer. Charlie's spinning move concludes with a bow to Edna that makes it seem as though the entire fight were merely a prelude to an elegant greeting.

The funniest moment in *The New Janitor* occurs near the end when lowly janitor Charlie happens onto a room where a corrupt bank employee has knocked a woman to the floor and is escaping through the window with stolen funds. The humor of this gag resides in Charlie's nonchalance when he comes upon this crime scene. A woman in trouble brings out a confident authority in Charlie. He smacks the man on the backside with his cane and points to the woman on the floor as though he were a manager telling an employee to pick up after himself. When the man pulls a gun on Charlie, Charlie looks at it blankly and then coolly kicks it out of his hand. Now Charlie points to the gun on the floor in the same calm, peeved way he had pointed to the woman, as if he were an increasingly annoyed teacher scolding a child. When the man takes a swing at Charlie, Charlie ducks. The man's blow, not finding its target, spins him around, providing Charlie with the opportunity to kick him in the behind and send him sprawling to the floor.

The hallmark of these scenes where Charlie defends women is this kind of economy of gesture. Charlie turns his behind to the man as he bends to pick up the gun and the man charges him but, in one of Chaplin's trademark gestures, Charlie, bent over, draws a bead on the man with his gun, upside down and from between his legs. Charlie is never out of control for an instant.

These moments occur over and over in Chaplin's films. Charlie dispatches three men trying to rob Edna at the beginning of *The Tramp* and defeats a crowd of twenty or so at the end of *Easy Street* (though aided there by the heroin he's accidentally imbibed) with a similar ruthless efficiency. In these fight scenes Charlie suffers no setbacks and wastes no punches; all his movements are calculated to dispel the problem with ease and efficiency. Charlie, by nature a coward, normally has a very ambivalent attitude towards fighting. But attraction to women amplifies his strength and intensifies his concentration. At these moments he fights with ease, sometimes even carrying Edna over his shoulder while he continues to vanquish her enemies, as he does in *Work* and *A Burlesque on Carmen*. This comic image conveys, at the same time, Charlie's superhero control at the moment and his childlike desire to carry his love object home like some big carnival prize. Chaplin also seems to enjoy the incongruous humor in Edna's behind being featured so in these moments of action.

The Flower

The symbol that is most associated with Chaplin's films, the flower, reflects the feminine side of Charlie as well. Throughout his films, Chaplin urges the relationship between Charlie and flowers. Charlie's incompetence at his job in *Pay Day*, for example, is prefigured by his arrival to work, late, and swooning over the smell of a lily which he then presents to his boss in the manner of a shy suitor, an example of Charlie either drastically misreading the rules of the masculine world or slyly mocking them.

Charlie often brings his love of flowers into the workplace, usually to the confusion of his bosses and co-workers. Charlie waters a display of women's hats with floral decorations with a watering can, as though they were a garden of flowers in *The Floorwalker*. Charlie's partner in crime, in *Police*, urges Charlie to hurry it up when they are robbing a house. Charlie's response is to madly dash around the room grabbing all the flower arrangements and stuffing them into his sack. In *The Rink*, Charlie throws flowers into the ridiculous drink he concocts during his bartender duties. In *Sunnyside*, salesman Charlie gently cradles the coarse men's socks Edna buys and elaborately wraps them as though they were a delicate bouquet of flowers. From very early on in Chaplin's films, Charlie seemed to have flowers on his mind.

More generally, Chaplin has a habit of bringing flowers into the sphere of his films' action whenever he can, as for example in *A Jitney Elopement*, when Charlie accidentally eats the flowers that represent the centerpiece of the table as though they were *hors d'oeuvres*, and in *The Pilgrim* where Charlie takes quite literally the sheriff's request that he go pick some flowers when the sheriff meant, in code language, to tell Charlie to escape from his custody. The mass murderer Monsieur Verdoux is a gardener and lover of flowers.

The flower, as a symbol, becomes more important in Chaplin's cinema as Charlie, in his later incarnations, becomes more of an idealized suitor, for example in *The Gold Rush* where Charlie keeps the rose that Georgia offhandedly gave him under his pillow. She later discovers the flower there, along with her picture, when she visits his little home.

We have to be careful, though, about drawing too strong a division between the early and later films with Charlie. Already in Chaplin's fifth film for Essanay, *A Jitney Elopement*, Charlie makes his first appearance in the film dreamily sniffing a flower while he casts his gaze towards Edna's window. In *The Tramp*, also from 1915, Charlie is too embarrassed to hand Edna a flower. Instead he kisses it privately and tosses it to her as he scurries away. Unfortunately it lands in a bucket of milk.

The Bank (1915) is the first film in which Chaplin puts the symbol of the flower to extended dramatic use. Charlie caresses the flowers he leaves for Edna along with a love note. After she rejects him, the dejected Charlie tries to throw out the now crumpled bouquet, but finds he is no more able to cast away the flowers than he is his love for Edna. He dejectedly tucks them in his jacket instead. So as early as 1915 we've arrived at that melancholy use of flowers that Gerald Mast felt was typical of Chaplin: "For Chaplin, flowers become surrogates for the real human beauty he wants to possess; he can at least hold a flower, if not the lady for whom it is intended."[5]

Mast's summary is certainly true of the scene in *Sunnyside* in which Charlie sees, through the window of Edna's house, his competition, the city gentleman, courting Edna successfully. As he watches this scene unfold, Charlie's hands unconsciously start to tug away the petals from the daisies he had brought for Edna, another of those moments in which Chaplin specializes: unconscious physical gestures implying interior sentiment. He doesn't drop the flowers though, he just walks away, no longer holding them for presentation but sadly at his side. Charlie often loses the girl but he almost always keeps the now tattered flowers. When Charlie can't have a woman's love, he settles for the consciousness of love kept alive by his suffering.

Charlie's offer of flowers to women communicates several things about him. They represent his childlike simplicity. If he wins women, it will not be through show or possessions but via something simple, close to earth. Charlie has little to offer a woman but a latent sense of aesthetics. And they represent his taste for the more delicate things in life, his appreciation of grace and delicacy. There's also a melancholy aspect to Charlie's flowers. Their temporality and fragility seem to comment on the hopelessness of Charlie's suit. Neither are likely to last long in this world. The flowers symbolize the transience of beauty in general, not just in Charlie's courtships. Flowers in Chaplin represent a small burst of beauty in an otherwise darkly urban, often Dickensian environment. That is why Monsieur Verdoux's love of flowers seems so in keeping with the tenor of Chaplin's cinema in general. Verdoux's delicate aesthetics exist side by side with murderous tendencies. Flowers, in Chaplin's films, are always waging a battle with the darker forces in life.

Needless to say, flowers bedeck almost all of Charlie's dreams and visions of paradise, the nymph dream in *Sunnyside*, for example, and the dream of heaven in *The Kid*. Flowers in Chaplin are hope, escape, beauty, love, women, heaven. And his constant proffering of them to women expresses his inherent chivalry, as do his heroic skills in arms against those men who are hostile to women. This chivalry of course contrasts neatly with Charlie's ragamuffin appearance. Charlie is a knight in Tramp's clothing, like Tennyson's Gareth, or any number of knights, sworn to secrecy as to their real identity and forced to endure all sorts of humiliations until their true nature is revealed.

It's in *City Lights* that Chaplin most develops the motif of the flower as a symbol of Charlie's understanding of, and relationship to, women. The use of flower in this film represents a good example of how Chaplin refined his art, taking ideas that he had used for years but working with them in a more careful, thorough way. In this film, flowers, women and love are conjoined in Charlie's love interest, a girl who sells flowers on the street. The flower is the dominant symbol of the film and serves as a framing device for the film as well. Charlie and Virginia meet when he buys a flower from her at the beginning and he is revealed as her anonymous benefactor when she brings him a flower at the end. Their relationship begins and ends via a flower held between them. It's Charlie bending down to pick up a wilted flower (a perfect match for his impoverished condition at that point in the film) in the gutter that causes him to stop at her shop before their reunion, as though the flower were guiding him back to her.

Flowers dictate the course of the film and during the course of the film flowers are never far from Charlie's mind. Charlie has gone down to the river quay to sit in silence and smell the first flower Virginia gave him when he comes across, for the first time, his suicidal rich friend. And he scampers back to collect the flower after he has steered his friend away from suicide at the quay. His moment of greatest happiness in his relationship with Virginia is when he is able, with his rich friend's money, to buy out all of her flowers and walk down the street with her, flowers in hand, her actual suitor.

Most significant of all the scenes involving flowers may be when Charlie is watching Virginia through her open apartment window while inhaling the odor of the flower she gave him. This scene expresses explicitly the idea that women are a kind of opium dream to Charlie. Charlie inhales the flower and sees the woman. The smell of flowers summons them when they are absent and intensifies his appreciation of them when they are present. Women are personifications of flowers, nymphs, like the young girls in the dream from *Sunnyside*.

Chaplin's Actresses

It might be worth noting one last aspect of Chaplin's attitude to women in his films that, again, I think has been underrated: how memorable the actresses are in his films, and how they avoid the pitfall of most films by male comedians of simply being bland "straight women" to the comedians' antics. It's a difficult subject to approach because Chaplin's representation of women in his film represents a kind of ode to youthful femininity and in his private life he is famous for having an unsavory penchant for young women under the legal age of consent. It's hard not to cringe at Lita Grey, who at sixteen became Chaplin's second wife, playing, at the age of twelve or thirteen (depending on different accounts), an alluring vamp in the dream sequence of *The Kid*.

And there's no doubt that the range of feminine beauty Chaplin celebrates is narrow. Lita in *The Kid*, the dancers in the *Sunnyside* dream, Merna Kennedy in *The Circus*, Virginia Cherrill in her threadbare skirt and torn sweater in *City Lights*, bare-

The simplicity and elegance of the gamin look Chaplin cultivated in his women co-stars is often underrated, perhaps because of the uneasy parallels to his personal romantic life. This image is from *The Circus* (1928) with Merna Kennedy.

foot Paulette Goddard in *Modern Times*—all of these women share a lithe, nymph-like beauty enhanced by the light simplicity of their apparel. There is no celebration of Rubensesque curves in Chaplin, no Fellini-like ode to womanly amplitude. Oversized women are objects of ridicule in his films, as are (it must be emphasized), even more often, oversized men. Chaplin's films reflect a fascination with the gamin and his inspiration would seem to be from the world of classical or classically inspired art. Bernini's evocation of Ovid's "Daphne and Apollo" comes to mind. Chaplin's ideal of feminine beauty is lithe, fetching, athletic, youthful and simply adorned. Like Daphne, she represents a fleeting erotic ideal, light on its feet, often difficult to grasp.

I wouldn't want to make a feminist argument for Chaplin's representation of feminine beauty in his films, any more than I would for Bernini's. I would only argue that Chaplin felt the beauty of the women in his films strongly and worked hard to express that beauty in a particular way. I've often marveled at how much more striking Goddard is in *Modern Times* than in any other film I've seen her in, how well the slight shift she wears suits her—a testimony to Chaplin's taste for Grecian simplicity in his women's costumes—how ingenious it was to have her traipse through the city for nearly the entire film barefoot, the only barefoot person in the city from what I can see, evoking at once her poverty and her femininity and making her seem as much nymph as street urchin. I can think of no other director who achieved so much elegance and beauty with so little extravagance in costume.

That's evident even in his last film, *A Countess from Hong Kong*, where Chaplin happens upon a rather unique look for '60s sex bomb Sophia Loren, quieting her expressive beauty by avoiding the bosomy dresses she normally specialized in and dressing her in a series of ill-fitting but fetching pajamas. Chaplin's women are memorably beautiful despite not engaging in the machinery of glamour in the Hollywood tradition. One of the reasons his women are so striking is the simplicity of his tastes, his sensitivity to the beauty of the women themselves. He lets their beauty breathe.

Another reason Chaplin's women come off so well is that Chaplin cared for the women themselves. For the most part Chaplin needed to work with women with whom he was personally taken and who were taken with him. And that mutual pleasure often shows on the screen. Edna Purviance, Georgia Hale, Merna Kennedy, Paulette Goddard—these women represent the great mass of his best silent films and he was involved romantically with them all. Usually, their film characters took their first name, underlining that, for Chaplin, there was not much difference between the actress and the character. The notable exception to the rule was Virginia Cherrill in *City Lights* who, unlike Goddard a few years later, found Chaplin a little long in the tooth and perplexed Chaplin by being immune to his charms. (Though she, too, felt that Chaplin didn't like her.) Their lack of chemistry caused fits in the shooting of that film, with Chaplin famously laboring, to the point of despair, to get the right response out of her in the scene where her character and the Tramp meet for the first time. She represents a real exception, though, as her performance is one of the greatest of the women in Chaplin's films.

Putting aside the question of whether it is advisable to be in love with your leading actresses, Chaplin *was*, throughout most of his greatest films, emotionally involved with his actresses and that involvement is reflected in their presence on the screen. In most of the films, the companionship of Charlie and his romantic interest is very persuasive. Charlie and Edna often seem to be having a good deal of fun on the screen, for example at the end of *The Immigrant* where he carries her laughing into the office issuing marriage licenses or at the end of *Burlesque in Carmen* where, the burlesque over, Edna and Charlie rise from their deaths, laughing with one another as Charlie demonstrates the fake knife used in their death scene.

Georgia Hale and Chaplin fell in love over the course of making *The Gold Rush*. Hale said she first became certain of Chaplin's love for her during the final scenes when they kiss on the ocean liner, and it's hard not to think of this when you see the warm, knowing but shy smiles they exchange before their kiss. Chaplin seems to have recognized what a personal moment he had registered on film when, years later, he excised the kiss from the revised version of the film, much to the dismay of Chaplin fans and critics. Or he may have thought that the kiss he recorded there was so genuine that it took him out of character. In that scene he does seem more like Chaplin than Charlie.

The same is the true of the ending of *Behind the Screen* where Charlie and Edna, in a very naturalistic close-up shot, sign off by mugging and kissing for the camera. The moment is so light-hearted, warm and naturalistic, and they seem so much themselves, that the camera seems really to have just recorded a moment in their lives rather than Charlie's. The scene takes Chaplin out of his character but it is of a piece with all the Edna-Charlie films where Charlie evinces a charming, protective warmth around Edna and Edna a touching flightiness and tender playfulness around Charlie.

And I think it's important to note that Chaplin, despite the aggressively masculine nature of many of his gags, registers with a female audience as well as, and usually better than, most any male artist I share with my students, whether from the world of literature or film. I think that's partly because of Charlie's inherently feminine nature, his unwillingness to strike conventional male postures and his spoofing of masculine pomposity. But I also think that it's partly because Chaplin aimed at making the women in his films into something beyond objects of desire. In Charlie's relationships with women, Chaplin aimed to communicate the joy of companionship. Charlie is never happier than when he is graced with a woman's company. Charlie so much wants to be with women, and to like women. Women, to him, represent a salvation from the barbarous crudity of the milieu into which he was born. And this barbarity is in many ways the product of a male-dominated culture. Women in Chaplin's films are more than erotic objects, they are personifications of a grace and kindness to which Charlie aspires. These ideas could not be expressed as successfully as they are if the women were mere erotic mannequins.

And, as we have seen, Charlie's courtship of women in many ways rests outside the boundaries of conventional attitudes of men towards women. Charlie is so vulnerable in his films, the women in his films so powerful. Charlie reveres them; they hardly notice him at all. Charlie courts from below, not above. He doesn't impress, but coaxes, wheedles, and charms. If he wins them, he does so not by means of masculine bravado, but by the ways of a child: teasing and amusing them or evoking their empathy. And, more often than not, he cedes the ground to other men. He doesn't expect to be liked and he's satisfied to love even when he's not loved in return. That's all the more impressive as we know what a healthy libido Charlie has. But even early on, in the randier incarnation of his earlier films, he showed a tendency to be stunned and overpowered by love, to not know what to make of it. And despite his powerful physical attraction to women, he often approaches them with great fear and awe. Charlie can be an aggressive flirt but when he really loves a woman he becomes an adoring child.

But, of course, he's not just a child with women. When he is allowed to express his affection for them, he tends to do it in a decidedly maternal way. How often does Charlie win a woman's affection by making her a meal, as he does for Edna in *The Vagabond,* Merna in *The Circus* and Georgia in *The Gold Rush*? In *The Vagabond,* as we have seen, he not only feeds Edna, he cleans her up and dresses her hair. Charlie often wins women not just by his vulnerability but also by taking care of them when they are vulnerable.

And as much as Chaplin reveres women, they are not stone goddesses in his films. Edna Purviance, for example, developed a charming personality over the course of her films with Chaplin. She is distressingly blank, dirty and nit-ridden in *The Vagabond.* She's charmingly clumsy in *A Dog's Life,* when she dances so poorly and furiously, despite supposedly being a professional dancer. She's comically flighty in the store scene from *Sunnyside,* where she can't remember what she came to buy. Charlie privately moons over Edna while watching her eat her lunch in *Pay Day,* but is snapped out of his romantic reverie when she puts some stinky cheese under his nose. Edna is very human. And in those scenes where she is a little childish and daffy, Edna elicits from Charlie a bemused reproof. He takes on a more mature, responsible air about him, sets himself to the task of helping her through her muddle. In those films where she reciprocates Charlie's feelings, she's less like a loved goddess than a fun play pal. She and Charlie enjoy themselves in the manner of a couple of children who are happy and free to scamper about in the warmth of their mutual love.

In the feature films, the Edna pattern is carried on most clearly in Charlie's relationship with Merna in *The Circus* and with Paulette Goddard's waif in *Modern Times.* In both of those films, Charlie is often parent-like in his efforts to take care of his love interests, though in *The Circus* he still harbors hopes that his love will be reciprocated whereas the relationship with Paulette Goddard in *Modern Times* is very ambiguous, as fatherly as it is spousal.

The characters of Georgia in *The Gold Rush* and the blind girl in *City Lights* are, in many ways, Chaplin's most complex portraits of women, because these two women have to really grapple with Charlie's love, with who this little man is and what it means to be loved by him. Georgia is far too cruel to represent a perfect idol of womanliness, though Charlie certainly treats her like a goddess. Here again, Charlie's courtship is outside the norm. He leaves that kind of thing to Jack, who is the epitome of the more conventional male suitor: big, handsome, bluff, confident, controlling. Charlie wins Georgia by loving her from afar and not asking anything in return; not by impressing her, but by gently, anonymously, like a knight of old, proving his love.

The blind girl in *City Lights* is something of a Victorian cliché for most of the film, the afflicted impoverished beauty, saved by a man's money and affection. But when her sight is restored, she turns into a more conventional girl. She hopes Charlie, who she has never seen, will turn out to be one of the rich handsome men who come to her shop. She harbors a young girl's fantasies of romantic suitors. Her expression upon seeing Charlie is the most complex of any woman in Chaplin's films. It's one of love, pity, gratitude and confusion. She sees that Charlie loves, and has loved, her more fully and better than any other man could and, yet, what to do with this distressed ragamuffin before her? And this is how Chaplin leaves it. Charlie doesn't win the woman, he doesn't lose her. The only thing we're certain of is her gratitude, which seems enough for Charlie.

If Chaplin is accused of sexism, it is usually because of his taste for the nymph, which while often charming in the faun-like, eternally youthful Charlie, was unseemly in Chaplin's life. This was another case of Chaplin trying unsuccessfully to be Charlie in real life. But it seems to me he is more susceptible to the charge of enjoying women, as a means to an end, not just for themselves, but as a kind of drug, a path to an elevated state. Think again of Charlie, sniffing the flower while staring at the blind girl in her window. Women often come to Charlie in an aroma of poetry. They introduce him to a world of gentleness and beauty that he could never find in his early consorting with men, but which his very early tendency for playacting and appreciation for aesthetics pointed him to. Charlie hangs out with women for the same reasons others smoke opium.

But even this criticism, of liking women as a means to an end, doesn't quite hold water. Remember that in *Pay Day*, stinky cheese awakes Charlie from romantic reverie. Chaplin does not allow Charlie to idealize women. In fact, the women in Chaplin's films, Edna in particular, are pretty good at taking pratfalls, falling to earth. And they can be cruel, egoistic, superficial in their love. They turn down Charlie's love as often as they accept it. Chaplin's films idealize feminine companionship, not women themselves. I'm thinking, again, of those scenes when, reacquainted with a lost love, Charlie greets her with an unbounded pleasure. In these scenes his hands are all over the girl, but in a way that expresses delight, not lust. And these are no dream girls, but real ones, as Charlie confirms by grabbing their hands, touching their arms, and drinking in their presence with hungry, childlike, delighted eyes.

Eleven

Charlie, Dogs and Children

Dogs

Dogs must also be accounted for as one of Charlie's allies. Chaplin built two films around Charlie's camaraderie with dogs, *The Champion* and *A Dog's Life*. In *The Champion*, Chaplin emphasizes Charlie's closeness to the dog in the scenes in which Charlie shares his meal with the dog and in which the dog runs into the boxing ring and helps Charlie vanquish his opponent by biting him in the rear. *A Dog's Life* begins with a touching montage that depicts Charlie and Scraps, the dog, as two of a kind, outcasts of society who we first see in the cozy nests they've created out of the detritus of city streets. Chaplin even puts a beat-up pair of Tramp-like shoes next to Scraps' bed to reinforce the parallel. The two are natural friends. Like Charlie, Scraps gets picked on by larger members of his species (they meet when Charlie saves him from a pack of dogs). Both are adept at stealing food. Several shots of Charlie and Scraps sitting on apartment stoops are anticipatory, in their pathos, of those in *The Kid*. At times *A Dog's Life* seems like a dry run for that film in its desire to establish a caring relationship between Charlie and another creature neglected by the world.

Charlie's dog-like identity is cleverly underlined in the dance hall scenes. Charlie is forced to hide Scraps in the voluminous back regions of his baggy pants in order to enter a dance hall that prohibits dogs. Scraps' tail protrudes through a hole in the seat of Charlie's pants, giving Charlie a wagging tail and making him a kind of mandog fusion, kin to the faun he suggests in so many other scenes. The close association between Charlie and dogs is reinforced in the film's mock idyll ending, where Edna and Charlie, a young couple in their dream home, beam, not over their own child's crib, as we are first led to believe, but over a litter of Scraps' puppies.

Chaplin also accentuated Charlie's dog-like nature in an early Keystone film, *His Prehistoric Past*. There, the animal cloak that Charlie wears brings out his dog-like tendencies. The fur hangs in the back in such a way as to create the illusion of a tail which Charlie has a good deal of fun spinning about and accentuating, particularly when he is flirting with young women. When his fur garment itches, Charlie scratches it with his leg, like a dog. When he comes out of the water, he vigorously shakes himself off, again like a dog.

Dogs appear consistently through Chaplin's films and they are invariably sympathetic. He protects one dog from the hungry Big Jim early in *The Gold Rush* and accidentally dances with another later in the film when he ties a rope around his waist to keep his pants up and finds a dog tethered to its other end. In *Modern Times*, he swallows a whistle and starts to hiccup, these whistling sounds drawing dozens of dogs to a party. Here, as in the dog fight scene from *A Dog's Life*, Charlie finds himself lost in a pack of dogs. And here, as in the dance scene from *A Dog's Life*, Charlie introduces dogs, those good-natured barbarians, into environments where they are not normally allowed. Dogs are his ilk, surrogate Charlies of sorts, bounding in where they are not wanted. Dogs find themselves at home in the chaos that surrounds Charlie, just as they do in the chaos introduced by M. Hulot in the Chaplin-influenced cinema of Jacques Tati.

Charlie is very much like an abandoned dog, a figure of great frailty and pathos, essentially good-natured and playful, loads of fun, but scrappy and hardened by penury. He will bite when up against a wall, and his good nature can flip easily into ferocious

Chaplin in a publicity shot for *A Dog's Life*. Chaplin had an instinctual rapport with dogs and derived a great deal of comic inspiration from them.

violence. Charlie also has something of a dog's indomitable good nature. There is, for example, much of the dog in the way Charlie walks down the road at the end of *The Tramp*, first forlornly but then, shaking off his sorrow, with a brisk scamper. Charlie has a dog's ability to always bounce back from his scraps. One of the reasons we like dogs so much is that they manage to arrive with such ease at a certain philosophical calm and contentment that humans have to work a lifetime to achieve. Every day is a red letter day for a dog. They need very little to be happy, a bit of food, some companionship and a breeze. Similarly, Charlie has absolutely nothing and that, generally, suits him just fine.

Dogs are also, like Charlie, very expressive of their feelings—no cat-like neutrality about them or Charlie—and when Charlie meets up with a girl he often is dog-like in his overt expression of affection. Charlie is incapable of hiding his feelings and is often taken advantage of for that reason. Many of Charlie's trademark moves are patterned after dogs. For example, Charlie often kicks in his sleep, in the manner of a dog dreaming of running. When he itches himself, his leg instinctively moves to scratch as well. He buries things, for example the rifle in *The Gold Rush*, like a dog with backward kicks. Like a dog, he panics when he has to walk on slick surfaces, for example, flailing madly as he crosses a waxed dance floor in *City Lights*.

And, like a dog, he's a food hound, always on the make for a treat, prone to stealing food whenever he has the opportunity, and in the manner of a dog, surreptitiously, with a great deal of fear and trepidation, but with a scoundrel-like persistence as well. When he gets food he often wolfs it down convulsively with the open-throated heaves of a dog, making it disappear with disturbing rapidity. Like a dog, when it comes to food, he knows his window of opportunity may be slight and so has learned to get rid of the goods fast. When he is caught in this kind of larceny, he's often removed like a dog, by the scruff of his neck. In the *City Lights* scenes where the butler removes Charlie from the house, Charlie suggests a dog in his uncontrollable scrambles to get back into a house from which he has been banished. Like a dog, Charlie is often barred entrance from, or kicked out of, respectable establishments, like the dance hall in *A Dog's Life* and the rich man's mansion in *City Lights*.

Charlie's movements are instinctively those of a dog. For example, he responds very sensitively to human contact. He approaches people warily and flinches easily, and dramatically when he does. Like a dog, he always anticipates a blow. His very demeanor bespeaks a long history of petty theft and overzealous retributions for those thefts. Often, when people approach him, he moves away from them in apprehension, maintaining the same distance from them that existed when they first started moving toward him. Like a dog, he's wary even of people who are kindly disposed to him.

For example, at the end of *City Lights*, Charlie smiles at the once-blind flower girl through the display window of her flower shop. But when she moves, in a moment of sympathy, to bring out to him a fresher flower than the one he holds, Charlie's face shifts to sudden apprehensiveness and he quickly scurries several steps past her door, his movements away from her mirroring hers towards him, exactly as a dog retreats when we advance. He doesn't run away entirely though, as dogs do not. They tend to hover on the outskirts of a situation, as though not entirely convinced there might not be some gain coming their way. This is the kind of scene that Minnie Fiske referred to when she wrote (though many years before *City Lights*), "[T]he manner in which he approaches the object of his affections, realizing the futility of his devotion, is very pathetic. It reminds one of a mongrel who, half boldly, half diffidently, lick's one's hand, hoping for a caress but fearing a kick."[1]

Fiske's comments highlight a couple of Chaplin's dog-like features. First she emphasizes how much Charlie's dog-like behavior is tied to his sense of pathos. Dogs are sometimes pathetic creatures, whose generosity of spirit is taken advantage of and who often meet cruelty with kindness. They are sociable creatures, more so than humans in many ways, and yet they can be coldly kicked to the side and segregated from the warmth of companionship, as Charlie is, for example, in *The Gold Rush* on New Year's Eve when he watches the festivities alone, through the window, shivering outside. Like a dog, Charlie is regularly left outside in the cold. Charlie, like a dog, is lovelorn, eager for affection, boundless in his display of affection, and yet that affection is frequently not returned. And Fiske notes how dog-like is Charlie's flitting back and forth between a bold temerity and a craven fear. Dogs are comical in their persistence that co-exists with, and survives, their epic sense of apprehension.

One of Charlie's most dog-like scenes occurs in *Behind the Screen* when he is filching a co-worker's meal during a lunch break, in this case a huge leg of mutton, or some such shank of meat, from which Charlie keeps sneaking bites. At first, the gag here is that typical one, often repeated in Chaplin's films, where Charlie sneaks bites, and gobbles them down quickly before the victim of his larceny can notice. The ultimate development of this gag is the extended scene in *A Dog's Life* where he steals sausages and cakes from the vendor played by his brother Sydney. As I mentioned above, this steal-and-gobble move of Chaplin's is already typical of dog behavior. Dogs are expert at seizing moments to sneakily grab food and at bolting down that food in seconds. In fact, another very dog-like moment is that in *The Circus* when Charlie, bite by bite, sneaks and gobbles away the pastry from a babe in arms. Dogs, too, kindly as they are, are reprehensibly open to stealing from small children when they have food in hand; in fact, they tend to home in on children, recognizing them as easy marks. Dogs, like Charlie, are good-natured but shamelessly amoral.

At one point in *Behind the Screen*, though, Charlie's dog behavior becomes unusually literal. Charlie has finally managed such good purchase on the man's shank of beef that boldness gets the better of apprehension and instead of releasing the meat when he's discovered, he growls like a dog at the man, and even snaps aggressively in his face twice. Here Charlie mimics that moment when a dog, having really sunk his teeth into some treat, abandons his congenital nervousness and commits to full-on aggressiveness and stubborn resistance. This moment echoes one in *His Trysting Place* when Charlie is gnawing on a bone, in the manner of a ravished dog at a soup counter. A man seated next to him, reaching for some seasoning, extends his arm before Charlie's face and Charlie bites him, just as a dog might when a person gets too close to his food.

Charlie's dog-like tendencies take over in fights as well, for example the fight that concludes *The Star Boarder* where Charlie takes a chomp out of his opponent's thigh as though it were a side of beef. At certain moments, when he's really fastened into a meal or a fight, Charlie can be ravenous and territorial. But, like a dog, separated from his quarry, he tends to become docile and friendly again. Neither Charlie nor dogs hold grudges. When the man in *Behind the Screen* finally tears the meat away from Charlie, Charlie laughs, conveying the idea that the growling was just a joke, a point he develops by putting his hands up in front of him and begging like a dog might, thereby capturing the way dogs, rogues that they are, segue from vicious aggressiveness to rank pandering in the blink of an eye.

Charlie, as I discussed more fully in my chapter on Chaplin's sense of balance, represents a collection of opposing tendencies held in delicate balance. Dogs appeal to Chaplin for the similarly interesting paradoxes of their nature. Charlie imitates both their territorial aggressiveness as well as their abject pandering. He often channels dog behavior when he's feeling rather sure of himself. For example, in *The Circus*, Charlie completes his thorough thrashing of Merna's suitor (in a dream sequence, of course) by turning his back and delivering several backwards kicks of dirt onto the fallen man. This dog-like backward kicking of dirt as a gesture of contempt is common in Chaplin's films. In *A Day's Pleasure* he is stuck in freshly laid tar along with two angry policemen. He escapes by leaving his shoes behind and walking out in his stocking feet, using one of the cops as a bridge. After he's free of the tar, he delivers a few backward swipes of dirt, hops in his car and drives away. As modest as dogs are by nature, they are impressively disdainful in these backward kicks that so thoroughly dismiss that which they leave behind.

In *The Kid*, the way Charlie chases away the driver of the orphanage vehicle, who had tried to take Charlie's child from him, is laughably like the aggressive posturing of a dog. Charlie chases the man furiously and then stops. But when the man he's chasing stops, Charlie advances a few more aggressive steps towards the man, who runs again and stops again. A third time Charlie makes a foray towards him with a fusillade of angry steps. As in the scene from *City Lights*, this is another imitation of how dogs, in retreat or pursuit, mirror the movements of their counterpart, expending only so much energy as necessary, always calculating their actions from a safe distance. This is classic dog behavior, standing your ground but also standing clear of a fight. Dogs often prefer threats like this, expressions of bombast, to actual fighting, just one more example of their comic blend of habitual viciousness and innate amiability.

At the same time, Charlie, like many dogs, is capable of sizing up a fight and knowing when capitulation is the best strategy. After Edna's father (Mack Swain) decks him four times in *The Idle Class*, Charlie falls to the ground before the father can administer a fifth blow, lying on his back and lifting his arms and legs in the manner of a dog signaling capitulation, all while carrying on their conversation from his prone position. In *Easy Street*, bully Eric Campbell stretches his arm before Charlie's face as he rolls up his sleeve, preparatory to striking Charlie. Charlie has already failed to fell the bully with several blows of his nightstick to Campbell's head, so he takes a new tack and kisses Campbell's hand in the manner of a pandering dog begging charity of his owner. Charlie, like a dog, is tough and scrappy but he's also shameless and never too good to pander if the moment calls for it.

Children

Chaplin incorporates the habits of children into his humor, just as he does those of dogs. Charlie has an affinity for both of these creatures; they are comical, powerless, often forgotten and disdained by society's figures of authority.

The Kid is one of Charlie's most emotional and successful films and Jackie Coogan joins Scraps in *A Dog's Life* and the host of neglected women in Chaplin's other films in a select group of types that Charlie cares for and defends. In fact, Charlie's relationship with the child in *The Kid* stands out as the most developed and highly detailed relationship in all of Chaplin's films. Women were Charlie's more standard partners but I can think of no Chaplin film in which Charlie's relationship with a woman is as carefully delineated as is his relationship with the kid.

Still, it has to be noted that Charlie's overall relationship with children is ambiguous. There are moments in other Chaplin films in which we spy an affinity between Charlie and children but they are not that numerous. In *Modern Times*, manacled to a policeman who is calling in his arrest, Charlie bides his time by buying cigars and chocolates he has no intention of paying for and passing the chocolates out to passing children. In *The Pilgrim*, only the child in the church congregation finds Charlie's rendition of the story of David and Goliath impressive. In these scenes, Charlie is seen as an ally to children in his lawlessness, his willingness to bend the rules on their behalf.

On the other hand, Charlie is often at odds with children. The newspaper boys in *City Lights*, for example, are unrepentantly cruel to Charlie at Charlie's lowest moment when he is shirtless, disheveled, and reduced to penury by his sacrifices for the blind flower girl. They shoot peas at poor Charlie, just as the boys do at the Chaplin character, King Shahdov, when he visits their school in *A King in New York*.

A King in New York demonstrates a particularly unsentimental attitude towards childhood. The school Shahdov visits is supposed to represent the acme of education innovation, an open school that encourages freedom of expression. The result is only boys who are even more poorly behaved than usual. (Yet another example of how the famously liberal Chaplin often built gags around a conservative point of view.) At one point Shahdov is horrified to see one boy pick his nose while baking cookies and use the same finger to press a single indentation into the cookie he makes, into which he proudly deposits the cookie's candy treat.

This unsentimental approach to children spans the entirety of Chaplin's films. Charlie is pummeled, *à la* W.C. Fields, by a spoiled child in *The Pilgrim*, steals candy from a babe in arms in *The Circus*, and cruelly kicks a boy who has done nothing but help him hold a ladder in *The Pawnshop*. One of the recurrent gags in Chaplin's cinema is that in which someone asks Charlie to hold a baby. Charlie rarely exhibits any warmth for the child in these moments. The payoff of these gags is that moment when, relieved of the child, Charlie tries to figure out what to do with his hands, now soiled by the baby's wet behind. In *Star Boarder*, Charlie's liaison with a married woman is made public by a bratty boy with a camera. Even in *The Kid* it takes some time for Charlie to warm to the child he finds. He tries, several times, to disembarrass himself of the child, even contemplating dumping him down into a sewer at one point.

Sergei Eisenstein wrote that the scene in *Easy Street*—in which Charlie scatters food for the many children of one impoverished couple as though he was scattering feed before chicken—reflected his distaste for children. "You see, I did that because I despise children," he quotes Chaplin as saying.[2] Eisenstein thought this statement was reflective of Chaplin's own childishness. His quote has an apocryphal air to it. It's contradicted by other statements by Chaplin and the physical evidence of Chaplin's behavior around children, even before he had his own. Both aural accounts and photographs testify to a strikingly warm relationship between him and Jackie Coogan on the set of *The Kid*. It's become common to link the pathos of *The Kid* to Chaplin's loss of his first child at that time but the warmth and success of the film is more likely due to the easy chemistry between Chaplin and Coogan, whose natural talent Chaplin admired immensely. Chaplin was by no means a perfect father and gets mixed reviews from his children as a parent but all of their reminiscences involve warm memories of Chaplin as a man who got an enormous charge out of his children, something we can see in the home movies of him hamming it up with them to their obvious delight.

The seed-scattering scene expresses more sympathy than contempt for the plight of children. Chaplin had a gift, a little bit like that of Luis Bunuel, of calling attention to social ills but via a light, almost cruel humor. He abjured self-congratulatory social commentary in favor of little stinging ideas like this one, calling attention to a social problem with a stringent humor that is perhaps more lasting in its effect by virtue of being a bit jarring. A gag like this has a melancholy undercurrent. It makes its point but does not descend to bathos. Rather, the humor is somewhat confrontive, causing us to laugh when we shouldn't and, consequently, sticking in our craw a little more effectively.

Actually, Eisenstein's theory that Chaplin disliked children because he was so much like one seems more accurate in regards to Charlie than it does Chaplin. Charlie sometimes has trouble with children because they perceive him, as he does them, as an equal. Charlie is a child himself. He is incapable of traditional paternalistic habits towards children, either of the disciplinary type or the smarmy appreciative type. In *The Pilgrim*, for example, Charlie administers some forceful kicks to the ill-behaved child when no one is looking. Charlie's run-ins with kids tend to reinforce our sense of Charlie's childishness. Adults don't act this way with children.

In the end, Chaplin's alliance with, or affinity for, children is most evident in how much his humor draws from them. It's striking how closely related the childlike aspects of Charlie's nature are to the essential ingredients of Chaplin's comedy. Chaplin often emphasized how important his small stature was in eliciting sympathy from the audience. Charlie seems as small as a child when paired with immense heavies like Eric Campbell and Mack Swain. And these heavies often discipline Charlie like a child, tossing him around by the scruff of the neck, lifting and holding him off the floor for extended periods, grabbing him by the ear when they lead him out of rooms, shaking him around effortlessly as though he were a large rag doll.

Chaplin recognized that his head was larger in proportion to the rest of his body and played that childlike feature up by styling his hair to increase the volume and by making his suit jacket tight so as to emphasize the narrowness of his torso. Dan Kamin notes how Charlie carries himself swaybacked with the gravity-free posture that a child shares with a dancer and often places his hands high on the back of his hips in the manner of a child engrossed in something. Charlie also often giggles like a child, sometimes at inappropriate moments, as for example when someone has had an accident or at some reference to sexuality. And when Charlie giggles, he often covers his mouth with his hand in the self-conscious manner of a child.

Hunger and food also play a significant part in Chaplin's films and this subject too ties into Charlie's childishness. Charlie is always on the make for food and particularly the kind of food that appeals to children: donuts, sweets, sausages and hot dogs. There are very few examples of healthy food in Chaplin's films. Charlie also has the eating habits of a child. In *The Kid*, he rolls up whole sticks of butter in his pancakes. In *Sunnyside*, he mashes so many sugar cubes (some twenty or so) into his coffee that he turns it into a kind of oozy paste, which he can spread on his bread as well as drink. Many of Chaplin's dining table gags revolve around Charlie's intemperate affection for sugar.

Like a child, Charlie has a child's rigid ethic when it comes to food distribution. Anyone who, as a child, has fought with their siblings over the exact portion of treats and desserts due them, identifies with the scene in *The Kid* in which Charlie counts out the pancakes like so many playing cards and, realizing he has one more than his son, cuts the pancake in half so that their portions are perfectly equal.

Many gags are developed in Chaplin's films around Charlie's undeveloped knowledge of table etiquette, for example in *The Kid* when, in his best *pater familias* posturing, he lectures Jackie about the proper way to slurp syrup from a knife. Charlie often thinks he understands dining etiquette more than he actually does. Charlie's boss watches in disbelief as Charlie drinks down his coffee sugar ooze in *Sunnyside*. Charlie, as he often does when enduring a stern male gaze, stiffens in his formality, here sticking out his pinky and drinking this absurd concoction with the grace of a duchess at high tea.

One of the most repeated comic situations in Chaplin's films is Charlie at a dinner table trying to cope with manners, rules and rituals that he doesn't understand. Formal dining can be a challenge for children, a test, as it is for Charlie, of their ability to conform. Charlie's discomfort with the dinner table is also a reflection of Chaplin's tendency to attack, Ibsen-like, those rituals most central to middle-class family life. Even today, newspapers routinely run articles on the essential importance of families dining together as a way to raise children properly. This is the kind of middle American wisdom and family normality that Chaplin never experienced and so always bristled at. Chaplin's dining scenes are just one way in which he expresses his annoyance with domestic norms and middle-class virtue. Charlie's childishness is tied into his critique of conventional mores. Children, like Charlie, are determined anarchists, and for them, dinner can be the site of their greatest showdowns with parents. Chaplin is on the side of their rebellion.

The Dining Scene in A Jitney Elopement

There are countless examples of Charlie at sea while dining. One nicely delineated scene is in *A Jitney Elopement* when Charlie, who has been mistaken for an aristocratic suitor, sits down to dinner with Edna and her father. It might be worth looking at in some detail as "Charlie at the dining table" represents one of Chaplin's most emblematic gags as well as one that touches on the childishness of his nature. The *Jitney Elopement* dinner scene is one of those scenes in Chaplin's earlier films that bristles with comic invention, where the eye can barely keep up with Chaplin's brisk comic business. The formalities of dining seemed to particularly incite Chaplin's comic imagination. The dinner table is an ideal place for his satire of pretense and for him to express his frustration with forced decorum. Formal dining unites two challenges for Charlie, the challenge of appearing to be a normal functioning member of society and the challenge of navigating a tangle of rules and rituals that he doesn't understand. Of course Charlie buckles under the pressure of these twin challenges. With his mind so deeply occupied with figuring out how to behave, his body is left to make all sorts of spasmodic and unfortunate decisions.

For example, as Charlie sits down to the table, Edna points with pride to the floral display at its center. Charlie notes the flowers appreciatively and then embarks on some witty banter, all the while picking one of the flowers, salting and eating it. This kind of thing happens to Charlie a lot. When he's putting all of his mental energies into something, here the pretense of sophistication, he often loses control of his bodily actions. He gets his wires crossed and so, in this instance, he confuses appreciating floral decoration with sampling *hors d'oeuvres*.

Eating the flowers is the first of many gaucheries on Charlie's part. Continuing to affect the air of the urbane guest, Charlie unfolds his napkin, blows his nose in it, folds it and tucks it in his suit jacket pocket, in the manner of a decorative handkerchief. Offered some bread, he surprises his hosts by taking the entire loaf. Again he becomes so engaged in social banter that he loses consciousness of what he's doing, this time endlessly carving at the loaf of bread he holds. By the time he regains his consciousness, he realizes he's carved the bread as one might peel an apple and has created a kind of springy bread coil, which he then plays like a concertina, a hold-over gag from his music hall days. Finally, tearing off a large piece for himself, he unconsciously uses that piece of bread as a napkin for the rest of the dinner.

After the bread gag, the dining miscues continue to come fast and furious. Again lost in chatter, Charlie absent-mindedly grabs two lumps of sugar and puts them in his soup. Realizing what he's done, he surreptitiously removes the wet lumps and puts them back in the sugar bowl, casting quick guilty looks at his dinner partners. He manages to salt his soup but only after accidentally salting his empty tea cup first. He has trouble working the pepper shaker and jarring it, sends a cloud of pepper towards Edna and her father, who have sneezing fits. When a servant brings Charlie his entree, a steak in sauce, Charlie, in one of Chaplin's favorite go-to gags, looks above him as if he suspects the sauce to be the product of a bird flying over him. Charlie cuts his meat correctly, but conveys the food to his mouth via his knife, after delicately posing the meat on his knife with his hand. In almost all of the dining sequences in Chaplin's films, Charlie exhibits an aversion to bringing a fork near his mouth. Eating with a knife is something of an obsessive compulsive disorder for Charlie, a habit he refuses to abandon. Here he shields his mouth with his hand so that Edna and her father can't witness this primitive habit.

Chaplin works several gags off the toughness of the meat cut. Charlie carves away at it so energetically that he mimes wiping his brow of sweat. In his frustration he finds himself stabbing at it as a murderer might a victim, and turning his back to Edna and tearing at it like a ravenous mongrel. Finally, he surprises his dinner mates by using it as a plate upon which he can be served other portions of food. The cool aplomb with which he proffers the meat as plate when offered a side dish suggests that he feels he has struck on a rather elegant solution to his problem with the tough meat. When the tea comes, Charlie gulps it too quickly, twice, and both times, in a visual gag, blows steam out of his nostrils. He reaches so deeply into the sugar bowl for lumps of sugar that his hand disappears to the wrist, at one time becoming lodged in the sugar bowl. When his hand reappears, it's with the customary baker's dozen sugar cubes Charlie likes to take with his coffee and tea.

The dinner table is one of those places where Charlie's essential inability to blend into conventional society is called out. But we don't laugh condescendingly at Charlie in his dinner sequences. We identify with him. The difference between Charlie and us is only one of gradation. We may not eat flowers nervously when we sit down to dine but we do worry about whether we understand which fork to use or whether we are elegant enough in our bearing for the snobby waiter at a fancy restaurant. Chaplin is a child at the dinner table but, we have to admit, at times, so are we.

Charlie: A Deviant Child

Charlie often exhibits the sincerity of a child. One of his childish traits is a susceptibility to tears. Even in *The Pawnshop,* one of those Mutual films where Charlie's persona is at its most cock-sure and aggressive, he can't help but weep over a bogus story a customer tells of losing his wife, a story that even Charlie suspects is meant only to jack up the amount the customer hopes to receive for the goods he pawns. When the minister and Edna try to save his soul in *Police,* Charlie is vulnerable to their emotional arguments, his face twitching from his effort to repress his tears. In *A Dog's Life* it is not the sad song that makes Charlie cry but simply the spectacle of people crying around him. Charlie often falls prey, in this manner, to the contagion of tears. Chaplin doesn't take this side of Charlie seriously, as he does the more profound sadness Charlie experiences when, for example, women jilt him. But Charlie's proneness to tears is Chaplin's way of comically pointing out, even in his early films, that Charlie has a vulnerable side, that his inner emotions run counter to his street-tough demeanor.

Charlie often conducts himself with the charming innocence and literal-mindedness of a child. In the *Easy Street* church service, Charlie considerately shares his hymnal with a babe in arms of no more than a month or two. In *The Pilgrim,* Charlie is touchingly surprised when the conductor points out that the ticket he has bought allows him to travel inside the train rather than in the berth below a stockcar where Charlie normally hitches a ride. When a man injured in a car accident is stretched out on the counter of the hotel where Charlie works in *Sunnyside,* Charlie goes about checking him in, even though the man is unconscious. The scene concludes with Charlie holding pen and register before the unconscious man, his look of befuddlement gradually transitioning into one of mild impatience. Charlie often charms us with his simple-mindedness, his inability to grasp how the world works.

But charming moments like this aside, Charlie tends to channel, even more, the devious side of children. Chaplin's films never fall prey to gauzy idealizations of childhood or the childlike mentality (hence the often cynical attitude towards kids in most of his films). Chaplin's comedy retains all the punk anarchy of childhood and jettisons moony sentiment about children, an attitude towards childhood that is, perhaps, predictable given his own tough childhood. Like a child, Charlie has a good deal of manic energy that he can't control. And in circumstances where it needs to be reined in, at the workplace or other places that demand decorum, that energy erupts in wild and destructive ways. Like a child, the more Charlie is asked to control himself, the less he is able to. All of Chaplin's cinema is, in a way, a development of the child's dilemma at the dinner table: what to do with all this energy when there is no place for it. The world does not have room for Charlie's energy. His elation soars too high, his roughhousing is too destructive.

Like a child, Charlie is a hopeless ham. He drives his fellow gamblers crazy with his elaborate baseball pitcher's delivery of the dice in *The Immigrant* and *His New Job*. When he enters the boxing ring in *The Champion*, he is met with the generic applause accorded a boxer entering a ring, but Charlie responds to that applause with the drama of a great stage actor, bowing deeply, blowing kisses, refusing to turn his grateful face from the crowd even as his managers carry him to the corner of the ring. Charlie has the child's tendency to always want to make more of, to have more fun with, the situation at hand than the adults do. He's always eager to amuse himself, and like a child, perpetually surprised and let down by adults' unwillingness to play along with him, frustrated by their lack of imagination and their joylessness.

And, like a child, Charlie loves to tease. In *The Pawnshop*, he annoys wealthy client Eric Campbell by repeatedly pretending to step on the hat that Campbell has deposited on the floor next to his chair. He poises his foot just above the hat and only when Campbell and his boss leap from their chairs in alarm, elegantly sidesteps the hat, as though his foot were carried away from the hat by a sudden gust of wind, all the while pretending to have not even noticed the effect his action had on the two men. Charlie loves to yank adults' chains. In almost all of Charlie's fight scenes he is reminiscent of a child whose parents are trying to catch him. He crawls through their legs and runs away from them. He comes up from behind and kicks them in the rear. He pops up behind barriers, appearing and disappearing like a jack in the box, playing peek-a-boo and taunting them.

The opening sequence of *A Dog's Life* is a quintessential example of Charlie as childish tease. In this exquisitely timed sequence, one of Chaplin's best, he taunts a policeman trying to capture him by rolling back and forth under a fence, sending the policeman scurrying back and forth on each side of the fence, trying to catch him. When the cop pauses on one side of the fence, Charlie, on the other side, grabs his leg from under the fence and unties his shoelace. When the cop ties that shoelace, Charlie's arm shoots out from behind the fence, in one of those whack-a-mole images Charlie specializes in, and unties the cop's other shoe. When the cop bends to tie that one, Charlie pricks him in the behind with a safety pin. When the cop gets stuck under the fence, reaching for Charlie, Charlie gets up, runs around the fence so that he is behind the cop and starts pummeling his exposed behind mercilessly. Having induced the cop to get up and chase him again, Charlie concludes this set piece of cruelty by taunting the cop from across the fence with a bratty end-of-show curtsy.

Of course Charlie's preoccupation with kicking others in the behind ties into his childish nature as well. Charlie has a childlike fascination with those aspects of the body of which no mention is supposed to be made. Whenever somebody rips the seat of their pants in Chaplin films, Charlie giggles like a child and, covering his giggle with his hand, looks out at the audience conspiratorially to see if they find it amusing as well. He has a child's instinctive sense that the best way to obliterate an adult's sense of dignity is to focus on the things they are most embarrassed by. The human behind represents a great temptation to a child. It sits there for all to see and yet you're not supposed to notice it. How is a child to resist attacking it?

A recurrent gag in Chaplin's films that highlights Charlie's childish brattiness is one in which a figure of authority tries to eject him from the premises. In *City Lights*, Chaplin does a wonderful imitation of a child eluding an adult when the butler tries to toss him from the rich man's mansion. In one scene, when the butler bars Charlie at the front door, Charlie twice tries unsuccessfully to rush by him; on the third effort he jukes him in the manner of a running back and escapes into the house. The butler races after Charlie, who immediately jumps onto an oversized chair that Chaplin obviously chose to accentuate his childlike size. There he kicks his legs like a toddler, and mocks him with a toothy giggle.

In *City Lights*, Charlie is like a mouse that keeps finding its way back into the house. In another scene, the butler drags him out of bed in the morning, ordering him to dress and depart. As he leads Charlie past a breakfast cart, Charlie, in the manner of a wayward toddler, grabs a muffin. While the butler snatches the muffin from Charlie's hand, Charlie grabs a grapefruit with his other hand. Charlie is impossible to corral, all arms, in a perfect imitation of a child moving with such protean energy as to rival the grasping skills of an octopus.

When the butler and his assistant try to grab the grapefruit, Charlie squirts grapefruit juice in their eyes. As the butler forcefully escorts Charlie out of the house, Charlie finds a pretext to pass a fruit bowl from which he takes an orange and banana. The butler, again in the manner of an annoyed babysitter, snatches the fruit away from Charlie and, while holding Charlie with one hand, replaces the fruit in the bowl with the other. But as he and Charlie turn, Charlie's other hand, from behind his back, snatches an orange and some grapes. Charlie resembles nothing in these scenes so much as an exasperatingly naughty little boy beyond the control of a harried keeper.

These scenes of childlike resistance to adult authority are odes to children's inspired waywardness, their unwillingness to go down without a fight, their protean energy, the way they lock into a fiendish stubbornness, the way they rise to a fight, their gift for exasperation, the creativity and humor in their mischief. These scenes represent a finely detailed homage to children's refusal to let the world have its way.

Charlie's Childlike Nervousness

Though Chaplin channels childhood behavior when he is feeling cocky, Charlie is often at his most childish when he is nervous. When, for example, he finds himself under the withering gaze of a co-worker or boss or in the midst of flirtations with women, Charlie devolves into an array of childlike tics—giggling nervously, drawing his head into his shoulders, making shy, indirect eye contact, shifting his body around anxiously, fidgeting to the point where he loses control of his body, which seems, at these moments, to act on its own volition.

Charlie gets particularly nervous, and hence childlike, when dealing with hostile men (and they are almost all hostile in Chaplin's films). In *The Champion*, for example, Charlie sits in a row of men awaiting interviews for a job as a boxer's sparring partner. A tough guy seated near Charlie practices his punches on a phantom opponent before him, with an intensity that catches Charlie's attention. After the boxer has convincingly mimed felling his imaginary opponent, Charlie decides to get in on what he, child that he is, perceives as fun playacting. He leans forward and, playing the role of referee, counts down to ten the boxer's imaginary defeated opponent.

Charlie's purpose is ambiguous here. Either he wants, in the manner of a child, to play the boxer's game with him, or he's gently mocking him for the melodramatic nature of his warm-up exercises. It's probably both. The boxer, however, is only baffled by Charlie's playacting. He looks at Charlie with that blank, humorless expression men usually reserve for Charlie's antics. Writhing under the man's uncomprehending stare, Charlie erupts into his trademark childlike gestures: a nervous, toothy giggle and manic shifting, shoulder shrugs, before, illogically, giving the man a slap in the face.

This is obviously the wrong thing to do but, as we saw in his behavior at the dinner table, the more nervous Charlie is, the more his body erupts in spasms of confusing behavior. The illogical nature of Chaplin's comedy is one of its attractions. We often puzzle over Charlie's actions, trace the subtle and convoluted psychology behind them. We sense, in those illogical actions, a reference to our own perverse psychology, the way we often, in moments of pressure, do exactly that which we should not, a situation with which children are particularly familiar.

The boxer, of course, responds to Charlie's slap by punching Charlie in the face. Over and over in Chaplin's films, Charlie gets in fights with men after he engages them in a spirit of childlike play, and they respond with a stern, unimaginative adult perspective.

Matters of sex also bring out a squirming, childish nervousness in Charlie. He is very childlike in his response to sex and romantic displays of affection. Like a child he seems only midway in his understanding of what all that means. A recurrent gag in Chaplin's films is one in which Charlie sees someone flirting and is filled with so much childlike embarrassment and nervous energy that he can't stop himself from expressing himself in a spasm of destructive physical energy. When he sees this kind of dalliance, he just has to hit someone or something.

In *The Gold Rush,* for example, Charlie is tickled by the sight of his partner Big Jim McKay (Mack Swain) flirting with a young girl. First, Charlie stares at them in vacant unconsciousness. Charlie is often stunned when he comes across sexual dalliance of this sort. Then, a kind of nervous embarrassment takes over. He starts to giggle and wag his finger teasingly at Jim. Next, the uncontrollable energy in his body starts to surge. He spins around, wags his finger knowingly again, and then, exiting, treats Jim to one of his trademark backward kicks to the face, though a kick administered with such gentle, dancerly dexterity as to amount to a kind of kiss by foot. As Charlie approaches the door, he can't help but run back and, giggling, give Jim one more poke in the back with his cane. Nothing reduces Charlie to a childlike state more quickly and thoroughly than a couple canoodling.

In *Twenty Minutes of Love,* Charlie happens across a couple kissing on a park bench. His facial expressions are hilariously diverse, ranging from open-mouthed incredulity, to nausea, to giggly embarrassment, to lewd desire, and even to surly anger, as if he's annoyed that it's not he who's being kissed. In moments like this, Charlie has absolutely no facial control or self-consciousness. His face is simply a barometer for an astonishing variety of surging emotions. Finally, Charlie responds to what he's seeing the way a child would: He mimics it. Turning the tree next to him into a surrogate lover, Charlie introduces himself, exhibits his pounding heart and finally embraces and kisses the tree rapturously. Charlie often turns to mockery and imitation when confronted by things that annoy him or make him jealous. After his tryst with the tree, he heads over to the bench to make trouble, bothering the suitors as a bratty sibling might. In parting, he smilingly delivers a couple of his backward kicks to the male suitor, as he does to Jim in *The Gold Rush,* Charlie's particular mimetic way of saying, "You dog, you."

Charlie often responds to these romantic scenes by pretending the nearest inanimate object is a human, with whom he will joke about what he is seeing or, alternately, make love to. In *The Fireman,* he is again the bratty younger brother when he imitates his boss (Eric Campbell), engaged in melodramatic love-making to Edna on her front porch. Charlie, off to the side a little, mimics the boss' effusive courting, using a potted plant from the porch as a love surrogate. He embraces the plant rapturously, strokes it as though it were made of fur, not bristly leaves, lifts it by its trunk, its pot hanging below, and buries his face into its branches. In *The Rink,* waiter Charlie is so tickled by the sight of a couple wooing in a corner table that he gives the kitchen door, through which he was about to enter, a playful shove, as though the door were a friend of his watching too. Of course on the other side of the door stands a waiter with a tray full of dishes. As I emphasized in my chapter on Charlie and women, sexual excitement often makes Charlie dangerous to be around. In *His New Profession,* he is taking care of a wheelchair-bound man with whom he is sharing a magazine. When they land on a photo of a girl in a bathing suit, Charlie becomes so excited he brings his cane down with a thud on the man's painfully wounded leg.

Charlie, of course, devolves into even more chaotic, childish nervousness when he is actually before a real woman. Women reduce Charlie to a collection of nervous ticks, shy smiles, flirtatious glances and teasing giggles. Sometimes he gets so excited by the proximity of a woman that he loses control of himself and, in the manner of a child who kicks the girl he likes, becomes too physically rambunctious.

For example, in *Work,* house painter Charlie bends over to pick up some painting equipment. Nearby a pretty maid is chatting on the telephone, idly flipping the feather duster in her hand. To Charlie's delight, she accidentally dusts Charlie's behind as he picks up his equipment in front of her. This leads to the typical exchange of giggles and flirtatious glances until Charlie's excitement gets the best of him and, with an innocent "aw shucks" manner, he returns her tickle, though to her face rather than her backside, and with a filthy paint brush.

In *By the Sea,* Charlie crowds a woman on a park bench, this time picking up a sliver on his backside as he does so. In the throes of his amorous excitement, he finds this little misadventure so comical that he not only brandishes the sliver before her but sticks her with it, an illogical action that, needless to say, does not advance his suit. Charlie's method of courtship is often like that of a boy in a playground, whose only means of conveying affection is through teasing physical aggressiveness.

But Charlie's childishness around women represents his salvation as often as it does his downfall. Charlie pursues women in the spirit of play rather than by conventional displays of masculine power. He teases and cajoles and tricks women into games. It's significant that, in *Modern Times,* the first thing Charlie and Paulette Goddard's waif do after they have filled their belly—their first night alone together—is to slap on roller skates. Charlie's default form of courtship is to entertain with his favorite party tricks, as he does in the famous dance of the rolls in *The Gold Rush*. He particularly likes to show off, when he meets a pretty girl, the small miracles he can accomplish with his hat and cane, as for example in *The Rink* when he tries, unsuccessfully alas, to impress a girl with his ability to make his hat appear to rise on its own volition. The comedy of the scenes in which Charlie strikes out with women in this manner is in the great contrast between how enormously pleased Charlie is with his tricks and how indifferent the woman is.

But Charlie's humor and playfulness often hit home with the women he approaches. The scene in *The Kid* where Charlie makes a move on a woman whose window he is repairing (she doesn't know he broke it) is illustrative of Charlie's technique with women and how he often finds success with them in humor. At first, Charlie makes a fairly conventional move on the woman, slipping his arm around her waist as he points out to her the attributes of his window repair. It's a typically masculine move and, consequently, ineffective. Charlie doesn't have a chance in the world of conventional masculine behavior. That's true of the workplace and of his romantic forays alike.

The woman removes his hand, admonishing him sternly while she does so. Charlie begs his innocence, arguing that she misinterpreted his intentions. While defending himself, he insinuates himself before her own outstretched arm, which she has since rested on the window sill. Having situated himself so that her arm seems to rest on his shoulder, he now picks up her hand, as she did his, with virtuous disdain, admonishing *her* for having been sexually aggressive with *him*. The joke makes her laugh and from that point on Charlie has won her over and the two engage in the jesting flirtation that Charlie lives for. It's charm and humor that win the day for Charlie, not masculine aggressiveness. In fact, the housewife is so taken with Charlie that she even begins to partake in his amorous roughhousing, poking him in the ribs just as he does the women he's keen on. Fortunately, she doesn't notice that Charlie just barely checks an impulse to respond in kind with his quite sharp hand trowel. Charlie's amorousness always lies just this side of chaos.

There is probably no greater example of the childish nature of Charlie's desire for romance than the *Gold Rush* scene in which Charlie tears his little cabin to shreds after he finds out that Edna and her girl friends will join him for dinner on New Year's Eve. Women bring out the mad child in Charlie. The most famous childlike gesture in Chaplin's mimetic lexicon might be his famous skip, arms out, knees raised high and splayed outward, the incarnation of a child's glee in a man's body. And Charlie is most often moved to this expression of elation by the proximity of women, as for example in the famous dream sequence with the nymphs in *Sunnyside*. It is the one Chaplin gesture that Italian actor Ninetto Davoli most emphasized in his spirited imitation of Chaplin in Pier Paolo Pasolini's *Decameron*, where he tries to emphasize the charming innocence of Chaplin's approach to women. It's the gesture that most conveys how happy women make Charlie. A great part of Charlie's charm is that he is as unrestrained as a child around women. Charlie's no cool customer when it comes to the ladies. For Charlie, romance represents the most fun a person can have.

Charlie's Childlike Playacting

Charlie also channels children's behavior in his love of games. As we have seen, there is perhaps no aspect of Chaplin's comedy more vaunted than his skill at transposition. In *The Pawnshop*, for example, Charlie examines a clock that a customer wants to pawn in the manner of a doctor examining a patient. Again we have to note how Charlie's childlike tendencies cut right through the core of Chaplin's comedy. His skill at transposition is reflective of his childlike nature. Charlie lives in a perpetual state of playacting, of imagination. He is constantly weaving fantastic scenarios from the most commonplace objects and situations. Like a child, he is always saying, "Let's pretend."

One of his favorite games is the beloved childhood game of playing house. No matter where Charlie finds himself, a grueling work situation or a disheveled slum domicile, he loves to pretend that he's the proprietor of a well-managed estate, as, for example, in *The Gold Rush* where he rises from bed in the morning to calmly and methodically pick stalactite-sized icicles hanging from the rafters of his frozen cabin as though he were gathering his morning fruit from a well-tended orchard.

Charlie is an adult with the imagination of a child. He has never lost his taste for play, never grown up. Fortunately, he is such a reprobate that Chaplin successfully skirts the Peter Pan risk of over-rhapsodizing about children. There's a mocking edge to much of Charlie's playacting. When, for example, the doctor is ministering to the out-of-town man who has had a car accident in *Sunnyside*, Charlie can't help but imitate the doctor's actions in the manner of a child who is unconsciously inspired to mimic the adult behavior he witnesses.

Again, we have to note how mimicry is Charlie's means of learning how things work, just as it is a child's. When the doctor takes the patient's pulse while looking at his pocket watch, Charlie tries to do the same. He grabs the patient's other wrist but has no watch with which to measure the pulse. He hurriedly grabs the patient's watch but in his rush to put it to use gets confused and puts the watch into his mouth as though it were a thermometer, another example of how Charlie's wires get crossed when he breathlessly tries to keep up with conventional behavior that he doesn't really understand. When the doctor finishes taking the man's pulse, Charlie removes the watch, shaking and reading it as though it were a thermometer. In this manner, Charlie takes the man's pulse and his temperature at the same time.

There's something innocent and childlike in Charlie's confused imitation of the doctor but there is also a double meaning. We know that the doctor is a fake because we've seen the elixir for curing horses in his handbag. Charlie's imitation of the doctor only echoes the farce the doctor himself is enacting. Charlie's role-playing tends to annoy adults (it certainly does the doctor here). They sense that he has caught on to their own playacting. Scenes like this bring to mind Chaplin's well-known remarks on children (among those that contradict Eisenstein's opinion that Chaplin didn't like children): "Despite the fact that I love children I find them difficult to meet. I feel rather inferior to them.... And one has to be on his best behavior with children because they detect our insincerity."[3] Children are truth-tellers and adults often would like to believe that children are misbehaving when actually they are doing what they can't stop doing, being honest. Chaplin's remarks here remind us that he doesn't model his humor on children in order to be cute and cuddly. Children do, naturally, what Chaplin took on as his vocation: highlighting the insincerity of adults, "mortifying the human sense of self-importance."

Charlie's childlike behavior around men is closely linked to his satirical attitude towards them. For example, in *Shoulder Arms* Charlie performs the stiff rituals of the changing of the guards—the ramrod posture, deliberate steps, robotic movements—with such exaggerated perfection that he seems to be making fun of them while he is, at the same time, doing them to his superior's satisfaction. He seems more a child playing soldier than an actual soldier. Comically, he maintains his stiff posture, even upon dismissal, so that he is unable to bend to pass through the small portal of his living quarters. Once inside his hut, he approaches his bed with the same exaggerated steps and sharp turns on the heel. He even maintains his ramrod posture in bed, which leads to his kicking a bunkmate in the head (the head of this man's bed is at the foot of Charlie's). When his bunkmate expresses anger, Charlie salutes him mechanically, carrying his changing of the guard routine right through to the last motion of his day.

There are several possible explanations of Charlie's behavior here. One is that he is a simpleton who can only understand the tasks asked of him in a literal way and is too slow-minded to realize when he is at ease. Another is that he is inherently childish and can't do anything in a work atmosphere without turning it into a game. Children will sometimes flout orders by performing them with exaggerated zeal. The third, and it's not inconsistent with the second, is that there is a spirit of malignant satire to Charlie. He performs his tasks to the letter of the law in order to mock them. The latter two seem closest to the truth of Charlie's nature. He affects a simplemindedness (that is not entirely an act, given how naive he often is) in order to more freely pursue his real agenda: to playfully mock the situation in which he finds himself.

Charlie is amused by adults' playacting and melodrama. Much of Charlie's playacting is an imitation of ours. Charlie, through his sensitivity to playacting and melodrama, emphasizes how much of adult reality is really a question of role-playing. He constantly urges the notion that there is a great deal more acting than we let on in the real world, that we are not so different from Charlie, nor so much more mature than children, that we too shift roles constantly and playact like children.

Twelve

Charlie and Men

If Charlie's allies tend to be outsiders and underlings—children, abandoned dogs, poor young girls—his enemies tend to be bulwarks of society. And, with the exception of some stuffy older society women, these are men: policemen, employers, co-workers, fathers.

Any discussion of Charlie's contentious relationship with men has to start by noting that Charlie, despite his identification with women and his often feminine behavior, has a strong masculine identity as well. He can be a tough guy, always spoiling for a fight. He often sizes up women's bodies with a cold and appetitive eye, and when he gets ahold of them handles them rather presumptuously. He carouses and drinks like a fish (though the drinking diminishes significantly as he ages). He has a variety of party tricks that testify to a masculine swagger. He can flick a spent cigarette over the top of his head and kick it with his back foot, make his hat look like it's doffing itself when he meets a young woman, gently tap a woman in the behind with his cane while looking like he hasn't moved, or coolly light a match on just about any appendage of a passing human body. Congenitally nervous, he can nevertheless be, at times, quite suave and, despite his surface frailty, a tough guy to bring down. He's a guerrilla warrior of sorts, and the more you push him around, the more he finds a way to pay you back. The more you try to take something away from him, the more stubbornly he clings to it. He has the appetites as well as the fighting skills of a junkyard dog.

And though he gentles considerably with age, even as late as *Modern Times* he continues to show remnants of his youthful combativeness. For example, in that film, Charlie, in prison, imbibes some cocaine and singlehandedly quells a prison riot, employing his trademark dodge, feint and strike warfare. Even in his latest incarnations Charlie can recover his masculine swagger though, like many an old gent, he needs a little stimulation to do so.

But Charlie is not a consistently tough guy, even in his earlier incarnations. Side by side with his combativeness and love of a good quarrel, Charlie exhibits a hair-trigger timidity even in his earlier films. Broke and homeless, Charlie has a very precarious hold on the world. He's never sure when he's going to be rousted, forever checking behind him to see if his backside is secure. His vagrancy, for which he is constantly being hounded, and his tendency to find his way towards trouble, have made him pathologically wary and anxious. In one of the trademark gags in Chaplin's arsenal, a male figure of authority needs only to raise his hand—say to comb his hair or wave—to make Charlie dodge an imagined incoming blow with lightning-like rapidity. Charlie is always in a state of nerves, ready to flinch at any sudden movement. He has the instincts of a beaten dog. He's been cuffed around in his time and it shows. Charlie does become softer with age. But you can see the same wild swing from masculine aggression to panicky fear in his early films as well.

In *The Floorwalker*, for example, Charlie is suspected of shoplifting by a store detective and clerk. The scene takes place near a water fountain. When the detective flashes his badge from inside his suit jacket, Charlie faints dead away from fear. But such is Charlie's mercurial nature that, before he hits the ground, he has the wherewithal to quickly turn the fountain handle and send a plume of fountain water shooting into the men's faces. His aplomb regained, he segues gracefully into a backward somersault and, exiting the scene, cockily tips his hat to the two men, who are still wiping the water from their eyes. This is Charlie's masculinity in a nutshell: a combination of abject fear and ruthless aggression, of unseemly cowardliness and elegant domination.

Throughout all of Chaplin's films, Charlie is characterized by this mixture of aggression and timidity that is held in careful counterpoise. Almost all of his fights with men are characterized by a mixture of frightened retreat and surly aggressiveness. He is both scared to death and unable to let go of a grudge, both meek and perversely antagonistic. Like many of us, he's often cowardly to authority's face, but refuses to accept the indignities he suffers at the hands of authority. And so he has a tendency to sneak back on it and kick it in the behind before he runs away. Like Dostoevsky's Underground Man, he's craven but indefatigable.

This mixture of dignity, fear, and surly aggressiveness is Charlie's master blend, and as representative as it is of Charlie's touching, pathetic nature, I think we're kidding ourselves if we don't recognize that Chaplin is satirizing the human species in general, our own manic blend of dignity and foolishness, heroic stance and dizzying fear, our own tendency to strike poses that we abandon far too easily and to meet defeat with a perverse, dogged resistance that is often as ridiculous and foolish as it is noble.

Satires of Masculinity

Though Charlie seems, at times, sincerely unable to understand the masculine world, there is some evidence in Chaplin's films that Charlie's ignorance about masculinity is willful, that he simply refuses to behave as a man is supposed to. When he chooses to satirize men, he does so with an unerring exactitude that betrays the subtlest comprehension of male behavior. It's only when he's sincere that he can't be the conventional male. When he's imitating or making fun of men, he has them down pat.

Charlie is particularly sensitive to the various roles men play in their battles with one another. Chaplin has a wide variety of very pointed comic bits that satirize the way men behave before, during and after a fight. Chaplin is particularly sensitive to the gestures of men who are spoiling for a fight. In moments of hostility with other men, for example, one of Charlie's trademark gestures is to half-remove his jacket

Chaplin and Ben Turpin in *His New Job*. Charlie is a much more belligerent and cantankerous fellow in his earlier films than in his later ones.

while thrusting out his chest and stepping towards his foe. In these scenes, the joke is that the jacket always remains halfway down his back, the arms in the sleeves. It's more a dance of intimidation than expressive of a sincere desire to fight, like the display aggressive birds put on with their feathers in their moments of territorial aggression. It's a mockery of men's empty bluster. This is one of Charlie's most repeated gestures, so instinctual that he does it almost unconsciously or spasmodically, just as he often doffs his hat at ridiculously inappropriate moments or kicks at people even when they have offered him no offense.

In *The Circus*, Charlie is also spot-on in his spoof of men's cock-of-the-walk behavior before a fight, as in the scene where Charlie squares off with his cruel circus boss. Engaged in an angry stare-down with the boss, he manifests a litany of aggressive, nervous tics. He leans towards the bully, straightening the bottom of his vest with curt, violent tugs meant to express his affronted dignity. Then he grabs a handful of hay from a nearby bale and scatters some at his enemy's feet, while solemnly breaking the remaining portion in his hand, in the manner of an Indian chief declaring war. Chaplin is expert at imitating this kind of behavior in which men, like dogs, mark their territory, their gestures signifying a great deal more comic bark than actual bite.

When Charlie does actually engage in a fight with other men, he does so in a manner that both reflects his athleticism and teases men for their pomposity. A great boxing fan and a natural athlete, Chaplin does a better-than-average imitation of a boxer: hands up, shoulders crouched, face protected, knees bent. His footwork is lovely too but it often gets the best of him by segueing into dance, as it does in several scenes from *The Pawnshop* where Chaplin cruelly pummels John Rand, alternating his boxing steps with elegant dance moves and shuffles. Chaplin often meets masculine aggression with effete mockery, sending up, rather than succumbing to, clichéd masculine behavior. Charlie's dancerly ease in his fight scenes lends them a sadistic elegance; Charlie often seems to be enjoying himself as he dances around his opponents, punishing them mercilessly.

Charlie's just as good at imitating the way men behave after fights. One of his go-to bits is the way men strut like roosters after they have shown another man up, in *Easy Street*, for example, after he has laid the neighborhood bully low by sticking his head in a gas lamp or in *The Gold Rush* when he mistakenly believes he (and not a falling clock) has knocked out Jack. In these moments, Charlie's swagger is full of fine, precise detail: He flexes his hands, checks his nails, hitches up his pants, straightens and tidies his waistcoat (Charlie's vest carries a great deal of dignity in his mind), dusts off his sleeves, barks orders, bends his legs athletically, arranges his hat dashingly, and lights a cigarette with elegant bravado.

Chaplin was just as amused by the slobbering bathos to which men descend when they conclude their quarrels as he was by their cock-of-the-walk displays of aggression before fights. Over and over in his films, Charlie's nemeses stick out their hand in friendship, with an unctuous sense of self-importance, after a quarrel. Charlie loves a good drama, so when men reach out to him emotionally like this, he warms to the role, meeting their bombast with his own overplayed pathos. The difference is that they are sincere while Charlie is playacting and only waiting, as he does when he stares neutrally at screaming bosses, for his next moment of payback.

In *The Kid*, for example, Edna convinces the neighborhood bully, with whom Charlie has been fighting, to shake hands and patch it up with Charlie. Charlie is happy to play the role of gentleman combatant and respond in kind. He, too, stiffly thrusts out his hand towards the bully, while looking away dramatically to the distance as though his emotions were too strong to trust eye contact. He gently wipes a tear away. No one will outdo Charlie in enacting the masculine ritual of dramatic reconciliations. Edna, citing the New Testament, even convinces the bully to turn his other cheek to those who have smote him (in this case, Charlie). The proffered cheek is too tempting for Charlie, however, who meets this act of contrition with a brick that he smashes over the bully's head. From this point on, the fight is much more to Charlie's advantage. Chaplin's overall sympathy for a kind of New Testament emphasis on forgiveness has always stood in paradoxical tension with Charlie's congenital indifference to the spirit of forgiveness. In all of these scenes, reconciliation is just a momentary game Charlie plays before he puckishly resumes a fight that only he is still spoiling for. He doesn't take this kind of male posturing seriously. He won't, at least, let it get in the way of winning a fight.

Feminine Responses to Male Aggressiveness

It's another curious aspect of Charlie's nature that he often exhibits feminine tendencies when he is threatened by men. As I discussed in my chapter on Charlie and women, he has a strongly pronounced feminine side. And that side tends to express itself strongly at certain moments of tension with men.

For example, in *City Lights*, Charlie, who has taken to boxing to raise funds for the blind girl he loves, finds himself in a locker room with the boxer (Hank Mann) he will oppose that night. Charlie tries to ingratiate himself to the stern boxer via a variety of coquettish gestures more characteristic of a woman trying to woo a man than one athlete befriending another: shy glances from a downturned face, nervous giggles, childish smiles, and that gesture Charlie often uses where he hunches his shoulders and ducks his head while intertwining the fingers of his outstretched hands. These gestures have no softening effect on Charlie's opponent, who stares at Charlie with the austere look of dull incomprehension men often wear when confronted by Charlie's enigmatic behavior. The only effect Charlie's eye-batting has on Mann is to drive him to a curtained changing room, suspicious as he is now about Charlie's sexual leanings.

Why does Charlie respond in a feminine way to men who threaten him? Well, first we have to note, again, how clueless Charlie can be about the rules of masculine behavior. He's good at imitating male behavior when he wants to make fun of it. But he has some real gaps as to how men behave in certain situations, like a locker room, where masculine ritual is emphasized. And, like many of us, Charlie has a strong streak of perverseness. He tends to do the opposite of what is expected of him. He is a nervous fellow and his default reaction, whether he's nervous around men or women, is to erupt in these giggles that are equal parts toddler and shameless flirt.

The motives behind Charlie's behavior are often shrouded in ambiguity. Sometimes he frustrates men by his slow-wittedness while we are left to wonder whether he isn't being purposely slow-witted in order to annoy them. Similarly, Charlie's feminine behavior can seem like a sincere eruption of nerves, but at other times appears calculated to annoy, as if Charlie knows this is the last thing expected of him and enjoys both the confusion this behavior engenders and the tactical advantage it provides.

In *The Cure*, for example, Charlie infuriates two of his nemeses by lobbing his shoes and clothing at them from behind the dressing room curtains where he changes into a swimsuit. The angry duo pull open the curtain in order to confront Charlie. The combination of being in his bathing suit, along with the flourish of the curtain opening, seems to put Charlie in the mind of a fashion model, and so he greets the open curtain in the pose of a men's swimwear model: one leg crossed before the other, chest out, look askance, straw hat on, cane in hand.

Charlie then quickly shuts the curtain on the two men before they even have time to react. They angrily pull the curtain aside a second time, revealing Charlie in a whole new pose, this time the coy, crouched, demure pose of a bathing beauty, a parody of *September Morn*, a popular female nude illustration of the era.[1] Charlie acknowledges their attention with flirtatious smiles worthy of Gloria Swanson before yanking the curtains shut again. The third time the men open the curtain, Charlie strikes a ballerina-like pose and leaps into the air in a flurry of entrechat kicks before landing in a graceful arabesque. He advances, *en pointe*, in tiny little staccato steps between the two men and then back into the dressing room, sending them kisses with sweeping balletic movements of his arms. The men now dazed, Charlie simply passes them by on the way to the pool without engaging in the slightest physical contact.

Charlie's feminine responses to masculine aggressiveness in this scene have nothing of the nervousness that he displays in the locker room in *City Lights*. Here the behavior seems to have two purposes. One is almost to mock masculine behavior by striking its opposite tone. Charlie won't stoop to playing the masculine fool. Moments of physical aggressiveness often bring out a taunting femininity on his part, as if he wanted to highlight how ridiculous men are when they strike masculine poses. The unpredictable feminine dances tend also to freeze his stunned aggressors in their spot, allowing Charlie, in this case, to walk off scot-free.

A similar moment occurs in *The Floorwalker* when the corrupt department store manager discovers Charlie with the briefcase filled with money that the manager aims to extort. The banker throws Charlie to the ground and Charlie pops up, not fighting but dancing, executing a series of balletic moves very much like the ones in *The Cure*. As the banker attacks Charlie, Charlie continues to dance and dodge at the same time, in the manner of a matador infuriating a bull.

And Chaplin uses feminine wiles to even more specific strategic effect in *A Woman*: A policeman has just witnessed Charlie push a man into the lake. Charlie, surprised by the cop's presence, quickly lapses into an ingratiating stance. He leans into the cop, looks up at him with coy, flirtatious eyes, strokes his shoulder with the crooked part of his cane, before hooking the cane behind his collar and flipping him into the water as well.

Chaplin was never one to run a gag into the ground, so Charlie's feminine responses to masculine aggression never mean exactly the same thing. In *The Adventurer*, when Charlie has contrived to fasten Eric Campbell's head between two sliding doors, the kiss he offers to Campbell's forehead seems aggressive, the icing on the cake that is Campbell's humiliation. In *The Floorwalker*, the department store manager (a double for Charlie) is so surprised to see his double that he holds Charlie's head and peers into his eyes. Charlie, a little nervous under this intense scrutiny, gives him a little peck on the lips, which he then quickly wipes on his sleeve, as if he mildly regretted the action. Here, in addition to expressing his nervous confusion, the kiss seems to mock a little. The banker has approached him in such melodramatic fashion that Charlie is put in mind of a romance. Charlie's comedy is always inspired by those who take a situation too seriously. In *Easy Street*, when he interviews to become a policeman, he is amused by the self-serious way the officers salute each other, which strike him as very much like blowing kisses to one another, a practice he happily accedes to.

Certain consistencies run through all these scenes, though: first an inability (that seems just as much a willful unwillingness) to understand the nature of male behavior. Second, there is an acute sense of how comic men are in their masculine bravado. Third, Charlie uses kisses as a means to contend with men, to gain advantage with them, sometimes before, sometimes during, and sometimes after fights. Invariably, the men are shocked and confused by Charlie's feminine wiles. No one has fought with them quite like this before. Just as it never occurs to Charlie that he has an obligation to fight fairly, so it never occurs to him that he has to pay obeisance to the conventionalities of male behavior when he fights. In fact, to flout those conventionalities provides distinct tactical advantages in a fight, not to mention great opportunities for mockery.

Charlie's Mode of Battle; Bottom-Kicking

Charlie understands men pretty well when it comes to mocking them. There his study of male behavior is acute. At the same time, he is more or less incapable of existing happily in a male world or in a situation that is governed by male rules of order. If, for example, Charlie fights according to the laws of masculine behavior, he loses. But if he is able to cheat, Charlie can beat up the biggest of men. Charlie is too poor, too small, too disadvantaged to respect rules and rituals when it comes to fighting. In the boxing matches in *The Champion* and *City Lights*, he dominates in direct proportion to how little the rules of the fight are being respected. The more out-of-control the fight is, the more dominant he is; the more it follows the rules of order, the more he loses ground. The only way he can succeed is through guerrilla warfare. When Charlie is miming boxing advice to his son in *The Kid*, we can discern from his visual signs that he is telling his son to poke his opponent in the eyes, punch below the belt and kick him in the rear end. Charlie is conscienceless when it comes to fighting.

Charlie has a good many tools at his disposal in his guerrilla warfare. He is expert at dodging punches, running away, and returning in a surprise attack. Like a good guerrilla warrior, he knows how to take advantage of his terrain. One of Chaplin's favorite gags during Charlie's fights with other men is to have Charlie pop up and down from his hiding places like a playful child or with the mechanical regularity of a tin target in an arcade shooting game. Charlie's battle method is to appear and disappear with lightning speed, running through doors and around corners, leaping through windows, appearing and disappearing, creating a dizzying maze for opponents. At the same time he is a master of immobility and can, also like a good guerrilla warrior, stand so still as to become part of the scenery, as he does in *The Adventurer*, where for one leg of a chase he does an excellent imitation of a floor lamp, or in *Shoulder Arms* where he perfectly mimics a tree. But of course Charlie's favorite weapon in his arsenal of tricks is the swift, unexpected kick to the behind.

Bottom-kicking is something of an obsession in Chaplin's cinema. Chaplin offers one of the better explanations of the significance of all the kicking of rear ends in his films in his autobiography, via some comments he recalled from an acquaintance of his, a Southern gentleman named Judge Henshaw. Henshaw praised Charlie's knowledge of the "essentials" of comedy. "You know," he told him, "that the most undignified part of a man's anatomy is his arse.... When you kick a portly gentleman there you strip him of his dignity. Even the impressiveness of a presidential inauguration would collapse if you came up behind the president and kicked him in the rear." Chaplin describes Henshaw "soliloquizing to himself" as he delivers his final thought on the subject: "There's no doubt about it; the arse is the seat of self-consciousness."[2]

This is a pretty good assessment of the meaning of Charlie's kicks to the behind. The kick, aimed right at the seat of self-consciousness, strips his opponents of their dignity. The kick to the bottom is one aspect of Chaplin's overall tendency, so primary to his cinema, to take the pretentious and self-righteous down a peg. Attacking his opponents' behinds is Charlie's way of undermining their pomposity. It's Charlie's great protest against the domination of snobs, bullies, and pedants. No one is so great that they can't be humbled in this manner. In Chaplin's films, to kick a man in his rear end is to win the battle, to dominate, to gain the day. Rear ends are like the flag in the game of flags, the ultimate goal of all this skirmishing.

Kicking is such an ingrained habit that Charlie often does it unconsciously and gratuitously. Charlie's leg kicks the way other people's eyes twitch. It's a default gesture, akin to his spasmodic doffing of his hat when he finds himself in nervous situations or the twirling of his cane when he is sexually interested in a woman. Charlie's body has a myriad of ways to outstrip the mind in its actions. The superfluous kick is one of Charlie's trademark gestures. Often when he shoos away animals or children, he adds a kick to their behind. Usually the kick doesn't land. The kick here, administered to these subordinate creatures, almost assumes a loving, solicitous quality, like a pat to the behind. In the footage of Chaplin and Jackie Coogan entertaining investors on the set of *The Kid*, we see that Chaplin finishes the little show he devised for the investors by sending Jackie off with one of these kicks that is never really meant to land.

Other times the superfluous kick is comically cruel and uncalled for. In *The Adventurer*, Charlie, on the run from a cop, mistakes the sound of the popping of a champagne cork for the report of the cop's gun. Mistake realized, policeman gone, he calms himself and resumes his disguise as a visiting dignitary, taking the arm of his hostess. But, on the way out, he administers a backwards kick to the behind of the entirely innocent butler who popped the cork.

I can't think of any film where more bottom-kicking goes on than *Sunnyside*. In that film, Chaplin communicates Charlie's abject subservience to his boss (Tom Wilson) by how patiently Charlie endures Wilson's repeated kicks to his behind. This film spells out clearly a law of Chaplin's cinema, that to be kicked in the behind by a man is to be owned by him. Chaplin works a good many variations on the bottom-kicking gag in this film. At one point, Wilson aims a kick at Charlie's seat but misses, banging his foot painfully on a bedpost instead. Charlie knows what he has to do. Seeing Wilson hopping in pain, he returns to the site where Wilson delivered the kick and willingly proffers his backside for a redo.

Later, Charlie gets in Wilson's way as Charlie pours coffee at their breakfast table. Wilson kicks Charlie's behind to move him out of the way. Being kicked in the rear is so much a part of Charlie's everyday life, though, that his face registers no acknowledgment of the kick. In fact, the kick only causes Charlie, whose face remains neutral, to neatly move his pouring to the second cup of coffee, as though he were a stuck needle on an LP that had been jarred back into place.

Later still, after the boss discovers Charlie sleeping on the job rather than tending his cattle, he literally drives Charlie home via a succession of kicks to the behind, each blow propelling Charlie forward. When the boss meets a neighbor on the road he doffs his hat, exchanges a few niceties and then returns to kicking Charlie down the road. Later, when Charlie arrives late to work, he stuffs some leaves in the seat of his pants to cushion the inevitable blows he is sure he will receive from his boss. He's perplexed when his boss doesn't kick him until his boss limps away and he realizes that injury prohibits abuse this day.

Sunnyside is not a typical Chaplin film. Charlie is more often the kicker than the kickee. At least he doesn't usually submit to the abject subservience he does in this film. But the film communicates the idea that runs throughout Chaplin's films, that a kick to the seat of the pants represents power in Charlie's world. It's a power Charlie enjoys to the full whenever possible.

Kicking behinds is such a recurrent part of Chaplin's cinema that he has ample opportunity to work variations on the gag. One of my favorite variations is that in which Charlie's enemy exposes his backside so fully that Charlie has enough time, not only to administer, but to savor the blow. In *His Trysting Places*, for example, Charlie's adversary (Mack Swain) bends over while flirting with a young girl, leaving his behind vulnerable to Charlie's attack. Charlie approaches the behind carefully. He gently lifts up the tails of Swain's coat in loving preparation, appraising the behind the way a waiter might a fine dish he has just laid before a customer. He places his arm on a nearby tree branch, steadying himself in anticipation of the kick. He cocks his foot, examines its readiness, warms it up a bit by flexing it and only then delivers the kick.

Similarly, in *The Floorwalker*, Charlie's adversary, a store clerk (Albert Austin), bends over. Charlie, again, preps his work scene, carefully lifting the tails of Austin's coat back, this time more in the manner of a scientist uncovering a lab specimen. He does a practice kick. He gently moves Austin's behind into place with the tips of his finger as though he were handling goods of rare value or setting up a baseball on a tee. He backs up, rolls up his sleeves (purposelessly), and hitches up his pants in readiness for the kick. Unfortunately, the store detective arrives at that moment and Charlie is forced to pretend, absurdly, that he is just admiring Austin's behind. He gently brushes away imaginary lint from one buttock, then the other. He replaces the tails, dusting them too as though he were a tailor arranging the suit's hang.

The Fireman has the same gag but with different detail. Austin, after kicking Charlie, has left himself vulnerable by bending over to attend to some task. Charlie scrutinizes Austin's behind for some time and then looks away, as though he were overwhelmed, even moved, by the opportunity. He returns his gaze to the behind a second time, this time resting his head on his arm in a gesture of reflection, as though contemplating the myriad alternatives available to him. He rolls up each of his pants legs carefully, readying himself for the kick, and just as carefully, almost ceremoniously, rests his hat on the bumper of the fire truck. There he sees an axe, which he picks up, measuring its heft and reflecting on its merit for the job he has in mind. This is one of those moments in Chaplin's films where we get a brief glimpse at just how potentially violent and chaotic Charlie can be, as for example in *The Kid* where he contemplates jabbing a woman with his quite sharp trowel. But he finishes by putting the axe down, electing instead to use his right foot, which he lifts and evaluates appreciatively before he employs it. Only then does he deliver the blow, which has gained a fine comic effect by this measured and detailed preamble.

Charlie does not need to kick others' behinds to rob them of their dignity. Charlie will often come across a bent-over person and will simply move the bent-over person to the side, via his behind, as though he were passing through a turnstile. Or he might sit down on the man's behind, using it as a kind of chair. Charlie's larger goal is not just to kick his adversary's behind, but to make that person aware that he has one, to reduce him, via his behind, to his most inglorious posture, to administer what Charlie feels is a badly needed dose of humility.

When he sits on a person like this, Charlie is also using his own behind as a weapon, heaping indignity upon indignity. Charlie often wields his own behind like a weapon. Even when the Tramp has reached the benign maturity of his later self in *City Lights* he is still apt to use his behind as a means of anarchistic protest. Of all the atrocities Charlie commits, in the opening of that movie, as he clambers around the sculpture that is being so reverently unveiled by the town's leading citizens, the most grievous has to be sitting on the face of the fallen Roman warrior represented in the sculptural grouping. In this moment, Chaplin expresses, very tidily and very forcefully, his sincere distaste for civic art and empty patriotic bombast.

Here again we are reminded of Chaplin's Shakespearean ability to range freely from moments as coarse as this one to the heartbreakingly delicate and lyrical moment that closes the same film. Even that final lyrical scene of *City Lights*, in which Charlie and the flower girl are reunited, is preceded by the newsboy's attack on Charlie's behind, when they taunt him by pulling at the underwear shred protruding from his behind when he bends over to pick up a flower. It's a prototypical moment for Charlie, a creature of poetry and gross matter, his nose in a flower, his backside dangerously exposed.

Work

Charlie's antagonism towards men gets its fullest play in the workplaces in which Charlie finds himself and where he wages war with both bosses and co-workers. One of the most recurrent scenarios in Chaplin's films, especially the early ones, is one that dates back to the routines of Fred Karno's troupe, Charlie haplessly wreaking havoc at a worksite.

Charlie is trouble at a worksite for a variety of reasons. First, to say that Charlie has no aptitude for work is a vast understatement. He is the spirit of anti-work. He is a gremlin, designed by nature to hinder work. Charlie is creative in his inability to work, ingenious in the way he doesn't work, prodigious and artistic in his inefficiency. In *The Rink*, for example, waiter Charlie's entire body gyrates as he mixes a drink in a cocktail shaker. The shaker, however, remains perfectly still. In this manner Charlie manages to play the role of bartender to great effect while simultaneously showing nothing for his efforts. This combination of playacting and unproductivity is Charlie's signature mix when he is in a work environment. In *Pay Day*, he drops into a hole in the ground with a shovel and works his shovel with vigor and expertise. His whole demeanor suggests a proficiency born from years of experience. And yet his shovel repeatedly emerges with only a few tablespoons of dirt on it. Charlie does an excellent imitation of a man digging productively; he just doesn't dig.

Much of Charlie's failure in the workplace is due to a slow-witted literal-mindedness coupled with an absolute inability to estimate the proportions necessary in a job. In *Behind the Screen*, for example, when moving props about, he carries a single pillow in an enormous wheelbarrow. In *The Tramp*, he waters fruit trees in the orchard with one quick spray from a watering can for each tree and tries to milk a cow by moving its tail like one would the arm of a water pump. In *The Circus*, he mops the sawdust floor and polishes the goldfish. In *The Bank*, when he finds that a letter he intends to mail is larger than the mail slot, he rips it in three parts and drops it in section by section. In *Sunnyside*, he seeks some lost cattle in tiny patches of shrubbery.

Often, the more Charlie applies himself to a job, the less successful he is at it. In *Police*, when Charlie's burgling partner (Wesley Ruggles) tells Charlie to "get busy" robbing the mansion, Charlie, as I mentioned earlier, starts darting around the room manically, grabbing flower vases from all over the room, dumping their flowers into his basket and then carefully replacing the vases in their original spot. At one point he even makes certain to get the last few drops of water in his basket before he sets the vase back in its place. He then hefts the basket to his shoulder as though he were carrying a load of iron, again taking a greater pleasure in playacting the job rather than actually doing it. This scene is one of the earlier ones in Chaplin's films that stresses Charlie's natural affinity to flowers. Charlie warms to a job when it conforms to his own sense of domesticity and aesthetics. Ruggles also gives Charlie a drill with which to crack open any safe he might find. Charlie immediately uses it to crack open the lock securing a piano cover. Part of Charlie's failure in work is that he does not share his co-workers' ideas of what is valuable in life.

Where Charlie does show innovation in the workplace is where it's entirely unnecessary. *The Bank*, for example, begins with Charlie arriving at the bank where he works. Carrying himself with his customary prim dignity, he seems to be a fairly important bank functionary, especially when we see that the first action of his work day is to open an enormous vault. Charlie executes three elaborate lock combinations before opening the massive vault door, only to pull out, from the depths of the vault, a mop and bucket. Only then do we realize that he is just the bank janitor.

Here again, the joke is one of proportion, Charlie wasting a great deal of energy to little effect, using a mammoth protective device for worthless objects. But the gag also points to how Charlie puts much more thought and effort to arranging his work than doing it, to the charming little domestic and decorative details of his routine. In *The Pawnshop*, Charlie has similar rituals involving his meager belongings. When he comes to work he checks his hat into a birdcage. His lunch is in the pawnshop vault. He stores his feather duster in an enormous suitcase. He's quite creative and detail-minded in how he sets himself up in his workplace, in this case taking advantage of all the curios that might be found in a pawnshop. In *The Rink*, before he sets off from his job as a waiter to a lunchtime visit to the skating rink, Charlie takes off his waiter's jacket and removes a suit jacket from the restaurant's oven where he has been steam-drying it.

Both of these tendencies in the workplace, the tendency to perform a role rather than actually execute it and the tendency to devise elaborate mousetraps of domestic routine, emphasize one of Charlie's biggest problems with work. He sees it as play more than work. His tasks often devolve into dance steps and he loves nothing more at the workplace than to roughhouse with his co-workers. He often gets increasingly playful and elated in proportion to his co-workers getting increasingly hot and bothered. And this roughhousing, like many a child's, results in devastating consequences to the physical environment of the workplace.

Charlie is always looking for a chance at work to amuse himself. In *The Pawnshop*, when he looks through the rungs of a ladder at co-worker John Rand, he starts to scratch himself in the manner of an ape behind bars at a zoo. When Edna calls him into the kitchen, he drapes a string of dough around his neck like a lei and starts strumming on a large wooden ladle as though it were a ukulele. He often only understands instruments of labor for their potential in play. In *The Tramp* the pitchfork it is, to him, an instrument tailor-made to prod behinds. Never would he think of using it for its conventional task.

Charlie is not just inefficient at the workplace, he's also destructive. One of the most recurrent plot devices in Chaplin's workplace skits is for Charlie to accidentally rain physical destruction upon the work environment via a series of accidents. Perhaps his most efficient means for destroying a workplace is to carry something of great length (a ladder most often, but anything will do—the tall column in *Behind the Screen*, the long pitchfork in *The Tramp*). While swinging it around carelessly, he destroys the things that are outside his peripheral vision. This destruction seems the result of Charlie's innocent incompetence. But Charlie tends to look on the fruits of his destruction with that same neutral gaze that he does a boss's tantrums. It's difficult to detect much surprise or guilt in that face and it's hard not to believe that this neutrality and seeming innocence masks at least an semi-conscious will to destroy.

Charlie only really enjoys work when he's broken it down some, eased its rigid restrictions. Well before Charlie traveled through the elaborate factory machinery of *Modern Times*, it was obvious that he represented, constitutionally, a monkey wrench in the organized framework of any male-dominated workplace. The scene in *Shoulder Arms* in which he parodies the rigid behavior of a military guard is an example of Charlie mocking the standardized behavior the workplace enforces on him, as is his inability to manage the escalator in *The Floorwalker*. Charlie is incapable of adjusting to the mechanized structures of the work world and so either mocks those structures or busts them apart, replacing them with an invigorating chaos. Once there is a good deal of rubble, Charlie, street urchin that he is, and accustomed to living in ruins, relaxes. Charlie needs a certain amount of chaos in order to truly feel comfortable.

The Anonymous Spectator of His Own Chaos

At certain moments, when Charlie's mishaps have resulted in chaos, Charlie will cleverly sidestep responsibility for his actions, foist the blame on others and escape to watch the ensuing chaos from a calm distance. In *Modern Times*, for example, waiter Charlie, walking into the kitchen through the door marked OUT rather than the one labeled IN, knocks over a waiter bearing a full tray of plates, food and drinks. Hearing the catastrophic crash of the waiter from the other side of the door, Charlie steps back from the door, letting another waiter, who was following behind him, enter the kitchen in his stead. This waiter receives the opprobrium due Charlie and a fight ensues between the two waiters, the fallen one and the mistakenly accused one. Only then does Charlie enter the kitchen, walking right between the two combating waiters with an innocent air of officious industry. He waits for his next order at a counter in the foreground of the frame with a kind of calm insouciance, looking into the air and strumming his fingers calmly, while in the background, the two waiters, victims of *his* ineptness, erupt into fisticuffs. Thanking the chef for his order with a smarmy politeness, he walks past the two combatants, carrying his tray of food and expressing a kind of surprised disdain for their disorderliness.

This gag, in which Charlie hides from the chaos he has wrought while letting other take his fall, is a favorite of Chaplin's. Anyone who has ever shirked responsibility or not owned up to some physical mishap can cringingly identify with the situation. But the gag also comments on how chaos seems to suit Charlie, to work to his advantage. When rules are upheld, Charlie is odd man out. When they are suspended, he rises in the ranks. Charlie often seems to glide happily on the currents of the chaos he creates.

This gag is not limited to the workplace, but any societal function which requires respect for decorum. In *The Rink*, Charlie, trying to right himself on his roller skates, knocks a man to the ground, who, in turn, trips another man. The ensuing row between these two victims of Charlie's ineptness draws the involvement of a skating rink official who kicks one of the two combatants out of the establishment. Charlie by this time is seated at some distance from the fray and, registered in that clever far shot Chaplin cited in his autobiography, watches it with a comic look of faux innocence.

In *The Adventurer*, Charlie, sharing ice cream with Edna on a balcony overlooking other guests at a party, drops a scoop of ice cream on the shoulder of a woman seated below. It then slithers down the back of her dress. Charlie, looking down, sees what he has done and, without mentioning his gaffe to Edna, beats a hasty retreat. He decorously leads Edna away from the balcony with a last nervous look down below at the mayhem he's caused and parks Edna and himself on a couch in the room just inside from the balcony. A second couple walks out onto the balcony that Charlie and Edna have just abandoned. This second couple looks down at the comic confusion of the lady below, who is fishing out the ice cream from her dress, and laughs at her, thus drawing the attention of the poor woman's husband, who assumes it was they who dropped the ice cream. Charlie and Edna, sitting just next to the balcony entrance, have a front row seat for what happens next. Charlie adjusts his tie guiltily as the husband charges onto the balcony and throws the laughing man into the room from the balcony. With the same calm decorousness that has marked his behavior throughout the scene, Charlie lends Edna his arm and gently leads her away from the fray, as though protecting her from this ugly spectacle which is, of course, all his own doing.

Police

Of all the men with whom Charlie has hostile relations, there are none that cause him more discomfort than the police. The police represent the letter of the law, trouble for a vagrant and petty grifter like Charlie. But policemen represent more than just law in Chaplin's films. They are a cosmic force of sorts that dictates to Charlie that he will never have rest. Charlie has no home. He is the perpetual odd man out, always on the move, and the police are the force that keeps him on the move. If he stops, even for a moment, he turns to find them glowering at him. He is never granted the luxury of stasis.

How many times does Charlie escape a scrape, catch his breath and then turn around to find a policeman looking at him sternly or eyeing him suspiciously, sending him off on a breathless run? Often Charlie doesn't even see the policeman; he merely senses his presence or makes contact with him before he knows he's there, leaning on the policeman, for example, when he meant to lean on a lamppost or reaching behind him to grab something and finding an officer's badge instead. Charlie can sense policemen subliminally, so powerful a place do they have in his consciousness.

Here, as in so many other aspects of Charlie's plight, we see a reflection of our own situation, a comment on human nature in general. Humans know no rest. Successes are brief and the majority of life is spent just keeping afloat. Call it the Greek side of Charlie. The best attitude is one of constant wariness. Don't ever be too pleased with yourself. "Count no man blest," as the chorus says in *Oedipus Rex*. Or, you might call it the Existential aspect of Charlie's life. Life is endless struggle. There is no panacea that offers more than temporary respite from the daily war of living.

One of the most notable aspects of Charlie's relationship to police is that it never occurs to him that he might reason with them. When he sees a policeman, he simply moves, rapidly, in the opposite direction, as though subject to reverse magnetism. Police are less men to him than they are human land mines to be avoided unquestioningly and at all cost. Charlie's aversion to police has little to do with whether he is actually guilty of a crime. When Charlie, after having picked up the abandoned child in the beginning of *The Kid*, puts the child back in the alley where he found him, he turns to find a policeman looking at him. Police tend to appear magically at Charlie's moments of indiscretion. The comedy of the bit lies in how Charlie turns around, on the dime, as soon as he sees the cop, picks up the child and walks away, with a nonchalant gait, casting only a single surreptitious glance at the cop as he parts, as if he had been planning all along on picking up the child.

In a similar scene from *Idle Class*, Charlie has been unjustly accused of pickpocketing by a man with whom he shared an outdoor bench. The man is throttling Charlie when a policeman approaches. Charlie could easily address two complaints to the policeman, one of being falsely accused, the second of assault. Instead, as soon as Charlie lays eyes on the cop, his body spasmodically erupts in a sprint in the opposite direction. Being guilty of a crime has nothing to do with Charlie's relationship with the police. He turns away from them with the same instinctual alacrity, whether he's the victim or perpetrator of a crime. Charlie has no faith that the police will treat him fairly, no faith that they will wait till he has done something wrong before they punish him, no faith that they are a force with which to reason. Police are the scourge of Charlie's existence, his instinctive bolting from then an implicit testimony to years of abuse at their hands, testimony to Charlie's absolute lack of faith in a just world.

It's worth noting that in both of the scenes above, the police, in chasing Charlie, direct him into a significant episode in the film. It's running from the police that brings John to Charlie's arms in *The Kid*. Charlie runs from the police and into the costume party where he will meet Edna in *The Idle Class*. It's police who chase Charlie into the big top early on in *The Circus*. Chaplin often uses a police chase to introduce the signal event in his film. Being chased by police represents Charlie's default existence. That's what he's doing up until Chaplin starts to tell the story he has in mind. Policemen represent the ogres that monitor the maze of city streets which Charlie must exist in, except at those moments when they chase him down some rabbit hole through which he discovers some adventure and a story for us.

It's usually police who make Charlie bolt in this manner, but not always. Charlie has a good sense of when to cut his losses with male figures of authority in general. In *Sunnyside* Charlie has chosen to court Edna by singing a song called "The Gallant Bandolero" which he also plays on the piano. Charlie sings it with comic bravado until Edna's father appears in a doorway behind the piano, presumably drawn there by the loud racket Charlie is making. Charlie isn't just embarrassed or chagrined by the father's presence; his response is more unequivocal than that. Seeing the father, he simply picks up his hat and heads directly for the door, casting a look or two back but otherwise assuming that courtship is over for the day.

In scenes like this, Charlie exhibits a beaten dog's aversion to figures of authority. There are certain men, he seems to understand, to whom there is no point talking, protective fathers, for example. Charlie often has to enjoy his romance on the run, just as he has to scarf down his food on the run, and often under the suspicious gaze of some man. This is one of the reasons that when Charlie gets a woman, or several women, to himself, he can barely contain his jubilation. Charlie relishes escapes from male scrutiny, never easy to come by.

Thirteen

Chaplin and Rhythm

Chaplin's skills as a filmmaker are often underrated because he is not characterized, in general, by a visual panache. His camera does not move a great deal, nor does he tend to create expressive angles in his shot composition. His filming technique is conservative. But what is demonstratively filmic about Chaplin's cinema is its sense of rhythm. If Chaplin is to be respected as a filmmaker, it has to be, to a great extent, as a master of rhythm. That was certainly T.S. Eliot's understanding when he wrote that Chaplin had "escaped in his own way from the realism of the cinema and invented a rhythm."[1] Chaplin felt that film "resembles the medium of music more than any other medium."[2] Good rhythm isn't as immediately arresting as powerful images, but it may be more important in building a film that lasts. Chaplin is not the only Hollywood pro who emphasized the musical properties of film. Hitchcock often spoke of directing via metaphors drawn from orchestral conducting. Rouben Mamoulian directed according to his belief that "rhythm was the greatest force in nature." He felt that a good studio film had its own complex rhythmic structure based on a triad of movements: those of the actor, the camera, and the editor.[3]

Studio-era Hollywood is characterized by a classical aesthetic that believes in sublimating art, the way art is sublimated in a Greek statue, expressing itself through a rhythm that is barely detectable to the conscious mind. The studio-era Hollywood film was an art form devoid, for the most part, of overtly serious ideas. And only a few of the directors were visual stylists. But all of the great directors had a good sense of rhythmic structure. The sophistication of some, Preston Sturges for example, is probably still under-recognized because they often sacrificed the more obvious virtues of visual display and weighty content for tight but lyrical rhythm.

Rhythm as the most significant constituent of filmmaking is an idea that ties together studio and art directors alike. Russian director Andre Tarkovsky, whose style could be described as anti–Hollywood in many ways (though he revered Chaplin), similarly felt that the "all-powerful factor of the film image is rhythm.... One cannot conceive of a cinematic work with no sense of passing through the shot, but one can easily imagine a film with no actors, music, decor, even editing."[4] And Robert

Bresson, the godfather of austere, demanding European art cinema (though also a huge Chaplin fan!), also emphasized "the primacy of rhythm" in film. "Nothing is durable but what is caught up in rhythms," he wrote, "Bend content to form and sense to rhythms."[5]

Rhythm in Mise-en-Scène

Chaplin came to Hollywood with a great sense of comedic rhythm, honed from years in acting and dancing troupes and particularly from his experience in Fred Karno's group of pantomime artists, which specialized in highly polished, well-practiced gags. But Chaplin quickly learned how to adapt that sense of rhythm to film, as he gained a sense of the quiet and small detail that the movie camera picked up. His cinema is filled with little gems of timing pitched perfectly to the intimacy of the movie camera.

One of my favorite bits in *The Bank* is as brief as it is quiet. Charlie, the bank janitor, has just been cruelly rebuffed by the object of his affection, Edna. He returns to his work station to find a fellow worker (Billy Armstrong) gussying himself up, presumably to impress the ladies at work. Armstrong fastidiously arranges his mangy tie, in imitation of the upscale workers of the bank. This annoys Charlie some as he has already suspected that it is his want of such upscale amenities as a tie that has scotched his chances with Edna. But Charlie is particularly irritated when Armstrong starts to comb his hair and moustache, alternately, with an intensity that might strike us as elaborate for any man, much less the comic-looking Armstrong. Charlie stares at this spectacle of narcissism for about five seconds with a dead, neutral expression that we know, from watching other Chaplin films, only masks a gathering storm of retribution. He seems to be just blankly watching Armstrong. But as his body stills, we sense an imminent eruption. A second later he kicks him out of the screen. In the tiny scene's epilogue, Charlie takes his seat and vents his spleen with a furiously bitter imitation of Armstrong tying his tie, an eruptive piece of little mimicry that passes by in the angry blur of a few seconds.

The key to the humor of this scene is the deadpan that Chaplin holds for five seconds or so before the kick, a kind of instinctual assessment of comic necessity, a calculation of how much time he needed to stare in mute annoyance before the violence of the kick would pay off in comic contrast. All this was done in one brief take and might be described as stagey were it not for the small scale of the scene, the way Chaplin registers extraordinarily slight facial gestures: the slight nausea that passes over his face when he sees Armstrong tying his tie, the anger nascent in his immobile face as he watches him comb his hair, the minutiae of hand movement in his angry imitation of Armstrong. The scene is characterized by good timing, but good timing pitched to the intimacy of the camera. Some of Chaplin's best gags, say the sausage-stealing scene from *A Dog's Life* or the scene from the same film in which, by substituting his hands for Albert Austin's, he makes the unconscious man seem animate, are scenes of great comic timing that are shot with an integrity of space and time that is stage-like but with a subtlety and intimacy of comic effect that could only be realized on the screen.

The rhythm of Chaplin's comedy becomes more rich and complex as he advanced as a filmmaker. He gradually arrived at a rich *mise-en-scène,* or arrangements of movement within a scene, that is characterized by complex choreography and expert timing. Take, for example, that scene in *The Idle Class* in which Chaplin plays an impeccably dressed dandy who has, that day, forgotten to put on his pants. As he enters the lobby, we shudder to see an older woman seated in the lobby, holding a pince-nez to her eyes, the perfect woman both to scrutinize and be shocked by the exposed gentleman. But just as Chaplin strides into the lobby, and just as the woman turns to note him, a worker passes by bearing a curtain rod from which curtains hang on either side and Chaplin is miraculously shielded, not only from the woman's gaze but any cognizance on his own part of his embarrassment. Three things—Chaplin, the woman's gaze, and the curtain—have converged to make this miracle happen. Chaplin doffs his hat to the woman from behind the curtain and she looks away.

Next, several people enter the lobby, including an attractive young woman who hangs around a bit in the foreground of the image. The worker bearing the curtains spins around some, contemplating the upper reaches of the lobby where his work is to be done, and in doing so exposes Chaplin again. But just as the young woman turns and walks towards Chaplin the worker spins back to his original spot and Chaplin is protected by the curtains a second time. The young woman turns back to where she was—she had forgotten something—and exits the scene in the foreground while the worker now takes his curtains and exits through a door in the left. Chaplin is left exposed once again. The older woman with the pince-nez turns her attention to him again, just as Chaplin enters a phone booth with wood paneling in the lower half of its door that protects him.

And so on. Chaplin came to be quite accomplished at this kind of elegant *mise-en-scène,* reminiscent of the carefully arranged scenes in the films of Jean Renoir and Max Ophuls, two Europeans whose films are characterized by long takes, elaborate arrangements of movement, and a charming, whimsical sense of rhythm. And he would influence long-take comic filmmakers like Jacques Tati and Otar Iosseliani who had the same propensity for showing how at certain moments, cosmic shifts occur, and the world arranges itself in the form of a well-choreographed dance.

Other times his carefully choreographed *mise-en-scène* has a slapdash, farcical quality. There's a nice example of Chaplin's fine timing in *mise-en-scène* in *The Pilgrim.* Charlie is forced to host a convict buddy of his, Nitro Nick (Chuck Reisner), at the home where he is a guest, even though he knows his ex-cellmate plans to rob this family that has been kind enough to offer Charlie harbor. Nick has his eye on a safe in the downstairs dining room. Charlie can't say anything or Nick will let the family know that Charlie is an escaped convict. So Charlie has no recourse but to keep a close eye on him the night he stays over at the family's house.

The scene I'm interested in takes place on the second floor landing of the house where Charlie, Nick, and the girl of the household (Edna Purviance), who Charlie is of course sweet on, all retire to bed. As Nick and Edna go to their respective rooms, Charlie opens and shuts his door without entering his room. Nick hears Charlie's door shut and reappears in the hall, intent on heading downstairs to rob the house. Seeing Charlie waiting for him in the hallway, he returns to his room.

Now Charlie tries a variation; he opens and shuts his door, again without going into his room, but this time scurries to a hallway chair across from his door where he can wait for Nick unnoticed. Again, Nick exits his room upon hearing Charlie's door close, this time looking through Charlie's keyhole to make sure Charlie is in his room and thus providing Charlie with the opportunity to kick him in the behind and order him back to his room.

Nick won't be cowed this time, however. He pushes Charlie aside and heads downstairs to find the safe. It just so happens, though, that he has pushed Charlie towards Edna's door. Charlie quickly avails himself of the opportunity to knock at her door. When the unwitting Edna opens it, he asks for a glass of water. Nick, having to maintain his facade, heads back to his room a third time.

I could go on with this scene but perhaps this small slice will suffice. The scene shows us a couple of things about how Chaplin achieves the rhythm he does. First, the scene is well-timed and choreographed, with everyone popping in and out of their doors like figures in a mechanical game. We see the same kind of mousetrap ingenuity in Charlie's "now you see me, now you don't" chases where he pops up in the most unlikely places, appearing and disappearing with a vermin-like rapidity that dizzies his opponents.

But we also see something here characteristic of Chaplin's later films. Over the course of his films, Chaplin got better and better at developing his gags, working variations on them. He doesn't fall into the lesser comic's habit of dull repetition. First, he dupes Nick with his door gag. Then he works a variation on it, hiding and kicking him. Then, when these strategies no longer work and Nick resorts to overt bullying, Charlie ingeniously arrives at the glass of water strategy. He keeps returning Nick to his room but it becomes more and more difficult with each effort. The stakes become higher, the pace more dizzying, the gags more complex and resourceful. Chaplin likes to create a motif and then spin variations off that motif, adding momentum and complexity to his rhythm, ratcheting up its pace.

Rhythm in Editing

As time went by, Chaplin learned to translate his gift for timing into film editing as well. Chaplin is often described as a genius, a habit that has led to feeble analysis of his films. But his genius was in many ways a product of his intense work ethic, the hours he logged looking at footage, figuring out what worked on film. He learned over the years to express his sense of comic timing through editing. The scene in which Charlie bolts from the lion cage in *The Circus* is a good example. This scene is funny because of its timing. And this timing, unlike the example from *The Bank*, is entirely dependent on editing.

In this scene, Charlie is trapped in a lion cage, but his panic subsides when the lion wakes and seems quite tame. Moments earlier, Charlie had frantically asked Merna to save him. As she unbolts the door, he sees an opportunity to impress her and so stays in the cage, showing off his nonchalance, even approaching the lion in a teasing manner. When the lion suddenly roars, Chaplin bolts comically, his abject fear a comic contrast to his calm seconds earlier. Chaplin follows Charlie's initial bolt from the lion's cage with four consequent shots.

The first is a shot, from outside the cage, of Chaplin running across the cage, from the right of the screen to the left, at a manic speed, and out the cage door. The speed of the shot is a gently accelerated to boost the comic effect of his abrupt turnaround. The humor here, again, is in how quickly he abandoned his confident swagger of seconds ago. The second shot is one of Chaplin running, wildly, directly to the back of the frame, through the grounds of the circus. The arrangement of the shot is clever since running directly to the back of the frame accentuates how much ground Chaplin is covering so quickly and also highlights the baggy seat of his pants and his splayed feet as he runs. The third shot is an incidental but important one of Merna exiting the cage and following Charlie. It's critical because it allows Chaplin to take our eyes off Charlie. The fourth shot is the best, and the payoff of the scene: Charlie at the tip of a 25-foot-tall tent pole, clutching for dear life.

Now, the time that transpired from the time we last saw him running to the time we see atop the pole (the length of the shot of Merna) is only a matter of a few seconds, not nearly enough time for Charlie to have even arrived at the pole, much less climbed to where he is. But that sped-up conception of time is what makes the scene funny. There's a cartoon logic here. Charlie was so frightened that he moved at superhuman speed. And since we didn't have to see it (via, for example a lame, sped-up technique) the comedy is not only plausible but elegant. In fact, part of its comedy is its very implausibility. We know it couldn't have happened but we love how neatly Chaplin made it seem like it did.

Here, Chaplin calculates just how little time he must let transpire to get this comic effect, just as in *The Bank* he's calculating how much time he needs to let roll with Charlie's neutral expression before he lets his kick fly. But the calculation here is about time implied by an edit rather than the real time of the held shot from *The Bank*. The sequence is also a good example of that other talent of Chaplin that I've explored earlier in the book, his ability to exploit ellipses, or gaps of information, in his films for comic effect. Not showing an action allows a director to play more freely with that action.

Chaplin's gift for rhythm via editing is probably most evident in his elaborate fight and chase scenes. Chaplin's editing of these sequences is notable for two aspects in particular. The first is that Chaplin got quite good at shifting from one scene to another in his fast-paced comic sequences so that not only does the editing not damage the velocity of the comic sequence, it actually intensifies that sequence. The second is that the cuts are immaculately matched.

As I mentioned earlier, Chaplin is famous for his lack of interest in continuity and for years deplored the necessity of a script girl, even when the importance of continuity had long been standard in the movie industry. Consequently, there are some whopping continuity errors in his films, particularly with props and costumes. Nevertheless, his greatest comic sequences are characterized by flawless continuity and match cuts. In chases, at least, where it was a case of comic timing, it seemed of vital importance to Chaplin to get his continuity right. Gags, like these, that rely on breakneck speed and breathless timing, fail if things are out of place. The scene in which Charlie frustrates a policeman who chases him, by rolling back and forth underneath a fence in the opening of *A Dog's Life* is an excellent example of both aspects of Chaplin's editing: the expert sense of timing and the fine matching of edited shots. The timing is superb with Chaplin rolling more and more quickly and the edits capture the roll on each side of the fence without a lag that would depreciate the comic effect.

The Chase in The Adventurer

The scenes from Chaplin's oeuvre which are most complex and developed in their rhythm employ both of Chaplin's timing skills—elaborate choreography and carefully rendered, lightning-fast editing. The boxing match in *City Lights* might be my nomination for the best example of skillful, developed rhythm in Chaplin's oeuvre, but there are many other examples, including the wild fight-chase sequences that conclude *Behind the Screen, Easy Street,* and *The Adventurer.* There is so much craft in these sequences that they render any short analysis impossible. And so I have reserved a later chapter just for an analysis of the musical virtues of the boxing sequence from *City Lights.* But the chase that concludes *The Adventurer* is also one of his great bravura exercises in rhythm and worth looking at for at least a few quick examples of how deftly Chaplin can interweave careful *mise-en-scène* with rapidfire editing to arrive at sequences of exuberant, triumphant rhythm.

The chase that finishes *The Adventurer* takes place in four contiguous spaces, two on the first floor of a building (an inner lobby and outer porch area) and two on the second (an upstairs recreational room and a balcony). This ups the ante, in terms of editing, as the characters enter and exit four different spaces, and, not only from left and right, but from above as well. And part of the success of the chase is the way Charlie and the police who chase him keep appearing out of nowhere. It's Chaplin's busiest and most vertical chase and utilizes three of the four edges of the frame, creating a greater sense of chaos and, quite literally, free fall.

It's also a highly edited chase as Charlie and his pursuers move rapidly between these four rooms. There are 14 cuts in between rooms. And the editing is top-notch. Much of the humor of the scene resides not just in Charlie's well-timed antics but in the timing of the cuts, in the way, for example, that Chaplin matches perfectly the velocity of Charlie as he charges from one room to that of him coming to a screeching halt in the next. Also, as in the rolling-under-the-fence scene from *A Dog's Life,* the cutting continuity is extremely well-polished, which is essential if the cuts are not going to mar the airtight architecture he's built, that mousetrap-like sense of everything happening with mechanical precision. The edits are the hinges in the mechanical apparatus that hold it together, and give the scene its final sense of machine-like perfection.

Within the edited scenes there is, of course, wildly conceived *mise-en-scène.* The cuts hold together, essentially, 14 different set pieces, each carefully choreographed. My favorite is the one where Charlie, having just leaped from the balcony to the porch and found a policeman there, charges back into the lobby of the building, the officer in pursuit. The choreography of this small segment of the chase is immaculate. Charlie races past Edna in the lobby and grabs a large lamp shade, placing it on his head and doing the best imitation of a standing lamp I've ever seen, before the cop enters the room. The gag capitalizes on Chaplin's unparalleled ability to stop on a dime, to move from frantic movement to absolute immobility in the blink of an eye. Pacing, in Chaplin's films, is a three-way dance between Chaplin, *mise-en-scène* and the editing, and his ability to go from movement to stillness and vice versa is a big part of how he arrives at such exhilarating and complex rhythms.

The cop races past Charlie, up the stairs, and exits through a door at the top of the stairs at the same moment that Eric Campbell, playing Edna's jealous suitor, enters from the left on the main floor, a small example of Chaplin's clockwork-like *mise-en-scène*. As Campbell starts to berate and even attack Edna (he's angry at her for having shown Charlie favor), Charlie is roused from his motionless lamp-stance. Charlie kicks Campbell, throws the lampshade on Campbell's head to blind him and punches him in the stomach, causing him to fall to the floor. Charlie steps on Campbell's ample belly as he returns to Edna, one of those casually brutish moments Charlie specializes in, in which he signals, in the most nonchalant way possible, as though he were not even doing it, absolute domination over a competitor. He picks up the lampshade off the floor, by now forgetting that it isn't a real hat, holds it over his chest, grabs Edna's hand and kisses her. Then he steps to her side and makes one of his trademark hammy gestures (like he does when he parts from Georgia in *The Gold Rush*), a gesture that suggests he is going away but will be back someday. Then, in what is my favorite gesture—because many of Chaplin's best gestures are his most absurd and least necessary—Charlie puts the lampshade back on his head and charges out the door, like a cavalry officer who has just kissed his girl goodbye and is heading off to battle. The cut finds him on the porch, shade still on his head, making one last dramatic gesture of self-glorification before he removes the lampshade to find himself before a policeman who has just dropped from the balcony above, as Charlie had moments earlier. And the chase is back on.

That entire sequence is just one of the 14 set pieces edited together to make this chase scene. It only takes 19 seconds, which explains why analyzing Chaplin's filmmaking can be so demanding. But it's important to recognize the significance of a scene like this in appreciating Chaplin's art. It's the very density of the scene, combined with its inspired musical pace, that makes Chaplin a competitor with the greatest art of all time. This scene's greatness is not in its visual elan (though the shots are very crisply organized) or in the depth of its content. Its greatness is in its musical qualities, the amount of details it crams into a small amount of space, and the ingenious rhythmical arrangement of those details. To those who are confused as to how critics can take a silent film comedian as seriously as they have Chaplin, I would say take a good look at this chase sequence, characterized by an explosive energy coupled with a delicate charm, by frantic, musical pacing, by ingenuity, resourcefulness and gathering energy. These are the characteristics not only of great filmmaking, but of great musical and dramatic art as well.

These highly choreographed and carefully edited scenes that witness Chaplin's pinpoint precision in timing, both in real space and via edited space, have much in common with music. Like music, they don't stop for us but rather pass by and with such rapidity and complexity that we are both exhilarated and overwhelmed by them, unsure of what we have just experienced. These scenes leave us wanting to experience them again, so that we might get a better hold on them or so that we might simply re-experience the pleasure. We want to replay them, as we do music, to enjoy them again and to get better at understanding them. Hence the long history of critics exhausting themselves, tracing the "logarithmic mazes" of Chaplin's gags, their musical structure. Writing on Chaplin is much like writing on music, where you also have to trace light and ineffable effects through the cumbersome media of words and to connect something devoutly content-less with the ideas it nevertheless implies.

It's also interesting how well these more "musical" scenes bear up to repeated viewing. Paradoxically, these scenes provide surprises but their pleasure is not dependent on surprise. "It is significant," wrote Andre Bazin, "that the best Chaplin films can be seen over and over again with no loss of pleasure—indeed the very opposite is the case.... [C]omic form and aesthetic owe nothing to surprise. The latter is exhausted the first time around and is replaced by a much more subtle pleasure, namely the delight of anticipating perfection."[6] Bazin here describes the pleasure in watching the chase from *The Adventurer.* The scene is enjoyable in its cold, machine-like precision, in its ingenious timing and architecture. Even after we know everything that will happen, we enjoy watching it. In fact, the more we know the scene, the more we marvel at its structure, the more we anticipate its movements. Becoming increasingly conscious of the architecture of Chaplin's best scenes only adds to the pleasure. To watch Chaplin, as in listening to great music, is to exalt in the display of form, to partake in an exquisitely delicate rhythm, something close to "perfection."

Fourteen

Dance

The particularly rhythmic nature of Chaplin's films is also emphasized by Chaplin's tendency to include dance in them. Even in his earliest films, Charlie had something of the dancer to him. As Dan Kamin has noted, there is something balletic in Charlie's essential look: "With his splayed feet, tilted-back pelvis, and regal bearing he presented a virtual parody of a classical ballet dancer."[1] And Chaplin had a strong, wiry body, by which he was able to convey weightlessness and to cheat gravity in a thousand little ways.

Like a dancer, Charlie is drawn to movement for movement's sake. He is not impressed by the utilitarian movements of the workplace, or of life in general. Charlie likes to play with movement and has a natural propensity for inessential, superfluous movement. He's like a child who doesn't find ordinary motion sufficient to contain the general sense of excitement within him. He needs to add extra moves to his motion. The everyday world doesn't have enough dance in it for him. And so Charlie is always amping up his motions, decorating them, with little skips, designs and tricks, like his trademark cane-play, his one-legged turns around bends and his variety of party tricks: rolling his hat down his arm, throwing a cigarette behind his back and kicking it backwards with his foot, bouncing his cane off a sidewalk. Charlie sees dance everywhere and this sense of the ubiquity of dance, of the tendency of dance to break out in all sorts of places, is no small part of the whimsy of Chaplin's films. Chaplin and Charlie both are very sensitive to our natural tendency to dance, our inherent attraction to expressive gestures. Chaplin's sensitivity to dance is part of his overall sensitivity to those moments where life escapes the utilitarian and chases the beautiful, those moments, in his mind, where life starts to exhibit rhythm, loveliness, artfulness and meaning.

In fact, you have to ask yourself what motion of Charlie's isn't dance-like. When Eric Campbell objects to Charlie spiriting away Edna for a dance in *The Count,* Charlie gently grabs Campbell's beard and elegantly pulls him aside. That done, he clicks his fingers at him and then thumbs his nose at him in a gesture that combines, at the same time, a tip of his hat. These are the sharply defined gestures of a dancer. Charlie is almost always exercising the bodily control and elegant self-consciousness of a dancer. When Charlie pulls a lever or hugs a woman, his leg flies up backward in a decorative pose. When he vanquishes a foe, he often finishes with a little dance, crossing his legs and bowing slightly. Charlie looks for any occasion to mix dance into his routine.

This was somewhat true of Chaplin in real life as well. "His movements are as piquant and precise as a ballerina's," wrote Thomas Burke in his account of the private Chaplin.[2] Alistair Cooke's description of the attractiveness of Chaplin's everyday motions is often quoted by biographers: "One of the permanent pleasures of being with him was to watch the grace and deftness with which he performed all physical movements, from pouring syrup to swerving like a matador just out of the line of an oncoming car."[3]

It is Chaplin's dancer-like quality, as much as anything else, that separates him from the other comedians of the day, all of whom seem much more a part of the real world than does Charlie, who brings a stage with him wherever he goes. Charlie is not cartoonish just because of his costume. His movements are not those of the quotidian world. Perhaps T.S. Eliot had this in mind when he wrote of Chaplin escaping the realism of cinema and inventing his own rhythm. Charlie is something less than an actual dancer but something more than a mere man. His art lies in a hybrid of dance and cinema, in the particular rhythm Chaplin invented.

Dance is one of those ingredients—along with pathos, music, Charlie's attraction to women and beauty, Charlie's increasing softness and melancholy—that Chaplin blends more freely into his mix as his films develop and which give his later films their greater artistic breadth. In the end, when we cite the most beautiful moments in Chaplin's cinema we often turn to scenes from his later films that involve dance: the dream in *Sunnyside*, the roll dance in *The Gold Rush*, the boxing sequence in *City Lights*, the assembly-line breakdown in *Modern Times*, the song and dance from *Modern Times*, the balloon sequence from *The Great Dictator*.

And these are just the instances where the dance is overt. As Chaplin developed as a filmmaker, he came to see the parallels between music and film more and more strongly and, as we have seen, the choreography of regular movement in his films becomes more dance-like. "Everything I do is a dance," he said in his 1966 interview with Richard Merryman. "In *City Lights*, with the blind girl, there is a beautiful dance. I call it a dance. Purely pantomime. The girl extends her hand with a flower. And the Tramp doesn't know she's blind. And he says, 'I'll take this one.' 'Which one?' He looks incredulous—what a stupid girl. Then the flower falls to the ground, and she goes to feel for where it is. I pick it up and hold it there for a moment. And then she says, 'Have you found it, sir?' And then he looks, and realizes. He holds it in front of her eyes—just makes a gesture. Not much. That is completely dancing."[4]

Chaplin defines, here, a kind of dance that is little more than carefully considered, drawn-out, elegant motion. This kind of dance is typical of his later films. The scenes in *City Lights*, in which Charlie first meets the blind flower girl and the later one in which the girl, her sight recovered, first lays eyes on him, are characterized by a slowed-down, balletic quality. These *City Lights* scenes are more hushed than the highly choreographed scenes from his earlier films, more overtly balletic in the solemnity of their rhythm, more plaintive and lyrical, with their emphasis on longing expressions and dramatic hand gestures. There are moments in these scenes of such dramatic posture that they alienate certain Chaplin aficionados who prefer the madcap, farce-like rhythms of chase scenes from earlier films and the less affected poses of the younger Charlie. Fortunately, though, Chaplin never lost the habit that he had from his earliest films on, to undercut grand gestures with embarrassing moments. And though the choreography in many of these later scenes is slower and more emotive, it rarely descends into bathos.

Overt Dances

Before these later films where dramatic action itself is often conceived in terms of dance, overt dance found its way into Chaplin's films in two ways. The first was via social scenes in which Charlie dances with a woman before a band, like the dance scenes in *The Count, A Dog's Life* and *Gold Rush.* These scenes allow Chaplin to do a couple of things. One is to ham it up quite a bit and to show off some of his most comical music hall dance moves. In these scenes Charlie is an entertainer and often the crowd of dancers around him is a surrogate audience, shocked at, or amused by, his antics.

Another thing Chaplin does in these sequences is display his exquisite, inherent sense of balance as a filmmaker; Charlie moves fluidly between irredeemable awkwardness and crowd-pleasing grace. In *The Count,* for example, Chaplin trots out a variety of charming dance moves, punctuated by pratfalls. The falls, which often result in dexterously accomplished splits, become part of the rhythm of the dance. At one moment the wax floor causes him to fall into a split but, with his cane, he hitches on to a chandelier and draws himself up with perfect ease and linear grace, never losing a beat in the measure.

Charlie's buffoonery often improves a dance rather than diminishes it. In this dance, Chaplin makes the point, as he does in other areas of his films, that improvisation enriches, that routine movement is more boring than movement enlivened by accident. It's part of Charlie's charm, and a result of Chaplin's deft sense of balance, that Charlie can be elegant and foolish at the same time, sometimes in a single gesture. At one point on the dance floor in *The Count,* Charlie exhibits great skill at a Charleston-like kick. But at the same time he keeps accidentally kicking him*self* in the behind. It's a moment of foolishness that can only be accomplished through athletic grace.

These dance scenes also often testify to Chaplin's compositional resourcefulness. He avoids repetition like the plague, one of the things that sets him above conventional comedians. He often builds these dance sequences as a series of variations on a gag. Like a musical piece, they unroll in several movements. Take a look at the scene in *The Rink* where he skates with, and tortures, his nemesis, poor Eric Campbell. The scene is structured very similarly to Chaplin's dance scenes and his skating here represents a dance as much as any of his ballroom moves do. I count six movements to Chaplin's choreographed punishment of Campbell in this skating scene, each of the six representing its own little dance move.

Charlie's first conceit is to rhythmically bounce off Campbell's enormous belly as though it is an inflated beach ball, but always returning to the belly as though he were tethered to it. The second is to avoid Campbell's wayward punch by dodging it and weaving tight little circles around him, in the manner of a matador who leaves only the minimum room between himself and the bull. The third movement occurs when Campbell grabs Charlie by the neck. Charlie holds on to Campbell in return and both of their feet slip and slide in synchronized panic as they try to bring each other down, finishing instead by creating a kind of one-bodied, four-footed perfectly timed manic dance. That Charlie is only pretending to have difficulty skating here becomes clear when he segues to his fourth dance idea, an elegant high-stepping dance in which he leads Campbell in waltzing twirls. Gaining some separation from Campbell, Charlie moves to a fifth dance variation, holding Campbell at bay with his cane to Campbell's belly as Campbell strikes wildly at Charlie, a target he can't reach. Charlie finishes this fifth stage of the dance with a nice flourish, pretending to bore a hole in Campbell's belly with his cane and then tapping the cane at its top as though he popping a pole into the hole he just dug. Finally, the sixth movement: Charlie hooks Campbell by the collar, leading him, like a chained hulking beast, in circles around the skating rink. He switches to pushing Campbell by a cane to the belly before finally sending him flying through a doorway to a spectacular fall in the cafe-bar that adjoins the rink. Six different means of torturing Campbell, all representing elegant dances distinct to themselves.

There's even a kind of coda to this dance scene. Charlie sends Campbell flying with such velocity into the bar-cafe that Campbell, entering the screen from the left, sends a waiter flying into a table of three guests on the right. All the guests fall down, like a bowling bowl might topple so many pins. Another waiter with a tray of food, heading from the bar in the back of the screen, towards the camera, trips over Campbell's fallen body, and a third waiter heading towards the bar, and away from the camera, does the same. It's a spectacular fall, as impeccably arranged as it is surprising in its chaos, the perfect pay-off to Charlie's gradual acceleration of torture. And it has to be replayed if you want to thoroughly relish its finest details, for example the nicely timed rhythm and visual symmetry of the three waiters' falls or the perfect annihilation of the table and three guests that the first waiter's fall represents.

The camera returns now to Charlie for one last little sign-off gag. After all this virtuosic footwork, after all the myriad opportunities for falling that his fight with Campbell provided, Charlie only falls now, and falls hard, when he has delivered himself of his charge and is observing Campbell's explosive fall from afar. It's typical of Chaplin's art that this little epilogue, this little rhythmic detail, also expresses an idea. Charlie tends to fare worse when he has time on his hands. Lost in warfare with some obese bully, he's a master of movement, a superhero of his own tricky brand of battle. But given a moment to rest and reflect, he reverts to awkward Tramp form. Charlie always flies higher when he's freed from the burden of consciousness. A moment like this, seemingly so incidental, represents a good example of the complexity of Chaplin's art. Charlie's fall here represents a crowning moment in an intense formal, rhythmic pattern and, at the same time, the subtle, wordless expression of a significant idea. It's Chaplin's great accomplishment to carry on a substantial conversation with us by means of elegant choreography.

This sequence is notable not only for its clever choreography, gathering rhythm and pitch perfect pay-off, but for its resourcefulness, its impressive spirit of invention. Chaplin is intent on not repeating himself. Each new moment must represent a new improvisation on the general theme of how Charlie might torture a competitor while skating, each a new sadistic dance move. Charlie moves from one experiment in physics to another like a kind of scientist-dancer. And as he does, there's an intensification of energy. How many new ways can Charlie find to torture this man before he sends him flying to oblivion? Where will it all end? The spectacular explosion of waiters that finishes this scene is the answer to that last question and the appropriate pay-off for a scene that seemed to be ratcheting its way to pure chaos.

Non Sequitur Dances

The second way in which dance often intrudes in Chaplin's earlier films, other than scenes in which Charlie literally performs dances with others before a band, are those in which Charlie breaks into absurd little non sequitur dances, dances that don't seem to be warranted by the situation, that are just pure expressions of exuberance. These are among the most charming dancing scenes in Chaplin's films because they are so curious, so uncalled for, so surprising. Kyp Harness has noted that Chaplin's gags, influenced as they were by the "broad behavioral surrealism of the British music hall," are "often nonsensical and audacious," characterized by a "cheerful illogic."[5] Chaplin's curious eruptions into dance certainly represent examples of this Surrealist bent in his filmmaking, this "cheerful illogic."

We see examples of this kind of dancing in some Essanay films like *Champion* and *Shanghaied* but, as critics have long noted, this kind of dance behavior really seems to burst out in the Mutual films, for example in *The Floorwalker, The Cure, The Pawnshop* and *Behind the Screen*. Critics have often suggested that Charlie's propensity for inane dance in these films is a reflection of Chaplin's happy artistic temperament at that time. Chaplin was at the height of his artistic powers during his stint at Mutual. He was enjoying mind-boggling wealth, popularity and critical acclaim. His confidence seems to brim over in these films in which he always seems to be just on the verge of dance.

What's most curious about these dances is how little they are motivated by the action of the scene. In *The Floorwalker*, department store manager Eric Campbell walks into his office to find Charlie happily sifting through the briefcase of money Campbell had extorted. Charlie does not provide a conventional reaction to being discovered by Campbell. We have just witnessed Charlie's delight over finding the money. At one point, as I mentioned earlier, he had even mimed diving into the briefcase as though it were a swimming pool. His joy at being wealthy seems too complete to even register Campbell as a threat. Campbell shoves Charlie to the floor but Charlie, absurdly, comes up dancing, not fighting, one of the most charming, comical dances in all his films. Chaplin's dance here, as it is elsewhere, is comprised of a kind of mock ballet, with quick backward steps *en pointe*, entrechats and twirls, but mixed with other steps closer to an Irish jig, a kind of rowdy but charming pseudo-ballet all his own.

It's not easy to account for Charlie's psychology here. He seems to be on such a sustained high from his discovery of the money that he, illogically, expects Campbell to share in his joy, to see by the charm and enthusiasm of his dance that he and his money are to be left alone. It will take a good amount of abuse to draw him from his giddy high and back to the dirty exigencies of combat.

There's an equally absurd moment in *Shanghaied* when sailor Charlie is taking a walk around the deck, having just escaped the punishment of a fairly sadistic boss. For no apparent reason, other than the influence of the sway of the boat, Charlie starts to fall into a sailor's hornpipe of sorts, the steps of which were no doubt left over from Chaplin's experience on the stage in his youth as one of a group of clog dancers. Charlie carries the dance into the kitchen where he works with the cook (John Rand). There the dance really takes off. Charlie grabs a leg of lamb that he swings wildly above his head and rhythmically slaps on the floor as well, by this time incorporating certain Russian folk qualities into the dance. As in *The Floorwalker*, there is no obvious reason for this dance. It comes out of nowhere and has no relation to the plot.

Whereas the more developed dance scenes in Charlie's later feature-length films will be characterized by charm and whimsy, the dances from these Essanay and Mutual films seem more an expression of cockiness. They are usually done to taunt and aggravate, or merely to show off. They frequently evolve out of fights and are often Charlie's way of mocking male posture and aggressiveness, making fun of the way men pose when they combat and responding to violence with art.

Fighting, with its ritualized gestures, points naturally to dance. The boxing sequences in both *Champion* and *City Lights* are two of Chaplin's finest, most densely packed set pieces and both fall naturally into an exploration of the relationship of fight and dance. And, of course, another glory in Chaplin films are the highly choreographed fight-chase scenes that get more and more carefully mapped out as Chaplin's comic ambitions and talents developed. The very best non sequitur dances, for example those in *The Floorwalker*, *Shanghaied*, and *The Pawnshop*, grow organically from or into fight sequences.

For example, in *The Pawnshop*, Charlie, carrying a ladder, accidentally slips the ladder around hated co-worker John Rand so that Rand is trapped within the rungs of the ladder, his arms immobilized. This represents an excellent opportunity for Charlie to pummel Rand at will and with great abandon. Since Rand can't fight back, Charlie even uses some particularly elaborate boxing moves, and he quickly seems as interested in showing off his fancy footwork as he does in actually striking Rand (though he continues to do that as well). Pretty soon, the rhythm of his boxing feet suggests dance to Charlie and, without even seeming conscious of what's happening, his feet transition to actual dance, first a variation on the sailor's hornpipe dance we saw in *Shanghaied* and then more graceful balletic steps in which he slides his feet left and right along the floor in great sweeping movements (all the while still managing to punch Rand). When a policeman shows up and Charlie needs to distance himself from his brawl, he segues fully into the dance, his arms abandoning their blows and joining his feet in large, graceful sweeping gestures that carry him away from the cop and back into the pawnshop. Back inside the shop, he carries on the dance for his own amusement with new airy embellishments of hand gestures until his boss appears and he returns to his regular cocky strut, itself a kind of dance.

Of course, Charlie doesn't just taunt with his dance. Dance has a strategic use for Charlie. He often immobilizes his opponents with dance, stuns them with the illogic of the dance. The men with whom Charlie contends cannot understand someone prone to this kind of behavior. In some ways, that's what provokes Charlie to dance. As I discussed in my chapter on Charlie and men, men make Charlie nervous and when he's nervous, Charlie, like the rest of us, is prone to doing exactly the opposite of what he should. He often lapses into airy entrechats in the midst of overbearingly masculine situations. His dances are in some ways an extended nervous tic, a part of his more general tendency to go confusingly feminine when squirming under a severe male gaze. But there's an anarchistic arrogance here as well, a kind of calculated lunacy. In these moments of dance explosion, Charlie is telling his nemesis that he's not tethered to the world of explicable behavior, that he doesn't necessarily feel compelled to make sense. He intimidates by a gentle insanity. When Charlie segues from boxing to ballet, his contenders are utterly flabbergasted and Charlie often exploits that vulnerability. Dance becomes a kind of tactical weapon. Charlie's purpose in dancing here is twofold: to freeze his nemesis in confusion and to mock his masculine posturing for good measure.

Work also inspires Charlie to dance. Chaplin was struck by the way the machine-like regularity of certain jobs often evokes dance, an idea he developed with some amplitude in *Modern Times*, where Charlie's work on the riveting line careens into a lunatic dance based on the turning of screws. Sometimes, if he can arrive at such an orderly rhythm in his job, he starts to enjoy it. By turning a job into a dance, he can make it somewhat more palatable.

Kitchens and food preparation can bring out the dancer in Charlie. Often in the kitchen, if he's asked to prepare food or wash dishes, he arrives at his own idiosyncratic way of doing things that can evolve into a dance, for example in *Shanghaied* where handling a leg of lamb puts him in mind of a circus performer juggling his enormous pins. Charlie's virtuosic stacking of bricks in *Pay Day* is preceded by several introductory balletic flourishes as Charlie announces to his workers and the audience that his brick-stacking will be artful as well as work. And, indeed, Charlie's stacking of bricks is as rhythmic and elegant in its mechanics as any well-practiced dance. Work has no attraction to Charlie in itself. Work has to somehow involve the imagination, or art, or musical rhythm to make it interesting to him. The brick-stacking scene in *Pay Day* is one of the few times we ever see Chaplin productive at work and that's because he gets to turn it into a kind of dance, to conduct the exercise according to his own sense of rhythm.

Melodrama can also provoke dance in Charlie. In *Behind the Screen*, a group of striking workers asks Charlie's boss (Eric Campbell) if he will join them. Campbell responds with an emphatic "no," puffing out his chest, holding up his chin and closing his eyes dramatically. He strikes the pose of a great orator, gesturing melodramatically to the ground with one hand, as if to say he will hold his ground, the other hand held at his waist with great dignity. He then holds this pose in statuesque glory.

When the workers ask Charlie, Campbell's assistant, if he will strike, Charlie imitates Campbell. Not so much because he wants to please Campbell or because he's anti-union, but more because, we suspect, he too would like to strike a dramatic pose. Charlie, like a child, is always entranced by exaggerated behavior and anxious to get in on any fun available. No, he announces dramatically, he will not strike. Charlie stiffens into the pose of the poised ballet dancer: ramrod posture, front foot perpendicular to back, the hammer he had been working with still in hand, poised dramatically to his side.

As the workers abandon the two, both Charlie and his boss hold their pose for a bit. But, after a few seconds, Charlie starts to wobble some. He glances, dog-like, at his boss, wondering what to do next. Finally, self-consciousness gets the best of him and, absurdly, inexplicably, he breaks into one of those hornpipe or clog dances that he likes so much. Then, just as absurdly and inexplicably, he freezes in a second pose, as though he were playing a game of statues. His hammer is raised in the air now, the pose vaguely martial. Charlie perceives his boss's actions as a child might, as though it must be part of a game. But when Charlie regresses to childish behavior, he's almost always mocking the subject he imitates as well.

Campbell regards him as all men with whom Charlie works do in these moments of his illogical lunacy, which is to say without a shred of understanding. That kind of disbelief not only does not deter Charlie, it seems to provoke him. The less Charlie gets the reaction he's looking for, the more he ratchets up his effort to get that reaction. And so he launches into an even more hectic dance, this time adding very precise arm gestures, in which he alternates, with clockwork precision, raising each arm to his head during the dance, a dance vaguely reminiscent of Hollywood versions of native American rain dances. Of course, he's still holding a hammer and so finishes the dance by conking himself in the head and falling into a chair.

Even a person in pain can suggest dance to Chaplin. In *Police*, Charlie drops a heavy mallet on Wesley Ruggles' foot, then starts to clap in time as Ruggles dances in pain. Charlie himself erupts into the same comic dance when he sits on a cactus in the *Sunnyside* dream and when he is shot in the behind in *Police*, a kind of manic hopping dance during which he flaps his arms like wings, as though trying to create an airflow that might assuage his pain. Physical movement in response to pain is itself a superfluous gesture, a situation in which we try to escape pain in an instinctive, if somewhat illogical way, through the expenditure of energy. Chaplin had the dancer's eye for those moments where we turn to dance because there is nothing else as satisfying, nothing else that fits the bill like those moments where our body outstrips our mind and we cope with life through repetitive movement.

The most obvious of these moments in which we are pushed to deal with a situation through stylized motion are those in which we experience a superabundance of joy; Chaplin had considerable expertise in rendering these moments as well. One thinks immediately of his trademark, foolishly happy prance—legs splayed out sideways as though he had the hips of a dog, knees kicking high, arms happily extended to the side—a childish dance that somehow expresses even more joy than children's dances do. Or one thinks of the many scenes of gleeful, chaotic, inspired destruction when a woman titillates Charlie or, even more dangerously, expresses affection for him. Charlie's body is always waiting an opportunity to launch itself into the stratosphere. For Charlie, a lovely woman is the greatest reason of all to dance.

Charlie, then, is not only ready to dance at the drop of a hat, he sees dance all around him. He is reminded of dance by a fight, a mechanical task, a person in pain, a moment of melodrama, the flirtatious glance of a girl. And when he senses dance, he seizes the opportunity and amplifies that dance, often to a lunatic extent. Charlie's dances are both an expression of joy at being liberated from the mundane world and a mocking challenge to those who won't liberate themselves, who have no feel for the pleasure and ubiquity of dance. Dance is Charlie's way of inviting others to loosen up, to drop their pretenses or, more precisely, to follow their pretensions to their full artistic extent. Needless to say, it's an invitation that, except for a few charming young women, is usually rejected.

As Charlie's character transforms over the years, so does his dancing. Charlie becomes a less cocky dancer. Chaplin turns to dance increasingly for dramatic effect, and less out of inchoate lunacy. Charlie becomes conscious of his charm and underlines it through dance. The dance in *Sunnyside*, though replete with many of his oddball and mock-ballet moves, is more bald-faced in its whimsy than earlier dances. The potato roll dance in *The Gold Rush* is charming and, within its context, heartbreaking. Chaplin's dances become less of a non sequitur, less improvisational, and more carefully choreographed. That kind of meticulously laid-out structure, with one clearly developed section or variation following another that we saw in Charlie's torturing of Eric Campbell in *The Rink*, becomes the norm and reaches its apogee in the boxing scene from *City Lights* where he accomplishes his most detailed and complex exercise in rhythmic composition. As his sense of unity improves, his sense of the structural necessities of a good film, the placing of the dance scenes becomes more purposeful. The riveter-gone-mad scene and the song-and-dance scenes from *Modern Times* are good examples of musical interludes that have a sound, organic spot in the film and advance its ideas as well as offering charming regressions to the film's action.

On the other hand, one of the reasons certain critics are particularly fond of the Mutual films is the chaotic charm of those moments when Chaplin breaks into dance, not because the storyline dictates it, or because it contributes to the thematic density of the film, but almost for the opposite reason, to blow the storyline to hell and simply present a moment of discordant, lunatic glee. There is an abstraction to these earlier films, that cheerful illogic to which Harness refers, an unwillingness to make sense of Charlie's behavior, that breathes life into them. Those little nutty dances are as enjoyable to Charlie as they are perplexing to his foes. In fact, he enjoys them because they are so perplexing. They are as expressive of his disdain for conventionality as they are of his enthusiasm for life.

Fifteen

Chaplin's Music

The essentially musical or rhythmic nature of Chaplin's art is emphasized also by how important a part music came to play in the latter part of Chaplin's career, when he began to score complex soundtracks for his films. It is ironic that the music Chaplin composed for his films has come to be seen as such a significant aspect of his cinema, considering he did not write a full film score until his penultimate silent feature. Only his final two silent films, *City Lights* and *Modern Times,* both made during the sound era, have original sound tracks. Of course, he went on to write a good many more film scores for his sound films but this book takes as its subject matter, for the most part, Chaplin's silent films, during which he developed the character of his alter ego, Charlie. And yet, even for a project of this scope, the role of music in Chaplin's films is important to consider.

First of all, *City Lights* and *Modern Times* represent two of Chaplin's greatest works, to many the apex of his craft, the films to which his art had been ascending for a decade and a half. Music plays a large role in both, thus in two of Chaplin's greatest works. But Chaplin also later penned plaintive soundtracks for his other great silent feature films, *The Kid, The Circus* and *The Gold Rush.* And when Chaplin fans point to scenes that are most important to them, that most persuade as to the power of Chaplin's films, they often turn to those sequences that involve music, just as they often do those that include dance. The scenes in which Charlie is threatened with losing his son in *The Kid,* the dance of the rolls in *The Gold Rush,* the boxing match in *City Lights,* the final moments of *City Lights,* Charlie's floor number in *Modern Times,* the final moments of *Modern Times*—these are some of Chaplin's greatest scenes, and they were either conceived in accordance to music or deeply enriched by music that was written later in Chaplin's career.

Chaplin continued to create impressive music and soundtracks till the end of his life. After *Modern Times,* as Timothy Brock has noted, Chaplin's "symphonic voice blossomed quite proficiently" in the soundtracks he wrote for *The Great Dictator,* the 1942 rerelease of *The Gold Rush, Limelight,* and *Monsieur Verdoux.*[1] Even those who are not enamored of Chaplin's sound films recognize the merits of their soundtracks. The most famous moment in *The Great Dictator,* the globe-balloon sequence, is a dance scored to Chaplin's music. *Limelight* won an Academy Award for Best Original Score after it was first shown in Los Angeles, 20 years following its original release. From the late 1950s on, Chaplin's scores were less complex, more oriented around simple songs and melodies. He scored several hit songs from his soundtracks: "Eternally" from *Limelight,* "Smile" from *Modern Times,* when the film was reissued in 1954, and "This Is My Song," from *A Countess from Hong Kong.*

He also created, with the help of composer Eric James, soundtracks for his First National films, many of which are charming and inventive. These scores aren't as sophisticated or complex in orchestration as the scores of the thirties and forties. As Brock notes, seven of Chaplin's scores were composed after the age of 80 and "late in his life the aging Chaplin became less involved with the infinite depths of the orchestra."[2] But the soundtracks to films like *The Kid* (composed in 1971) and *A Woman of Paris* (composed in 1976), while simpler, are still startlingly innovative and moving. Even soundtracks that appeal less to pathos, like those to *Pay Day* (composed in 1973) and *The Pilgrim* (composed in 1959), are subtle works that draw out Chaplin's comedy and deepen its effect. They improve rather than detract and intensify the films' "Chaplinesque" feeling.

The Nature of Chaplin's Musical Talent

Chaplin's strong affinity for music has been well-established. There is a standard accounting of Chaplin's music development among biographers: First, they quote his Aunt Kate recalling Chaplin's rhythmic response to music as a toddler, then Chaplin's own emotional description in his autobiography of his "awakening to music" during a moment in his childhood when he heard a clarinet and harmonica version of "The Honeysuckle and the Rose" in the streets of Kensington Cross.

A sensitivity to music seems to have been pretty likely, given Chaplin was born to two music hall performers. His first steady professional job in entertainment was when he was nine years old as one of the "Eight Lancashire Lads" who performed a meticulous kind of folkloric clog dancing, echoes of which we see in Chaplin's dances in his films. It took Chaplin six weeks of practice to master this dance before he could perform it, the first example of what would be the standard of his career, a strong work ethic combined with a gift for execution. Chaplin was born and raised in an element of music and dance.

Chaplin took up the violin and cello in his teens and also played the piano and the huge organ he had installed in his Hollywood home. He seemed to have a natural affinity for music, as he took to these instruments without instruction. He played them well, though without great virtuosity. He had an enthusiast's knowledge of classical music and several of his co-composers describe him citing composers—Puccini or Gershwin or Debussy—when he sought certain musical effects in his soundtracks. Many of his greatest friends, particularly in his later years in Switzerland, were from the world of classical music. Even before he took up the burden of penning his own soundtracks, he oversaw the compilation of music meant for live accompaniment of his silent features, such as *A Woman of Paris, The Gold Rush,* and *The Circus.* In 1915, just a year after his film debut, he established the Charlie Chaplin Music Publishing

Company and released sheet music to several songs that were moderate successes. Curiously, then, Chaplin's musical career began and finished with writing popular songs, with his more ambitious orchestral scores sandwiched between, in the '30s and '40s.

Chaplin could not read or write musical notation and freely confessed his amateur status, though sometimes he affected more musical knowledge than he had. Once he told David Raksin, his co-composer on the soundtrack of *Modern Times*, that a phrase "should be played vrubato." Raksin writes that he took the new word that Chaplin's had coined as "a real improvement upon the Italian word, which was much the poorer for having been deprived of the 'v.'"[3]

Raksin is as honest about Chaplin's musical naiveté as he is appreciative of Chaplin's musical accomplishments. He may gently mock Chaplin for mispronouncing musical terms but he could also be protective of Chaplin's musical reputation. He recalled a party at which Chaplin introduced him as "the fella who wrote the music of *Modern Times.*" Raksin recalls scolding Chaplin for his excessive humility, telling him "that it was not true and that it was indiscreet of him to say so, because there were already too many people in Hollywood who were eager to challenge his integrity."[4]

It took critics some time to arrive at a balanced view of Chaplin as a composer, one that didn't overrate or underrate his accomplishments, but there is now a pretty solid sense of how he worked on his soundtracks and what the value of his contributions were. Chaplin muddled the discussion when he summed up his musical contributions to *City Lights,* when the film came out, in a pretty well-known quote that is somewhat accurate but, like his comment at the party, far too humble: "I really didn't write it down. I la-laed and Arthur Johnson wrote it down, and I wish you would give him the credit, because he did a very good job."[5] Timothy Brock, who has restored many of Chaplin's scores and performed them live, often laments this well-known bit of humility: In his mind, it has provided fodder for those who are cynical about Chaplin's musical accomplishments and obscured our understanding of just how subtle and complex Chaplin's scores are.[6]

In one way, Chaplin's quote is a fairly legitimate summary of his method. He would come to his soundtrack sessions with his arrangers armed with a fund of melodies that the arrangers then helped him develop orchestrally. This area of the co-composer's job—that of developing "a few notes or short phrases" into orchestral movement of some breadth and variety—is the part of being a musical collaborator to Chaplin that Raksin felt had been routinely underrated by those who celebrate Chaplin as a musical genius. Raksin was frustrated by certain critics (he was particularly irritated by Chaplin biographer Theodore Huff) who think that "composing consists of getting some kind of micro-flash of an idea, and that the rest of it is mere artisanry." By the "rest of it," he meant the elaborate orchestral developments and variations for which he and Chaplin's other co-composers were responsible.[7]

But at the same time, Raksin emphasized, "neither did [Chaplin] feed me a little tune and say, 'You take it from there.' On the contrary, we spent hours and days, months in the projection room, running scenes and bits of action over and over, and we had a marvelous time working on the music until it was exactly the way we wanted it—and by the time we were through with a music cue we had run it so often that we were certain that the music was in perfect sync."[8] In other words, Chaplin did a great

Chaplin with David Raksin, the composer with whom he scored *Modern Times*.

deal more than "la-la" a few tunes and leave the rest to his composers. Raksin writes that he was too young and experienced at the time to realize that other composers did not work the way Chaplin did, that most of them simply used a timing sheet and a stop-clock. Brock, too, notes that Chaplin and Raksin's lengthy four-week session working on the soundtrack was "unheard of by studio standards." Chaplin's soundtracks are noteworthy, at the very least, for the amount of work and time he put into them. They also typify his independent approach to film. Chaplin had the time and money to do it his way.

But the value of his contributions to his soundtracks is also underlined by the way in which all the soundtracks have a similarly distinct sound, regardless of Chaplin's collaborator. Carl Davis, another of Chaplin's co-composers, asks, "If it was being written by other people, how is [it] that the 'Chaplin style' maintains itself through widely differentiating and widely changing arrangers? There is a line that goes through, no matter who the composer is."[9] Huff makes the same point, that a Chaplinesque quality "was discerned and commented upon in the music, despite the fact that it was arranged and orchestrated by other hands." Huff goes so far as to delineate the nature of the Chaplin sound: "[I]t shows a fondness for romantic waltz hesitations played in a very rubato time, lively numbers in two-four time which might be called 'promenade themes' and tangos with a strong beat."[10] Brock notes also that no matter who the associate, "the musical structure and approach remains distinctively his own. The term 'Chaplinesque' is more and more frequently used by musicologists as a point of reference to his chordal and melodic structures, and it is certainly not by accident that every Chaplin film both looks, and sounds, like Chaplin."[11]

This kind of tension between the author of a film and his collaborators has been the subject of debate in studio-era criticism for generations now and it's usually politically correct, in this post–Auteurism era, to side with the collaborators' point of view. But so often it happens, in the way that Davis describes, that a great Hollywood director will work with experts in their field and yet arrive at a vision that is more the director's than the experts'. Hitchcock was not a clothes designer, and he worked with different designers, and yet arrived at a vision of women's fashion that is associated with his name alone, and that still lands him in fashion magazine spreads. He also came from the visual side of production and was dependent on finding good screenwriters to help him with his scripts. Many of these screenwriters complained about his chary acknowledgment of their contributions. And yet a Hitchcock script has a certain feel to it no matter who works on it with him.

Chaplin's soundtracks are singularly his own for the same reason Hitchcock's scripts are his own: because Chaplin oversaw the soundtrack preparation with an unusual zealousness, just as Hitchcock was always intimately involved in the process of smelting a writer's words into the sights and sounds of his films. Chaplin's soundtracks are impressive because, as Raksin notes in great detail, Chaplin was there for the entire ride, suggesting orchestrations and tucking his musical ideas with great precision into the rhythm of his films, a rhythm he had already established through his fine comic timing and elegantly choreographed *mise-en-scène.*

Perhaps most important is Raksin's reference to the two "having fun." Devising a soundtrack seems to have been a labor of love for the musical Chaplin, a means of accentuating the rhythms of his films and making more manifest their subterranean emotions. "Very little escaped his eye and ear," Raksin wrote, "and he would say that melody ought now to move 'up' rather than down (or vice versa), that it ought to be in some other register of the orchestra than the one in which I had put it, or that the accompaniment ought to be 'busier.'"[12] We can feel, in Raksin's account, Chaplin feeling his way through orchestration with an amateur's vocabulary but a visionary's confidence.

And it's clear he was unstinting in the labor he put into his soundtracks as well as in the demands he made on those with whom he worked on soundtracks. Chaplin's son, Charles Jr., observed several of Chaplin's musical collaborations and noted that "if the people in his own studio had suffered from Dad's perfectionist drive, the musicians ... endured pure torture."[13] Chaplin and Arthur Johnson spent six weeks on the soundtrack to *City Lights* and, according to Theodore Huff, finished with a score of 150 pages and 95 musical cues, "not counting the passages where the music follows or mimics the action in what is generally known as 'mickey-mousing.'" Huff notes that "nearly twenty numbers in the score could be published as separate and original works,"[14] highlighting what is probably Chaplin's greatest natural musical gift, and one not to be overlooked: his gift for melody. And *Modern Times* was a much more complicated affair than *City Lights*, with 64 musicians rather than the 30 that performed on the soundtrack to *City Lights.* Raksin, Charles Jr. says, worked "an average of 20 hours a day, lost 20 pounds and was so exhausted that he couldn't find strength to go home but would sleep on the studio floor," a description, no doubt, tinged with hyperbole, but generally reflective of Chaplin's drive when it came to his soundtracks.[15]

Timothy Brock writes of starting his restoration of the soundtrack of *Modern Times* for orchestral performance by confronting "the pencil-written manuscript of the fully orchestrated score [that] stood nearly half a meter in height. There were five archival boxes of just player's parts alone." Brock discusses one small segment of the film, the one in which Charlie is drawn into the cogs of a large machine, a scene that takes 68 seconds in total but which "contains 14 tempo changes, 9 meter changes, 27 synch points (places where the music sharply mimics the precise movement of the actors or their actions). Each of these 27 synch points had been meticulously laid out to not only narrate the action, but by the benefit of linear musical construction, every shot flowed with a natural consequence."[16]

All of this tells us a couple of things. First, that Chaplin applied the same exhaustive work ethic to making music that he did to recording images. And that Chaplin's music is so resonant, not because he was a musical genius, but because he had a good head for melody and musical emotion and worked at his music as hard as he did his comedy, taking above-average musical knowledge, capitalizing on the resources at hand and, through those resources, creating a sound that, paradoxically, was completely his own, though he never could have arrived at it himself.

There have not been many actor-composers or director-composers in film history, much less an actor-director-composer like Chaplin. It was an immense advantage to Chaplin that he could put into music something of the emotional mix he was trying to accomplish with Charlie's comedy. As the director *and* composer he had a rare opportunity to create music that was organic to the feel and purpose of the film. One of the strengths of his music is how well it suits his films, how it seems to emanate from the same emotional well. As David Robinson noted, "Something of the universal appeal of Chaplin's screen character emerged in his composition as well."[17] There is a good deal of Charlie in Chaplin's music. Even years after Charlie has disappeared from Chaplin's cinema, we detect his presence, that particular blend of pathos and comedy that he represents, in Chaplin's later soundtracks.

Whether in his comedy or his music, Chaplin had a gift for simplicity, for getting to the heart of things, for touching a wide array of people by trafficking in the most essential of human situations and emotions. "It's all simple music," he said of the soundtrack to *City Lights*, "in keeping with my character." Petula Clark, who made a hit out of "This Is My Song," also praised Chaplin's "simple and direct approach to music. Charlie was not an educated musician. He was not clever in that way and that perhaps was a good thing. Charlie's music went straight to the heart."[18] Like many veterans of the Hollywood studio era, Chaplin came to lament the loss of simplicity in post studio-era filmmaking. Studio-era Hollywood valued a well-treated simple story rather than one characterized by web-like complexities, either of plot or thought. This is even more true of silent films which had an international audience and so sought an effect that was simple, immediate, universal. Chaplin's music is all of these things.

What the success of Chaplin's soundtracks reveals is that he is about something more than his physical comedy, that there is something essentially Chaplinesque in his comedy that corresponds to a mood or feeling, an attitude towards life. Here we are again at one of those moments where we have to compare Chaplin to his contemporaries. The important question is not "What other comedian could write music as well as act and direct?" though of course none could. The versatility of Chaplin's talents has long been established. But the fact that Chaplin had musical talent doesn't make his films great any more than the fact that he was excellent at roller-skating does. The question is, what other comedian could distill the essence of his films into the ineffable form of music? What other comedian's films were characterized by a strong- or emotional-enough abstract feeling even to try to do that? Chaplin's music isn't great because he was such a great musician but because he had something great to say in musical form.

Understatement and Counterpoint

The success of Chaplin's soundtracks is also due to their understatement, their complexity and use of counterpoint. He complained of musical arrangers who wanted to underscore funny moments with funny music. That kind of associative musical accompaniment grates quickly. For evidence of that, take a look at the many Chaplin films still circulating in which distributors tried to supplement Chaplin's humor by assigning what they took to be appropriate sounds for his slapstick comedy, say the sound of a kazoo for someone slipping; the effect is numbing. Chaplin's point is well-taken. The less you underline comedy, the more effective it is. He thought music should, at least in part, work against the grain of the filmed scene. He praised the music that his mentor Fred Karno chose for his music hall numbers, noting that they would often use "beautiful boudoir music" for scenes of great squalor, "just purely as satirical and as a counterpoint; and I copied a great deal from Mr. Fred Karno in that direction."

In *A Woman of Paris*, for example, the scene in which Marie, having rediscovered her love for Jean, laments to Pierre about her life as his kept woman, studiously avoids the melodramatic music that we might have thought it called for. Instead, Chaplin scores it with a breezy, upbeat dance, characterized by a light, relentlessly forward-moving rhythm. The score is more in keeping with Pierre's cynically humorous response to Marie than it is with her depression. The music mocks the heroine of the film more than it indulges her, suggesting, with Pierre, that her ennui is a passing thing, that she herself doesn't know what she wants. The lighthearted approach to Marie's despair is no small part of what makes this film interesting. We identify strongly with Marie and we don't take her or her love for Jean lightly. But Chaplin also identifies with Pierre's humorous, detached worldliness. The film's music reflects its complexity, here teasing the character with whom we more strongly identify and empathize.

In *Pay Day*, Chaplin will go all through all sorts of comic hijinks typical of his workplace comedies: misappropriated lunches, injuries from a hot poker, and various other absurdities wrought by the unceasing service elevator. And yet all of this is scored to a mildly sad, whimsical, lyrical piece that, to my mind, anticipates some of Jean Constantin's music for Truffaut, music that aims to capture sadness, humor and charm all at once and to wrap it in a package that, in its simplicity, never strays from the quotidian. (Since the film was scored by Chaplin in 1972, it isn't inconceivable that Chaplin was influenced by Constantin.)

We are struck by how well the slapstick comedy in *Pay Day* does on its own, when left to its own devices, in the midst of a lyrical soundtrack that really only finds its match in those few minutes where Chaplin's humor borders on the poignant, for example where Charlie, like a stray sparrow, is eating the fallen crumbs from the lunch shared by Edna and her father. In writing music for the First National films, Chaplin was sensible enough to understand that there was not the basis in most of these films (*The Kid* being the obvious exception) for great strains of emotion. But, at the same time, Charlie was moving, in these films, towards his later sentimental self. The more sentimental Charlie is there in snatches throughout these films, and the music that Chaplin later wrote for these films draws out their nascent melancholy deftly.

Chaplin's retroactive soundtracks always seem, in this manner, to be elaborations of his original film work. When directors tamper with films years after the film has been created, the results are not usually impressive. We have ample evidence of that today in reissues of celebrated directors' reedited versions of their films. Even Chaplin was not immune to tampering with his films unproductively, as for example in the addition of narration to the 1942 version of *The Gold Rush* and, to my mind, in his deletion of material from *The Kid* in the last version he released. But Chaplin's musical tampering with his films rarely went amiss. It tended to enrich those films, to draw out and accentuate their "Chaplinesque" feelings.

The soundtrack to *The Pilgrim* (written in 1959), for example, is excellent but doesn't aim for the deep pathos of the soundtracks to *The Gold Rush* and *City Lights*, two of Chaplin's richest and most complex orchestral works. Whereas in the 1970 reissue of *The Circus*, Chaplin deepened the pathos of the film, adding the plaintive little opening song "Swing, Little Girl" (which he sang himself in the touchingly thin voice of an old man), *The Pilgrim* begins with, of all things, a cowboy ballad, "Bound for Texas," introducing right away the lighter aims of the film and reflecting Chaplin's sense of the film (not always grasped by the viewer) as a Western.

That said, Chaplin's music is never too far from the plaintive in *The Pilgrim*, for example in its final moments when Charlie is too witless to realize that a benevolent sheriff is actually inviting him to escape his custody when he directs Charlie's attention to the Mexican border nearby and tells him to go pick some flowers there. Chaplin wrote some charming music for this scene with, as was often his wont, tango rhythms that reflect the scene's light comedy. But the tango is mixed with more lyrical passages played on the accordion that seem drawn more from the melancholy balladry of Mexican folk music. Those melodies underscore Charlie's touching naiveté in this scene. Chaplin's score expresses Charlie's duality, his comedy and his charm. But the effect is much more lighthearted than the great musical effects in *The Gold Rush* or *City Lights,* as is only fitting for *The Pilgrim,* one of Chaplin's greatest, but less emotionally ambitious, films.

Despite Chaplin's emphasis on counterpoint, there are many points in his orchestrations where he underlines the action with more direct correlatives to the orchestra. But if these moments aren't characterized by a counterpoint, they are subtle nonetheless. One of the musical highlights from his *Modern Times* soundtrack represents an example of direct sound on image scoring. Charlie has just learned that jobs are available at a nearby factory. He is so elated at the opportunity to earn money so that he can help Paulette Goddard's waif, that he immediately bolts to the factory, accompanied by frenetic orchestration, in which some strings are swirling with bee-like chaotic flights while others are pounding out a martial rhythm. A horn sounds out a triumphant solo to accompany Charlie's race across the bleak no-man's-land between his hovel and the factory.

It's typical of Chaplin's meticulous orchestration that just as Charlie plunges into the crowd of men gathered outside the factory looking for jobs, the horn solo intensifies, rising in pitch and quickening in tempo, creating a sense of near-panic as Charlie powers through a crowd of hundreds. But just as Charlie reaches, and slips through, the closing gate—the last job applicant to be admitted—this bombastic orchestration is cut off abruptly, the orchestra arresting itself with a comically abrupt, high-pitch slide of the violins, as though a conductor had called a halt in the midst of a practice session.

The comic effect of his scoring is not easy to describe. Chaplin seems to be mocking his own score. It's all buildup and no payoff. The violins almost seem embarrassed to be exposed when the music stops. And their embarrassment corresponds to Charlie's as he shifts from manic attack on the gates to the prim, self-conscious carriage with which he passes the men watching him from the other side of the fence, all of whom he has just slyly cheated of a job. The musical point seems to be that dramatic situations sometimes resolve themselves with an almost comic lack of drama.

One of the most interesting one-on-one musical effects Chaplin employed in his soundtracks occurs in that scene from *A Woman of Paris* to which I earlier referred, in which Marie expresses her frustration with being a kept woman to the playfully amused Pierre. Pierre, as he teases and cajoles the moody Marie, intermittently picks up a saxophone that's lying nearby and doodles with it. It's a nice touch on Chaplin's part, typical of his gift for translating psychology into tactile action and expressive of Pierre's boredom, his unwillingness to take Marie seriously, and his desire to playfully coax her from her mood. In short, introducing Pierre doodling with a saxophone is already an example of good filmmaking.

But fifty years later, when Chaplin scored the film, he managed to heighten the significance of the saxophone in the scene. Chaplin made the interesting decision to score those moments where Pierre plays the saxophone with actual saxophone music, so that Pierre takes on the role of a soloist in a saxophone concerto. The effect is charming. Since Pierre only picks up the saxophone here and there, and for small bits at a time, his contributions to the orchestration represent light and haphazard improvisation. They provide little playful and errant interjections that complicate the soundtrack, providing it interesting off-rhythms and bursts of fey charm. And of course, they contribute to that feeling Chaplin had wanted to convey originally in the film, of Pierre's particular mix of charm, humor, and cruelty.

Of course, analysis like this implicitly accepts that we should take Chaplin's later soundtracks, some added 30 to 50 years after the film was made, as intrinsic to the film. Chaplin's films certainly represent a unique case in film history. Few directors have returned to their films years later to add soundtracks. But I, for one, always prefer to watch Chaplin films with his own soundtracks. Chaplin's skills as a filmmaker diminished with age, the advent of sound and the disappearance of Charlie from his films, but his music continued to evolve meaningfully. And he continued, via his music, to have access to the emotions that made his silent films great. Music became the means for him to continue to express his emotions in a wordless manner, when the film industry no longer allowed him to. The effectiveness of Chaplin's later music, highlighted by the increasing awkwardness of his later films, testifies to the affinity between silent film and music, both mediums that snap their fingers at the importance of words.

That Chaplin's music was always a fruitful addition to his films also testifies to the simplicity and universality of the central Chaplin emotion, that emotion that Charlie's personality encompasses and which is often referred to as "Chaplinesque." Though he lost Charlie, the "Chaplinesque" spirit that Charlie represented was something Chaplin had access to his entire career. But we sense it more in the music he wrote in the later part of his career than in the later sound films he made. Sound film and his own age had both proved to be insurmountable barriers to his tapping into, visually, the charming pathos of Charlie after *Modern Times*. It was through his music, a language that was not dependent on words or images, that the spirit of Charlie most endured.

Sixteen

Two Musical Sequences

In this chapter, I examine two famous *City Lights* sequences, the ending and the boxing match. They are two of Chaplin's most popular sequences, and so carefully constructed that they beg for a stand-alone, moment-by-moment analysis.

I also chose the two pieces to complement one another. One, the boxing sequence, is an example of Chaplin's great gift for choreographing physical comedy into a kind of sophisticated dance. Chaplin's fights are probably his most recurrent comedic gag and they are where we can see a great deal of his filmic ingenuity. The ending to *City Lights*, on the other hand, might be the greatest example of his films' appeal to pathos, his sublime mixture of comedy and sadness. The two, combined, testify to Chaplin's twin genius for a highly choreographed comedy of almost mathematical elegance and a pathos that is as heart-rending as it is subtle.

City Lights represents the first film that Chaplin scored with a soundtrack and so both sequences are also excellent examples of his rhythmic or musical approach to cinema. Both are to be appreciated, not for the overt expression of their ideas, but for their formal elegance, their strong sense of structure, their sophisticated rhythm, both in sound and image, their arrangement of movement as a kind of dance, and their meticulously orchestrated soundtracks. The analysis here, then, represents an extension of the ideas in the preceding chapters on rhythm and dance in Chaplin's films.

But placing this analysis at the end of the book allows us also to look back on certain ideas emphasized throughout the book and to weave those ideas into the analysis here, showing, I hope, just how much goes into a single Chaplin sequence. This kind of exhaustive analysis can also be hard on the reader and so it seems the right course to place it at the end where it can be taken or left by readers, who might by this time be mildly addled by the many scenes I have led them through. Both clips, I might add, are readily available online and reviewing them might be helpful in following my readings of the scenes (the boxing sequence, in particular, represents a marvelous accumulation of blink-and-you-miss-it details).

The Ending to City Lights

The final sequence of *City Lights*, in which Charlie is dramatically revealed to the once-blind young girl as her heroic benefactor, provides an excellent example of Chaplin's meticulous arrangement of music to image. Appropriately set in autumn, this melancholy sequence comprises the last five minutes of the film. It opens with the flower girl, her sight restored thanks to the sacrifices of Charlie. She is arranging flowers at an upscale flower store that, presumably, she and her grandmother own, her days of suffering behind her. Once a hawker of modest posies, the girl now is surrounded by the rich floral arrangements of her Main Street business. The music that opens the scene, fittingly, is a fairly upbeat version of the lyrical tango "La Violetera," a popular 1914 song about a girl who sells flowers, that Chaplin has used as the film's central theme. Here it is given a more energetic rhythm, with castanets and tambourines, that suits the girl's new and happy circumstances.

After establishing the girl's new success, Chaplin cuts from the flower shop to the streets outside where a forlorn Charlie will make his first appearance in the sequence. Chaplin continues the "La Violetera" theme but, as Charles Maland notes in his excellent study of the scene, when Charlie appears, the music shifts from moderato to andante and to a lower key, thus evoking a sadder feel.[1] As impoverished as Charlie has always looked in Chaplin's films, he has never looked as worn as he does at the end of *City Lights*. Fresh out of prison for a sentence he didn't deserve, but which he gained in earning the girl her funds, he doesn't even have a shirt to wear beneath his tattered suit jacket. His pants are shredded.

Charlie appears around the corner where the girl once sold her flowers. He is stooped and devoid of the prim alertness that has been his trademark. The more melancholy version of "La Violetera" accompanies him as he revisits the spot where he first bought a flower from the girl. The girl and her flower stand gone, Charlie settles for tearing off a sprig from a shrub poking through an iron railing next to the place where she once sat. The scene is typical of that aspect of Chaplin's art upon which I have often commented, his ability to trace psychic states via incidental action and physical detail. Here the torn piece of shrubbery is a melancholy substitute for the flower that Charlie recalls the girl handing him when they first met.

As the scene returns to the girl in her shop, the "La Violetera" theme returns to its brisk, confident version. This version serves as background as the girl serves a wealthy young man in top hat and tails who she had hoped might prove to be her anonymous benefactor. "I thought he had returned," she says to her grandmother, after the man leaves the shop, priming our anticipation of her meeting, soon to come, with her real benefactor, Charlie. Chaplin establishes in these back-to-back scenes that both she and Charlie are dreaming of each other in the moments before they meet, heightening our anticipation of the moment.

A moment of silence intrudes in the soundtrack, as Chaplin cuts back to Charlie on the street, window shopping. The "La Violetera" theme disappears and Chaplin turns to another theme, the second in this sequence, what critics have come to refer to as "the promenade theme." The music here is the loping, upbeat piece that appears many times in the film, usually when the film is picking up its pace and Charlie is in a hopeful mood. The first time we heard it was when Charlie first encountered the newsboys who like to have their fun with him. Those boys will be teasing Charlie again momentarily, so it's a book-end piece; the theme appears a few minutes from the ending of the film just at it had a few minutes into the film, and under the same circumstances and at the same place.

In this scene, the newsboys notice, and find comical, the remnant of material sticking out from a hole in the seat of Charlie's pants, making it look as though Charlie has a white tail. The scene is reminiscent of that moment in *A Dog's Life* when the tail of a dog protrudes from a hole in the seat of his pants, making Charlie appear to be a hybrid of dog and man. The more light-hearted music is the right accompaniment to the boy's equally light-hearted teasing of Charlie, as they shoot peas at him. But the music has a more melancholy pace and feel than it did earlier in the film. Just as we've never seen Charlie so tattered, so we've never seen him quite this down in the dumps. His only response to the boys' taunting is a kind of glum, wounded annoyance, the irritation a sick animal might express. The antics of the dog-man from *A Dog's Life* are a distant memory. This is Charlie approaching the end of his career.

This musical piece carries us to a point in the sequence where Charlie discovers a discarded rose in the street. There's a nice bit of the kind of quiet, but elegant, long-take *mise-en-scène* that often goes unnoticed in Chaplin's films here. As Charlie slumps down the street, he walks by the flower shop where we see, though he does not, the love of his life working in the display window. Within the same shot, a young woman from the flower store crosses before Charlie and sweeps some debris from inside the store into the street. Charlie spies a wilted flower in the midst of the debris and bends to pick it up. As Charlie does so, the boys attack, jackal-like, yanking away the material that sticks out from the seat of his pants (presumably a tattered shred of his underwear), and Charlie chases them away indignantly.

All this takes place in one carefully choreographed take. In this manner, Chaplin unites, visually and in one shot, the boys' bit of tomfoolery with Charlie's looming reunion with the girl. He creates a complex visual environment that does what long takes with careful *mise-en-scène* are supposed to do: allow us to look around, to weave together, ourselves, different planes of carefully laid-out visual information. Chaplin is, in many ways, one of the early progenitors of the kind of long-take *mise-en-scène* that Andre Bazin trumpeted and which finds its apotheosis in the elegant choreography of directors like Max Ophuls, Vincente Minnelli and William Wyler. This kind of filmmaking provides the viewer both a complex visual scheme and the freedom to explore it. More specifically, in this particular scene, Chaplin continues to prime the pump, visually bringing together Charlie and the girl, who we know are already thinking of each other, before they even know it and giving the viewer that little surge of excitement that comes with anticipation and dramatic irony.

When Charlie sees the flower, "La Violetera" returns, signaling a return to the story of Charlie and the girl and the flowers that always seem to bring them together. But the tambourine and castanets that had made it so upbeat earlier have departed. Now it's carried more plaintively and only by a few violins. The single flower, as I have discussed, is the central symbol of the film. Charlie met the girl buying a flower from her and they will be reunited over a single flower momentarily. Every stage of their relationship in between had been demarcated in reference to flowers.

After Charlie chases the boys away, Chaplin hits upon a lovely piece of comedy:

Charlie blows his nose in the ragged piece of underwear that he has grabbed back from the boys and places it in the front pocket of his suit coat, in the manner of an elegant handkerchief. Even in his most down-and-out moments, Charlie has the ability to create domestic comforts out of the detritus of his poverty.

The altercation with the boys has deposited Charlie directly in front of the large flower shop window. Charlie's back is to the window and he doesn't know that the girl he loves and her co-worker are watching him in amusement through the window in the background of the image. The shot here is well–thought out, a testimony both to Chaplin's compositional skills and his gift for elegant but economical *mise-en-scène*. Charlie is in the foreground to the left, the two women at some recessive depth to the right. In this manner, Chaplin has both seamlessly moved from the slapstick with the boys to the emotional encounter with the girl, and united Charlie and the girl in one image before they've reconnected. The effect is, again, one of dramatic irony; we see the girl Charlie loves before he does, as Chaplin continues to quietly build anticipation in his audience. Charlie and the girl's rediscovery of each other is so powerfully registered in this sequence, in part because Chaplin has taken his time building up to it, and pointed towards their reunion in so many ways before it actually occurs.

Charlie turns to the flower store window, where the girls are giggling at him. As Charlie turns, Chaplin cuts to a shot of Charlie from inside the store, through the window, and from a point of view just behind the flower girl's head, so that he can film Charlie's discovery of her face-on and from her point of view. Charlie turns from railing at the boys and slowly arrives at a point where he sets eyes on his beloved. At this point, Chaplin makes one of his wisest decisions in this portion of the soundtrack. As Charlie's eyes find the girl, the "La Violetera" theme terminates. Chaplin opts for absolute silence at the moment when Charlie rediscovers the girl. This moment will be paired with a corresponding moment of silence, moments later, when she, in turn, will realize who Charlie is.

These silences have two powerful effects. First, they underscore moments that Chaplin knows are so fascinating to us that musical accompaniment would be distracting and superfluous. Secondly, the silence makes us hear the music that follows it more acutely. The silence sets up the music that Chaplin most wants to register, the music that accompanies revelation. After this first, brief silence, the violins return, not with the "La Violetera" theme but with what Huff describes as a "violin caprice"[2] and Maland a "beautiful violin recitative ... framed by the rest of the string section with a harp obbligato."[3] The violin invades our consciousness more fully because of the silence that precedes it. Also coming, as it does, out of silence, the violin mimics the experience of revelation. It pierces the silence, ascends and gently flutters about in a way that perfectly communicates the dawning of Charlie's tender surprise and happiness at that moment. The violins here do not describe what we are seeing but what Charlie is feeling.

Charlie's dumbfounded expression changes into a childlike, nervous grin of rapt adoration. Charlie, of course, knows who the girl is, and his face expresses his delight, but she still only thinks he's an amusing hobo. Noticing that the petals are falling from the flower he salvaged from the gutter, the girl signs to him, through the window, that she would like to replace his flower with the fresher one in her hand. Charlie is still too stunned by his discovery to even respond to her offer; he just stares at her in daft happiness. She adds a coin to her offer; still no response from the hypnotized Charlie.

When she gets up to bring the coin and flower out to him, his rapt expression finally breaks into one of fear and panic. He scurries past the door of the flower shop, as if to run away, his actions the default ones of a person who has routinely been hounded by suspicious store owners. But she calls him back. He turns to her and, realizing what she is offering, smiles and reaches out for the flower, in one of Chaplin's most self-consciously balletic poses in the scene. Up until now, the piece had been a violin solo, but as Charlie reaches out for the flower, a second violin very touchingly joins the first, underlining Charlie and the girl's union. One of the harp beats is timed to match the moment she hands the flower to Charlie. Little moments like this of meticulous orchestration abound in Chaplin's scores, and testify to those lengthy, grueling sessions that he made his musical arrangers and orchestra endure.

The girl then grabs Charlie's hand and puts the coin in it—and recognizes the touch of Charlie's hand as that of her old friend and benefactor. This little hobo is the man of her dreams. This is the moment of revelation that the entire film has built to, and, again, Chaplin wisely opts at that moment for silence. Her moment of revelation earns this silence just as Charlie's moment did earlier. Chaplin holds the silence even longer this time. And the silence here has the same effect of the earlier silence. It underlines the drama of the girl's discovery and also creates a lovely emptiness for the subsequent music to quietly grow into. That music is a devastatingly emotive piece, reminiscent of a Puccini aria, but played by four violins.

Timothy Brock feels that, despite the derivativeness of this musical piece, it has all the earmarks of a Chaplin composition, representing Chaplin's fondness for, and skill at, composing with strings.[4] I can well understand what Brock means because the way music shivers out of silence, the time Chaplin takes to introduce it, the thin plaintive quality it has because it is only violins—these are all expressive of Chaplin particular manner of carefully relishing emotion. After reading Raksin's and other composers' accounts of the way Chaplin worked, it is easy to see him conducting this scene, drawing the music out of the silence oh so quietly, and at a delicate high register that effectively underlines both the girl's dawning recognition and the poignancy of her emotions. Chaplin's success with music in his films has to do with his lovely sense of melody and his workman's knowledge of the orchestra and orchestral music, but above all it has to do with his delicate sense of pathos, his own particular way, with the help of a composer, of finding his way to moments of sublime emotion, emotions that are already there in the actors' performance but which music gives him a means to enhance.

It seems extraordinary that Chaplin was dissatisfied with Virginia Cherrill's performance. The subtlety of her expressions in this final close-up is vital to the success of the scene. It's not only one of the best bits of acting any actress ever did for Chaplin, it's one of the best bits of acting in silent film history. Chaplin, the director, deserves credit for the scene as well, as we can recognize Chaplin's ideas and body movements in nearly every one of Cherrill's actions. Chaplin had thought of firing Cherrill at one point and arranged a screen test of the final scene of the film with Georgia Hale, with whom he planned to replace Cherrill. Hale's screen test reveals how meticulously mapped out the flower girl's mannerisms are here, how much they were calculated by Chaplin himself; there's little left to chance or improvisation. There's already something of a choreographed dance going on here, in the arrangement of the girl's gestures, even before Chaplin brings music to the scene.

First, as she recognizes Charlie's touch, the girl's face expresses a dawning awakening. This awakening gradually gives way to a sad sympathy as the realization of the truth seeps in. When she asks "You?" she holds her hand to her face and the nervous gesture, as well as her expression, suggest a kind of panic and loss as she realizes that this ragamuffin is her dream lover. When he nods yes, her hand moves in a protective gesture to her throat and her eyes wince in pain a little, more, it seems, in realization of what Charlie has done for her than in sadness for the diminution of her fantasy. We see here Chaplin's ability, expressive of the best of silent film technique, to communicate his ideas via hands and eyes.

When Charlie notes, "You can see now," her expression becomes one of steadier, calmer sympathy. She seems to have settled into the truth of what has happened. Her face conveys a more resolute feeling of affection for Charlie as well as a sense of gratitude. "Yes, I can see now," she says, her words expressive of both her new eyesight and new understanding of who it is that has helped her. She catches her breath (one of those tiny gestures that it was Chaplin's great talent to understand the camera would capture) and holds Charlie's hands near her chest with both of her hands. She seems on the verge of tears, yet Cherrill's gestures here are extraordinarily delicate; a shudder of emotion seems to pass through her like wind through the leaves of the trees.

If Chaplin's highest aim was to express, as he told Will Durant, "a smiling sadness," a combined sense of "death and loveliness," this scene has to be counted as one of his greatest successes. He managed to arrive at a rather powerful concoction of sentiment here. The girl is overjoyed to find her benefactor. That he is poor as he is only deepens her sense of his generosity. She is, at this moment, even more grateful than she was before. But she has so many things to be sad about: that her fantasy of a storybook lover is dashed, that the man she loved is as destitute as this, that she accepted all this largesse without knowing that he was actually worse off than she, that their relationship going forward is a profound question mark. Hence the expression that mingles empathy, pain and confusion. Love that encompasses painful empathy and a profound sense of loss: This is the kind of mix in which Chaplin specialized.

The violins that accompany the girl's dawning awareness of who Charlie really is are held in suspension throughout almost the entirety of this interlude. The music gradually adds complexity but refuses to break open in emotion. When Charlie nods yes to her question "You?" a viola joins the violins. When he asks "You can see now?" cellos arrive. Basses follow. But it's only when she holds Charlie's hand to her breast and answers "yes," affirming that she *can* see, and Chaplin cuts to the final image of the film, Charlie's look of childlike pleasure mixed with nervous apprehension, that the music breaks open and ascends, that the instruments, as Maland writes, "display their widest array of color and sound."[5]

We see and hear, in this scene, the evidence of the concentrated study Chaplin put into his soundtracks with his co-composers. It's interesting that the soundtrack in this scene is characterized by such pinpoint precision and fine emotional delicacy, when the editing in terms of visual continuity is a bit lazy. As I've mentioned before, the shot of Charlie from behind in this scene, with rose and hand by his lapel, does not match Charlie in close-up with rose and hand near his mouth. It's curious that Chaplin's comic scenes, his chases for example, are often characterized by pinpoint match-cuts. Even this final sequence is characterized by a graceful editing that carefully weaves together the Tramp's presence on the street with the girl's in the shop. But by the end of the scene, Chaplin's concern with rhythm, music and emotion is well nigh obsessive. Visual continuity seems something he can't be bothered with.

I would also note that the success of Chaplin's soundtrack in this sequence is due not only to the quality of the music and its orchestration, but to its understatement, the way it elegantly accommodates the images. The ending to *City Lights* represents a five-minute scene with four different pieces of music, which in turn are subject to fine variations, and all employed with taste and understatement. But of the three heartbreaking moments in this sequence, two are moments of silence where image is given full sway. And the third—the scoring of the girl's revelation about Charlie—is notable, not only for its subtle music phrasing, but for how the music draws out and gently amplifies the very quiet visual details that Chaplin's camera managed to capture.

The Boxing Match from City Lights

This is one of Chaplin's most popular sequences, even among non-aficionados, if its popularity on YouTube is any indication. The glory of the boxing sequence is that, though it is one of Chaplin's most breezily and effortlessly entertaining sequences, it is also characterized by rigorous craft and meticulous planning, by what Billy Wilder described as "that kind of architectural structure that is completely forgotten once you see the movie."[6] If you want to know why Chaplin became so famous, why we take him so seriously, these six and a half minutes have nearly all the answers. And the great fineness and delicacy of humor here, the spot-on timing and etching in miniature, seem less the result of spontaneous genius than of studied craft, of a choreography nearly mathematical in its calculation, the result of grueling labor and tireless preparation.

The fight sequence is perhaps best understood through its musical structure. The sequence divides neatly into five sections: the preamble to the fight, round one of the fight, a brief interlude between the boxing rounds in which Charlie hallucinates that the young blind girl for whom he fights is with him, round two of the fight and the finale where Charlie finally suffers defeat. Each of these sections has its own musical motif, though the two boxing rounds share the same theme.

The Preamble

The first sequence is announced by the rousing orchestral piece with tango rhythms and momentous horns that had opened the film and which reappears at certain exciting moments in the film, and at moments when Chaplin is picking up the action again after quieter sequences. Here it serves nicely to express both the excitement before a boxing match and the challenge awaiting Charlie. The comic theme of this first section is Charlie's absolute lack of comprehension of the rules of boxing and, more generally, the world of male competition. Charlie has no idea how a boxer conducts himself and so approaches the role with touching humility. He carries his oversized water pail himself as he walks to the ring, presenting the image of a nervous child heading off, with lunch pail, to his first day of school. After climbing through the ropes into the ring, he exhibits a touching politesse, uncharacteristic of the boxing ring, holding the ropes open for his entire entourage. Just as in *The Pilgrim* he doesn't understand that the ticket he bought actually allows him to travel inside the train, rather than in storage as is his custom, so here he doesn't understand that a boxer gets to be the center of attention. For all his pluck and bravado, Charlie is, by nature, touchingly unassuming and humble.

Charlie has no understanding of the nature of relationships in the masculine world of physical competition, so when one of his handlers loosens his boxing trunks and massages his belly he is nervously affronted, wary of a sexual assault. While the referee briefs him and his opponent (Keystone veteran Hank Mann) on the fight, Charlie is so nervous that Mann has only to scratch the back of his head to make Charlie flinch dramatically. This hyper-sensitivity to the slightest movement is just one of many characteristics that he shares with dogs. Like them, and other creatures of the wild, Charlie has always to remain on the defensive. His life is a constant defense against potentially hostile forces that he doesn't fully understand.

Charlie arrives at his first moment of ease when the referee instructs him and his opponent to shake hands. Charlie is so immensely relieved by this one sign of normal human friendliness that he goes on a binge of handshaking—with the boxer, the referee, all of his opponents' handlers, and finally his opponent again, tipping his bowler hat (which Charlie is still wearing, along with his ratty suit coat) until his annoyed managers finally haul him back into his corner.

This ill-timed politeness is a classic Chaplin gag, pointing to two aspects of his art: first its inherent femininity. Charlie's appeal to women is at least partially explained by his inability to play by the rules of masculine discourse, his tendency to meet bluff displays of masculinity with a naive, puppy-like friendliness that, in the end, disarms that masculinity, makes it look puffed-up and foolish. The bit also points to the very confident mockery that actually resides just below the surface of the Tramp's seeming befuddlement. The Tramp may be the most frightened person in the ring. But Chaplin's point is clear: The real objects of ridicule are the idiotic and inhumane masculine rituals that rest outside the understanding of someone as essentially good-natured, playful and civilized as the Tramp.

Round One and the Central Motif

The musical preamble quiets as Charlie takes his seat and this silence is followed by the ringing of a bell signaling the beginning of round one. Chaplin introduces a new musical piece here, the most recurrent motif of the entire sequence and its anchor of sorts. It's a quick-paced, Rossini-like piece with anxious strings. David Robinson calls it "hurry music."[7] Dan Kamin describes it more carefully as a "rapid rhythmic tattoo, or ostinato, played by the strings."[8]

This hurried, rhythmic string piece accompanies the central comic motif of the sequence, Charlie's comical, dance-like boxing strategy. Charlie's fighting method is to mirror Mann's movements, hopping back and forth on his feet, as Mann does, to the point of inducing a kind of rhythmic hypnosis in both Mann and the referee so that all three, at a certain point, find themselves hopping back and forth on their feet in rhythm to the quick string movement. Charlie also protects himself by positioning himself behind the referee so that the ref becomes a kind of unwitting middleman in a three-way folk dance. When the ref tries to step out from between the two boxers, Charlie takes the opportunity, guerrilla fashion, to wallop Mann. When Mann strikes back, Charlie deftly dodges the blow and then, in an expression of rank cowardice, clutches Mann for dear life, at one point spinning Mann around, holding him from behind and administering of couple of savage blows with his knee to Mann's behind. When the ref halts the fight for a moment to lecture Charlie on the inappropriateness of his behavior, Charlie listens dutifully, but the second the ref's back is turned he does exactly what he has done before, taking advantage of the screen the ref has just unconsciously set to sock his opponent one more time.

This is the essential movement of the boxing sequence, its central leitmotif: a rhythmic dance (accompanied by the quickly sawing strings) that induces stupor in the two other men, punctuated by Charlie's little guerrilla attacks from behind the ref (which are accompanied by little piccolo variations that break free from the violins). Sometimes Charlie darts out from behind the ref to administer a sucker punch. Sometimes, when Mann swings at him, he ducks and holds onto him. This is the essential dance of the piece, off of which Chaplin will spin increasingly complex improvisations and variations.

After the kicks to Mann's behind, Charlie returns to his base attack. The ref starts the fight again, Charlie seeks refuge behind the ref again, and the three are off on their rhythmic dance again, the fighters facing each other, the ref unable to get out from the middle as Charlie cunningly hangs behind him. At a certain point, the ref does free himself from the dance and assumes a more traditional place outside the actual fight. But by this time Mann has been so hypnotized by the rhythm of Charlie's movements that he suffers a temporary lapse of consciousness and does not even notice that he and Charlie are now dancing face to face without the ref as intermediary. Charlie takes that opportunity to pummel him. Mann is stunned and, at this point, Charlie utterly dominates the fight.

Chaplin here enters into a variation of one of his favorite repeated gags. Often Charlie, through his guerrilla techniques in fighting, will so discombobulate his opponents and then pummel them with blows that they are reduced to a kind of still-standing unconsciousness. At this point Charlie becomes a kind of gourmand of punishment, relishing each moment of his dominance, approaching each blow with the concentration and creativity of an artist. Having, by his blows, reduced Mann to a semi-comatose state, Charlie now takes the time to decorate his physical attack. He runs a circle around him before administering a blow. He arranges Mann's body like a sharpshooter might the object of his target practice, then retreats to the corner of the ring, so that he can get a running momentum before leaping into Mann's chest, knocking him down. He works so many variations into his physical assault that he suggests the improvisations of a scientist in his laboratory.

The gag in which Chaplin barrels into his dumbstruck opponent's chest is particularly instructive in understanding Chaplin's work habits. The running jump is preceded by a medium close-up of the ref watching the fight, the purpose of which is to divert our attention from the fact that in the next sequence Chaplin has attached a wire to his waist that will allow him to lift off the mat when he sails into Mann. Chaplin uses this special effect quietly and efficiently. He stays on his feet well into his charge. The wire lifts Chaplin's feet off the ground only momentarily, just as he leaps into Mann. This gag attests to Chaplin's care in using special effects. The careful cut and the minimal use of the effect mask the effect well. The wire allows just a little more oomph to Charlie's flight, a little relief from gravity, but doesn't disturb the naturalist feel of the piece. This is the kind of small, studied effect—etching on the smallest scale—that resulted from Chaplin's obsessive study of rushes and pathological tendency for retakes. Chalk it up to Chaplin's exquisite sense of balance as well: Charlie's as mean as a junkyard dog but as graceful as a dancer.

This gag is finished off in classic comic tradition. After watching Charlie sail into his opponent twice, the ref steps in front of the fallen boxer and orders Charlie to desist, only to receive the third knockdown blow himself. Chaplin follows here the time-honored tradition of the rule of three. As Billy Wilder often advised, introduce the gag, extend it a second time, pay it off the third. There is a rhythm to this sequence that precedes the musical overlay, a rhythm of comic principle, a rhythm which is often as ineffable in meaning and its inherent logic as musical rhythm is.

The first round finishes with Charlie suddenly forfeiting his dominant position. Mann finally lands a blow and Charlie, stunned, spends the remainder of the round desperately trying to stay on his feet. First he reels backward, arcing around the ring in a very specific comic dance move that he will reprise in round two of the fight: a perpetual backward fall, with one leg up in the air, his body tilted backward at a sharp angle from the floor, always on the verge of a fall that never quite happens.

Charlie's confidence having given way to rank cowardice, he careens from person to person, clutching anyone and anything that can protect him from Mann's blows, including Mann himself (three times), the corner stanchion of the ring (which he clings to like a nestling contemplating its first flight) and finally, as the bell rings, his own manager (whom he holds with such desperation that he has to be carried to his corner, another handler lifting his feet).

The transformation from vicious aggressor to craven coward again attests to Chaplin's exquisite sense of balance. It's the complex marriage of his many contrary tendencies that makes the Tramp such a rich character, but these oppositions tend to have meaning beyond delineation of the Tramp's rich hybrid nature. They also tend to comment on universals of the human condition. Who hasn't feasted on success, warmed to the role of victor as though it were a God given destiny, only to find themselves, in the blink of an eye, confronted with sweaty failure once again? Like the rest of us, the Tramp has his triumphs but they are short-lived and not to be trusted.

A Brief Interlude

Once the nearly unconscious Charlie reaches his corner seat, the flighty piccolos of the ostinato fade to silence. One of Charlie's handlers brushes back his hair, trying to soothe him. Here again we see Chaplin's technical competence as he effects one of his seamless dissolves, far better than the typical dissolve of its day in its pinpoint precision. The manager brushing back Charlie's hair dissolves into the blind flower girl for whom Charlie fights. Charlie, buffeted by Mann's blows, is having a delusional vision and it is she, in his imagination, who soothes his brow. He grabs her other hand between his two boxing gloves and kisses it over and over. Accompanying the dissolve are a few languorous bars, accompanied by harp, of the film's central love theme, the only time that theme appears in the fighting sequence. This little musical interlude represents the midway point of the sequence. The preamble and round one are finished, round two and the finale are still to come. It's a little oasis, a breathing spot where Chaplin reminds the Tramp, and us, why he's in this boxing ring, a dream in which the battered Tramp can refresh himself. As the music fades, Virginia dissolves back into Charlie's handler who is distinctly uncomfortable with Charlie's romantic advances on his hand. This is the second time Charlie and his handler have had an uncomfortably intimate moment, though this time it's Charlie who is the mistaken sexual aggressor—a little comic payback for his earlier prudishness.

Round Two and the Return of the Ostinato

This brief romantic interlude lasts only half a minute or so before round two is announced and the vigorous ostinato with little flights of piccolo reasserts itself. Chaplin returns to the central musical motif of the sequence and, at the same time, Charlie returns to the central dance motif of the pieces, his three-way rhythmic dance with Mann and the ref, in which he hides behind the ref, only popping out now and then to land cheap blows on Mann or, if his blows haven't landed, clutch him desperately. Chaplin starts with the familiar, establishing his base motif, but he will quickly work variations on that standard theme. Chaplin, having taught us how to read the dance in round one, is confident now that he can switch things up more rapidly and with more complexity. He not only ratchets up the tempo in the second round but increases the variety of the gags; there is an uptick in both speed and invention, creating a dizzying effect. The audience who can barely keep up with what they are seeing.

The first break in the central pattern comes when Charlie, through a few deftly choreographed movements, confuses Mann, who finds himself now the middleman in the three-way dance. He's still staring at the ref and he's still locked in the hypnotic dance, but Charlie has now snuck behind Mann. Charlie waits for Mann to gain cognizance of this change and to turn around to Charlie, who at that moment administers a powerful sucker punch. The variations from this point on are fast and furious. Mann, in turn, swings at Charlie who ducks and clutches the ref in one of his desperate hugs. Mann aims for Charlie again but Charlie ducks just in time and Mann socks the ref, who staggers into Mann's arms. It's the same dance we saw last round but with the participants exchanging roles: Charlie behind Mann this time, rather than the ref; Charlie clutching the ref rather than Mann; Mann swinging at the ref rather than Charlie. Charlie is something of an expert choreographer, entertaining himself with new variations of the dance. And the improvisations have their effect on the movie's audience members who, having been set up to have certain expectations of this boxing dance, are delightfully surprised to see the coordinates of the dance mixed up in unexpected new equations.

Charlie, seeing Mann and the ref locked in a hug, takes the opportunity to pretend he's the ref, pulling them apart and encouraging them to fight fair. The ref, confused by the blow he has suffered, even takes a swing at Mann before he realizes he has been manipulated by Charlie into transforming himself from ref to boxer.

The ref recovers from his stupor, regaining his authority and pointing out to Mann that Charlie, not he, is his opponent. Charlie's strategy exhausted, he switches in a moment from sadist to rank coward again. Charlie now runs circles around the ref trying to escape Mann before, in his desperation, arriving at a new scheme. He rings the ringside bell, thus ending the round himself. The ref quickly realizes what he's done and rings the bell again. The fight is back on.

This is one of my favorite gags in the piece because of the way it highlights the razor-sharp precision and quiet understatement of Chaplin's comic skills. The funniest aspect of Charlie ringing the bell is the way he "sells" his con, immediately walking off to the corner (though not too quickly) with the calm gait of a worker knocking off for lunch at the sound of the noontime whistle. Everything in his demeanor communicates that this was the legitimate ring of the bell. But just as funny is how quickly he drops this pretense when the ref rings the bell, leaping back into the ring with Pavlovian immediacy, fierce energy and unquestioning obedience to the legitimacy of the bell.

There is a good deal of Chaplin's art in these few seconds, moments that are as funny the fifteenth time as they are the first. We marvel, first, at Chaplin's comic virtuosity, conjoining in one moment the leisurely movement of a boxer at the end of a round with the fierce energy of a boxer at the beginning of the next. The humor resides in the lightning-fast turnaround. We also get a kick out of the Tramp's indifference to the roles he plays, his willingness to take on and abandon roles at the drop of a hat. You have to admire his spirit of improvisation. He puts his all into his con but drops it as soon as he's found out, moving without a moment of hesitation to the next role. The bell provides Charlie with the opportunity to do what he loves most: to play, to show off how quickly he can drop and assume roles. He's taken the boxing match and turned it into a kind of party game that tests participants' skills of improvisation.

Back in the ring, Charlie resorts to his standard base approach, the three-man dance we are very familiar with, ref in the middle again, as he was in the first round, again reminding us of how musical this sequence is, always finding its way back to its refrain before spinning off in new directions. Then Charlie makes the clever step that tricks Mann into being the middle man in the dance, now hopping in rhythm face to face with the ref. This too we've already seen, at the outset of round two, a second established motif.

But now Chaplin works a very clever innovation off that second motif. Charlie, confident, stands behind Mann ready to sock him when Mann turns around, just as he had before. He whirls his boxing gloves in anticipation of a choice haymaker. We look forward to him clocking Mann but good, just as he had the first time. But Chaplin's technique in this boxing sequence is to surprise us with variations, not numb us with repetition, and he's set up the same scenario as before only to deviate from it. This time, as Mann turns around, he does so in the midst of an almost unconsciously administered right hook that catches the overconfident Charlie unaware. Charlie's energetic practice swings only serve as the perfect comic introduction to Mann's devastating blow. Charlie, like other great comic figures, is a better fighter when he improvises than when he plans. As with all of us, too much time to think is ruinous for him.

Charlie falls backward, tracing an arc to his right around the ring. It's the same quasi-dance we saw last round, with Charlie always on the verge of falling down but always just able to stand on one foot at about a 50-degree angle from the floor. Mann hits him again, this time from the left, and Charlie traces the same arc in the opposite direction, again emphasizing Chaplin's careful choreography: first an arc to the right, then its mirror image to the left.

What follows next is a moment of wonderfully ineffable humor. Having landed a right and a left, Mann, also with a great sense of symmetry, aims to finish Charlie off with an uppercut, right down the middle. But this third blow, illogically, zaps Charlie with energy, transforming him (again with lightning-like rapidity) into a fast-skipping boxing machine. It's one of the funniest moments in the entire sequence and it's not easy to explain why. Part of it is the rapidity of Chaplin's change from near-defeat to prize pugilist. Part of it is the element of surprise. That this blow would revitalize Charlie is as unforeseen as Mann's blow catching Charlie was seconds earlier. We're as blindsided as Mann is. Chaplin keeps returning to established motifs, setting up expectations and then reversing them. It's this constant succession of variations and surprises, always expressed by the chaotic piccolos of the score that gives the second round its ratcheted energy, its quality of controlled ascension to chaos.

The gag is also funny because, like so many of Chaplin's best gags, it seems to tap into an eternal law of nature: that street urchins like Charlie (or any of us, for that matter) discover surprising resources at the moments just before abject failure. Of course the boxing match has already illustrated a corresponding point as well, that we are most vulnerable to unhappy surprises at moments of success.

Charlie is now a whirling dervish of a boxer, pummeling Mann to the point of dropping him. But, in a moment of exquisite timing, just as Charlie rears back to deliver the knock-out blow, Mann rears back too and, in a mirror image of each other, both administer right hooks and fall to the ground. The referee tries to administer the count to ten that would end the fight but both boxers frustrate his efforts by alternately staggering to their feet before falling to the mat again, forcing him to turn from one boxer to the next, constantly restarting his count. By now we have accumulated quite a few highly symmetrical gags: Charlie's stagger to the left and then to the right, followed by an uppercut up the middle; the mirror image take-down of both boxers; their perfectly timed, alternating rise and fall as they try to recover themselves. If the scene lacks some of the free-flowing chaos of some of Chaplin's earlier boxing sequences, it more than makes up for it in its virtuosic calculation that is as mathematical as it is musical.

Both boxers on their feet again, Chaplin finishes off the match with his last gag. In the course of some grappling with Mann, Charlie gets the rope that rings the bell tightly tangled around his neck so that every time Mann fells him, the bell rings and the boxers think the round is over. But when Charlie then skips to his corner, the taut string around his neck rings the bell again and the round seems to recommence. The key to this gag is, again, Charlie's unfailing devotion and response to the bell. There's something charmingly empty-headed in the way Charlie happily skips to the corner on the first ring of the bell, quite confident the round is over, only to come rearing back like a fierce animal when it rings again, as though he were a trained dog or incapable of even the slightest bit of long-term memory. Here, though, the lightning-fast transformation isn't so much due to cocky role-playing as much as a reflection of how addled he's become by this point in the fight. Here he is not the clever trickster but the sad-sack Tramp doing his best to survive a situation he doesn't understand.

Finale

There's little left in the sequence after the bell gag. As the referee finally untangles Charlie from the bell rope, Chaplin silences all music, signaling to the audience rather dramatically that the blow that will finally fell Charlie is coming. This little ellipsis of silence lends a note of gravity to Charlie's defeat, separating the event from the rest of the fight, which has been comically set to music. As Charlie hits the mat we are introduced to the last musical movement of the sequence, a slow, triumphant piece for echoing horns, half Duke Ellington, half "Taps," that signals the Tramp's defeat. With the preamble, the ostinato and the musical interlude that accompanies Charlie's vision of the girl, that makes four distinct musical pieces used quite purposefully in this roughly six-and-a-half–minute sequence. A short interlude of incidental orchestration ensues as Charlie is removed from the ring and laid on the locker room table, his gloves hung above his head. Charlie regains consciousness temporarily but one of the gloves falls on his head, and such is the precariousness of Charlie's condition that the soft blow of the glove knocks him out again, allowing the funereal horns to announce themselves one more time. Here the boxing sequence concludes finally.

Conclusion

No single clip from a Chaplin film is going to summarize his art entirely. *City Lights'* boxing sequence, for example, has little of the pathos that Chaplin mixed into his comedy and that was, perhaps, the crowning triumph of his films. But this sequence is almost shocking in the wealth of its gags and the pinpoint precision of its art. It's an excellent microcosm of Chaplin's art and tells us a great deal about what there is to value in his films.

First, the meticulously laid-out gags, developed with mathematical precision, testify both to Chaplin's intense work ethic and his keen analytical sense of what the camera can capture. This is the work not of an inspired genius but a careful craftsman decorating his work with as much fine detail as he can. And the fineness of the detail, these delightful bits that pass in a nano-second, remind us that we are dealing not just with an inspired mime, but an inspired mime who had the most sophisticated understanding of the camera's ability to register quiet, deft gestures that are nearly invisible to the naked eye. It's the minutiae of Chaplin's films that delight audiences, the sleight of hand we can barely register as it passes by, much less explain. It's from these jam-packed marvels of miniature that all the celebrity followed. Here is Chaplin's genius, except it's not genius, it's craft—the careful work of an extraordinary comic actor, probably the greatest the screen has seen, but, even more importantly, one of the earliest filmmakers to understand the capabilities of this "prodigious heaven-sent machine," as Bresson put it, the movie camera.[9]

The sequence also reminds us that Chaplin's art is essentially one of rhythm, something that has frustrated critics who want to convey the seriousness of his filmmaking through analysis of its content. The sequence is effective in no small part because of Chaplin's soundtrack but the music only amplifies the preexistent rhythm of the piece, which is very sophisticated in its use of recurrent motifs and of complications and innovations that spin off those motifs. The sequence gathers in pace and energy, only repeating itself when Chaplin wants the audience to collect itself via the central ostinato motif before he shoots off in even wilder variations. And it gradually ratchets up these variations as the piece evolves. It doesn't just accelerate in pace, it accelerates in innovations, so that round two is conducted at a giddy, liberating pace, the effect being of so many fireworks being shot off from a central base of operation.

And yet the sequence, despite being silent filmmaking that principally expresses itself in rhythm, is also curiously rich in meaning. Charlie's manic role-playing touches on the superficiality of the postures we adopt in life. And so many of Chaplin's gags have resonance, in surprisingly sensitive ways. Charlie's manic flutter between cowardice and confidence, for example, is familiar to the rest of us poor humans who careen wildly between confidence and distress. When he is surprised by Mann's blow despite his well-executed plan to attack Mann from behind, we are reminded how often our failures come when we are most sure of ourselves. When Mann's uppercut unleashes a comically surprising abundance of boxing energy in Charlie, we are reminded of how often we succeed when we least expect to. Both gags point to the slight control we have over life, how difficult it is to understand and manage, how much of managing life is to live, like Charlie, in a spirit of improvisation. Add this to the seemingly endless list of paradoxes that define Chaplin's cinema: a mathematical sense of precision culminating in an ode to spontaneity.

Chapter Notes

Introduction

1. Graham Petrie, "So Much and Yet So Little: A Survey of Books on Chaplin," *Film Quarterly* (Spring 1973), cited in Richard Dyer MacCann, *The Silent Comedians* (Metuchen, NJ: Scarecrow Press, 1993).

2. David Robinson, *Chaplin, His Life and Art* (London: Penguin, 2001).

3. See for example Kenneth Lynn, *Charlie Chaplin and His Times* (New York: Simon & Schuster, 1997); A.J. Marriot, *Chaplin: Stage by Stage* (Herts, UK: Marriot, 2005).

4. The following are some recent examples of scholarship that might be seen as fitting into this trend in Chaplin criticism: Charles Maland, *Chaplin and American Culture* (Princeton, NJ: Princeton University Press, 1989); Stephen Weissman, *Chaplin: A Life* (New York: Arcade, 2008); Simon Louvish, *Chaplin: The Tramp's Odyssey* (New York: St. Martins Press, 2009).

5. Gerald Mast's study of Chaplin in *The Comic Mind* (New York: Bobbs-Merrill) remains, to my mind, a touchstone for this strain of Chaplin criticism, as does Dan Kamin's more recent *The Comedy of Charlie Chaplin: Artistry in Motion* (Lanham, MD: Scarecrow Press, 2011).

6. Charles J. Maland, *Chaplin and American Culture* (Princeton: Princeton University Press, 1989).

7. Peter Bogdanovich, *Who the Devil Made It* (New York: Knopf, 1997), 395.

8. Thomas Burke, "A Comedian," in *City of Encounters* (Boston: Little, Brown, 1932), 145.

9. Waldo Frank, "Charlie Chaplin, a Portrait," *Scribner's Magazine* 86, no. 3 (1929).

10. Gerald D. McDonald, *The Picture History of Charlie Chaplin* (Franklin Square, NY: Nostalgia, 1965), cited in Kamin, *The Comedy of Charlie Chaplin*, 39.

11. Kevin J. Hayes, ed., *Charlie Chaplin Interviews* (Jackson: University Press of Mississippi, 2005), 80.

Chapter One

1. Thomas Burke, "A Comedian," in *City of Encounters* (Boston: Little, Brown, 1932), 138.

2. Simon Louvish, *The Tramp's Odyssey* (New York: St. Martin's Press, 2009), 357–58.

3. David Robinson, *Chaplin, His Life and Art* (New York: McGraw-Hill, 1985), 160.

4. Ibid., 159.

5. Theodore Huff, *Charlie Chaplin* (New York: Arno Press, 1972), 125, 117.

6. Waldo Frank, "Charles Chaplin, a Portrait," *Scribner's Magazine* 86, no. 3, 243.

7. Winston Churchill, "Everybody's Language," in *The Essential Chaplin*, ed. Richard Schickel (Chicago: Ivan R. Dee, 2006), 210.

8. Stephen Weissman, *Chaplin: A Life* (New York: Arcade, 2008), 272.

9. Gilbert Seldes, "I Am Here Today," in Schickel, ed., *Essential Chaplin*.

10. Scott Eyman, *Ernst Lubitsch: Laughter in Paradise* (New York: Simon & Schuster, 1993), 104.

11. Louvish, 178.

12. Lillian Ross, *Moments with Chaplin* (New York: Dodd, Mead, 1980), 50.

13. Burke, 149–50.

14. Kenneth Lynn, *Charlie Chaplin and His Times* (New York: Simon & Schuster, 1997).

15. Jeffrey Vance, *Chaplin: Genius of the Cinema* (New York: Harry N. Abrams, 2003), 367.

16. George Wallach, "Charlie Chaplin's *Monsieur Verdoux* Press Conference," in *Charlie Chaplin Interviews*, ed. Kevin J. Hayes (Jackson: University of Mississippi, 2005), 105.

17. Robinson, 412.

18. Kevin J. Hayes, ed., *Charlie Chaplin Interviews* (Jackson: University Press of Mississippi, 2005), 27.
19. Burke, 140.
20. Charles Chaplin, *My Autobiography* (New York: Simon & Schuster, 1963), 497.
21. Burke, 150.
22. Robinson, 579.
23. Andrew Sarris, "The Most Harmonious Comedian," in Schickel, ed., *Essential Chaplin*, 55.
24. Gerald Mast, *The Comic Mind* (New York: Bobbs-Merrill, 1973) 122.

Chapter Two

1. Gerald Mast, *The Comic Mind* (New York: Bobbs-Merril, 1973), 70.
2. Graham Petrie, "So Much and Yet So Little: A Survey of Books on Chaplin," *Film Quarterly* (Spring 1973).

Chapter Three

1. David Thompson, "The Demon Tramp," in *The Essential Chaplin*, ed. Richard Schickel (Chicago: Ivan R. Dee, 2006), 61.
2. Andrew Sarris, "The Most Harmonious Comedien," in Schickel, ed., *Essential Chaplin*, 53.
3. Benjamen de Casseres, "The Hamlet–like Nature of Charlie Chaplin," in *Charlie Chaplin Interviews*, ed. Kevin J. Hayes (Jackson: University Press of Mississippi, 2005).
4. Burke, 143.
5. Ibid., 146–47.
6. Walter Kerr, *The Silent Clowns* (New York: Knopf, 1973), 83.
7. Letter to Yvette Guilbert, quoted in Stephen Weissman, *Chaplin: A Life* (New York: Arcade, 2008), 272.
8. Francois, Duc de la Rochefoucauld, *Maxims* (London: Penguin, 1959), 89.
9. Graham Greene, *Modern Times*, in Schickel, ed., *Essential Chaplin*, 226–27.
10. Jeffrey Vance, *Chaplin: Genius of the Cinema* (New York: Henry N. Abrams, 2003), 236.

Chapter Four

1. Charles Chaplin, *My Autobiography* (New York: Simon & Schuster, 1964), 356.
2. Walter Kerr, *The Silent Clowns* (New York: Knopf, 1975), 84.
3. George Wallach, "Charlie Chaplin's *Monsieur Verdoux* Press Conference," in *Charlie Chaplin Interviews*, ed. Kevin J. Hayes (Jackson: University Press of Mississippi, 2005), 105.
4. Benjamin de Casseres, "The Hamlet-Like Nature of Charlie Chaplin," in Hayes, ed., *Charlie Chaplin Interviews*, 47.
5. Kerr, 92.
6. Chaplin, 497.
7. Harold Clurman, "Oona, Oxford, America and the Book," *Esquire* 6, no. 3 (Nov. 1962), 182.
8. "A Comedian Sees the World," *Woman's Home Companion* 61 (Jan. 1934), 86.
9. David Robinson, *Chaplin, His Art and His Life* (New York: McGraw-Hill, 1985), 530.
10. Chaplin, 470.
11. Francis Wyndham, "Chaplin on the Critics, the Beatles, the Mood of London," in Hayes, ed., *Charlie Chaplin Interviews*, 145.
12. 459.
13. Harry Carr, "Chaplin Explains Chaplin," in Hayes, ed., *Charlie Chaplin Interviews*, 80.
14. Chaplin, 396.
15. Thomas Burke, "A Comedian," in *City of Encounters* (Boston: Little, Brown, 1932), 167.
16. "Verdoux Press Conference," in Hayes, ed., *Charlie Chaplin Interviews*, 111.
17. Robinson, 529.
18. Robert Nichols, "Future of the Cinema: Mr. Charles Chaplin," in Hayes, ed., *Charlie Chaplin Interviews*, 81.
19. "From Rags to Riches," in Hayes, ed., *Charlie Chaplin Interviews*, 99.
20. Robinson, 383.
21. Ibid., 591.
22. Hayes, ed., *Charlie Chaplin Interviews*, 81.
23. Chaplin, 291.
24. "Chaplin on the Critics," in Hayes, ed., *Charlie Chaplin Interviews*, 144.

Chapter Five

1. Dan Kamin, *The Comedy of Charlie Chaplin* (Lanham, MD: Scarecrow Press, 2008), 36.
2. Gerald Mast, *The Comic Mind* (New York: Bobbs-Merril, 1973), 67.
3. Charles Chaplin, *My Autobiography* (New York: Simon & Schuster, 1964), 153.
4. Ray W. Frohman, "Charlie Chaplin," in Kevin J. Hayes, ed., *Charlie Chaplin Interviews* (Jackson: University Press of Mississippi, 2005), 44.
5. Mary Porter, "Charlie Chaplin, Cheerful Comedian," in Hayes, ed., *Charlie Chaplin Interviews*, 10.
6. Interview with Richard Merryman, cited in Jeffrey Vance, *Chaplin: Genius of the Cinema* (New York: Harry N. Abrams, 2003), 364.
7. Robert Bresson, *Notes on the Cinematographer* (New York: Quartet, 1986), 112.
8. Ibid., 97.
9. Robert Nichols, "Future of the Cinema: Mr. Charles Chaplin," in Hayes, ed., *Charlie Chaplin Interviews*, 81–82.
10. Walter Vosges, "Charlie Chaplin: Rather a Quiet Little Guy Who Takes His Pantomimic Art Seriously," in Hayes, ed., *Charlie Chaplin Interviews*, 31.
11. "Introduction: The Tramp Transformed," in Richard Schickel, ed., *The Essential Chaplin* (Chicago: Ivan R. Dee, 2006), 12.
12. Schickel, ed., *Essential Chaplin*, 88.
13. Bresson, 20, 26.
14. Stephen Weissman, *Chaplin: A Life* (New York: Arcade, 2008), 171.
15. Kyp Harness, *The Art of Charlie Chaplin* (Jefferson, NC: McFarland, 2008), 4.
16. Kamin, 21–22.
17. Gilbert Seldes, "I Am Here Today," in Schickel, ed., *Essential Chaplin*, 108.
18. David Robinson, *Chap-*

lin, *His Life and Art* (New York: McGraw-Hill, 1985), 312.
19. Lillian Ross, *Moments with Chaplin* (New York: Dodd, Mead, 1980), 15, 17.
20. Vance, 362.
21. Hayes, ed., *Charlie Chaplin Interviews*, 31.
22. Scott Eyman, *Ernst Lubitsch: Laughter in Paradise* (New York: Simon & Schuster, 1993), 105.
23. Hayes, ed., *Charlie Chaplin Interviews*, 120.
24. Robinson, 613.
25. Ibid.

Chapter Six

1. David Robinson, *Chaplin, His Life and Art* (New York: McGraw-Hill, 1985), 304.
2. Charles Chaplin, *My Autobiography* (New York: Simon & Schuster, 1964), 211.
3. Robinson, 304.
4. Scott Eyman, *Ernst Lubitsch: Laughter in Paradise* (New York: Simon & Schuster, 1993), 104.
5. Ibid., 211, 286.
6. Ibid., 130.
7. Peter Bogdanovich, *Who the Devil Made It* (New York: Knopf, 1997), 244–45.
8. Kevin J. Hayes, ed., *Charlie Chaplin Interviews* (Jackson: University Press of Mississippi, 2005), 96.
9. Gerald Mast, *The Comic Mind* (New York: Bobbs-Merrill, 1973), 78.
10. Chaplin, 255.
11. Bogdanovich, 71.
12. Ibid.
13. Robert Bresson, *Notes on the Cinematographer* (London: Quartet Books, 1975), 39, 67.

Chapter Seven

1. Charles Chaplin, *My Autobiography* (New York: Simon & Schuster, 1964), 209.
2. Kyp Harness, *The Art of Charlie Chaplin* (Jefferson, NC: McFarland, 2008), 7.
3. David Robinson, *Chaplin, His Life and Art* (New York: McGraw-Hill, 1985), 385.
4. Ibid., 565.
5. Ella Winter, "But It's Sad, Says Chaplin, It's Me," in Kevin J. Hayes, ed., *Charlie Chaplin Interviews* (Jackson: University Press of Mississippi, 2005).
6. George Stevens, Jr., *Conversations with the Great Moviemakers of Hollywood's Golden Age* (New York: Knopf, 2006), 159.
7. Ibid., 319.
8. Ibid., 159.
9. Richard Schickel, ed., *The Essential Chaplin* (Chicago: Ivan R. Dee, 2006), 11.
10. Gerald Mast, *The Comic Mind* (New York: Bobbs-Merrill, 1973), 65.
11. Chaplin, 151.
12. Schickel, ed., 101.
13. Richard Merryman interview with Chaplin, cited in Jeffrey Vance, *Chaplin: Genius of the Cinema* (New York: Harry N. Abrams, 2003), 362.
14. Girish, "Received Ideas in Cinema," *Comparative Cinema*, 24 June 2008 (http://girshsambu.blogspot.com).
15. Mast, 66.

Chapter Eight

1. George Stevens, *The Great Moviemakers of Hollywood's Golden Age* (New York: Knopf, 2006), 112.
2. Gerald Mast, *The Comic Mind* (New York: Bobbs-Merrill, 1973), 93.
3. Richard Schickel, ed., *The Essential Chaplin* (Chicago: Ivan R. Dee, 2006), 24.
4. Mast, 76.
5. Walter Kerr, *The Silent Clowns* (New York: Knopf, 1979), 346.
6. Francois, Duc de la Rochefoucauld, *Maxims* (London: Penguin, 1959), 37.
7. David Robinson, *Chaplin, His Life and Art* (New York: McGraw-Hill, 1985), 261.

Chapter Nine

1. Dan Kamin, *The Comedy of Charlie Chaplin* (Lanham, MD: Scarecrow Press, 2008), 116.
2. David Robinson, *Chaplin, His Life and Art* (New York: McGraw-Hill, 1985), 211.

Chapter Ten

1. Dan Kamin, *The Comedy of Charlie Chaplin* (Lanham, MD: Scarecrow Press, 2008), 29.
2. Ibid., 18–19.
3. "The Demon Tramp," in Richard Schickel, ed., *The Essential Chaplin* (Chicago: Ivan R. Dee, 2006), 61.
4. Robert Nichols, "Future of Cinema: Mr. Charles Chaplin," in Kevin J. Hayes, ed., *Charlie Chaplin Interviews* (Jackson: University Press of Mississippi, 2005), 83.
5. Gerald Mast, *The Comic Mind* (New York: Bobbs-Merrill, 1973), 72.

Chapter Eleven

1. David Robinson, *Chaplin, His Life and Art* (New York: McGraw-Hill, 1985), 21–11.
2. Jeffrey Vance, *Charlie Chaplin: Genius of the Cinema* (New York: Henry N. Abrams, 2003), 73.
3. Ibid.

Chapter Twelve

1. Dan Kamin, *The Comedy of Charlie Chaplin* (Lanham, MD: Scarecrow Press, 2008), 60.
2. Charles Chaplin, *My Autobiography* (New York: Simon & Schuster, 1964).

Chapter Thirteen

1. Quoted in Gilbert Seldes, "I Am Here Today," in Richard Schickel, ed., *The Essential Chaplin* (Chicago: Ivan R. Dee, 2006), 108.
2. Robert Nichols, "Future of the Cinema: Mr. Charles Chaplin," in Kevin J. Hayes, ed., *Charlie Chaplin Interviews* (Jackson: University Press of Mississippi, 2005), 80.
3. George Stevens, Jr., *The Great Moviemakers of Holly-*

wood's Golden Age (New York: Knopf, 2006), 175–76.

4. Andre Tarkovsky, *Sculpting in Time* (New York: Knopf, 1986), 113.

5. Robert Bresson, *Notes on the Cinematographer* (London: Quartet, 1986), 58.

6. Andre Bazin, "Charlie Chaplin," in Schickel, ed., *The Essential Chaplin*, 88–89.

Chapter Fourteen

1. Dan Kamin, *The Comedy of Charlie Chaplin* (Lanham, MD: Scarecrow Press, 2008), 100.

2. Thomas Burke, "A Comedian," in *City of Encounters* (Boston: Little, Brown, 1932), 135.

3. Alistair Cooke, "Fame," in Schickel, ed., *Essential Chaplin*, 134.

4. Cited in Jeffrey Vance, *Chaplin, Genius of the Cinema* (New York: Henry N. Abrams, 2003), 361.

5. Kyp Harness, *The Art of Charlie Chaplin* (Jefferson, NC: McFarland, 2008), 18.

Chapter Fifteen

1. Timothy Brock, "The Intimate Score of the Tramp Composer: Restoring Music for *City Lights*," June 7, 2013, http//www.timothybrock.com.

2. Timothy Brock, Modern Times, TimothyBrock.com.

3. David Raksin and Charles M. Berg, "Music Composed by Charles Chaplin: Auteur or Collaborateur?" *Journal of the University Film Association* 31, no. 1 (Winter 1979), 49.

4. Ibid., 50.

5. David Robinson, *Chaplin, His Life and Art* (New York: McGraw-Hill, 1985), 412.

6. Brock, "Intimate Score."

7. Raksin, 49.

8. Ibid.

9. Vance, 348.

10. Theodore Huff, *Charlie Chaplin* (New York: Arno Press, 1972), 235.

11. Brock, Modern Times.

12. Raksin, 49–50.

13. Robinson, 471.

14. Huff, 237.

15. Robinson, 472.

16. Brock, Modern Times.

17. Robinson, 412.

18. Vance, 348.

Chapter Sixteen

1. Charles Maland, *City Lights* (London: BFI, 2007), 91.

2. Theodore Huff, *Charlie Chaplin* (New York: Arno Press, 1972), 238.

3. Maland, 93.

4. Brock's thoughts here are cited in Maland, 97.

5. Maland, 100.

6. Peter Bogdanovich, *Who the Devil Made It* (New York: Alfred A. Knopf, 1997), 370.

7. Robinson, 412.

8. Dan Kamin, *The Comedy of Charlie Chaplin* (Lanham, MD: Scarecrow Press, 2008), 129.

9. Robert Bresson, *Notes on the Cinematographer* (London: Quartet Books, 1986), 112.

Bibliography

Bogdanovich, Peter. *Who the Devil Made It*. New York: Knopf, 1997.

Brownlow, Kevin. *The Parade's Gone By*. New York: Knopf, 1968.

Bresson, Robert. *Notes on the Cinematographer*. London: Quartet, 1986, 58.

Brock, Timothy. "The Intimate Score of the Tramp Composer: Restoring Music for *City Lights*." June 7, 2013, http//www.timothybrock.com.

Burke, Thomas. *City of Encounters*. Boston: Little, Brown, 1932.

Chaplin, Charles. *Charlie Chaplin's Own Story*. Edited by Harry M. Geduld. Bloomington: Indiana University Press, 1985.

_____. *My Autobiography*. New York: Simon & Schuster, 1963.

_____. *My Life in Pictures*. New York: Grosset and Dunlap, 1975.

Chaplin, Charles, Jr. *My Father, Charlie Chaplin*. New York: Random House, 1960.

Clurman, Harold. "Oona, Oxford, America and the Book." *Esquire* 63, Nov. 1962.

Cooke, Alistair. "The One and Only," in *Six Men*. New York: Knopf, 1977.

Epstein, Jerry. *Remembering Charlie*. New York: Doubleday, 1989.

Eyman, Scott. *Ernst Lubitsch: Laughter in Paradise*. New York: Simon & Schuster, 1993.

Frank, Waldo. "Charlie Chaplin, a Portrait." *Scribner's Magazine* 86, no. 3, 1929.

Gehring, Wes. *Charlie Chaplin: A Bio-Bibliography*. Westport, CT: Greenwood, 1983.

Haining, Peter. *Charlie Chaplin: A Centenary Celebration*. Berkshire, UK: W. Foulsham, 1989.

Harness, Kyp. *The Art of Charlie Chaplin*. Jefferson, NC: McFarland, 2008.

Hayes, Kevin J., ed. *Charlie Chaplin Interviews*. Jackson: University Press of Mississippi, 2005.

Huff, Theodore, *Charlie Chaplin*. New York: Arno Press, 1972.

James, Eric. *Making Music with Charlie Chaplin*. Lanham, MD: Scarecrow Press, 2000.

Kamin, Dan. *The Comedy of Charlie Chaplin: Artistry in Motion*. Lanham, MD: Scarecrow Press, 2011.

Kerr, Walter. *The Silent Clowns*. New York: Knopf, 1973.

Lieberman, Evan A. "Charlie the Trickster." *Journal of Film and Video* 46, no. 3 (Fall 1994).

Lyons, Timothy. *Charles Chaplin: A Guide to References and Resources*. Boston: G.K. Hall, 1979.

Louvish, Simon. *Chaplin, The Tramp's Odyssey*. New York: St. Martins Press, 2009.

Lynn, Kenneth. *Charlie Chaplin and His Times*. New York: Simon & Schuster, 1997.

MacCann, Richard Dyer. *The Silent Comedians*. Metuchen, NJ: Scarecrow Press, 1993.

Maland, Charles. *Chaplin and American Culture*. Princeton, NJ: Princeton Press, 1989.

Manviel, Roger. *Chaplin*. New York: Doubleday, 1978.

Marriot, A.J. *Chaplin: Stage by Stage*. Herts, UK: Marriot, 2005.

Mast, Gerald. *The Comic Mind*. New York: Bobbs-Merrill, 1973.

McCabe, John. *Charlie Chaplin*. New York: Doubleday, 1978.

McCaffrey, Donald W., ed. *Focus on Chaplin*. Englewood Cliffs, NJ: Prentice Hall, 1971.

McDonald, Gerald D. *The Picture History of Charlie Chaplin*. Franklin Square, NY: Nostalgia, 1965.

Mitchell, Glenn. *The Chaplin Encyclopedia*. London: B. T. Batsford, 1997.

Nysenholc, Adolphe, ed. *Charlie Chaplin: His Reflection in Modern Times*. Berlin, NY: Mouton de Gruyter, 1991.

Petrie, Graham. "So Much and Yet So Little: A Survey of Books on Chaplin." *Film Quarterly*, Spring 1973.

Raksin, David, and Charles M. Berg. "Music Composed by Charles Chaplin: Auteur or Collaborateur?" *Journal of the University Film Association* 31, no. 1 (Winter 1979).

Robinson, David. *Chaplin, His Life and Art*. New York: McGraw-Hill, 1985.

Rosen, Philllip. "The Chaplin World-View." *Society for Cinema and Media Stories* 9, no. 1 (Autumn 1969).

Ross, Lillian. *Moments with Chaplin*. New York: Dodd, Mead, 1980.

Schickel, Richard, ed. *The Essential Chaplin*. Chicago: Ivan R. Dee, 2006.

Smith, Julian. *Chaplin*. Boston: Twayne, 1984.

Sonnenberg, Ben. "Chaplin and Women," *Grand Street* 5, no. 1 (Autumn 1985).

Stevens, Jr., George. *Conversations with the Great Moviemakers of Hollywood's Golden Age*. New York: Knopf, 2006.

Tarkovsky, Andre. *Sculpting in Time*. New York: Knopf, 1986.

Vance, Jeffrey. *Chaplin: Genius of the Cinema*. New York: Harry N. Abrams, 2003.

Weissman, Stephen. *Chaplin: A Life*. New York: Arcade, 2008.

Index

Academy Awards 18
acting, Chaplin's approach to 69–72, 74, 76–80, 162–7
actresses, Chaplin's 162–7
Adair, Gilbert 105
The Adventurer 107, 142, 190–2, 197, 205–7
Agee, James 14
Aldrich, Robert 117
American Film Institute 116
Armstrong, Billy 134, 201
Austin, Albert 25–6, 28, 72–4, 193, 201
Auteurism 221

Baker, Nellie Bly 51, 78, 117, 122
The Bank 58, 72, 82, 120, 128, 134, 146, 151, 154, 161, 194–5, 201, 203–4, 214
Barrie, James 14
Barry, Joan 15
Baudelaire, Charles 20
Bazin, André 68, 109, 116, 207, 229
The Beatles 12
beauty, Chaplin's concept of 61–4
Beethoven, Ludwig van 11
Behind the Screen 27–8, 40, 48–9, 71, 87, 113, 120, 135, 152, 165, 171, 194, 196, 205, 212
Bergman, Henry 13, 50, 59, 114, 158
Bergman, Ingmar 100
Bernini, Gian Lorenzo 164
Betjeman, John 24
The Bicycle Thief 60
biographers, Chaplin's 1–2, 18–19

biography, Chaplin's 1–2, 11–24
Blackmail 105
Blanke, Henry 83
Bloom, Claire 23
Bogart, Humphrey 80
Bogdanovich, Peter 8
bottom-kicking gags 191–5
Boucher, Francois 109
"Bound for Texas" 224
Brahms, Johannes 23
Brando, Marlon 79
Brecht, Bertolt 14
Bresson, Robert 8, 68–71, 80, 91, 201
Brock, Timothy 217–20, 222, 231
Brooks, Louise 16
Brownlow, Kevin 66–7, 79, 87, 113, 129
Buñuel, Luis 174
Burke, Thomas 8, 11, 16, 19–20, 37–9, 46, 55, 62, 209
Burlesque on Carmen 29, 160, 164
By the Sea 181

Cagney, James 80
camera: Chaplin's sensitivity to 65–9; movement of 101–3; restrained use of 96–8
Campbell, Eric 33, 44, 72–4, 91, 108, 172, 174, 178, 181, 190, 206, 208
Capra, Frank 13, 116
The Champion 27, 96, 168, 178, 179, 191, 212–3
Chaplin, Charles (father) 12
Chaplin, Charles, Jr. 222
Chaplin, Charles Spenser:

belief system of 53–65; childhood 12; children and 172–4; empathy of 59–64; fame 13–6; financial success 12–3; musical talent of 217–23; neutral expressions of 69–72; politics of 1, 16, 18, 47–52; radicalism of 56; romantic life 15–6; world events and 16–18
Chaplin, Hannah 12
Chaplin, Michael 24
Chaplin, Sydney Earle (son) 79
Chaplin, Sydney John (brother) 73–4, 76, 135, 171
Charlie (the Tramp): balanced nature of 129–44; childishness of 174–84; children and 27–9; chivalry 159–60; companionship and 62; cruelty of 132–5; dance 208–16; dining 175–7; dogs and 168–72; domesticity of 30–6; femininity of 153–7, 188–90; food and 135–7; liquor and 141–4; love and 156–9; masculinity of 185–6; men and 185–99; playfulness of 27–9, 183–4; police and 191–9; sexuality of 147–53; women and 145–60; work and 194–6
Chekhov, Anton 57
Cherrill, Virginia 72, 78, 107, 162, 164, 231–3
Chou En-Lai 14
Churchill, Winston 14

Index

The Circus 6, 33, 45–6, 58–9, 61, 95–6, 98, 100–3, 111, 118–20, 128, 133, 158, 163, 166, 171–3, 187, 194, 198, 203, 217–8, 224
City Lights 6–7, 11, 14, 21–2, 27, 33, 35, 41, 44, 46–7, 56, 58–62, 72, 78–9, 82, 86, 88, 92, 95–6, 104–5, 107–8, 112, 114, 116–7, 120, 122–3, 135, 137, 140, 144, 151–3, 162, 164, 166, 170, 172, 179, 189–91, 194, 205, 209, 213, 216, 219, 222–5; boxing sequence in 233–241, ending of 227–233
Clark, Petula 223
Classicism, Chaplin's 94
Clurman, Harold 61
Cocteau, Jean 14
Constantin, Jean 224
Coogan, Jackie 13, 32, 54, 77–8, 174, 192
Cooke, Alistair 209
Cooper, Gary 71, 80
The Count 13, 33, 91, 95, 143, 149–50, 153, 208, 210
A Countess from Hong Kong 4, 21, 64, 79, 122, 137, 164, 218
Crane, Hart 14
criticism, of Chaplin 1–6
Cubism 14
The Cure 29, 74, 107, 129, 142, 144, 159, 189–90, 212

Dadaism 14
dance, Chaplin and 208–16; "non-sequitur" dances 212–6
Davies, Marian 15–16
Davis, Carl 221
Davoli, Ninetto 182
A Day's Pleasure 172
The Death of Ivan Ilych 60, 62
Debussy, Claude 218
Delacroix, Eugène 102
The Decameron 182
DeMille, Cecil B. 66
DeSica, Vittorio 80
Dickens, Charles 55, 86, 125, 161
Dietrich, Marlene 71, 80
A Dog's Life 6, 25, 32, 42, 72–4, 95, 103–5, 120–1, 137, 135–6, 166, 168–71, 173, 177–8, 201, 204–5, 210, 229
El Dorado 83
Dostoevsky, Fyodor 186
Dough and Dynamite 25, 48–9
dreams (in Chaplin's films) 125–8

Durant, Will 61–2, 232
Dwan, Allan 88

Easy Street 43, 50, 73, 95, 122, 124, 127, 138, 160, 172–3, 177, 188
editing, Chaplin's 107–9; in *The Adventurer* 203–7
Edward, Prince of Wales 14
Eight Lancashire Lads 218
Einstein, Albert 8, 14, 55
Eisenstein, Sergei 98, 107, 109, 173–4, 183
El Dorado 83
elimination from accumulation 81–6
Eliot, T.S. 14, 200, 209
Ellington, Duke 240
ellipticism, Chaplin's gift for 86–97; in conveying sound 91–3
"Eternally" 218
Existentialism, and Chaplin's films 58–60, 64, 145, 198
Eyman, Scott 77

Fairbanks, Douglas 21, 67, 150
Fellini, Federico 163
Fields, W.C. 173
The Fireman 181, 193
Fiske, Minnie Maddern 137, 171
The Floorwalker 33, 133, 138–9, 149, 160, 186, 190, 193, 212–3
flowers, in Chaplin's films 160–2
Ford, John 2, 100, 116–7
Fragonard, Jean-Honoré 109
Frank, Waldo 8
The French New Wave 3, 94
French Symbolism 91
Freud, Sigmund 14, 43

Gandhi, Mahatma 14
Garbo, Greta 82
Gardiner, Reginald 78
Gershwin, George 218
Getting Acquainted 147
Gilbert, Billy 78
Gilbert, Jack 78
Goddard, Paulette 24, 48, 86, 109, 126, 136, 163–4, 166, 225
The Gold Rush 6, 13, 21–3, 31–2, 43, 46, 56–61, 69–70, 72, 95, 100–2, 104, 109–10, 116, 118, 120, 125, 128, 136–7, 154–5, 158, 160, 165–6, 169–71, 180–83, 188, 206, 209–10, 216–8, 224
Golgotha 50, 95
The Great Dictator 16, 18, 21–3, 44, 78, 114, 122, 209, 217–8

Greene, Graham 14, 48
Grey, Lita 148, 162
Grierson, John 97
Griffith, D.W. 21, 49, 66, 86, 88, 95, 110, 117

Hackett, Francis 127
Hackman, Gene 97
Hale, Georgia 164–5, 231
hands and eyes, a cinema of 69–73
Hardy, Thomas 47
Harness, Kyp 71, 212, 216
Hawks, Howard 83, 116
Hemingway, Ernest 18
Henshaw, Judge 191
His New Job 152, 178
His New Profession 113, 152, 181
His Prehistoric Past 155, 168
His Trysting Place 171, 193
Hitchcock, Alfred 3, 13, 79, 86, 105, 116–7, 200, 220
Hitler, Adolf 16, 23
"The Honeysuckle and the Rose" 218
Hoover, Herbert 14
House Un-American Activities Committee 2–3, 16
Huff, Theodore 13, 219, 221–2, 230
Humanism 50, 131
"Hungarian Rhapsody" 23
Huxley, Aldous 14

The Immigrant 2–3, 6, 12, 25, 27, 44, 46–7, 58, 66, 81, 92, 95, 104, 107, 109, 120, 122, 137, 139, 146, 157, 164, 178
Insley, Charles 51
Intolerance 66
Iosselianni, Otar 202

James, Eric 218
Jeffers, Robinson 14
A Jitney Elopement 152, 160–1, 175
Johnson, Arthur 19, 219, 222
Johnson, Ben 17
Joyce, Peggy Hopkins 16
"just selection," Chaplin's gift for 81–6

Kamin, Dan 65, 74, 131, 141, 150, 153, 208, 234
Karno, Fred 12, 20, 35, 53, 71, 77, 194, 201, 223
Keaton, Buster 4, 8, 94, 97, 100, 102, 114, 123
Keller, Helen 14
Kennedy, Merna 162–4
Kerr, Walter 39–40, 53–6, 58–9, 123
Khrushchev, Nikita 16

The Kid 6, 13, 21, 29, 31, 34, 37, 39, 41, 46, 49–50, 53–4, 58, 60, 75, 77–9, 87–8, 95–6, 100, 112–3, 116, 120, 126, 132, 136, 146, 148, 151, 154, 157, 161–2, 168, 172–5, 182, 188, 191–3, 198, 217–8, 224–5
Kid Auto Races 41, 78
A King in New York 16, 21, 24, 38, 49, 173

La Rochefoucauld, François de 43–4, 124, 132
Laughton, Charles 79
Laurel, Stan 20, 71
Leachman, Chloris 17
Léger, Fernand 14
Lehár, Franz 86
LeRoy, Mervyn 97–8
lighting 141–4
Limelight 21, 23, 79, 97, 111, 122, 137, 217–8
Loren, Sophia 79, 164
Lourié, Eugène 97
Lubitsch, Ernst 3, 77, 83–4, 86, 116
Lynn, Kenneth 18

Maland, Charles 5, 7, 228, 230
Mamoulian, Rouben 82, 200
Manicheism 131
Mann, Hank 234–41
Mann, Thomas 14
mannerism 90
Marcus Aurelius 36
masculinity 185–99; feminine responses to 188–90; satire of 186–8
The Masquerader 146, 154
Mast, Gerald 24–5, 65, 86, 98–9, 109, 116, 121, 161
materialism, Chaplin's 56–7, 135–44
Maupassant, Guy de 51, 57, 124, 132
Mayakovsky, Vladimir 14, 83, 85, 117
McCarey, Leo 6, 115
McCarthyism 2, 18, 24, 55
McDonald, Gerald D. 8
Menjou, Adolphe 501, 76, 78–9, 84
Merryman, Richard 209
Miller, Arthur 60
Minnelli, Vincent 229
mise-en-scène, Chaplin's 201–3
Mitchum, Robert 83
Modern Times 2–4, 6, 10, 21–2, 34–5, 44–5, 47–8, 55, 57–8, 86, 98, 100–2, 109, 114, 120, 122, 126–7, 136, 144, 146, 151, 155, 157, 164, 166, 169, 173, 181, 184, 196, 209, 214, 216–8
Modernism 55
Mon Oncle 106
Monsieur Verdoux 5, 18, 20–1, 23, 34, 55, 61–2, 98, 137, 217, 222, 225–6
Moscovich, Maurice 78
Mussolini, Benito 11

naked statue gags 151–3
Napoleon 11, 16
Naturalism 6, 132
Negri, Pola 16
New Historicism 2
The New Janitor 159
The New Testament 64, 188
Newman, Paul 79
Niblo, Fred 6
Nichols, Dudley 2
Nichols, Robert 110
Niebuhr, Reinhold 64, 131
A Night Out 29–30, 141, 143
Nijinsky, Vaslav 14
Normand, Mabel 147
Notes from the Underground 186

Oakie, Jack 78
"Oedipus Rex" 198
Oliver Twist 55
One A.M. 141, 144
O'Neill, Eugene 15
O'Neill, Oona 15
Ophuls, Max 202, 229
Ovid 57, 98, 164

Pasolini, Pier Paolo 69, 182
pathos, Chaplin's sense of 116–21; letting the air out of 121–5
Pavlova, Anna 14
The Pawnshop 6, 25–7, 68, 74–5, 94–5, 121, 133–4, 146, 155, 173, 177–8, 183, 188, 195, 212–3
Pay Day 44, 88, 91, 100, 113, 122, 139, 160, 166–7, 194, 214, 218, 223
Peck, Gregory 79
Petrie, Graham 1, 25
Picasso, Pablo 14, 21
Pickford, Mary 21
The Pilgrim 6, 27, 42, 50, 86, 91, 95, 138, 142, 146, 155, 160, 173–4, 177, 202, 218, 224–5, 234
Playtime 106
Police 34, 39, 49, 91, 99, 110, 133, 138, 142, 146, 155, 160, 173–4, 177, 202, 218, 224–5, 234
Priestly, J.B. 63
psychology, Chaplin's gift for 42–7

Puccini, Giacomo 218, 231
Purviance, Edna 46, 88, 134, 146, 164–6, 202

Queen Christina 82

Rachmaninoff, Sergei 14, 62
Raksin, David 219–21, 231
Rand, John 74, 134, 188, 195, 213
Raye, Martha 23
Reisner, Chuck 202
Renoir, Jean 202
rhythm, Chaplin's sense of 200–7, 233–41; in editing 203–7
The Rink 32, 38, 41, 71, 99, 101, 103, 160, 181–2, 194–5, 197, 210–2, 216
Rivera, Diego 14
Robinson, David 1, 2, 12, 78, 81, 83, 222, 234
Rococo art 126
Romanticism, Chaplin's 29, 58, 61, 64, 125
Roosevelt, Franklin 14
Ross, Lillian 14
Rossini, Gioachino 234
Ruggles, Wesley 92, 110, 195, 215

Sarris, Andrew 22, 37
Sartre, Jean-Paul 12, 60
satire, Chaplin's 37–51; social 47–51; of upper class 38–40; of working class 40–2
Scheuer, Philip 63
Schickel, Richard 68, 98
Schoenberg, Arnold 14
Schopenhauer, Arthur 63
Schwaab, Charles 12
The Seagull 97
Seldes, Gilbert 75
Sennett, Mack 20
Sermon on the Mount 50
The Seventh Seal 100
Shakespeare, William 53, 122, 194
Shanghaied 212–3
Shaw, George Bernard 14
Sherwood, Robert 14
shot composition 98–106; large-scale composition 99–101
Shoulder Arms 16, 33, 89, 95, 103, 105–6, 110, 112, 184, 191, 196
Sjöström, Victor 6
small gestures, a cinema of 67–76
"Smile" 14, 218
sound films, Chaplin's 21–4
sound, innovations in 114–5
sound tracks, Chaplin's 219–26; *City Lights* 227–41

special effects, Chaplin's 111, 114
Spender, Stephen 14
Stagecoach 2
Stalin, Joseph 14
The Star Boarder 171, 173
Steinbeck, John 14
Stoicism 36
Straub, Jean-Marie 8, 69, 109
Stravinsky, Igor 14
studios, Chaplin's 13, 20–1
Sturges, Preston 200
Sunnyside 40, 49, 60–1, 82, 88, 91, 109, 112, 120, 125–6, 133, 154–6, 160–2, 166, 175, 182–3, 192, 194, 198, 209, 215–6
Surrealism 14, 55
Swain, Mack 138, 154, 172, 180, 193
Swanson, Gloria 79, 189
"Swing, Little Girl" 224

Tarkovsky, Andrei 69, 200
Tati, Jacques 22, 105–6, 169, 202
Tennyson, Alfred 61, 162
Terris, Tom 156

"This Is My Song" 14, 218, 223
Thomson, David 37, 153–5
Those Love Pangs 155
The Three Stooges 23
Tolstoy, Leo 41, 47, 60, 131
Toulouse-Lautrec, Henri 105
The Tramp 72, 117–8, 120, 122–3, 137, 146, 160–1, 170, 194, 196
transformation gags 25–36
trompe l'oeils 103–6
Trouble in Paradise 86
Turpin, Ben 187
Twenty Minutes of Love 180

United Artists 4–6
United States Steel Corporation 12
unity, Chaplin's sense of 94–6
The Unknown Chaplin 87, 113, 129

The Vagabond 27, 32, 57, 82, 91, 101–3, 118, 120, 137, 146, 154, 166
Vaughan Williams, Ralph 121
"La Violetera" (Padilla, Montesinos) 228–30

Von Sternberg, Joseph 97
Vosges, Walter 68, 77

Wagner, Richard 121
Wayne, John 80
Welles, Orson 12, 80, 110, 117
Wells, H.G. 14
West, Rebecca 16
Wilder, Billy 97, 233, 236
Wilson, Edmund 14
Wilson, Tom 154, 192
Winter, Ella 97
A Woman 134, 154–5, 190
A Woman of Paris 5–6, 13, 16, 50, 76–9, 83–6, 90–1, 96, 100, 110, 140, 215, 223, 225
Woollcott, Alexander 14, 63
Work 29–30, 100, 109, 14, 138, 152–3, 160, 181
Wyler, William 229

YouTube 23, 233

Zelig 13

www.ingramcontent.com/pod-product-compliance
Lightning Source LLC
Chambersburg PA
CBHW081549300426
44116CB00015B/2811